ODESSA

State and Opposition in Military Brazil

Latin American Monographs, No. 63
Institute of Latin American Studies
The University of Texas at Austin

Consuela

898-8234

Steve

" Frank 884
3682

277 office

6210

2097

mesa vista

STATE AND OPPOSITION IN MILITARY BRAZIL

By Maria Helena Moreira Alves

University of Texas Press, Austin

Second Paperback Printing, 1990

Requests for permission to reproduce material from this work should
be sent to:
  Permissions
  University of Texas Press
  P.O. Box 7819
  Austin, Texas 78713-7819

∞ The paper used in this publication meets the minimum requirements of
American National Standard for Information Sciences—Permanence of Paper
for Printed Library Materials, ANSI Z39.48-1984.

Library of Congress Cataloging-in-Publication Data

Alves, Maria Helena Moreira, 1944–
  State and opposition in military Brazil.

  (Latin American monographs; no. 63)
  Includes index.
  1. Brazil—Politics and government—1974. 2. Brazil. Exército—Political
activity. 3. Brazil—National security. I. Title. II. Series: Latin American
monographs (University of Texas at Austin. Institute of Latin American
Studies); no. 63.
F2538.25.A48   1985   320.981   84-13151
ISBN 0-292-77617-9

To the memory of my mother, Branca de Mello Franco Alves.
Her faith and her unending devotion to the cause of justice
taught me to understand the Living Church.
To my father, Márcio de Mello Franco Alves.
Thank you for sharing with me your political experience.
Above all, thank you for caring.

Contents

Figures

Tables

Appendix

Acknowledgments

I wish to express my gratitude to M.I.T. professors Brian Smith, Peter Smith, and Josh Cohen for their advice and support throughout the writing of an early version of this book. My most special appreciation goes to my husband, A. P. Simonds, for his invaluable theoretical help in the many long discussions we have had. I would also like to thank Margaret Keck for the important work of editing the first version of this manuscript, which she accomplished with precision and insight.

A special thanks, as well, to those who have helped in the compilation of the data, transcription of the interview tapes, and gathering of information: Marcos César Suzano Andrade, my research assistant; Marília Faria and Fernando Andrade, who transcribed the interviews; Modesto da Silveira, who helped obtain valuable information from Congress and the Confederação dos Trabalhadores na Agricultura (CONTAG). Many other people contributed anonymous but important data on different aspects of the national security state. Conversations with political leaders, religious leaders, and members of the various opposition sectors were essential for insight into the aspects of the dialectic between state and opposition. A most important contribution came from leaders in the trade unions and from the people of Nova Iguaçú and São Bernardo do Campo. Their daily courage and devotion allowed me to glimpse the difficulties of opposition in a repressive context.

Although not all contributors are mentioned in this final version, I am grateful to all who gave me their time and the benefit of their experience by subjecting themselves to long conversations and interviews on sometimes difficult subjects. A special thanks to those within the military who helped me understand the difficult position of democratic-minded members of that sector.

The study resulting in this publication was funded by a fellowship granted by the Social Science Research Council and the American Council of Learned Societies. However, conclusions, opinions, and other statements in this publication are my own, and not necessarily those of the councils. Although many provided invaluable help in this work, the final responsibility is, of course, entirely mine.

Foreword

Those who know Maria Helena Moreira Alves will recognize that this book, *State and Opposition in Military Brazil*, is the highest point—although perhaps that was not her original intention—of the work she has carried out in order to study and explain the Brazilian political phenomena of the last twenty years. This she does with undeniable success.

From her first publications, in her articles and in the talks she has delivered, Maria Helena has developed, on an increasing scale, a critical study of the implications, ever more important, of the ideology of national security as developed by the Superior War College and that ideology's relationship to the national environment. The result of that ideology was a military state programmed with the aid of technocrats and corrupt civilian leaders who pursued political power and developed the means by which this power could be maintained.

State and Opposition in Military Brazil, on the one hand, gathers a large amount of empirical data so as to describe the current political scenario of the country. On the other hand, the book accentuates the perplexity of an opposition that, having been deprived by and large of legitimate political leadership as a consequence of its forced retirement from the decision-making process, cannot develop a sufficiently clear perspective to bring about a decisive turnabout with the consequent installment of a democracy built on a popular base.

Taken in its totality, the elitism of Brazilian public administration, and its defense of the interests of an exploitative minority, have become important factors for the stability of the regime—for the political parties, by and large, reflect this generalized picture—which today may even be able to weather, without danger of more profound changes, the return of the military to the barracks.

It is within this framework that Maria Helena analyzes all of the popular and social movements after 1964. She pays particular attention, with the keenness of an attentive observer, to the popular movements that organized and surfaced above all in São Paulo, under the leadership first of workers in the industrial park of Osasco and then, a decade later, in the highly industrialized ABCD area (Santo André, São Bernardo, São Caetano, and Diadema), where the largest automobile factories in Brazil are located.

Responsible sectors of civil society, especially a church politically active and frankly opposed to the regime, responded to the awakening of the political consciousness of the working class when it began to organize the union opposition movement that began immediately after the student protests of 1967. Students and workers were subject to ferocious repression by the security forces, eliciting thereby the support of sectors of civil society.

Meanwhile, politicians like Magalhães Pinto, Carlos Lacerda, Juscelino Kubitschek, and others, together with those who were in exile, as was the case of former president João Goulart, attempted to find the path to a new reconciliation so as to open the possibility of the re-establishment of civilian power. They formed what was called the "broad front" but saw their efforts undone by acts of force. These efforts reached a climax with the issuance—under the pretext of some offense to the armed forces in a speech delivered to Congress by Congressman Márcio Moreira Alves—of Institutional Act No. 5 on 13 December 1968. AI-5 was followed on 17 October 1969 by Constitutional Amendment No. 1, imposed by a military junta that took power so as to, from that point on, institutionalize a military regime in the country.

Her strong vocation as a researcher, added to her position as personal witness to the present-day history of Brazil, allows Maria Helena not only to narrate the empirical facts with certainty but also to interpret them in light of the ideology of national security prevalent in the country. She shows, with objectivity, how the political, economic, and social system developed over time, and how it bestowed privileges on a techno-bureaucracy that used military power as the precondition for the establishment of a new economic and social order, firmly anchored in concepts of security and development. The goals of that techno-bureaucracy, in time, proved completely false, based as they were on a model of development that, instead of leading the country forward, brought it to a halt and imposed an exaggerated security that transformed Brazil into a veritable war zone.

The repressive apparatus, with the National Security Council, the controlling organization of all state activities, as its highest expression, reduced the opposition to almost nothing, or, perhaps more clearly, to a minimum. But, after the Médici government, it began to restructure itself and act within the consensual opposition party (the MDB, Movimento Democrático Brasileiro) and, after the so-called *abertura* opened the possibility of new parties, developed organization with parties such as the

PMDB, the PT, the PDT, the PP, and the PTB. The short-lived PP attempted to represent the interests of the business community; the PTB was to serve as a balance between the opposition and the state for the maintenance of the status quo.

Maria Helena's book narrates, with the perceptiveness of the historian and analyst, the events that occurred throughout the different military governments. She shows the attitude of the power holders in a dialectical relation between the state and the opposition. The book also shows how this process led to decompression, in the last moments of the administration of Ernesto Geisel, demonstrated by the abolition of censorship, and the later opening up of opportunities for organizing political parties and, in the administration of João Figueiredo, the granting of amnesty and the re-establishment of direct elections for state governors.

Particularly emphasizing the movements of the working class, she studies closely the awakening of political consciousness, after the ABC metalworkers' strikes at the end of the 1970s and the beginning of 1980, and the development of a new party, the Partido dos Trabalhadores, which attempts to gather working-class support for a new project so that, as a group and for the first time in Brazil, it can break with political tradition and attempt to construct a party founded on popular bases that are conscious of their importance in the building of a new Brazilian nation.

On the other hand, she does not forget the role of the church (the CNBB and the CEBs) and of civil organizations (the OAB and ABI, for example), which were responsible for the final granting of political amnesty and for the struggles that forced the state, here and there, to liberalize. This was the case, for example, in the electoral campaign of 1982, when the opposition parties, in spite of the control measures the regime developed, were able to win considerable power in Congress and the governments of ten of the most important states.

Since then there has been evidence of the bankruptcy of the military state, which has caused inflation rates never before reached, an accelerated recession, administrative corruption that cannot be compared to any other period in the history of the country, and a social debt that has reached a critical level, as evidenced by unemployment, low salaries, hunger, and by a lack of health or education assistance for the population. The solutions can develop only when the people become organized in political parties or in the various representative organizations, thereby strengthening civil society, and become active participants in the political process, as well as in the current economic and social processes.

Maria Helena's book, having the attributes of a serious historical and critical study of an entire epoch, is a decisive contribution to all those who wish to inform themselves adequately so as to be able to find solutions to Brazil's problems. She shows that, by analyzing the evolution of events as they developed in this mistaken takeoff in the construction of a "great power," built mainly on the dreams of a military group, one may draw conclusions and lessons for a new Brazil, where democracy can exist and not be a mere intellectual exercise.

It remains for us to find out how to use these lessons, without reinstating, in new dress, a regime that has already been institutionalized; rather, we should give to the people, within the framework of a real conception of political representation, the power to debate freely the solutions so as to encourage a profound assessment of the suggestions for changes in ways that can enlarge the possibility of popular participation in the important decisions that interest all of the Brazilian people.

Hélio Bicudo

(*Author's note*: Dr. Hélio Bicudo is a jurist and member of the Archdiocesan Justice and Peace Committee of São Paulo, author of several books on law, human rights, and police violence. He became an important figure in Brazil when, in 1971, as a state judge in São Paulo, he was responsible for uncovering the activities of the "Death Squad" and bringing the principal parties to trial [they were saved by a piece of legislation, known as the "Fleury Law," passed by the Médici government to save Colonel Sérgio Fleury, the leader of the Death Squad, from the gallows]. Dr. Bicudo's book *Meu depoimento sobre o Esquadrão da Morte* became a landmark publication for law and human rights.)

State and Opposition in Military Brazil

Part I. The Doctrine of National Security and Development

Introduction: Dependency and the National Security State

It is the purpose of this book to examine the relationship between the state and the opposition in military Brazil, which has shaped the complex political and social mechanisms of domination in that country since 1964. These processes of change are located, however, within a wider context: they must be understood in relation to the particular role that the Brazilian economy has played in a world economic system. The growing penetration of international capital after the mid-fifties shaped an alliance of multinational capital, associated-dependent national capital, and state-owned capital. By the end of that decade, Brazil was involved in a process of development characterized by a condition of dependency based on an "economic tripod" (*tripé econômico*) that was strengthened after the military takeover of 1 April 1964.[1]

A brief examination of the idea of "dependent development" will make it easier to appreciate the significance of this context to recent social change in Brazil. In its fundamental economic sense, "development" denotes the expansion of a society's productive capacity. More broadly construed, it refers to the whole range of changes in technological, social, political, and cultural practices that accompany and (in differing degrees) facilitate such expansion. An economic system can be called "autonomous" when it is able to generate its own growth, a circumstance that requires above all the ability to create new technology, to expand the capital goods sector, and to control its financial and banking system. Dependent economies, in contrast, function at the periphery of a world system in which the resources for self-generated growth are concentrated elsewhere. In the extreme case, the dependent economy is limited to the role of supplier of raw materials to the advanced industrial economies. Even when not wholly locked into this role, the international market severely limits the possibility of developing the technological, industrial, and financial capacity requisite to self-generated growth. Hence, peripheral industrialization occurs essentially as a distorted reflection of the expansion of the advanced economies.

Peripheral industrialization is based on products which in the center are mass consumed, but which are typically luxurious consumption in dependent societies. Industrialization in dependent economies enhances income concentration as it increases sharp differences in productivity without generalizing this trend to the whole of the economy: whereas the production of cars, televisions, refrigerators, and the like types of goods is based on modern technology, important parts of food products, textiles and other goods that constitute the basic consumption for the masses are still based on more traditional technology and relations of production. The wages of technicians, managers and specialized workers, although not directly determined by productivity, are incomparably higher than those earned by peasants or workers employed in traditional sectors. Thus, industrialization in the periphery increases disparity of income among wage earners accentuating what has been called in Latin America the "structural heterogeneity."[2]

It must be stressed that a situation of dependency does not necessarily mean permanent underdevelopment and economic stagnation. What it does imply is, at best, a skewed process of development: major social problems, such as regional inequality, severe maldistribution of income, high rates of unemployment, and greatly depressed living standards for the majority of the population, remain unresolved.

The condition of dependency thus entails a complex relationship between local capitalist development and the expansion of a worldwide capitalist system, with the result that control over the process rests with actors and institutions that are both internal and external to the nation.

We conceive the relationship between external and internal forces as forming a complex whole whose structural links are not based on mere external forms of exploitation and coercion, but are rooted in coincidences of interests between local dominant classes and international ones and, on the other side, are challenged by local dominated groups and classes. . . . Of course, imperialist penetration is a result of external social forces (multinational enterprises, foreign technology, international financial systems, embassies, foreign states and armies, etc.). What we affirm simply means that the system of domination reappears as an "internal" force, through the social practices of local groups and classes which try to enforce foreign interests, not precisely because they are foreign, but because they may coincide with values and interests that these groups pretend are their own.[3]

In this way, dependency implies the development of "clientele classes" whose interests are associated, by means of joint ownership and formal cooperative arrangements, to foreign capital and who therefore actively support international penetration of the national economy. The essential nature of dependent capitalism can thus be understood only in the context of the relations of domination that characterize the international system.

Dependent development and the specific international and national interests associated with it provide the essential backdrop for understanding the military and civilian conspiracy that toppled the constitutional government of João Goulart on 1 April 1964.[4] This conspiracy was the direct consequence of a series of tendencies and contradictions that had been gathering force. Goulart's government had imposed a series of restrictions on multinational investment that included strict policies of control over profit remittance, payments for technological transfers and royalties, as well as antitrust legislation and negotiations over the nationalization of major foreign corporations. It also pursued a nationalist policy of supporting and directly subsidizing private national capital, mainly that part that was not associated with foreign capital.

In the late 1950s and early 1960s, the mobilization of previously excluded sectors of the Brazilian population had significantly increased. Rural unions and peasant leagues grew in agricultural regions.[5] Urban workers organized within both the official trade union structure and parallel networks that extended coordination across different job categories. The Goulart period was a fertile one for working-class organization; the government sought the support of workers and provided a political climate that allowed deeper and more effective forms of organization to develop. Decentralization of the political and economic system gave states real autonomy in decision making within their territories (this was especially significant in Pernambuco, under the administration of Miguel Arraes, and in Rio Grande do Sul, under the administration of Leonel Brizola[6]). While the power of multinational and associated sectors of national capital continued to expand, increasingly well-organized groups demanded participation in and reform of Brazil's highly skewed social structure. The rapid organization of the working class and the peasantry frightened the upper classes, which had never before been forced to make even minimal concessions respecting such matters as wages, working conditions, or even trade union organization. The example of Cuba intensified the fear of a revolution that would topple the system and produce serious losses for both national and multinational capital.

The system of formal democracy that had been in existence in Brazil since the end of the Estado Novo in 1946 became subject to constant institutional crisis.[7] The increased participation of hitherto marginalized sectors of society brought forward political demands and interests that were irreconcilable within a system of dependent capitalist development. In this sense we can say (following Jürgen Habermas) that "fundamental contradictions" were brought to the surface:

We can speak of the fundamental contradiction of a social formation when its organizational principle necessitates that individuals and groups repeatedly confront one another with claims and intentions that are, in the long run, incompatible. . . . As long as the incompatibility of claims and intentions is not recognized by the participants, the conflict remains latent. Such forcefully integrated action systems are, of course, in need of an ideological justification to conceal the asymmetrical distribution of chances for the legitimate satisfaction of needs. . . . As soon as the incompatibility becomes conscious, conflict becomes manifest and irreconcilable interests are recognized as antagonistic interests.[8]

With the expression of such irreconcilable interests, the institutions of formal democracy proved increasingly unable to resolve the contradictions. Competing parties and groups outbid one another in their search for voter support, with the consequence (again noted by Habermas, though in the very different context of advanced industrial capitalism) that popular expectations were brought to the point of an "unavoidable gap between the level of pretension and the level of success, which would lead to disappointments among the voting public."[9]

In such cases, a government may be unable to cover the costs of its own legitimation and faces a crisis in its formal democratic institutions. It was in response to such a crisis that Brazil's clientele classes played a crucial role in creating and enforcing an authoritarian form of capitalist state. And it is in this context that the ideology of national security can be understood as a tool the ruling classes, associated with foreign capital, utilize to justify and legitimize the continuation, by nondemocratic means, of a highly exploitative model of dependent development.

The immediate antecedent of the takeover of state power was a well-orchestrated destabilization policy, which involved multinational corporations, associated-dependent Brazilian capital, the U.S. government, and Brazil's military—in particular, a group of military officers of the Superior War College (Escola Superior de Guerra, ESG).[10] Documentation has recently become available that shows that the U.S. government, through the Central Intelligence Agency, acted in coordination with civilians and military officers—members of the clientele classes—to plan the destabilization of the Goulart government.[11] This conspiracy was implemented through civilian cover institutions, particularly the Brazilian Institute for Democratic Action (Instituto Brasileiro de Ação Democrática, IBAD) and the Institute for Research and Social Studies (Instituto de Pesquisas e Estudos Sociais, IPES). The ESG coordinated the actions of the civilian and military conspirators.[12] The needed ideological justification for the takeover and for the modification of state structures to enforce an authoritarian variant was provided by the Doctrine of National Security and Development taught in the ESG.

The Superior War College was founded in 1949, with the help of French and American advisers, to train "high-level personnel to direct and plan for national security."[13] Its role was expanded that same year to include the development of a "method to analyze and interpret political, economic, diplomatic, and military factors that condition strategic conception and planning."[14] The development of cold-war theories led to an emphasis on the interpenetration of political, economic, psychosocial,[15] and military factors in formulating national security policy, and a high priority was increasingly assigned to training in development theory. Because of the high level of training provided at the ESG, it became known as the Sorbonne of the military establishment.

' Alfred Stepan points out that the ESG differed from its American counterpart in two principal ways: first, the military in Brazil paid particular attention to the theory of "indirect attack" by the Soviet Union and the danger of subversive or revolutionary warfare; second, the ESG included not only military officers, but also upper-class civilians among its regular staff, visiting scholars, conference-givers, and student body. Civilian participation tended to increase through the years. Between 1950 and 1967, of 1,276 ESG graduates, 646 were civilians.[16] After the takeover, ESG graduates occupied most of the important posts within Brazil's political and economic structures. Graduates of the ESG included 599 top military officers, 224 major industrialists, 200 top-level bureaucrats and ministers of state, 97 heads of governmental agencies, 39 congressmen, 23 federal and state judges, and 107 professional technocrats.[17]

Among the prominent civilians active in the ESG prior to the coup were Octávio Gouvea de Bulhões, Roberto de Oliveira Campos, Mário Henrique Simonsen, and Antônio Delfim Netto. They would all later occupy posts as ministers of state.[18] Military and civilian members of the ESG also increasingly used the IPES/IBAD complex to develop projects and draft programs and directives for alternative government policies. Particular emphasis was placed on developing plans for the administration of capitalist development.[19] The Brazilian military and its technocratic allies specifically rejected laissez faire capitalism, espousing, rather, a model that combined Keynesian regulatory measures with state capitalism. The ESG/IPES/IBAD complex became, in effect, a think tank and an efficient parallel bureaucracy for planning a new state.[20] Many of the proposals developed in the late 1950s and early 1960s at the ESG were later incorporated into legislation. For example, David Carneiro's suggestion, in 1959, that the number of political parties be limited and that party fidelity be enforced in voting, was later incorporated into Institutional Act No. 2 (1965) and the Party Fidelity Bill (see chapter 3). Another question discussed in ESG conferences was the negative effects of decentralization of political and economic power on capitalist economic development; centralization of power in the federal government became a hallmark of the post-1964 state.[21]

Perhaps the most important function of the ESG/IPES/IBAD complex prior to the takeover was the design and implementation of an intelligence network, considered necessary for an effective and centralized state. The coordinator of this effort was General Golbery do Couto e Silva. A number of military officers of the ESG were regular staff members of the

IPES and worked full time with General Golbery in designing the security information network and in developing the sophisticated Doctrine of National Security and Development. Prior to the takeover, this group had already compiled a dossier of complete and detailed information on over four hundred thousand Brazilian citizens.[22] René Dreifuss has documented the way in which the ESG/IPES intelligence network was extended to sectors of civil and political society. Covert information agents worked among students, trade unions, peasants, the press, in cultural organizations, in the Catholic church, in universities, and even in middle-class civic associations.[23] These agents were responsible for gathering information necessary for the planning and coordinating network of the conspiracy— the "Informal High Command"—which was set up at the IPES and headed by General Humberto Castello Branco.[24] The ESG/IPES complex kept in close touch with American officials and was funded by many international and national corporations.[25] It was the nerve center of the destabilization campaign.

General Castello Branco became the first president of the new state. His cabinet was almost entirely composed of members and associates of the ESG/IPES/IBAD complex. In addition, the staff and members of the class alliance institutionalized in the three main think tanks occupied most secondary administrative posts.[26] Once in control of all levels of power, the civilian-military clientele class alliance proceeded to implement its plans and build a formidable state apparatus to support its power monopoly. How this apparatus developed and what kind of state was in fact established are the main questions this work investigates.

The ideology of national security contained in the Doctrine of National Security and Development was an important tool for the maintenance of state structures intended to facilitate associated-dependent capitalist development. The Doctrine of National Security and Development, as taught in the ESG and other military schools, must be understood in its entirety. As it was constructed in Brazil, it is an integrated body of thought that includes a theory of war, a theory of internal subversion and revolution, a theory of Brazil's role in world politics and its geopolitical potential as a world power, and a particular model of associated-dependent economic development that combines Keynesian economics and state capitalism.

The Doctrine of National Security and Development has been used to justify the imposition of a system of controls and domination. It does not require the support of the masses to legitimize state power, nor does it attempt to elicit such support. Neither does it contain a theory of racial supremacy or the need for empire, as does Fascist ideology. Nonetheless, the Doctrine of National Security and Development does foresee the state's obtaining a degree of legitimacy based on continued capitalist development as well as on its function as defender of the nation against the threat of "internal enemies" and "psychological warfare."

The state also seeks legitimation by linking the concepts of economic development and internal security. The government slogan, "security with development," connects associated-dependent capitalist development and the defense of internal security from the "enemy within." The emphasis on the constant threat to the nation from hidden and unknown "internal enemies," in turn, produces a climate of suspicion, fear, and divisiveness among the population that enables the regime to conduct repressive campaigns that would not otherwise be tolerated. In such a manner, dissent and class antagonism can be controlled through terror. As such, the doctrine is an ideology of class domination and has been instrumental in justifying the most violent class oppression.

One of my main purposes is to examine the ways in which the Doctrine of National Security and Development has been used to shape the structures of the state, to impose specific controls upon civil society, and to provide a blueprint for governing Brazil. In reality, the doctrine is a complete world view, a Weltanschauung.[27] Its totalizing character leads to a dynamic of absolute control, the search for absolute security. In the name of anticommunism, the doctrine, with its particular emphasis on internal security, leads inexorably to the abuse of power, arbitrary arrests, torture, and the suppression of all freedom of expression. It tends to re-create a kind of state that General Golbery has termed the new Leviathan, "the supreme *Leviathan* . . . the uncontested owner of the planet Earth and of the human spirit."[28] The Doctrine of National Security and Development's permeation of state structures has led to the transformation of Brazilian society during the last twenty years of military rule. We must, therefore, be concerned with understanding the evolution of the national security state in Brazil since 1964. In a broader sense, I will be attempting to explain the totality of this type of capitalist state and the characteristics that have been imprinted on the structures of the state and on civil society.

A major claim of this book is that the character of the national security state can only be understood in relation to the dynamic process of its interaction with forms and structures of opposition movements within civil society. Both the structures of the state and the forms of opposition are continuously transformed in the ongoing efforts of each to control, check, or modify the other. Hence, their relationship is essentially a dialectical one. The concept of dialectic will be used to denote the centrality of this dynamic conflict, by which each part of the totality becomes transformed and reconstituted by the other. The focus of this study, therefore, is the explanation of how state structures were built over time and developed largely in reaction to the constant and changing pressures of organized opposition. Although the theoreticians and planners of the national security state were armed with a general blueprint of development and of state formation, the actual structures and controls have taken on a dynamic of their own. The very need to control society as a whole, implicit in the Doctrine of Internal Security, has meant that the structures and mechanisms of control must be constantly changed in order to re-establish conformity.

The constant need to change or rebuild the structures of coercion has produced four serious contradictions, which have become characteristic of the organization of the national security state. The first is a tendency to lose control of bureaucratic growth, particularly of the repressive apparatus, which has been able to build its own power base independent of the executive. Second, the national security state is unable to eliminate the opposition completely. Each campaign against one sector of the opposition brings new and previously uninvolved sectors into the fray, in protest against the use of force. Third, the attempt to eliminate dissent by force ignores the real grievances; dissent is thus not eliminated, but only displaced from one sector of civil society to another. For this reason, the national security state is inherently unstable and tends to become increasingly isolated. The long-range tendency is for the state to become the province of a small elite group, which keeps civil society and even its own ranks under control through increased use of physical force. Fourth, because it is unable to eliminate the causes of dissent, and thus to control and contain the opposition, the national security state is haunted by contradictions, which produce a situation of ongoing institutional crisis. In addition, the shifting control mechanisms and the application of physical violence create a gap between the language of legitimation by means of democracy and the reality of oppression. Ultimately, the deep legitimacy crisis that results from this gap, together with the institutional crisis, undermines the stability of the state.

In addition to crucial factors that determine the actual formation of state structures and their relationship to the opposition, other issues of concern and theoretical importance will be discussed in the course of this analysis. Some of the questions I examine have not received sufficient attention in the literature on the post-1964 Brazilian state:

1. What kind of economic development have the clientele classes in power envisioned and implemented, and what is the connection between this particular economic model and the system of control the state has institutionalized?

2. With what degree of success has the original blueprint of governmental rules—which General Golbery do Couto e Silva called the master plan—been applied in forming the actual structures of the state and the mechanisms of social and political control?

3. How did the national security state react to challenges from organized opposition

groups, and what has been the effect of their relationship on the formation of the state itself?

4. How did the changes in the mechanisms of control affect the opposition? Was it eliminated? Did strategies and tactics of resistance change? Was the actual constituency of opposition groups affected? Did new groups join, or was the opposition limited to one ideological or class-based sector of civil society?

5. What are the basic concepts of the Doctrine of National Security and Development, and what has been the impact of this ideology on state formation? To what extent did the basic premises of the doctrine permeate the thinking and practice of those in power so as to imprint a specific seal on state policies?

6. What is the connection between the concepts of the Doctrine of National Security and Development and the different state reactions to opposition challenge?

7. Finally, how do the complex mechanisms of control and information gathering work? How does the repressive apparatus function? What are the interconnections between the various organizations?

My method for analyzing the dialectical relations between the state and the opposition draws on a number of sources. First, I examined major documents, analyses, and historical studies, which have become available recently in various publications, in works sponsored by the Catholic church, the Brazilian Bar Association, and the Brazilian Press Association. There is a wealth of information now available in Brazil in the form of personal memoirs of military leaders of the government as well as of participants in the various opposition activities, including those engaged in armed struggle. Second, I have relied strongly on primary source materials, such as the official congressional and state records (in the *Diário Oficial da União*), and governmental registers of all legislation and acts of the government. I have obtained statistical data from government records such as the censuses, the publications of the Instituto Brasileiro de Geografia e Estatística (IBGE), the *Anuário Estatístico do Brasil*, and electoral data from the electoral courts, published by the Superior Electoral Tribunal. In addition, I utilized military material, speeches, and studies of the various branches of the armed forces, including the basic textbook of the Superior War College. For the study of opposition, I found invaluable documentation in the archives of the Ordem dos Advogados do Brasil (Brazilian Bar Association, OAB), the Associação Brasileira de Imprensa (Brazilian Press Association, ABI), and the Conferência Nacional dos Bispos do Brasil (National Conference of Brazilian Bishops, CNBB). Labor union documentation includes union newspapers, leaflets, assembly and meeting records, and statistical information published by the Departamento Intersindical de Estatística e Estudos Sócio-Econômicos (Interunion Department of Statistical Studies, DIEESE).

Finally, I conducted, during a period of four years, extensive formal and informal interviews with members of both the opposition and the government. I interviewed members of the Catholic hierarchy as well as Catholic lay organizers and participants in a variety of church-related organizations. For information on the labor unions, I relied on interviews with rank and file and leaders of the labor unions in the "new union movement," as well as with participants in the strikes of 1978, 1979, and 1980. Participant observation and interviews have also aided my analysis of the different neighborhood organizations and civic associations in urban areas. Extensive interviews with members of opposition and government political parties were the source of much of the material in the discussion of political party organization. Interviews with active-duty military as well as with retired or purged members of the military have supported my examination of the mechanisms used to control the military and of the policy interpretations of the military. Finally, my analysis of the activities of the Brazilian Bar Association and the Press Association was based on interviews with editors, journalists, writers, lawyers, and the presidents of the two associations.

1. The Doctrine of National Security and Development

Origins of the Doctrine

Margaret Crahan has traced the origins of national security ideology in Latin America as far back as the nineteenth century in Brazil and the beginning of the twentieth century in Argentina and Chile.[1] She links its origins to theories of geopolitics, to anti-Marxism, and to conservative Catholic social thought as expressed in such organizations as the Opus Dei in Spain and the Action Française in France.[2]

With the advent of the cold war, elements of the theory of total war and inevitable confrontation between the two superpowers were incorporated into national security ideology in Latin America. The specific form it took in Latin America emphasized internal security in the face of the threat of "indirect action" by communism. Thus while American national security theoreticians stressed total war and nuclear weapons strategy, and the French, well into the Algerian War, focused on limited warfare in response to the Communist threat, Latin Americans, concerned with the growth of working-class social movements, emphasized the threat of internal subversion and revolutionary warfare. In addition, Latin American national security ideology, particularly as it developed in Brazil, was specifically concerned with the link between economic development and internal and external security.

A number of works are available on the ideology of national security in Brazil.[3] In this chapter I shall concentrate on the work of General Golbery do Couto e Silva, by far the most influential Brazilian theorist, and on the teachings of the Superior War College.

An analysis of ESG textbooks, particularly the *Manual básico da Escola Superior de Guerra* (the basic textbook), is an important tool for understanding the Doctrine of National Security and Development, because of the *Manual básico*'s importance in professional and ideological training for both top-level Brazilian military and highly placed civilian technocrats in the state's administrative bureaucracy. Such analysis is essential for understanding the development of the national security state and the reactions of holders of power to challenges from the opposition.

I have already referred to the priority given to the development of an integrated body of thought concerned with state planning and security and development policy. I have also discussed the important role the ESG played in incorporating top-level civilians, as students and in the regular or visiting faculty of the college. The ESG thus cemented a military-civilian network that institutionalized and disseminated the Doctrine of National Security and Development. This network, organized as the Association of Graduates of the Superior War College (Associação dos Diplomados da Escola Superior de Guerra, ADESG), conducted conferences, study sessions, debates, and courses all over Brazil, spreading ESG principles and doctrines to other key military and civilian political actors.[4]

The ESG has influenced the curriculum in other military schools in Brazil. Alfred Stepan notes the spread of the doctrine particularly to the Escola de Comando do Estado Maior do Exército, ECEME, the top-level training school for the military high command. Stepan traces the following developments: in 1956 the ECEME curriculum made no mention of conferences on counterinsurgency or internal security strategies; by 1961 courses on national security had become more prevalent; by 1968 the ECEME curriculum included 222 class hours devoted exclusively to the discussion of internal security doctrine and another 129 class hours devoted to the analysis of nonclassical forms of warfare. Only 21 hours were devoted to traditional military topics such as territorial defense against external aggression.[5] This becomes highly significant in that, to be promoted to general or to hold any command post as an officer in Brazil, one must be a graduate of the ECEME.

As elaborated in the *Manual básico*, the school's doctrine has evolved from a partial definition of internal and external security to a more global vision of national security integrated with economic development. The regulations currently in effect state that the ESG shall be concerned chiefly with the "Doctrine of Political National Security and Development." The *Manual básico* further distinguishes between what it defines as a "political doctrine to be applied to the country as a whole," the "military doctrine," and the "information doctrine." The political doctrine is to be developed exclusively and with "absolute freedom in formulation and directives" by the Superior War Faculty of the ESG. The military doctrine, on the other hand, is to be elaborated under the direct supervision and responsibility of the High Command of the Armed Forces (EMFA). As to the information doctrine, the ESG has no particular responsibility for the actual "production of information." The methodology of intelligence gathering is entrusted to the National Intelligence School (Escola Nacional de Informações), which is connected to the National Intelligence Service (Serviço Nacional de

Informações, SNI) and which trains top-level intelligence agents.[6]

It is important to note this apparent division of labor among various organizations that develop and gather information on internal security questions. The ESG, although not directly involved in the production of information, does deal with what it defines as the "doctrine of the *utilization* of information" (emphasis in original). The *Manual básico* explains that this doctrine falls within the responsibility of the ESG because information is used in the context of the political doctrine, which is the exclusive concern of the ESG.[7] The ESG thus plays the role of the think tank for the Doctrine of National Security and Development.

Basic Concepts of the Doctrine

The ESG, in collaboration with the IPES and IBAD, formulated the Doctrine of National Security and Development over a period of twenty-five years. It is a comprehensive and coherent body of theory that contains both ideological elements and guidelines for networking, information gathering, and political-economic planning of government policy. It provides a basis for establishing and evaluating structural components of the state as well as for periodic program development and policy planning.

National Security, Internal Security, and the Opposition

The Doctrine of National Security and Development begins with a theory of war. The teachings of the ESG envisage different kinds of war: total, limited and localized, subversive or revolutionary, and indirect or psychological.

The theory of total war is based on cold-war military strategy, which defines modern-day war as total and absolute. Because of the immense destructive power of nuclear weapons and the inevitable confrontation of the two superpowers—the United States and the Soviet Union—the theory concludes that war is no longer limited to the territory of the warring nations or to specific sectors of the economy or population. General Golbery do Couto e Silva states the concept as follows:

Today, the concept of war has been expanded . . . to the entire territorial space of the belligerent states, thus involving the whole economic, political, cultural, and military capacity of the nation in the enormity of the struggle. All activities are focused on one single aim: victory and only victory. No distinction is made between soldiers and civilians, men, women, and children; they face the same danger, and identical sacrifices are demanded of them. They must all abdicate the secular liberties, which had been won at such high costs, and place them in the hands of the state, the all-powerful lord of war. . . . Above all total war has eliminated the time scale, incorporating in itself the time of prewar and postwar, which are in fact now only extensions of one sole and continuing state of war.

Thus, from the strictly limited military war we have now moved to *total war*, economic, financial, political, psychological, and scientific. . . . From a total war we have gone to *global war*, and from the global war we finally have the *indivisible*, the *inescapable war* and—why not recognize it?—*permanent war*. The "white war" of Hitler or the "cold war" of Stalin has taken the place of peace so that, really, there is no longer a clear distinction between where peace ends and war begins.[8]

Because the United States and the Soviet Union are irrevocably involved in a total war, which cannot be fought actively because of the possibility of complete destruction of both nations, contemporary war, according to this theory, takes several forms: nuclear war, the total or unlimited form of war; and limited or localized wars, where the two superpowers meet to test their power to control certain limited territories, but stop short of total nuclear war. Furthermore, contemporary war can be declared or undeclared; the latter specifically applies to insurrectionary and revolutionary warfare.[9]

Classical, or conventional, war is politically declared and is by nature limited. It is conceived basically as a war of external aggression, or a war that is conducted between states, and in which one nation declares war on another as a reaction to an external attack. Thus, in the case of conventional war, the total productive capacity and population of a nation is mobilized to unite it around the fight against aggression by another nation. Up to World War II, this was the most common form of warfare and it is, by definition, a war of defense and offense, but of a population united against a defined *external* enemy.[10]

Undeclared, or nonclassical, warfare, on the other hand, is a war of indirect aggression: "It may include armed conflict within a country and between parts of its population." The ESG textbook defines it as a war of "internal subversion." The concept used includes both *insurrectional* warfare and *revolutionary* warfare. These concepts are further defined as follows:

Insurrectionary warfare: an internal conflict in which part of a population attempts to depose a government by the force of arms.
Revolutionary warfare: a conflict, normally internal, that is stimulated and aided materially or psychologically from outside the nation, generally inspired by an ideology. It attempts to gain state power by progressive control of the nation.[11]

The *Manual básico* also makes clear that the concept of revolutionary warfare does not necessarily involve the use of armed force. It includes any action by an organized opposition with enough strength to challenge state policies. In addition, it is linked automatically to Communist infiltration and to indirect action on the part of international communism controlled by the Soviet Union. It is here that the concept of "ideological frontiers," as opposed to "territorial frontiers," of warfare becomes an essential concept in the theory. In revolutionary warfare, the war of ideology replaces conventional interstate war within the geographical frontiers of a nation. This point is basic to the theory of the internal enemy and of indirect aggression. According to the ESG,

Communist revolutionary war is of the second type in our definition of nonclassical warfare. The Communist nations, in their eagerness to expand their domination of the world, avoid becoming engaged in a direct confrontation. Thus they apply a particular strategy—one in which the *psychological* weapon is most utilized. They exploit the possibilities and the vulnerabilities of a democratic society by surreptitiously and clandestinely acting to weaken it and to induce submission to their sociopolitical regime.

A principal characteristic of Communist revolutionary war is the involvement of the population of the target country in a gradual, slow action—both progressive and continuous—which aims at the conquering of minds. It encompasses all aspects, from the exploitation of existing discontent and protest—with the incitement of the population against the constituted authorities—up to the actual organization of dominated and controlled zones or territories. They may use the method of guerrilla warfare, of terrorism and other irregular tactics where persons who are nationals of the country itself are then turned into the combatants. They may also use devious, nonarmed tactics.[12]

Hence, revolutionary war takes psychological and indirect forms so as to avoid armed confrontation and attempts to win over the minds of the people and slowly sow the seeds of rebellion until the population is incited against the constituted authorities. Since revolutionary war is undeclared and is carried on secretly by external forces of international communism, combatants are recruited from among the population of the target nation. Thus by definition the entire population becomes suspect, composed of potential internal enemies, who must be carefully sought out and uprooted.

National security planning, and particularly efficient intelligence gathering on the activities of all sectors of political and civil society, is therefore crucial to the proper defense of the nation itself, for, according to ESG theory, international Communist forces orchestrate and carefully plan propaganda campaigns and other forms of ideological manipulation, which are then secretly implemented in the target nation so as to win over sectors of the population and weaken the government's ability to react. This, in sum, is the indirect action strategy of communism.[13]

According to the *Manual básico*, the main focus in the Third World has to be on revolutionary warfare rather than on the possibility of limited or total war. The Soviet Union, in this view, sees revolutionary warfare as the most effective way of carrying out its own imperial destiny, which depends on gaining control of Third World countries:

In countries of weak national power, where the political structures are unstable, the *indirect action strategy* of aggression is much more effective, for it may potentially increase antagonisms and pressures inside the country. Thus, it is also evident that attention to *internal national security* must be an important priority, especially where, in addition to the conditions described, one also finds geographical conditions that reinforce this factor.

In nations with a low state of development, there can be a climate of insecurity that may be exploited and may allow the growth of influence or domination, whether it be in the political arena, or in economic, psychosocial, or military arenas.[14]

The strategy of indirect action mandates the establishment of different fronts within the population as well as of a particular method of psychological propaganda and ideological control. According to the definition, there are two kinds of target public. The internal public includes active-duty military personnel, military in the reserves or civilians working in military ministries, as well as the military police and other paramilitary forces. The external public is composed of students, trade union leaders, print and electronic media, influential social groups such as intellectuals, professionals, artists, and members of various religious orders. This grouping also includes organized sectors of political and civil society, such as organizations of workers, students, peasants, and associations such as clubs and neighborhood committees.[15] The indirect strategy endeavors to exploit dissent among civil and political groups and to gain control of leadership positions in order to impose a climate of active opposition to the government. The psychological campaign encourages the population to engage in direct opposition, to sympathize with the claims of the opposition, and eventually to incite revolt against the constituted authorities. The main problem for the state in confronting communism's indirect strategy is that, potentially, the enemy could be anywhere.

Internal security, defined as follows, is thus the top priority for those in power in an underdeveloped nation:

Internal security involves aspects of *national security* that have to do with internal manifestations or demonstrations of dissent, antagonisms, and pressures. It encompasses all actions that may be carried out by the state so as to preserve the constituted powers, law, order, and guarantee the threatened national objectives. Therefore, internal security includes any and all measures carried out within the country aiming at the elimination of pressures and antagonisms of any origin, form or nature. . . .

Internal security is an integral part of the concept of national security. Its specific field of action is with antagonisms or pressures: be they external, internal, or external-internal. It is not important to consider their nature: they might be political, economic, psychosocial, or military. Nor is it important to consider the variety of forms the dissent may take: violence, subversion, corruption, trafficking in influence, ideological infiltration, economic domination, social disaggregation, demonstrations, and breach of sovereignty. Whenever any antagonisms or pressures are producing an effect within national frontiers, the responsibility to fight them, overcome them, neutralize them, or reduce them is understood within the framework of the actions and planned programs that we define as the policy of internal security [*política de segurança interna*].[16]

Considering the definitions of "antagonisms" and "pressures," the theory of internal security presents the national security state with a far-reaching justification for control and repression of the population in general. It can even be said to provide a moral incentive, since the rigorous enforcement of internal security is a mission comparable to defense of the nation from occupation by a foreign army. Furthermore, the hidden nature of the threat makes it all but impossible to establish limitations on repressive actions. The national security state itself—and often those sectors most intimately linked to the repressive apparatus—ultimately determines who constitutes the internal enemy, and which opposition activities constitute antagonisms or pressures. Thus responsibility for the control of subversive or revolutionary activities gives the military forces practically unlimited power over the population.

Such a doctrine clearly poses a substantial threat to the protection of human rights. When it is impossible to determine exactly who is to be considered an enemy of the state and what activities are defined as permissible or judged to be intolerable, there can no longer be any guarantees of due process of law, the right of defense, or freedom of expression or association. Even if such formal rights remain in the constitution, in practice they exist only at the discretion of the repressive apparatus of the national security state. All citizens are suspect and are considered guilty until they can prove their innocence. Such a reversal is the root and cause of the serious abuses of power that occur in Brazil.

Another important point to emphasize here is that the theory of the enemy within requires that the government build two types of defensive structure. First, the state must create an apparatus of repression and armed control able to enforce its will and coerce the population if necessary. Second, the state must set up a formidable network of political intelligence, to pinpoint the enemies, the opposition sectors that may have become infiltrated by "indirect" Communist activity. All of this further implies the centralization of the state's power in the federal executive to operate the vast internal security apparatus. It also follows that those sectors most intimately linked to the actual running of the intelligence and repressive forces are the de facto holders of power within the national security state.

In his writings in the mid-1950s, General Golbery do Couto e Silva was already discussing this "counteroffensive strategy." He argued that the need for an intelligence/information network was a consequence of the inescapability of total war, of a permanent war whose corollary was subversive or revolutionary war. A strategy had to be developed to counter the enemy's (i.e., communism) use of infiltration and psychological warfare—of "propaganda and counterpropaganda, dissemination of tempting ideologies, of suggestive slogans for internal and external use, persuasion, blackmail, threats, and even terrorism."[17] Consequently, the counteroffensive had to move away from classical military strategy and concentrate on new techniques of counterintelligence and counterpropaganda and develop similar strategies of offensive action. Developing a new strategy in the face of permanent cold war led to what Golbery already at that time was calling the "Grand Strategy":

We have, in the highest levels of national security, a strategy—which has been called by many the Grand Strategy or the General Strategy. It is an art that comes under the exclusive competence of the government and that must coordinate, within a basic strategic concept, all of the political, economic, psychosocial, and military activities that may lead to the achievement of the objectives that embody the national aspiration toward unity, security, and growing prosperity. To this strategy are, thus, subordinated other strategies, whether they be military strategy, or political, economic, or psychosocial strategies. . . . The Grand Strategy is like the theory of war that provides its foundation: it is indivisible and total.[18]

Golbery held that a government must be organized around effective implementation of the grand strategy. The state must have full power to organize the infrastructure necessary for national security, and particularly to guarantee internal security. He developed a theoretical model of the governmental structures that ideally should perform this task by drawing the connections between the various state organizations entrusted with carrying out the crucial "Policy of National Security" (see fig. 1).

The construction of the "ideal" structures envisioned by General Golbery was entrusted to the network of intelligence and represssion created after the takeover. Some twenty years after he outlined the policy, these concepts were reiterated in the ESG textbook used in the basic training of those who were to run the apparatus. Thus we find in the definitions provided by the ESG's *Manual básico* some of the main concepts that Golbery had used in his theoretical development of the grand strategy:

National policy is the global process that orients the government in order to achieve the primordial functions of the state. . . . In its widest expression, *national policy* is the formulation of the permanent national objectives. . . .

National policy may be subdivided into two aspects: *development policy* and *security policy*.

National development policy aims at the orientation of the government in the sense of strengthening its power to achieve the goals of the national economic objectives.

National security policy is the art of advising the national power so as to guarantee the conquest and the maintenance of the national objectives.[19]

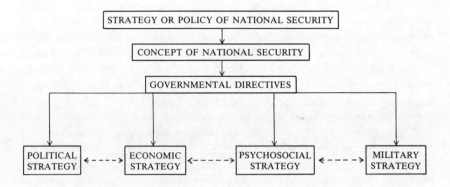

Source: General Golbery do Couto e Silva, *Conjuntura Política Nacional, O Poder Executivo e Geopolítica do Brasil* (Rio de Janeiro: José Olympio Ed., 1981), p. 26.

Fig. 1. National Security

Together, the development policy and the security policy constitute the national policy, elsewhere in the ESG textbook termed the "national strategy." Further clarification of the national strategy is provided by its definition as "the art of preparing and applying the national power of the state to counteract existing or potential obstacles that impede the achievement or the maintenance of the objectives that are determined by the national policy of the government."[20]

These "existing or potential obstacles," in turn, result from a variety of causes, ranging from lack of material resources or problems in the international markets, to unfavorable political circumstances that cause internal "adverse factors," "antagonisms," and "pressures." The different levels of difficulty encountered by the state are carefully defined in the textbook's discussion of the grand strategy:

Obstacles [óbices]: are obstacles of any kind—material or spiritual—which may arise from structural, conjunctural, natural conditions or be the result of the human will. They impede the attainment and the maintenance of the national objectives.

Adverse factors [fatores adversos]: are obstacles—internal and external—that are in opposition to the efforts of the national community in its desire to reach or maintain the national objectives.

Antagonisms [antagonismos]: are obstacles of a peculiar form. They are the expression of a deliberate, intentional, and otherwise dissenting activity. As such, they question the attainment or the maintenance of the national objectives.

Pressures [pressões]: are obstacles of an extreme degree in which the dissenting and disputing will becomes manifested by its capacity to counteract the power of the government in an organized fashion.[21]

Depending on an assessment of the political conjuncture, the grand strategy must plan counteroffensive actions specifically targeted at eliminating or neutralizing the effects of each of the different levels or degrees of opposition activity. The actual techniques for handling each level of opposition discussed in the ESG text vary. Counteroffensive techniques range from daily routine security measures, such as checking documents, surveillance, and other methods of intelligence gathering, to emergency measures and total mobilization of the power of the armed forces to deal with situations defined as "pressures," that is, an organized and powerful challenge to the power of the government. This strategy, as we shall see later, helps to explain the violent reaction of the state to the metalworkers' strikes in São Bernardo do Campo in 1980 and the subsequent targeting of social movements linked to the Catholic church—particularly in the countryside and in the *comunidades de base* (basic Christian communities). These movements have been defined as "pressures," which require total mobilization to neutralize their effect and the danger they represent for national policy. Dealing with pressures may involve the establishment of "emergency areas" that allow the state to use its full coercive power. According to the ESG textbook, pressure situations that require "emergency actions" are defined as those resulting from "war or the imminence of war, internal insurrections, civil disturbances, illegal strikes, floods, fires, and other situations of public calamity."[22]

Government directives primarily concern the different counteroffensive actions required to deal with obstacles. These directives also provide the specific strategies defined by the *Manual básico* as the political, the economic, the psychosocial, and the military, for dealing with the different areas involved in the control of antagonisms or even pressures. The political strategy defines state goals and directives for the neutralization of obstacles, antagonisms, or pressures within the political sphere—the executive, the legislature, the judiciary, and political parties.[23] The economic strategy is concerned with both the private and the public sectors of the economy. This area is further subdivided into specific policies for the primary, secondary, and tertiary sectors. In essence, the economic strategy is concerned with the compilation of the basic information necessary for a coherent economic development policy, integrated into the policy of national security.[24] The psychosocial strategy, for the purposes of national security policy, is defined in the textbook as concerned with the institutions of civil society: the family, schools and universities, the mass media, trade unions, the church, private enterprise. The grand strategy must plan specific strategies for dealing with obstacles, antagonisms, and pressures from each of these areas.[25] The military strategy, finally, is designed to control the navy, army, air force, and all the paramilitary units of Brazil's extensive military organization.[26]

For the counteroffensive to be effective against each specific area of potential opposition, there must be periodic conjunctural analyses to determine the appropriate policy to be applied to a particular target. It is then possible to decide how much coercion is required to deal with the level of opposition encountered in each of the sectors just described. The correct dose of coercion depends on the degree of "nonconformity" that exists (*oposição* or *contestação*).[27] The *Manual básico* provides guidelines for making such a determination according to (1) number of nonconforming nuclei; (2) intensity of activity; (3) quality and size of membership of nuclei; (4) emotional repercussions of their activity among population; (5) proportion between the number of nuclei that represent a direct challenge (*contestação*) and the opposition nuclei; (6) proportion of voters who are members of the government party; (7) proportion of votes obtained by government party and votes obtained by opposition; (8) quantity, quality, and degree of actual penetration of opinions into the main currents of public opinion.[28]

The greater the potential for organization and penetration of opposition nuclei in public opinion, the graver the threat to the state. At a high level of organization, the opposition no longer represents an obstacle or antagonistic activity, but rather enters the more serious category of pressure, thus requiring a greater degree of coercion.

In summary, the planning and running of the national security state involves the development of government directives for determining policies and structures for the control of every area of political and civil society. To carry out the program, it has been necessary to take full control of state power, centralize it in the executive branch, and place those closest to the information network and the programming of internal security policy in key positions in government. In later chapters, I shall explore how this was put into practice and how the specific controls for each of the specific areas of opposition were developed in constant dialectical relationship with the opposition.

Brazil's Role in an International Context

The second important element of the Doctrine of National Security and Development is the way in which it sees Brazil's particular place in the arena of world superpower confrontation. The most influential of the geopolitical studies that explore this question has been General Golbery's *Conjuntura política nacional*, whose argument I shall briefly summarize.

According to Golbery, geographical conditions determine, in large part, a nation's destiny. The power of the nation and its ability to achieve full economic development depend on its resource endowment, and even political and strategic alliances among nations are related to and partially determined by geographical position. In a climate of total and permanent war, there is no room for neutrality. The superpowers are engaged in a life-and-death struggle; the technology of modern warfare collapses time and geographical barriers. Since there is no way to remain outside, all nations must take sides. The side taken is already to a large extent geographically determined. Because of its geographical position, the Latin American continent is clearly committed to the United States' camp, and is thus inevitably within its sphere of influence and control. The economic power of the "Giant of the North" forecloses the possibility of neutrality for Latin America; manifest destiny impels Latin American nations to join the United States in the general defense of the West against the threat of Communist expansion, represented by the imperial ambitions of the Soviet Union.[29]

General Golbery argues that Latin America is of crucial importance within the framework of Western alliances, particularly to the United States, and that, within Latin America, Brazil is the most important partner. He goes so far as to assert that the Western industrialized nations and the United States "cannot survive without the alliance of the nations of Central and South America," for a number of reasons, including the need for Latin American support in the United Nations, provision of strategic materials, control and protection of maritime traffic and ocean routes to Africa, collective security, and demographic resources for army conscripts in extracontinental operations.[30] Brazil's superiority in this partnership derives from its geographical position (in terms of control of the South Atlantic), its vast natural resources, particularly in strategic minerals, and its large population. Although accepting the necessity of subordination to the Giant of the North, Golbery nonetheless claims the bargaining position of a privileged ally. In arguing that Brazil should command a high price because of its privileged situation, Golbery states that

when we see that the United States negotiates, using the weight of dollars, immense amounts of aid in order to gain the support and cooperation of undecided people or even frankly hostile nations of the Western European region, in the Middle East, or in Asia—it seems to us to be only just that we should also learn to bargain at high prices and to use the fact that we, as a nation, hold the trump card.

We should use this to obtain the necessary means to develop our land . . . and to carry out our mission. We may also invoke a "manifest destiny" theory, especially since it does not collide directly with that of our bigger and more powerful brother in the North.[31]

This viewpoint is widely held by the military. It helps to explain why Brazil has followed an independent foreign policy and has even come into conflict with the U.S. government. Brazilian military leaders believe that the highest price should be paid for the continuing support of Brazil and its integration into the general framework of the Western alliance. In addition, the military clearly has some imperialist ideas of its own, particularly as regards the relationship between Brazil and other Latin American nations. Thus it has taken a "pragmatic approach to foreign relations." The military clearly believes in the manifest destiny of Brazil, in its geographically strategic position, and in its potential to achieve superpower status.

The Economic Model of the Doctrine

The third important element of the Doctrine of National Security and Development is its economic development component. An analysis of the writings coming out of the ESG helps to clarify the economic model envisaged in the doctrine.

First, there can be no national security without a high degree of economic development. A nation's security requires the development of productive resources, industrialization and effective utilization of natural resources, extensive transport and communication networks to integrate a vast territory, and the development and training of a skilled labor force with technical know-how. Thus among the most important factors in a nation's security are its capacity for accumulation and absorption of capital, the quality of its labor force, the development of science and technology, and the efficacy of its industrial sectors.[32] Industrial development is indispensable to national economic policy. The ESG textbook defines the goal of economic development to be the achievement of complete integration and complete national security, particularly as an underdeveloped nation is especially vulnerable to the indirect strategy of the Communist enemy. One counteroffensive strategy is therefore a rapid takeoff in economic development, to gain the support of the population.

Although the rapid takeoff is the aspect most emphasized in the ESG classroom materials, General Golbery's writings focus on a slightly different aspect of economic development. In terms of overall continental and national defense in the context of Western defense strategy, economic and infrastructural development in Brazil are essential to counteract the extreme vulnerability resulting from the country's vast empty spaces. Golbery terms the uninhabited and undeveloped expanses "paths of penetration," which must be effectively "plugged." He therefore argues not for an economic policy geared toward eliciting the support of the population, but rather for one aimed at the integration of the national territory. This integration would follow three distinct phases:

First phase: To firmly establish the basis of our continental prominence by binding the Northeast and South to the Central nucleus of the nation while at the same time guaranteeing the inviolability of the vast expanse of unpopulated interior by effectively plugging all possible paths of penetration.
Second phase: To colonize the Northwest, starting from the basis of the Central

platform, in order to fully integrate the Center-West peninsula into the Brazilian whole.

Third phase: To flood the Amazon region with civilization, in particular the frontier areas, starting from the advanced base that is to be constructed in the Center-West and following a coordinated and planned strategy of development along the large river.[33]

Infrastructural improvements must include communication networks, highways, and railways, which would crisscross the region. The rail services must first be removed from the control of subversives and then carefully administered. The nation should also develop the navigational potential of its rivers and ensure the security of its ocean ports. These improvements would be completed in the first phase of the economic development strategy. The second phase would involve the occupation of the "heartland" in the interior of the Central region, which includes the states of Mato Grosso, Goiás, Paraíba, and the valley of the São Francisco River as well as the valleys of the large Amazon tributaries, especially the Araguaia and the Tocantins. The third phase would then move from the interior heartland to the conquest of the Amazon region. Thus, the entire development-security effort must move from the firm control of the essential Central plains, and from the pole of Manaus, in such a way as to form a protective "concentrical area of maneuver."[34] Golbery sees the integration and development of the interior plains and of the Amazon region as necessary for all "national security maneuvers," thus requiring that special attention be paid to these areas, which have been neglected for too long and which are vulnerable to penetration.

It is essential to keep in mind that, under the Doctrine of National Security and Development, military defense rather than the population's basic material needs is understood as the primary objective of economic development. Development of the vast expanses of Brazil's interior and the Amazon, for example, is desirable mainly as a means of plugging up possible paths of penetration, not as a way of raising the standard of living in the area. This is particularly true of development programs in the central plains regions along the banks of the great Araguaia and Amazon rivers. It is, of course, precisely in the central interior region and in the Amazon that Brazil's greatest mineral wealth, one of General Golbery's strategic "trumps," is to be found. The main focus of the economic model is the strengthening of Brazil's productive potential so as to increase its bargaining power in the global geopolitical arena. Benefits that might accrue to the population in the process are secondary to geopolitical considerations in setting priorities.

To increase industrial production, a military-industrial complex is to be encouraged and developed. The most desirable model for bringing about industrialization is considered to be the capitalist one. The ESG textbook explicitly analyzes capitalist relations and pays close attention to the contradictions and problems Marxist theory raises. The manual concludes that Marx was mistaken mainly because he did not foresee the potential regulatory power of the state, developed in Keynesian economics, as a way of managing the capitalist system and of eliminating problems while conserving benefits. National Security Doctrine theorists in Brazil explicitly reject laissez faire capitalism. They do not believe in the "magic of the market," but consider this to be an outmoded form of capitalist economic development that is neither viable nor desirable today, especially in the context of a developing nation. It is here that the Brazilian theoreticians seem to differ most from their Chilean and Argentinian counterparts. Brazilian theoreticians argue the need for a strong state, able to apply a variety of fiscal incentives, tax inducements or penalties to regulate the model of economic development in an almost completely centrally planned economy. Modern capitalism, the ESG claims, must pursue an economic model based on strong state interference in regulatory planning and programming of the national economy and in direct production or infrastructural investment, both of which may be combined with direct appropriation of natural resources.[35] The model is thus closer to state capitalism than to laissez faire capitalism. "Liberal capitalism" is a folly leading directly to the kinds of problems that Marx studied; the regulatory potential of the state makes it possible to overcome these contradictions and realize the full power of the development of the industrial capacity of a nation.[36]

Military practice since 1964 has been fairly consistent with this analysis. State participation in planning and regulating the economy after 1964 has reached unprecedented levels of centralization, and state involvement in direct production, and in exploitation of mineral resources through state-owned corporations, has also increased dramatically.[37]

In summary, the economic model includes these major elements. It is a model of capitalist development based on an alliance among state, multinational, and local capital. The ESG textbook explicitly considers the contribution of multinational corporations to be by and large positive in the economic development of a nation, in spite of the fact that it may generate considerable internal opposition.[38] Security, as an element in the "development with security" concept, implies the need to control the social and political environment so as to provide an attractive climate for multinational investment. Social peace is also necessary for the achievement of maximum rates of capital accumulation in order that rapid economic growth reach a "takeoff" stage of development. The security element in the model implies the need to occupy the Central plains of the interior states bordering the Araguaia, São Francisco, and Amazon rivers so as to guarantee frontier defense and effectively plug up paths of penetration, which may be vulnerable to Communist aggression. Economic development is not geared to basic needs, and development policy is not particularly concerned with the establishment of priorities for a rapid amelioration of the living standards of the majority of the population. Education programs, according to the ESG, should be concerned mainly with training technicians to participate in the process of economic growth and industrialization. Other basic-needs programs, such as low-cost housing, community health, and basic primary education, are low priorities. Ultimately, the economic model is designed to augment Brazil's potential as a world power. For such primordial and all-important goals, the ESG textbook emphasizes, the sacrifice of successive generations may be necessary.[39]

Part II. The First Stage of Institutionalization, 1964-1968

2. The Foundations of the National Security State *—Operation Cleanup—*

In the early morning of 2 April 1964 a special session of the Brazilian Congress was called to declare the presidency vacant. Until a new president could be elected, the speaker of the house, Congressman Ranieri Mazzilli, would fill the post. In reality, he was a figurehead, and de facto power was in the hands of the High Command of the Revolution, composed of General Arthur da Costa e Silva, Vice-Admiral Rademaker, and Brigadier Correia de Mello.[1] The High Command of the Revolution issued a series of statements setting forth the program of the new government. The new ruling military junta promised to "restore legality," reinforce the "threatened democratic institutions," and re-establish the "federative composition of the nation" by breaking up the excessively centralized power of the federal government and returning power to the states. Above all, it promised to "eliminate the danger of subversion and communism," and to punish those in government who had become rich through corruption.[2]

The military-civilian coalition appealed to the population for support and justified its actions on the basis of this program. But the quest for internal security by eliminating the "enemy within" came into conflict with the stated goals of restoring legality and reinforcing democratic institutions. The measures taken to purge everyone who had been linked to social movements and to the previous government led to the institutionalization of the national security state, beginning in the early days under the High Command of the Revolution, with the passage of Institutional Act No. 1.

The contradiction between declared goals—reinforcing democracy and restoring legality—and the need for increased repression to smother dissent became the root of the permanent legitimacy crisis that has plagued the national security state. The coalition in power did not have a ready-made model for all the structures of the new state; it had only elaborated doctrine, an ideology, on which it based its political thinking. The economic interests of the class alliance that supported the takeover combined with elements of the doctrine to impose an authoritarian character on the state. But the actual construction of the national security state was the result of a dialectical confrontation with the opposition. The state was formed by means of a continuous process of reformulating plans and regulations and expanding the scope of coercive power.

Institutional Act No. 1

The institutional act was drafted in secret and published on the afternoon of 9 April 1964, only seven days after the takeover.[3] The authors made the justification and intent of the act clear in the preamble:

TO THE NATION

Today's institutional act could only have been drafted by the commanders-in-chief of the army, navy, and air force, who—in the name of the victorious revolution and with the support of the majority of the nation—now propose to begin a new government and to provide it with the indispensable institutional framework with which to carry out its mission of economic, financial, political, and moral reconstruction. . . .

The victorious revolution needs to institutionalize itself. . . . Only the victorious revolution may make the rules and regulations that will constitute the new government and provide it with the powers and juridical instruments that will ensure its effective power to rule in the interests of the country.

In order to demonstrate that we do not intend to radicalize the process of revolution, we have decided to maintain the Constitution of 1946. We have limited ourselves to amending it in the part that deals with the powers of the president of the republic. . . . In order to further reduce the powers that rightfully belong to this victorious revolution, we have also decided to maintain the national Congress—only establishing certain limitations on its power.

Thus, it should be clear that the revolution does not intend to legitimate itself through Congress. On the contrary, it is Congress that is made legitimate by this institutional act, which could only result from the inherent and revolutionary exercise of constituent power.[4]

There was clearly a felt need to institutionalize a new apparatus to support the "revolution." Already in the preamble of the first institutional act, authority is defined not as coming from the people but from the de facto exercise of power. It is the executive that "chooses" to maintain both the constitution and the national Congress, but that places serious restrictions on both. Congress is to derive its legitimacy not from its electoral mandate, but from the de facto power whose locus is in the executive. This is entirely consistent wih the content of the Doctrine of National Security and Development.

Nonetheless, since the doctrine was not widely known by the public at the time, the institutional act came as a shock to those who had supported military intervention out of a belief that its intention was to restore democracy. The press reaction to the act was almost unanimously negative.[5] In effect, Institutional Act No. 1 broke apart the tacit support for the military-civilian coalition and gave birth to the dialectic of opposition and state.

The act severely limited the powers of Congress; legislative power was to a large extent transferred to the executive. Article 3 gave the executive the power to introduce constitutional amendments and limited congressional debate on such amendments to thirty days (later changed to forty days). Congress did retain the right to reject the amendments within this period by a majority vote of both houses. Article 4 created the legislative measure known as the *decurso de prazo*, by which "urgent" bills introduced by the executive are automatically approved unless Congress decides otherwise within thirty days (later changed to forty and then to sixty days). This measure is particularly important in that a simple government filibuster for the required period can guarantee the automatic approval of any bill the executive considers urgent. Article 5 transferred exclusive competence in financial or budgetary legislation to the executive. Article 6 transferred the authority to decree a state of siege from Congress to the executive, reserving for Congress only the right to reject or approve the move within an allotted time period.[6] Most important of all, the act temporarily eliminated parliamentary immunity, thereby giving the executive the power to cancel summarily the electoral mandates of representatives at any level of government. This procedure became known as the *cassação de mandato* and was widely used for a variety of purposes.

The institutional act contained measures for control of the judiciary and for the suspension of individual rights to allow the clean-up operation a free hand. Article 7 suspended constitutional and legal guarantees of job tenure or job security for a six-month period. Thus the state, upon "summary investigation" and within the fixed period established by the article, could "fire or dismiss, transfer or put in reserve or put in force an early retirement" of civilian bureaucrats or military personnel. This article facilitated purges of the state bureaucracy and kept under control those sectors of the military that disapproved of present policy, or that were linked to the previous period. All public employees were covered under this article. The last paragraph also established that judicial competence would be "limited to extraneous formality, the juridical consideration of the facts being considered prohibited."[7] Article 8 established that special inquiries would be conducted into the activities of those considered to have committed a crime "against the state, its property, public or social order, or engaged in acts of revolutionary war." Such inquiries could apply to individual cases as well as to collective action.[8] This article laid the basis for the Military Police Inquiries (*Inquéritos Policial Militar*, IPMs), which tried thousands of people. Unlike article 7, however, this article did not specifically preclude juridical consideration of the substance of the case, thus allowing the judiciary to play an important liberalizing role in this period. Article 10 allowed for the cancellation of the electoral mandates (*cassação de mandato*) of federal, state, and municipal representatives as well as of the political rights of any citizen for a period of ten years. Cancellation of political rights eliminated the right to vote, to run for office, and to participate in political party activities.[9] The act included a list of those who were to lose their electoral mandates and have political rights cancelled immediately. Former president João Goulart headed the list, followed by forty members of Congress. Another one hundred persons were specifically named as losing political rights for a ten-year period.

Finally, the act included an early attempt to institutionalize the mechanism of transference of executive power. The first Electoral College to choose the president of Brazil indirectly was composed of a carefully trimmed federal Congress of 326 deputies and 62 senators. General Humberto Castello Branco received 361 votes and was inaugurated as president on 15 April 1964, replacing the military junta that had ruled as the High Command of the Revolution for the first month of the national security state.

The passage of Institutional Act No. 1 thus effectively laid the first important legal foundations for the implementation of the Doctrine of National Security and Development. It was considered to be such an important juridical instrument for the institutionalization of the new state that Luís Viana, himself a member of the Castello Branco government, could state that, "without it, the civilian-military movement of March could be considered a coup d'état or a simple revolt to remove or substitute people in the command posts of government."[10]

"Operation Cleanup"

The foundations laid, the military was now in a position to pursue its program along the lines set forth in the grand strategy of the Doctrine of National Security and Development. Beyond the general activation of the repressive forces of the new state, this policy—in conformity with the principles of the doctrine—targeted particular, strategically sensitive areas of possible opposition: political, economic, psychosocial, and military. The economic strategy, which in practice required an entirely new planning and administrative program, will be discussed in the following section. Here I shall examine some of the main features of initial efforts to activate the repressive forces and to secure state control over the political, military, and psychosocial areas—a set of policies that the military called by the code name *Operação Limpeza* ("Operation Cleanup").

The Activation of Repressive Forces

The general counteroffensive of the grand strategy was conducted primarily within the institutional framework of investigations called Military Police Inquiries (IPMs). On 27 April 1964, the Castello Branco government issued an executive decree-law that officially established the IPMs (already in the institutional act).[11] Special investigating committees were set up at all levels of government, in all public ministries, agencies, state corporations, federal universities, and other organizations connected to the federal government. The Military Police Inquiries were to examine the activities of employees—civilian and military—at municipal, state, and federal levels to identify those engaged in "subversive" activities. The IPMs constituted the legal mechanism for the systematic search for absolute security and elimination of the enemy within. Once an inquiry was completed, the alleged involvement of the accused person or persons was examined by the chief of the department to which the accused were connected. The final decision concerning punishment was up to the president, the state governors, or the mayors. Once decided, a decree establishing the particular form of punishment had to be published in either the federal *Diário Oficial da União* or in the official registers of the states and municipalities.[12]

The IPMs became a source of de facto power for the group of colonels designated to head or coordinate the investigations. These composed the first core of a nascent repressive apparatus and the beginning of a pressure group of hard-line officers within the national security state. Because, at that time, a decision could be reviewed by the judiciary, the state and federal supreme courts often reversed the decisions of the IPMs. This established a growing confrontation between the traditional legal structure and the parallel extralegal or "revolutionary" structure. The colonels of the IPMs became increasingly strident in their protest against such judicial autonomy and eventually forced the executive to broaden the measures of control over judges and over the judiciary itself.

IPMs also came to serve local political interests. Some UDN (União Democrática Nacional) politicians who consistently lost elections took the ultimate recourse of accusing their political adversaries of "subversive" activities, which involved them in an ongoing IPM in order to eliminate unwanted political competition. This was the case, for example, in the state of Goiás, where Governor Mauro Borges, himself a colonel, was forcibly removed from office and had his political rights canceled for ten years because of accusations of Communist infiltration made by Irapuan Costa Júnior, then a professor, but soon to become the governor of the state of Goiás.[13] Since such accusations were not subject, particularly in the case of *cassação*, to the test of holding up in court and to the decision of a neutral jury, such local power struggles were frequent.

Lacking any formal juridical basis, the IPMs were bound by no fixed rules of evidence or standards of proof. The colonels themselves often established the legal precepts on which to base their decisions. The evidence of public opinion was sufficient, to some, to prove subversive or revolutionary activity that warranted punishment: "When the fact is public and notorious it is independent of proof—as is established in the general premises of law that have abolished the system of 'legal certainty,' thus freeing the judge from having a text prejudice." This explains some of the conclusions of the best-known IPMs of that period. Professor Rodolfo da Costa e Silva, of Goiás, for example, was condemned because "he participated in various conferences promoted by the Academic Center where he talked about political themes, all strongly subversive, a fact that is related to us by the witness Dr. Irapuan Costa Jr." Engineering professor Elder Rocha Lima was charged simply with "being really a Communist, subversive, and agitator, as is well known by public opinion." Another accused person, Maristela Duarte Mendes, a housewife, denied any participation in politics, but was accused nonetheless and found guilty because "the reality of the facts negates her denial of her activities. She visited Russia and has friendly ties with people considered to be extremely communistic as is well known in the gossip that circulates throughout the city of Anápolis." Guilt by family association was common: Edson Germano de Brito, for example, was found guilty of "being notoriously subversive and a Communist agitator, as is the case of the entire family of the Germano de Britos in the state of Goiás," and public employee Mauro Campos Neto was considered a Communist because "his father was always a militant of the Communist party and taught him this as a child."[14]

Mere accusation in an IPM was sufficient to begin a series of persecutions that sometimes included imprisonment and torture. The number of people involved in the hundreds of IPMs is extremely difficult to establish. The data are dispersed in the *Diário Oficial da União* and the registers of all the different states and municipalities. Considering that Brazil had at that time twenty-two states and over thirty-five hundred municipalities, and that the IPMs were installed in all government agencies and departments, institutions of learning, and in corporations directly or partly owned by the government, the gathering of complete information is practically impossible.

Operation Cleanup was not limited to purges of political and bureaucratic offices. From the outset, pressure mounted in military circles for more direct repression of the population. Lists of those who should be expelled, purged, or arrested were compiled in military barracks. Luís Viana recalls,

Already on the fourth of April, in answer to a question, fourteen officers of the Escola de Comando do Estado Maior sent their lists and suggestions to the military commander of the school, considering it to be indispensable that the electoral mandates and the political rights of all Communist, nationalist, and activist deputies be canceled. It also urged the purging or arrest of all who were considered criminals or who had committed acts "threatening to the democratic liberties and to the rights that are established by the constitution."[15]

These officers were integrated into the extreme right-wing group of hard-liners who, departing from the long-term viewpoint of the ESG strategists, favored greater quantities of immediate force.[16] The hard-line sector coalesced around the minister of war, General Arthur da Costa e Silva, and used him as an instrument of political pressure on the government's decisions.

In the immediate aftermath of the military takeover, a vast campaign of search and arrest was launched throughout the nation. The army, navy, and air force were mobilized according to established counteroffensive techniques to conduct the large-scale operations of "sifting with a fine-tooth comb" and "fishnet." Roadblocks were set up and house-to-house searches conducted for persons included in previously prepared lists. The aim was to clean up all of those connected to the previous government, to political parties considered to be Communist or highly infiltrated by Communists, and to the social movements of the pre-1964 period. Particularly targeted were trade union leaders, peasant leaders, intellectuals, teachers, students, and lay organizers of the Catholic movements in the universities and the countryside.

During the first months after the takeover, reports indicate that perhaps as many as 50,000 persons were arrested in the country as a whole.[17] A precise accounting is impossible, since search-and-arrest techniques (*arrastão* and *pente fino*) included arresting anyone who could not prove he or she was not a suspect or who did not have valid identification documentation.[18] In addition, part of the strategy of intimidation involved temporary arrest— usually followed by beating or violent treatment for a few hours—and quick release before habeas corpus writs could be filed. In this manner the military avoided the supervision of the legal system and could act almost without limit to its power. Some published reports suggest the magnitude of Operation Cleanup. *Time* magazine, for example, reported that during just one week at least 10,000 persons were arrested—4,000 of those in the city of Rio de Janeiro.[19] The *Correio da Manhã* daily published lists of names of persons under arrest. Careful counting for May shows 1,655 prisoners listed.

By the end of 1964 the extent and the violence of the repression in Operation Cleanup had become a matter of international concern. The International Commission of Jurists, in Geneva, issued a formal report in September 1964 condemning the government for the continuing imprisonment of eight thousand persons as well as for the imposition of press censorship and the cancellation of electoral mandates.[20]

Prisoners were held in makeshift prisons. The large football stadium of Rio de Janeiro, the Maracanã, and a number of navy ships, such as the *Custódio de Mello* and the *Raul Soares*, were turned into gigantic, temporary prison camps. The prisoners were also kept in military barracks and at the military police headquarters of various states.[21] Slowly, reports of the widespread use of torture leaked to the press. These reports spurred a large press campaign to force the Castello Branco government to investigate the allegations of torture of political prisoners. The *Correio da Manhã* spearheaded a press campaign and denounced the widespread use of torture, particularly in the states of Rio de Janeiro, Pernambuco, Rio Grande do Sul, Minas Gerais, São Paulo, and Goiás.[22] Journalist Márcio Moreira Alves, of the *Correio da Manhã*, was sent as a special correspondent to Recife to investigate the allegations of torture. He was smuggled into a prison and was able to compile testimony and witness firsthand the wounds inflicted on various prisoners. As a result of his investigation, articles were written with details of torture techniques as well as the location and names of those primarily responsible. A detailed account of torture in different states, based on his investigations and those of committees of lawyers and journalists, was published in a carefully documented book, *Torturas e torturados*.[23]

Eventually, General Castello Branco ordered an investigation, which was headed by General Ernesto Geisel, then chief of military staff. Although the investigation ended because of "insufficient proof," torture was in fact temporarily controlled and significantly diminished. The press campaign against torture in 1965 was thus the first example of an organized public opinion movement sufficiently forceful to occasion modifications in the strategies of the national security state. It also served to turn others from active support of the nascent repressive apparatus and state policies.

The Political Strategy

Political strategy, according to ESG doctrine, concerns surveillance and control of political parties, the legislature, the judiciary, and the executive. In the initial stage, the judiciary suffered much less direct interference than the other branches of government. Political crimes remained within the jurisdiction of civil courts, and after the completion of an IPM, the investigation of cases was ultimately turned over to the judiciary for legal processing. In fact, the judiciary maintained a high degree of independence, which included the granting of habeas corpus to political prisoners. The cases that caused most direct conflict with the fledgling repressive apparatus involved the granting of habeas corpus to Governors Miguel Arraes of Pernambuco and Mauro Borges of Goiás. Even so, the judiciary was not immune to the cleanup operation, and forty-nine judges were purged in 1964.

Use of *cassação*, however, showed that the legislature and the political parties were important targets of Operation Cleanup. As a result of these purges, political representation within the legislative branch was completely transformed. As the data in table 1 show, the Partido Social Democrático (PSD) and the Partido Trabalhista Brasileiro (PTB) were by 1962 the largest parties in Congress. The PTB increased its representation steadily in every election after 1945, until it surpassed in strength the old conservative UDN, which remained fairly stable over the period. Alliances formed by the PTB and PSD were unbeatable in elections and sufficiently strong to circumvent much of the stalemate in Congress over political and social reforms.

Of the forty members of Congress who lost their mandates in the first list, which accompanied the enactment of Institutional Act No. 1, eighteen belonged to the PTB, four to the PSP, three to the PSD, three to the PST, and three to the PDC. The remainder had no party affiliation listed. Subsequent lists of *cassações* brought the total number of purges for 1964 in Congress to fifty. In addition, the PTB lost four alternate deputies and the PSD lost one senator, Juscelino Kubitschek, during that first year. The effect was to change the composition of Congress and weaken its potential for resistance of the legal initiatives of the executive.

In the state assemblies, there was a similar tendency to target those parties most identified with past social movements. In 1964 forty-three members lost their mandates by force of Institutional Act No. 1: thirty-one from the PTB, seven from the PSD, and others who had no party affiliation listed. Of eleven alternate members of the state legislature who lost their mandates in the first year, eight belonged to the PTB. At the municipal level, of ten aldermen removed from their posts in the first year of the national security state, four belonged to the PTB and two to the PSD.[24]

These figures show that, although the main target of the attack was João Goulart's party, the PTB, the PSD also suffered from the attempt to break the coalition and to intimidate remaining liberal representatives into quiescence or subdued protest. Thus the policy of *cassação* served two important functions: it intimidated Congress through the "demonstration effect" of what could happen to those who rebelled, and it significantly reduced the potential for legislative coalition between the two major parties, the PTB and the PSD. The UDN was completely spared in the purges. As an extremely conservative party, it would provide the main congressional basis of political support for the new state.

Purges of the civilian bureaucracy were a further significant component of Operation Cleanup, for they served both to eliminate opposition and to open up positions for personnel more closely identified with the policies of the new state. The effort to purge the civilian bureaucracy of those connected to the previous populist period reflected the desire to modify

Table 1
Party Representation in Congress

Party	No. of Seats				
	1945	1950	1954	1958	1962
PSD—Social Democratic Party (Partido Social Democrático)	151	112	114	115	122
UDN—National Democratic Union (União Democrátia Nacional)	77	81	74	70	94
PTB—Brazilian Labor party (Partido Trabalhista Brasileiro)	22	51	56	66	109
PSP—Social Progressive party (Partido Social Progressista)	4	24	32	25	22
PR—Republican party (Partido Republicano)	7	11	19	17	5
PDC—Christian Democratic party (Partido Democrata Cristão)	2	2	2	7	20
PTN—National Labor party (Partido Trabalhista Nacional)	0	5	6	7	11
PST—Social Labor party (Partido Social Trabalhista)	0	9	2	2	8
PL—Liberation party (Partido Libertador)	1	5	8	3	3
PRP—Popular Representation party (Partido de Representação Popular)	2	2	3	3	4
PSB—Brazilian Socialist party (Partido Socialista Brasileiro)	0	1	3	9	4
PRT—Republican Labor party (Partido Republicano Trabalhista)	0	1	1	2	3
MTR—Labor Reform Movement (Movimento Trabalhista Renovador)	0	0	0	0	4
PCB—Brazilian Communist party (Partido Communista Brasileiro)	14	0	0	0	0
No party or coalition	6	0	6	0	0
Total seats	286	304	326	326	409

Source: U.S. Army, *Area Handbook for Brazil, 1964* (Washington, D.C.: U.S. Government Printing Office, 1964), p. 314.

basic economic policy. It is significant that the purges were most severe in the sectors of the state bureaucracy most directly responsible for social and economic policy; by far the most extensive purges occurred in the Ministries of Public Works, Labor, and Finance (see table 2). The demonstration effect of insecurity and fear further quieted opposition in the civilian bureaucracy. For every one person punished after inclusion in an IPM or simply by the application of Institutional Act No. 1, there were others who were also included but who temporarily escaped the hatchet. As was the case with the legislature, this element of insecurity would suffice to silence most protest.

The Military Strategy

The control of the military is an area of particular and specific interest to the national security state. A series of control mechanisms were created to limit political participation and to enforce hierarchical standards severely so as to guarantee the predominance of the views of those officers holding power. Purges were directed mainly against officers with influence or

Table 2
Purges of the Civilian Bureaucracy

Organization	No. Purged		
	1964	1965–1967	Total
Ministry of Public Works	505	5	510
Ministry of Labor	219	0	219
Ministry of Finance	275	0	275
Ministry of Mines & Energy	48	2	50
Ministry of Agriculture	23	2	25
Ministry of Foreign Relations	6	0	6
Ministry of Commerce & Industry	89	0	89
Ministry of Justice	49	91	140
Ministry of Health	40	1	41
Ministry of Education	67	15	82
Extraordinary Ministry of Coordination of Regional Programs	29	0	29
National Council of Telecommunications	0	3	3
Municipal government of Brasília	28	3	31
Urban Company of the New Capital of Brazil	30	0	30
Total	1,408	122	1,530

Source: *Dossier do Ministério da Aeronáutica.*

command over troops and were concentrated on those who had resisted the conspiracy against João Goulart's government on the grounds that the armed forces were sworn to protect and defend the constitution. Such officers (the *legalistas*)—even if many disapproved of Goulart's policies—had insisted that the transfer of presidential power should be legal.

The purges of the armed forces in the first year had a dual function: to eliminate all military personnel who were closely associated with the previous government, and to establish the predominance of the ESG and the extreme right wing. It was necessary to eliminate members of the democratic, nationalist sector of the military, who might oppose policies that intensified overt repression and favored multinational corporations. The rapid elimination of these groups from the armed forces was essential, thus the largest number of purges occurred in 1964, as may be seen in table 3. It is also noteworthy that the most extensive purges occurred in the army, the branch that could more effectively challenge the holders of power. The figures in table 3 refer only to the officer corps of the three main branches of the armed forces, as compiled in the *Dossier* of the air force. They are, in addition, indicative only of those who were punished by application of the powers of Institutional Act Nos. 1 and 2.

Repression of the troops was also severe, but there are few reliable figures to indicate the magnitude precisely. It is suggestive that, in the first months of 1964, some two thousand sailors were arrested. Sailors were a specific target of the counteroffensive, for many had participated in a revolt against their immediate officers during the Goulart period.[25] Sergeants, who also revolted against their superiors in the events immediately preceding the

Table 3
Purges of the Officer Corps

Branch of Armed Forces	No. Purged		
	1964	1965–1967	Total
Army	505	5	510
Navy	335	9	344
Air Force	360	14	374
Total	1,200	28	1,228

Source: *Dossier do Ministério da Aeronáutica.*

coup, were another sector severely repressed.[26] As more military officers withdrew their support of the policies of the national security state, the network for controlling the internal public had to be enlarged. Thus the repressive apparatuses and the intelligence network had to be extended down to every regiment and every battalion so as to maintain tight political surveillance over the members of the military forces and the military police.

The mechanism of *cassação* was used against the officers of the "internal" public with one aggravating circumstance: when a member of the military was punished under any of the institutional acts or their complementary acts, he would be declared legally dead. This essentially means that he automatically lost all military benefits acquired in the course of his career—pension, retirement benefits, promotion pay, health and education benefits, aid to children, and the like. The wife of a "dead" military officer would then receive a government widow's pension and would qualify for the regular aid to widows with dependent children. Clearly, this meant a considerable loss of income, for the widow's pension is much smaller than the actual pay of a career officer. In addition, when a military man had been *cassado* and removed from his occupation, it also became very difficult for him to find a civilian job. According to a general I interviewed who had been *cassado*, the limitations imposed were so severe that his only remaining right, in practice, was that of paying income tax. During the conversation he added, smiling, that for sixteen years he had insisted on writing on his income tax form, "I am dead." It should be noted, finally, that this bizarre punishment intensifies the effect of the culture of fear among the military and makes the deterrent effect of stories of persecution and punishment more powerful, thereby enhancing the potential for political control.

In addition, the military is ruled by a special military code, which establishes the legal structure and penalties for crimes tried by military courts. Besides the regulations in the military code, the members of the internal public are subjected to the internal disciplinary regulations (*regimento disciplinar interno*) in each of the separate branches of the armed forces and in the military police. These statutes control the political activities of the members and prohibit, among other things, any public statement of a political opinion.

The Psychosocial Strategy

The psychosocial strategy of Operation Cleanup focused especially on the social movements that had gained strength in the years prior to the military-civilian coup d'état. Military search-and-arrest maneuvers were conducted in universities, in the labor unions, in the peasant leagues, and in the many different Catholic movements of workers, peasants, and students.

In April 1964 the minister of education, Flávio Suplicy de Lacerda, officially installed the special investigating committees that established the IPMs in all Brazilian universities, and the Ministry of Education became directly involved in the hiring and firing of university personnel. Military authorities, through the Ministry of Education, insisted that IPMs were necessary to root out Communist agents, who utilized institutions of learning to "win the minds" of the people in accordance with what military authorities believed to be the indirect strategy of the Soviet Union. A Special Investigation Committee (Comissão Especial de Investigação Sumária, CEIS) composed of professors, chancellors, and other administrative personnel, appointed by the authorities, was established in each university for the purpose of conducting the purges.[27]

Troops invaded the University of São Paulo and almost completely destroyed the College of Philosophy, causing damage that was estimated at ten million cruzeiros. Participants and professors described the situation in the university as one of "terror and fear." One of the professors recalled the experience:

The university went through a thorough cleansing. . . . A letter was sent to the army. No one knows in detail what this letter contained. It was anonymous. However, right after receiving this anonymous letter, the army took all necessary steps to "clean up" the University of São Paulo.

We were not the only ones to suffer. The University of Brasília was invaded and completely destroyed by the troops. In the whole country similar actions happened. It seems to me it was like the French Revolution.[28]

The University of Minas Gerais (UFMG) was put under direct military intervention, and a military chancellor was appointed to run it for the first year. However, the protests became so loud that the minister of justice was forced to acquiesce and remove the appointee.[29] The list prepared for the UFMG purges included the names of over four hundred professors and researchers, but internal opposition was so strong that the actual number dismissed was in fact much smaller.[30]

Perhaps the most serious case of interference, however, was at the University of Brasília. During the government of João Goulart, the University of Brasília had pioneered efforts to integrate the curriculum and the needs of a developing society. The military considered this curriculum subversive and Communist-inspired, thus the complete dismantling of the University of Brasília and its reshaping was a primary goal of the groups that took power in 1964. Just one day after the takeover, troops invaded the university, arresting professors and all members of student organizations on the premises.

The political importance of the student organizations centralized in the National Union of Students (União Nacional dos Estudantes, UNE) made it a primary target of the psychosocial strategy of the cleanup operation. Student organizations were not to be allowed to engage in politics and were to be confined to the arrangement of recreational activities or to administrative concerns of student life. The UNE, however, primarily represented the students as a political pressure group vis à vis the government; hence, Operation Cleanup moved immediately against it. On 1 April, the same day as the coup, troops attacked the UNE headquarters in Rio de Janeiro and burned it to the ground. Students were arrested by the hundreds at all universities, and the UNE was officially banned and dismantled by the military government.[31] A new structure for student organization was developed—controlled by its ties to the Ministry of Education.

However, the forceful banning of the UNE and the enactment of legislation for the control of students spurred a resurgence of opposition within the student movement, in spite of repression. The student population's support of the UNE, in fact, increased after the enactment of the Lei Suplicy, which dissolved the organization. According to a former president of the UNE, Jean Marc von der Weid, the strictness of the controls was beneficial to the opposition groups:

What legally existed was a faculty union and a university union, but the state and the national union were now prohibited. This was because they created a new organization called the National Directory of Students. This organization was controlled by the Ministry of Education which alone could convene meetings, and the meetings were held in the Ministry of Education in Brasília.

In reaction, the banned UNE organized clandestinely a national referendum to see if the students accepted the controls and restrictions, or if they wished to support an illegal UNE. Approximately 98% of the students voted to support the illegal organization.

The other measure of the government that helped us was that voting became obligatory. The government forced all students to vote in the local level organizations for they wanted to bring out the "silent majority" which they assumed was against the leadership of the UNE. But this had the result of forcing students to participate and discuss the elections. Thus the program of the government for the universities could be discussed and criticized so our position was enormously reinforced.[32]

The UNE organized a parallel structure of representation and held its meetings and congresses clandestinely. It was instrumental in building a forceful student movement of direct opposition to the military, a movement that rose to the forefront of the political arena in 1967 and 1968.

The psychosocial strategy of Operation Cleanup also included the labor unions and the peasant leagues.[33] The former were structured in corporative organizations by a Labor Code copied from Mussolini's legislation for control of unions; the latter were independent associations of peasants. The leagues' chief goal was to win land titles and other rights for rural workers. They made up a system of rural unions that also fought for agrarian reform and a more equal distribution of land. The government was convinced that Communists had infiltrated the peasant leagues, and moved to have them disbanded. Their leadership and many members were arrested and included in the IPMs. The rural union structure was reshaped and brought under the jurisdiction of the Labor Code, thus submitting the independent rural movement to the corporative control of the Ministry of Labor.

In the case of labor unions, all that was necessary was to apply fully the Labor Code's control provisions, a legacy of the Estado Novo period, when Fascist influence was strong. One of these provisions allowed the ministry to intervene in trade unions and remove the elected officials from office by simple decree-law, with no appeal. The decree-law was published in the *Diário Oficial da União*, and the new officials were appointed directly by the Ministry of Labor. The ministry also had the power to annul elections, cancel the candidacy of any union leader, and both grant and withdraw legal recognition of trade unions.

During the populism period (1946–1964) these mechanisms were not applied with severity, because of the political cost to government. The Labor Code's union structure nonetheless remained intact; it was never reformed, not even during the Goulart government. Thus when the civilian-military coalition took power in 1964 it found a ready-made repressive legal framework for the control of trade unions and effectively used it.

In 1964 there were 7 confederations, 107 federations, and 1,948 urban workers' trade unions in existence.[34] The cleanup operation removed officers in 452 unions, 43 federations, and 3 confederations during the first year of the national security state.[35] Three other unions suffered a disguised form of intervention (*intervenção branca*, or "white intervention"), wherein elected officials were removed from office without the publication of a specific decree. One election was canceled because of alleged subversive activities, and the government abolished one labor union entirely.[36]

The 1964 interventions were generally justified with one of three different reasons: that the union, federation, or confederation officers had disappeared, and thus the ministry presumed abandonment and intervened to appoint new officers to run the unions; that the union officers were active subversives; or that the military commander of the region had been forced to "occupy the premises of the trade unions to avoid subversive activities." Under military occupation a union could not perform its normal functions and thus required the intervention of the Ministry of Labor. Often interventions simply ratified the de facto act of a local military commander or delegate of the regional labor court. According to the testimony of political actors, the arrest of union leaders was often the explanation of their "disappearance."[37] Newspaper accounts at the time provided names of arrested union leaders not accounted for by the police, including, in the State of São Paulo, the presidents of the Cubatão Petrochemicals Union, the São Paulo bakers, the oil workers, port workers, urban transport workers, longshoremen, port administration employees, São Paulo and Santos metalworkers, São Paulo bank workers, journalists, construction, graphic, and maritime workers. Intervention was concentrated in the larger unions: 70 percent of unions with more than five thousand members suffered intervention; 38 percent of those with one thousand to five thousand members, and 19 percent of unions with fewer than one thousand members.[38]

In Minas Gerais, between 1 April and 5 May 1964 there were twenty-eight interventions in urban trade unions, all of which were preceded by the Belo Horizonte Military Command's occupation of union headquarters. Union officers were either arrested or went underground. In Rio Grande do Sul the military occupied the unions and interrogated their officers about participation in the activities of the Comando Geral dos Trabalhadores (CGT), the central union organization, which had been set up as a structure parallel to the Labor Code prior to 1964.[39]

The situation in Rio de Janeiro was equally severe. Troops occupied the Rio Metalworkers', Naval Shipyard, and Bank Workers' unions. The minister of labor, Arnaldo Sussekind, decided to intervene immediately in at least 40 unions in the state of Guanabara in April 1964. These interventions were intended to uncover ties between the CGT, which the military was convinced had links to international communism. According to press reports, São Paulo was the worst hit: by June 1964 the government had ordered interventions in 270 workers' organizations in the state, including unions and federations.[40]

Rural unions, which were incorporated into the Labor Code in 1963, were also hard hit: 90 percent of the rural unions that organized between 1963 and 1964 were closed down, particularly in the State of Pernambuco.[41] Finally, all parallel interunion organizations that had been set up outside the auspices of the Labor Code were abolished by decree. These included the CGT and the Brazilian Confederation of Christian Workers (Confederação Brasileira de Trabalhadores Cristãs, CBTC).[42]

The case of the unions demonstrates the ability of the national security state to take advantage of existing controls, such as those provided by the Labor Code, as well as to create new structures when necessary. Control of the unions was necessary for the implementation of the wage-control policies, which were to be a foundation of the new economic model.

Structuring the New State

The three most important measures structuring the national security state in the first year were the creation of the National Intelligence Service (Serviço Nacional de Informações, SNI),[43] the administrative reforms that came with the first Government Economic Action Program (Programa de Ação Econômica do Governo, PAEG), and the wage-control policies. Building the new state involved institutionalizing the intelligence network necessary to control the enemy within and laying the foundations of the economic model.

The Creation of the National Intelligence Service

According to the *Manual básico*, information on internal security is required for the identification of "antagonisms and pressures" and for the surveillance of opposition activities to "permit the government to take the necessary measures to identify, neutralize, or annul" them.[44] Internal security is thus dependent on information, "precise information as to the reality of the political situation in the nation, the truth of the facts, the characteristics and intensity of the manifestations and the effects of antagonisms and pressures as well as the prediction of possible future events. A system of permanent organization of security information, which is adequately structured and manned by specially trained personnel, constitutes one of the most essential instruments for the planning and exercise of internal security."[45]

One of the first measures taken to institutionalize the new state was the creation of the SNI. President Castello Branco insisted that the SNI was intended to be not a secret police, but rather a means of "improving the efficiency of the executive, keeping it well informed on what is going on in the country so that it can act with confidence and opportunely." And, he added, "the SNI bears no resemblance to an agency of propaganda or indoctrination. There is no reason to see in it the potential for an institution of terrorist spying."[46] Whatever the initial intentions, the dynamics of the system and the quest for absolute security did make the SNI into an agency for spying on citizens; in a situation in which it was impossible to isolate the enemy within, all were suspect.

The SNI was formally created by Decree-Law No. 4341, on 13 June 1964. It was to be an advisory agency for the executive branch, responsible not to Congress but to the National Security Council and the president. The law established explicitly that the SNI must cooperate with the National Security Council in "all matters pertaining to national security." Its main purpose would be to "collect and analyze information pertinent to national security, to counterinformation, and to information on internal subversive affairs."[47]

In practice the SNI has come to be a de facto political power that is almost as important as the executive itself. All of the SNI chiefs have been extremely powerful men within the national security state, and many have become president. General Golbery do Couto e Silva, creator and first director of the SNI, has been one of the most powerful men behind the scenes, often referred to as the "gray eminence" of the state. Generals Garrastazú Médici and João Batista Figueiredo, both chiefs of the SNI, were later appointed president of the national security state; indeed, the occupant of that post is generally regarded as the most likely successor in the presidential chain.

The SNI has been an effective agency for intelligence and political control from the beginning. By law, it has one central agency located in Brasília, and regional agencies in each state and in all territories.[48] A regulatory law of 10 December 1964 set up the organizational structures of the SNI, regulated its budget, and specified its mission, defined as

the promotion and carrying out of the tasks of evaluation and integration of information; . . . to distribute such information among the various branches of the government; to establish all necessary connections with state and municipal governments, with private and state-owned enterprises, and to draw up certain plans, which must include:
1. the planning of strategic information;
2. the planning of internal security;
3. the planning of counterintelligence.[49]

By law, the SNI is not required to publish information, reveal its organizational structure, or discuss the functioning of its agencies. SNI personnel and agents may be drafted from other ministries or government departments, or from civilian or military bureaucracies, by a simple requisition from the SNI chief. The SNI director has the status of a government minister and is a member of the cabinet. He is appointed by the president, with the approval of Congress.

The SNI chief may also use secret "unpaid or paid service and collaboration of civilians, military personnel, public employees, or any other person to carry out specific and special missions."[50] Military personnel assigned to the SNI are considered to be on "special military mission" and are entitled to special merit. Civilians in SNI service have the right to a special reward, which is to be determined annually by the president.[51]

The SNI budget is the responsibility of the general secretary of the National Security Council and is established by the Ministry of Finance. The law that set up the SNI also established the amount of its first budget: two hundred million cruzeiros, equivalent at the time to about ninety million U.S. dollars.[52] The SNI is accountable only to the president, and thus reinforces the executive at the expense of the judiciary and the legislature, which have no power to supervise its operations. The SNI is as powerful an agency as the executive, and at every crisis point over the last seventeen years, it has exerted considerable pressure on the president.

The SNI is of particular interest here as an institution of the national security state. The juridical framework of the state was established by Institutional Act No. 1, but the creation of the SNI was the first legal application of the Doctrine of National Security and Development and laid the foundation for the immense repressive apparatus that was to develop.

The Economic Program

One of the first measures of the Castello Branco government's administrative reform was the creation of the Ministry of Planning and Economic Coordination (Ministério de Planejamento e Coordenação Econômica), which, as Dreifuss points out, "was a veritable reserve of the IPES."[53] The ministry was to coordinate the planning of and implement the economic model by facilitating foreign investment and increasing the rate of capital accumulation. The first economic team was composed of the minister of finance, Octávio de Bulhões, an economist of the Chicago school who was an active participant in the ESG/IPES conspiracy, and Roberto de Oliveira Campos, a former ambassador in Washington, with strong ties to U.S.-based multinational corporations.

The government's first Economic Action Program, of 1964-1966, established the fight against inflation as one of its main priorities. Three strategies were considered: the imposition of a tight credit policy for the private sector; the reduction of the deficit; and a wage control policy.[54] The policies of the Bulhões-Campos team combined a strong stabilization program guided by a strict monetarism and a series of decisions aimed at encouraging foreign investment.[55] Monetarist inflation-fighting techniques called for a temporary industrial recession coupled with the freeing of prices, which government subsidy during the Goulart years had kept artificially low. Gasoline, rent, wheat, and paper, in particular, were items that Roberto Campos decontrolled to further restrict the available money supply. Free market forces were also used to eliminate inefficient capital. Thus a reduction in the effective protection level and an end to subsidized credit during liquidity crises made it easier for foreign—especially American—firms to acquire bankrupt Brazilian companies.[56] The resulting denationalization of the economy has been a major characteristic of the Brazilian economic model. Foreign investment figures overstate the benefit to the country's economic development in that much of that investment has been applied to the purchase of existing facilities rather than to the creation of new productive capacity.

To attract foreign capital, Campos also pushed for an agricultural policy that would quiet fears concerning agrarian reform. He favored policies that would encourage production of export crops rather than cash crops for internal consumption.[57]

Campos and Bulhões wanted to eliminate all sources of tension between

Brazil and the United States with respect to regulation of foreign investment. Resolution of the cases of the American and Foreign Power Company (AMFORP) and the Mineração Novalimense (Hanna Corporation) was a priority, and other pending nationalization cases were also to be speedily resolved so as to establish "the new welcoming spirit toward foreign investment." But the most important early step taken to reassure foreign investors was the repeal of the Profit Remittance Law (Law no. 4131), which had been passed in 1962, over the vigorous objection of foreign investors and the U.S. embassy,[58] but which was not signed by President Goulart until January 1964. Five months after the takeover, a new regulatory law on profit remittance and registration of foreign capital, investment, and reinvestment, and the regulation of interest, royalties, and payments for technical assistance was forced through Congress under the *decurso de prazo* mechanism. Law no. 4390 (29 August 1964) placed no limit on the percentage of registered capital that could be remitted as profit. The only exception was an 8 percent limit on profit remittance of capital invested in the production of goods and services for luxury consumption. There was no limit on repatriation of capital. Reinvestment of profits was also legally treated as original capital.[59] A further incentive allowed foreign firms to reduce their tax on profits from 30 percent to 15 percent, if profits were set aside in a fund for reinvestment in industrial facilities. In addition, all machinery or equipment imported for use in projects considered to be of interest to the country's development were classified as direct foreign investment and were not taxed.[60]

The economic team's overall program was aimed at rationalizing the economy by concentrating capital in the more efficient industries and encouraging the penetration of more efficient and modern multinational capital. This aim was consistent with the tenets of the Doctrine of National Security and Development with regard to the beneficial effects of multinational investment; that is, the best chance for Brazil's development was for the country to become a priority area for foreign investment.

Wage Controls

Legislation aimed at controlling strike activities and regulating wage increases as a step toward an overall wage-control policy was considered necessary to attract foreign investment. The Antistrike Law (Lei de Greve, Law no. 4330) was passed on 1 June 1964. It amended the 1946 Constitution (which had guaranteed the right to strike) by defining the conditions under which a strike would be considered legal. Public employees or employees of state-owned corporations and agencies were expressly forbidden to strike. Strikes in "essential" services were also prohibited, as were strikes considered to be of a "political, social, or religious nature" and solidarity strikes.[61] The definition of what constitutes a political strike was left to the government.

Outside of these areas, strikes for "better working conditions or wages" were allowed but subjected to conditions that made them, in practice, virtually impossible. Most strikes declared legal by the labor courts since 1964 have involved corporations that had not paid their workers for more than three months. Some of the bureaucratic requirements for legalizing a strike are so burdensome and expensive that their fulfillment is beyond the reach of many unions. In his study of labor relations in Brazil, Kenneth Mericle shows that the government can generally prevent a strike simply by strictly applying the requirements written into the Antistrike Law:

The public Attorney can request the intervention of the Regional Labor Court during the five day strike notice period required. Employers can also initiate Court intervention 30 days before the previous Court decision or collective contract expires. . . . In practice, interest disputes over wages and working conditions are settled by Court decisions before strikes can occur. Strikes are authorized in only two situations, both of which involve violations of Court decisions or of labor agreements by employers: 1. strikes are allowed to gain back salaries when employers are behind in payments and 2. strikes are permitted when employers are not paying the wages declared in a Court decision.[62]

The Antistrike Law must be understood in the context of the Labor Code. Article 723 of the Labor Code stipulates that workers cannot strike under any circumstances without the prior authorization of a regional labor court. Penalties for unauthorized strikes include suspension or dismissal of striking workers without compensation, the removal of the union leadership from office, heavy fines, and even outright cancellation of the union's legal mandate. Kenneth Erickson points out that the full application of the Antistrike Law in combination with the Labor Code's regulations has rendered practically all strikes illegal. From 154 strikes in 1962 and 302 in 1963, the number fell to 25 in 1965, 15 in 1966, 12 in 1970, and none in 1971.[63] Between 1973 and 1977 there were only 34 strikes and slowdowns.[64] Since 1978 the "new labor movement" has strongly challenged the Antistrike Law, but it is still in effect.

The wage-squeeze policy (*arrocho salarial*) was first established with the Finance Ministry's Regulation No. 10, which established the formula to be used in calculating wage levels.[65] Under this regulation, the size of a wage increase depended on three factors: the average real wage of the workers in the twenty-four months preceding the increase; the estimate of anticipated inflation (*resíduo inflacionário*) for the twelve months following the increase; and a factor based on an estimate of the annual rise in productivity. Wages were to be readjusted once a year. The regulation was to apply to all government employees. Decree-Law No. 54018, passed in July 1964, extended the wage policy to the entire public sector, including state-owned corporations or corporations in which the state held majority control. A detailed formula for automatic calculations of wage increases was formalized at that time, and in September, another regulatory measure further refined the calculation techniques.[66] Over the years, the wage policy has consistently underestimated the anticipated inflation rate as well as the rise in productivity, such that wage levels have fallen significantly in real terms.

Conclusion

In its first year, the national security state put into effect a combination of measures aimed at removing any potential opposition nuclei from the political, economic, and social arenas. With these measures, it also laid the first coercive and economic foundations of the new state.

Operation Cleanup, authorized by Institutional Act No. 1, thoroughly purged the civilian and military bureaucracies and used the IPMs to root out any citizen who might organize opposition to policies being implemented. The cleanup operation was generally and specifically targeted, in keeping with the strategies of the National Security Doctrine, which divided society into different compartments to be individually controlled.

Economic measures were likewise aimed at removing impediments and providing the first foundation for the development process envisaged by the Doctrine of National Security and Development. The primary goals were clearly the attraction of foreign multinational capital and the establishment of a wage-control policy to maximize the rate of exploitation and thereby increase profit.

The force of the repression and the rapidity with which the new state's strategists moved to implement policy left the opposition in disarray. This, in turn, allowed the new state a wide area in which to maneuver for further measures to deepen its organizational structure. The creation of the SNI, for example, was a crucial step for the formation of the repressive apparatus and for the effective organization of an intelligence network necessary in the quest for internal security. The disarray of Congress and of most other political sectors enabled the Castello Branco government to eliminate the weak congressional attempts at resistance to the institutionalization of this important mechanism of political and social control. Thus by the end of the first year, the fledgling national security state was in place and the basis established for the broader control measures that would become necessary in the following years.

3. Building New Control Mechanisms: Institutional Act No. 2

The Constitution of 1946 stipulated that gubernatorial elections were to be held in October 1965 in eleven states.[1] The Castello Branco government, to reassure the public of its democratic intentions, promised to stick to this timetable. Moreover, as the end of the period of extraordinary powers under Institutional Act No. 1 approached, the government officially began a policy of "return to normalcy," promising the end of Operation Cleanup and the IPMs and a gradual political opening. Representative democracy and the balance of power between the three branches of government were to be restored. This policy emphasized the role of the civilian-military coalition as the "savior of democratic institutions." At the same time, the government moved forward with its economic program, removing further barriers to the free flow of foreign investment by enacting a decree-law to the effect that "foreign capital invested in Brazil shall enjoy the same legal status as domestic capital."[2]

The stabilization policy had contradictory effects: although it succeeded in lowering inflation from the 1964 high of 87.8 percent to 55.4 percent in 1965,[3] it caused a deep recession, demonstrated by a negative growth rate (−4.7 percent) in the industrial sector.[4] New wage regulations were passed, extending the measures imposed on the public sector to the private sector.

In this context, the opposition began to accumulate sufficient force to threaten the government with defeat in the October 1965 elections. The population's mood had changed considerably since April 1964. A public opinion poll conducted by MARPLAN in Guanabara exposed alarming results: when asked if they approved of and supported the policies of the new government, 63 percent answered no, 18 percent had no opinion, and only 19 percent were in favor.[5] The October elections began to take on the character of a plebiscite on the economic, social, and political policies of the new national security state.[6] Hard-line sectors of the military began to apply pressure on the government to suspend the elections. Although the gubernatorial elections were, in fact, held, opposition victories in key states resulted in a closing of the political opening—ending the first cycle of liberalization. In this chapter I shall examine the policy changes that formed the background for political debate, the gubernatorial elections of 3 October 1965, and the resulting state crisis, which produced Institutional Act No. 2.

New Labor Controls

In 1965 the national security state took the offensive against labor by extending its wage-control policy and intensifying its repression of trade unions. The extension of wage controls was perhaps the most significant act of state economic strategists during this period. The maintenance of market wage relations in the private sector, where collective bargaining between unions and capital owners still determined wage levels, had prevented the sharp drop in wage levels that the strategists considered necessary for the success of the stabilization program and the establishment of a positive investment climate. Law No. 4725, passed on 13 July 1965, extended the wage-squeeze policy to the private sector. This legislation represented an unusual step for a capitalist state: direct intervention in and control of wage determination in the marketplace. Its preamble outlined the government's justifications:

The anti-inflationary policy that the government has pursued is aimed at achieving a reasonable stability in prices by 1966. Its success depends on the development of a coherent and uniform salary policy both for the public sector of the economy and for the private sector.

The salary policy that has already been established was throughly observed in the public sector and in all enterprises subject to government control. In the private sector, however, although labor courts have accepted the annual spacing of salary raises, the practice of salary readjustments at the rate of inflation—and sometimes even higher than inflation—became the norm.

This situation developed because of a lack of appropriate legislation to regulate the private sector. Since experience has demonstrated that salary raises at the level of— or above—the rate of inflation are incompatible with an anti-inflationary program, it is now necessary to extend to the private sector of the economy the regulations that discipline and control salary raises that have already been successfully applied to the public sector.[7]

This law marked the beginning of a comprehensive salary control policy known as *arrocho salarial* (wage squeeze), which is still in effect. It established a readjustment formula that took the average real wage of the twenty-four preceding months and added to it a percentage calculated from the rise in productivity; this would set the wage for the next twelve months. This formula was modified six months later, when projected inflation rates were restored into the calculation of wage increases.[8] In 1966 decrees that established that the index for wage increases would in future be dictated by the executive eliminated what flexibility had been left by loopholes in the 1965 wage law.[9] This would be the only index admissible in the labor courts for determining readjustments. Productivity rises, however, would still be based on the productivity rate of the particular firm involved.

Collective bargaining was reduced to the discussion of fringe benefits, working conditions, and the additional wage increase based on productivity rates to be added to the official index. According to a study by DIEESE, corporations tended to use the automatic wage settlement to refuse to discuss wage questions with unions; "thus," the study concludes, "bargaining sessions between industrialists' associations and labor unions became a dialogue of the deaf. When the workers' representatives presented their wage demands, the corporations' representatives would simply say that they were forbidden by law to respond." From this time on, the number of agreements between unions and corporations diminished, and solutions were sought through collective bargaining suits (dissídio coletivo) in the labor courts.[10] Determination of wage scales thus became depersonalized, a technical calculation carried out not at the bargaining table, but by impersonal and pressure-resistant state agencies like the National Monetary Council and the Planning Secretariat (SEPLAN).[11]

Although official policy had promised a "return to normalcy," because the development model espoused in the Doctrine of National Security and Development was based on a high rate of labor exploitation, the repression of labor could not be relaxed. To neutralize and control opposition to its severe wage-control policy, the government stepped up its attack on trade unions. By the end of 1965, it had intervened in 358 unions, had removed the leaders of 6 others, had cancelled 3 union elections, and had completely dissolved 7 other unions.[12]

In spite of these attacks, the labor movement (spurred by the seriousness of the Wage Law) gathered a coalition that included even the deeply purged National Confederation of Workers in Industry (CNTI) and the Confederation of Workers in Education and Culture (CONTEC) to conduct a campaign against the extension of wage controls to the private sector. The trade unions jointly drafted a series of proposals and amendments to the original draft of Law No. 4725, and these were introduced into congressional debate. Although the government retained a sufficient majority in the purged federal Congress to block all of these changes, the effort helped unite the labor movement and provided labor leaders a first experience in working with opposition politicians to attempt to influence legislation drafted by the executive of the national security state.

Power Struggles within the State

By curtailing possibilities for dissent channeled through established representative institutions such as labor unions, student organizations, and professional associations, the national security state forced a pattern of dissent that has become characteristic in Brazil: elections cease to be a periodic mechanism for choosing representatives and become instead an act of protest, a vote of no confidence in the policies of the state. Under such conditions, the parties that are most identified with antigovernment positions become the beneficiaries of discontent and the conduits of dissent. In the 1965 gubernatorial elections, this plebiscitary function was already apparent. Students, intellectuals, labor leaders, and others who had felt the effects of repression most directly seized on these elections as an opportunity to register protest. Thus the very timetable of the electoral process as well as the routines of party selection of candidates were transformed into a heated battle between the opposition and the hard-line groups within the state.

The officers in charge of the Military Police Inquiries became the core of a growing hard-line group, which was pressuring for the continuation of the extraordinary powers granted by Institutional Act No. 1 and for the postponement or cancellation of the October elections. The heads of the investigating committees resented Castello Branco's commitment to stopping the wave of purges the IPMs brought about. They organized themselves into a pressure group within the state and asked the government to take the following actions: institutionalize control over the judiciary, particularly the Supreme Court, by removing from its jurisdiction the deciding of political charges brought against civilians by the IPMs and putting those cases in the province of newly created military courts; extend the discretionary powers of Institutional Act No. 1, so that Operation Cleanup could be completed with the arrest of "subversives and corrupt people"; and cancel the October elections.[13] The hard-liners were particularly upset by the fact that there were no explicit prohibitions against the candidacy of persons who had been prosecuted under Institutional Act No. 1 but whose political rights had not been taken away. The hard-liners wanted comprehensive legislation that would permanently prevent undesirable opposition from participating in elections at any level.

The pressure from the hard-liners caused a serious political-military crisis within the state. Other officers protested the attempt to curb the freedom of the electoral process and publicly voiced their disapproval. Some even resigned command posts in protest. This was the case, for example, of the head of SUDEPE (the Superintendência de Desenvolvimento de Pernambuco), General Mário Reis Pereira, who openly summarized the views of the dissenters: "If the Revolution had followed its original purpose of getting the country out of anarchy, the government would not have to fear the judgment of the people on their ballots."[14] Castello Branco finally made a firm commitment to hold the elections, and hard-line IPM Colonels Pina, Osnelli, and Martinelli resigned their posts, charging that the government was not living up to the commitments required for internal security.[15]

Three gubernatorial candidates in particular struck the hard-liners as intolerable provocations. The first was the Brazilian Labor party (Partido Trabalhista Brasileiro, PTB) candidate for the governorship of Guanabara, Marshal Henrique Teixeira Lott. Although a military officer, Lott was a nationalist who had taken a firm stand against the conspiracy to overthrow the Goulart government. His candidacy was easily declared illegal by using a new residence requirement included in the Electoral Reform and Party Statute package, passed as an amendment to the Constitution of 1946, which stipulated that a candidate for governor, lieutenant-governor, senator, federal or state congress, must have been a resident of the state for four continuous years.[16] Marshal Lott was a resident of Teresópolis, just outside the state of Guanabara.

With the invalidation of Lott's candidacy, the PTB chose Hélio de Almeida, who had been transportation minister in the Goulart government. Although the IPMs had not managed to convict him, even after repeated efforts, the IPM colonels considered his candidacy intolerable.

The third undesirable candidate was Sebastião Paes de Almeida, a congressman from Minas Gerais for the Social Democratic party (Partido Social Democrático, PSD). Paes de Almeida was also labeled "subversive" by hard-line military sectors. In his case, there was a particularly aggravating circumstance: public opinion polls in Minas predicted that he would win the gubernatorial election by a wide margin.[17]

The opposing groups within the state negotiated a compromise: the gubernatorial elections would be held as scheduled, but a strict law would be drafted to prevent the candidacies of undesirable persons. Luís Viana Filho, then chief of the civilian household of the government, comments on the internal battle:

From the first moment of the struggles we could feel that the solution lay in an ineligibility law. Milton Campos, minister of justice, was entrusted with the drafting of such legislation, . . . which was introduced in Congress on June 22.

It was easy to get rid of Hélio de Almeida: all we needed was an article in the law that would make ineligible for any electoral post those who had been ministers of state in the period between 23 January 1963 and 31 March 1964. We afterwards found that the net had been made too wide, for with it we would also eliminate General Kruel. Thus a substitution was introduced to make the stipulation more specific by exempting from this regulation those who had been in military ministry posts. This was the way we found to see former minister Carvalho Pinto and General Kruel excluded from the law. They had both aided the civilian-military movement that deposed Goulart. The law also excluded from elections the former secretaries of state of any governor who had his mandate suspended or cancelled.[18]

The Ineligibility Law was thus carefully tailor-made.[19] Hélio de Almeida reportedly commented, with justification, that the law had one particular and certain address: Avenida Vieira Souto, 340, where he lived.[20]

Getting rid of Paes de Almeida was more difficult. The Ineligibility Law had an article that prohibited the candidacies of "people who are being *accused* of crimes against the democratic order, against public property, and of abusing economic power during elections" (my emphasis). According to Luís Viana Filho, the government had hoped to eliminate the candidacy of Paes de Almeida (who had the full support of Juscelino Kubitschek) by virtue of this article, for he had been accused by the military of using his vast fortune to finance his own candidacy. The plan failed, however, for Congress was able to amend the law to stipulate that only those *convicted* of such charges could be considered ineligible. Under hard-line pressure, President Castello Branco simply applied his veto power to reapply the original terms:

In order to stop the candidacy of Paes de Almeida . . . the first step was the partial veto of section "i" in Article 1 of the law approved by Congress. This read that those ineligible would be "all who had been convicted of having compromised themselves directly or by using others in the exercise of abuse of their economic power in elections." The president simply vetoed the four words "been convicted of having." Without these words it was easy for us to get rid of the PSD candidate.[21]

The fact that the Ineligibility Law had clearly been tailored to eliminate specific candidacies became a major campaign issue for opposition parties. The legitimacy that Castello Branco's government had hoped to gain by holding the elections suffered accordingly. As Congressman Nelson Carneiro put it, the Ineligibility Law had been written in such a manner that "every citizen could be considered unfit to exercise the electoral mandate."[22]

Other constitutional amendments were also clearly targeted at particular members or sectors of the opposition: "It is no secret that these constitutional amendments are meant to placate the IPM colonels. . . . One of these new amendments will restrict the right to a special court and immunity to the period in which the electoral mandate is actually being exercised. Once this amendment is passed, Mr. Miguel Arraes and Mr. Mauro Borges can be arrested and the Supreme Court will be unable to help them."[23]

It should be emphasized here that these laws introduced a pattern of political crisis-management in the national security state. Legislation, particularly electoral legislation, was drafted and implemented to solve particular political crises and eliminate individual candidates or foci of opposition. This lent a certain ad hoc quality to the process of institution building; designed to deal with problems of the moment, these measures nonetheless became integrated into the overall legal framework of the state. This pattern brings out an important analytical point: although the Doctrine of National Security and Development did provide a basis for a state program, it did not provide a complete blueprint for institution building. The controls that the state instituted evolved gradually, and in dialectical response to potential or actual opposition. Furthermore, this crisis-management pattern (particularly in the case of electoral legislation) undermined the legitimacy of the new state and contributed to its inherent instability. On the one hand, the state had to continue to invoke the legitimation function of elections, for this is tied to the promise of restoring democracy, which was the original justification for the takeover of power. On the other hand, the state cannot risk losing elections—at any level—for its repression has made elections into plebiscites on its policies. It thus continually rewrites electoral legislation to ensure that undesirable candidates are eliminated and that the government party or candidates always win. But in so doing, it undermines the legitimating function of the elections, so that with every new electoral contest the legitimacy of the state diminishes.

The Elections of 3 October 1965

Gubernatorial elections were held on 3 October 1965 in the states of Pará, Maranhão, Rio Grande do Norte, Paraiba, Alagoas, Minas Gerais, Guanabara, Paraná, Santa Catarina, Mato Grosso, and Goiás. In Guanabara, after the two PTB candidates, Marshal Teixeira Lott and Hélio de Almeida, were disqualified, the PSD and PTB formed a coalition to support the candidacy of Francisco Negrão de Lima, a close associate of former president Juscelino Kubitschek. Although he was not particularly liked by hard-liners, they had been unable to prevent his running.[24] The voting in Guanabara confirmed the dissatisfaction with the government, which had already shown up in MARPLAN public opinion polls. An unusually high turnout gave Negrão de Lima 582,000 votes, approximately 52 percent of the votes cast and an absolute majority. He received nearly 140,000 more votes than the next highest candidate, Flexa Ribeiro of the National Democratic Union (União Democrática Nacional, UDN).[25]

With the disqualification of Paes de Almeida, the PSD in Minas Gerais chose as its candidate another associate of Kubitschek, Israel Pinheiro, the first mayor of Brasília. He received 855,000 votes, against 690,000 for the UDN candidate, Roberto Resende. Magalhães Pinto, one of the central figures in the civilian-military coalition, supported Resende.[26]

In Paraná, the government candidate obtained nearly 52 percent of the votes cast, thus winning over the PSD-PTB candidate, Munhoz da Rocha. However, in neighboring Santa Catarina, a PSD opposition candidate, Ivo Silveira, won easily over the government-supported UDN candidate. A PSD opposition candidate also carried the state of Mato Grosso with 53.3 percent of the vote. In the remaining gubernatorial races, the government-supported candidates won.[27] The opposition thus won absolute majorities in the four most industrialized and important states in which elections were held: Guanabara, Minas Gerais, Santa Catarina, and Mato Grosso. In a fifth state, Alagoas, no candidate received an absolute majority; in such cases, by law, the federal government appoints an *interventor* to serve a full term.

Although the government candidates won in the majority of state elections, these were states where victory was less politically significant— rural states where local bosses traditionally control votes. In rural areas dominated by large plantations (*latifúndios*), rural peasants are often completely dependent on the landowner, and their votes are captive. A system has developed, known as the "electoral corral" (*curral eleitoral*), in which peasants are given transport to the voting areas, a free lunch, and transport back to the farms. In some cases they can even bargain over the price of their votes. Thus it has been easier for conservative local politicians, who hold a virtual monopoly of power in a particular region, to keep rural states under control. The national security state's reliance on clientelistic voting patterns in rural states is a pattern established in the 1965 elections that has grown more pronounced over the years. The industrialized states, particularly state capitals and cities with over 100,000 inhabitants, have been opposition strongholds, and, as we shall see in later chapters, this has been a significant factor in political developments and in the dialectic between state and opposition.[28]

The elections in Guanabara and Minas Gerais caused particular concern because the margin of victory of Kubitschek's candidates demonstrated his strong electoral influence, even though he himself had been stripped of political rights for ten years and was unable to run for office. Within the national security state, hard-liners returned to the offensive. They insisted that the Castello Branco government intervene in the two states, annul the election results, and appoint new governors. The ensuing political-military crisis was solved by a compromise between the leaders of the opposition in Guanabara and Minas Gerais: the elected candidates would be allowed to take office, but the federal government would have the right to appoint the states' secretaries of security.[29]

This was an astute move. The coalition in power was aware that the states' security, or police forces would have been a significant political trump card in the hands of the opposition. Magalhães Pinto, as governor of Minas Gerais prior to the 1964 takeover, and Carlos Lacerda, as governor of Guanabara, had both used their police forces effectively to aid the military coup. The lesson was not lost on the military, which did not wish to see the same instrument turned against it. Therefore, the military police of the individual states were placed under the direct control of the army and commanded by a general. In this way both the state police forces and the state military police came to be controlled by the federal government in an increasingly centralized repressive apparatus.

But hard-line pressure did not end with the compromise. When the crisis within the state reached proportions serious enough to threaten the overthrow of the Castello Branco government, the president was forced to take steps to satisfy the hard-line officers.

Closing the Political Opening

The government first tried to push a constitutional amendment through Congress that would have considerably weakened the judiciary and further curbed the powers of the legislative branch. But this time the usually quiescent Congress rebelled. According to Luís Viana Filho, the government applied intense pressure for the approval of this amendment. Within the national security state, it had already been established that, if Congress rejected the amendment, Institutional Act No. 2 would be passed by executive decree. A political crisis developed following indications that Congress might refuse to comply in its own demise, and hard-line pressure on the president became intense:

Gradually, the institutional act became unavoidable, since, in spite of the pressure put on Congress for the approval of the government proposals, there was no guarantee that we would succeed in reaching our objectives. The last polls conducted in the Congress indicated that there would be only 174 votes in favor of the government's project. There were rumors that the opposition had decided it would "pay to see." At the same time, we had the clear awareness that if the president did not do something concrete to counterbalance the electoral defeat he would fall.[30]

Clearly the preferred course of the more enlightened ESG/IPES group was to secure the rubber stamp approval of the Congress for a proposal that would otherwise have to be achieved by force—and thus at the cost of state legitimacy. Congress, however, refused to play and forced the hand of repression.

Castello Branco finally decided not to wait for the congressional vote. The day before the plenary session on the constitutional amendment was to be held, he issued Institutional Act No. 2 by decree. Like its predecessor, Institutional Act No. 2 began with a self-justifying "Manifesto to the Nation." The civilian-military movement that took power in 1964, the manifesto explained, was "an authentic revolution" that aimed at the "establishment of a new state." As such, the "revolution could invest itself of constituent power in the name of the people."[31] Furthermore, the preamble promised, the "revolution was not over and would continue." The justification of the preamble made explicit reference to premises basic to the Doctrine of National Security and Development—particularly in reference to the danger of the "enemy within." The new act was required, it claimed, because "subversives and agitators" were now attempting to "challenge the revolutionary order itself." The activities of these "agitators," it continued, made it "impossible for the government to fulfill its original pledge of bringing an end to the economic chaos." The government was paralyzed because the activities of the subversive elements "made it impossible for the government to achieve the necessary order and stability with which to complete its program of economic development."

In fact, the entire preamble was a clear statement of intentions: social tranquility, defined as the total absence of opposition, is essential for the implementation of the economic model of development. One could say that the government's slogan, "Desenvolvimento e Segurança" ("Development with Security"), was born with Institutional Act No. 2. Furthermore, it should be noted that the manifesto changed the definition of the "enemy within" to include not only all those who had been connected to the previous defeated government, but also the considerably broader category of all who challenged "the revolutionary order itself," that is, all members of any opposition.

The measures included in Institutional Act No. 2 can be divided into three categories: those aimed at controlling the federal Congress, with the consequent strengthening of the executive branch; those aimed particularly at the judiciary; and those intended to control political representation. To bring Congress under control, Article 2 reduced the number of congressional votes needed to approve a constitutional amendment introduced by the executive from a two-thirds majority to a simple majority; Article 4 transferred to the executive exclusive competence in budgetary matters and in regulation of the armed forces; Article 5 limited congressional debate on any bill to forty-five days and maintained the mechanism of *decurso de prazo*, by which executive-initiated urgent bills must be considered within thirty days or be automatically approved; Article 13 transferred to the executive exclusive power to declare or extend a "state of siege"; Article 30 gave the executive the right to issue complementary acts and other decree-laws; and Article 31 gave the executive the authority to close the federal Congress, State Assemblies, and Municipal Chambers. During a period in which Congress was closed, the executive would have the right to legislate on all matters.

To limit the powers of the judiciary, Article 6 amended the Constitution in the following manner: (a) it increased the number of Supreme Court justices to sixteen, to be appointed by the president; (b) it stipulated that federal judges were also to be appointed by the president; and (c) it stated that political crimes against the state could only be tried by the Supreme Court if they were not under the direct jurisdiction of the military courts. Article 8 provided that civilians charged with crimes relating to national security were to be tried by military courts. In addition, the special forum provided for governors and secretaries of state would be eliminated, and they too would be tried by the Military Supreme Court. Article 14 suspended the tenure, job security, and nontransferability of judges stipulations in the Constitution. This, of course, opened the way for more purges of the judiciary. Finally, Article 19 made acts and decisions based on Institutional Act No. 2 not subject to appeal or legal recourse in the judiciary.

The increase in the number of Supreme Court justices was intended to guarantee a majority in matters of interest to the executive. The appointment of federal Supreme Court and Federal Court judges by the president, together with the suspension of guarantees to judges included in the Constitution, allowed the executive a much greater degree of control over the decisions of the judiciary. The transfer of political trials on national security questions to the military courts was clearly a response to the pressures of the hard-liners; it eliminated the recourse that had allowed many of those tried by the IPMs to escape the final hatchet. Finally, as predicted, the elimination of special forums for governors and cabinet members would allow the hard-liners to arrest people like former governors Miguel Arraes and Mauro Borges, to whom the Supreme Court had previously granted habeas corpus.

Institutional Act No. 2 placed important restrictions on political representation. Article 9 established that the president and vice-president were to be elected indirectly by a special Electoral College composed of the federal Congress, and no longer chosen by direct popular vote. In addition, the electoral process was to be open and by voice vote, thereby eliminating the secret ballot and increasing military control over the delegates who chose the president. Article 15 re-established the executive's power to cancel the electoral mandates and political rights of citizens for ten years. A complementary paragraph stipulated that the places of legislators who had lost their mandates would not be filled; a quorum would be determined by the number of places effectively occupied. This article enabled the executive to transform the legislative at all levels both *qualitatively*, by cancelling electoral mandates of opposition members, and *quantitatively*, in that the government could always obtain a majority simply by canceling the necessary number of opposition legislators. This technique was sometimes used to ensure control over state assemblies.

Article 16 regulated the activities of *cassados* and all others who had been or would be punished under either of the first two institutional acts. It severely limited their rights by canceling their right to a special forum as a prerogative of office; suspending their right to vote or participate in trade union elections; prohibiting comments on political matters or participation in political activities; allowing the state, when it considered such measures to be necessary for national security, to determine where they would live, limit their freedom of movement, and prevent them from going to places considered to be "inconvenient."[32] This article, which became known as the "Statute of the *Cassados*," was clearly intended to eliminate from political life or trade union activities all those the national security state considered part of the "enemy within."

Finally, in Article 18, the institutional act abolished all existing political parties. New parties would be formed according to the stiff conditions laid down in the Party Statute and Electoral Code of 15 June 1965 (Law 4740), and would be regulated by later complementary acts.[33]

Institutional Act No. 2 was signed on 26 October 1965, only twenty-four days after the gubernatorial elections. It was the price paid for the inauguration of Negrão de Lima in Guanabara and Israel Pinheiro in Minas erais. However, as with Institutional Act No. 1, the legal validity of this act was to be limited (it was to last only until 15 March 1967, the end of Castello Branco's term in office). It provided the state with room to maneuver in several ways. First, it permitted the repressive apparatus to complete the cleanup operation that had been interrupted by Castello Branco's "normalization" policy in 1965. Second, the abolition of political parties and the strict requirements for the establishment of new ones forced the opposition to concentrate all its energies on rebuilding the representative structures. Finally, growing repression combined with the new electoral controls gave birth to a debate within the opposition on the efficacy of organizing within legal institutions under such circumstances.

On 20 November 1965, the government passed Complementary Act No. 4, which established regulations for political parties.[34] New parties had to be formed by at least 120 federal deputies and 20 senators within a period of forty-five days after passage of the act. The names of the abolished parties could not be used for the new ones. The stringency of this regulation was eventually softened, because the government feared that under the circumstances the opposition would not find enough legislators willing to risk loss of their mandates by forming an opposition party, and it was not in the interests of the national security state to set up a one-party system. For legitimation purposes, the state wanted a "responsible opposition party," whose role would be to provide the government with "constructive criticism." Thus the new regulations required only that the party unite as many members of Congress as possible into a single organization. The various opposition parties banded together to form the Brazilian Democratic Movement (Movimento Democrático Brasileiro, MDB). The party supporting the government was named the Alliance for National Renovation (Aliança de Renovação Nacional, ARENA).

Conclusion

The year 1965 began with a relative easing of the repressive pressures applied by Institutional Act No. 1. Although President Castello Branco began an official party of return to normalcy, localized and specifically targeted repression continued. In particular, a pattern emerged that was to prove a continuing characteristic of liberalization cycles under the national security state: class-selective repression. The state intended to ease repression of the elite sectors of the opposition primarily. In the space opened by the liberalization, political parties organized energetically and effectively to challenge the state's control of the executive offices of state governments. The labor movement, in contrast, continued to suffer severe attacks from the state in the form of trade union repression and the new policy of *arrocho salarial*.

The national security state was never able to make its strategy of class-selective repression fully effective, but nonelite sectors could often effectively exploit the space elite groups won as well. The realization that the repressive apparatus was a continuing threat to all—even during periods of its relative relaxation—encouraged opposition unity. It is clear, nonetheless, that such class differentiation was fundamental to the aims of the national security state, for only on such a basis could it reconcile the contradiction between its need for democratic legitimation and its reliance on a highly exploitative economic model.

The closing of the liberal cycle with the passage of Institutional Act No. 2 points to a further characteristic of the national security state: it began to form a parallel power base within its own legal framework and that of the repressive apparatus. Those sectors of the power coalition charged with the maintenance of internal security increasingly saw their purpose and goals as contradictory to those of other sectors more concerned with the need to institutionalize the state on a more permanent basis of population consent. "Slaves do not make good combatants," General Golbery had once warned. The ESG/IPES sector was well aware of the fact that force alone is self-defeating as a basis for a stable state; the need for flexible mechanisms of control, however, was antagonistic to the policies required to implement the Doctrine of National Security and Development. The tension created by the state's need to legitimize itself through the institutionalization of flexible mechanisms of control and the need for direct repression was the heart of the permanent conflict between the two groups.

Finally, 1965 was also important in terms of the state's institutionalization. The provisions of Institutional Act No. 2 provided a framework in which to pursue the destruction of old state structures and the building of new ones. The end of the political parties threw the opposition into considerable disarray and enabled the government of Castello Branco to deepen measures aimed at long-term institutionalization of the state.

The result, as we have seen, was a clear victory for the sectors for which internal security was the first priority. Ultimately, the quest for absolute security became irreconcilable with a return to legality, and the enactment of Institutional Act No. 2 closed the first cycle of liberalization.

4. Constitutional Reform and the Institutionalization of the New State

1967

The abolition of political parties presented the opposition with a challenge that not only absorbed most of its energy but also fragmented the loose coalition built for the 1965 elections. Internal debate consumed the opposition as it sought alternative tactics.

The state had clearly recovered the offensive. Within the legal framework set up by Institutional Act No. 2, Operation Cleanup was reinstated to finish the purges interrupted by the brief liberalization. The economic model was further refined during this period, with new wage control regulations and with the drafting of a comprehensive wage program: the Time-In-Service Guarantee Fund (Fundo de Garantia por Tempo de Serviço, FGTS). The FGTS was designed to replace existing job security provisions and to create a special fund to be used for capital accumulation.

Some of the attention of state planners was devoted to regulatory measures in the political arena. The formation of new political parties required complementary legislation as well as delicate political negotiations to avoid divisions in the ranks of the ruling sectors, which were to form one party. And Institutional Act No. 3 would provide new electoral mechanisms to avoid the periodic chaos surrounding gubernatorial elections.

The main priority of the state during this period, however, remained the problem of its permanent institutionalization. The imminent end of Castello Branco's term in office made it imperative that the national security state institutionalize its structures. The need to mold a stable state apparatus capable of managing the succession set the context for the confrontations that took place during this period between the ESG/IPES group and the hard-liners. To legitimize such an apparatus, it seemed advisable to the former that the institutional acts be incorporated into a body of constitutional law. Thus, the drafting of a new constitution took on paramount importance.

Time-In-Service Guarantee Fund

The persistence of job security guarantees from the pre-1966 labor laws lessened the impact of the wage-control legislation the new regime passed. These earlier guarantees had stipulated that workers with one to ten years of service in the same company were legally entitled to indemnity payments when they were laid off without just cause. The indemnity payment was to equal one month's salary for each year of service to the company. Furthermore, workers with more than one year of service were entitled to thirty-days' notice prior to dismissal and to one month's extra pay as indemnity (e.g., a person with five years' service would receive six months' indemnity pay). The sums involved discouraged corporations from initiating large-scale layoffs. Workers with more than ten years of service in the same company achieved job "stability," and could be dismissed only if the employer could prove in court that the worker was guilty of serious misconduct.[1] If the employer lost the case in court after attempting to discharge a worker with job stability, he or she was required by law to rehire the worker and cover all legal costs, as well as full back wages. If the worker agreed, the employer could avoid rehiring him or her by paying twice the indemnity rate.

To some extent, the pre-1966 job security legislation had prevented the problems of mass layoffs and other problems that highly mobile capital can cause, as in "runaway shop" situations, where capital is transferred from one region to another in search of higher profits. The pre-1966 job security legislation was, however, a source of irritation to multinational corporations, which wanted the freedom to set wage levels and to move investment capital to wherever labor costs were lower and profits therefore higher. The legally required payment of indemnities to fired workers limited the free flow of capital and its potential profitability because of the high cost of plant closings. In addition, "job stability" meant the maintenance of a higher base wage than was desirable for the application of the indexing measures included in the new wage-control legislation. Thus, from the point of view of multinational corporations, the job stability system was a severe drain on capital. I should point out here that the government's wage-control system set the *maximum* indexed increase that could be given to workers once a year. It did not, however, set the *minimum*, which the federal government decreed periodically. Negotiations between trade unions and employers often involved the question of the base wage for a particular job category. With the job stability system in effect, it was difficult for employers to force "stable" workers to accept a lower salary, and such workers could not be fired for that reason alone without incurring significant expense for the employer. Job stability had been a victory of the unions in past years and limited the impact of wage-control legislation.

The Time-in-Service Guarantee Fund (FGTS), enacted in September 1966, was designed to replace the job stability provisions of the previous labor legislation.[2] The new program did not recognize job stability of any kind and greatly reduced the immediate cost of discharging workers. Employers could now discharge an employee with ten years of service without a special court hearing and without just cause. The time-in-service distinction was completely eliminated.

The manner in which indemnity payments were made was also significantly altered. Under the FGTS program, employers must deposit 8 percent of the worker's monthly wage to an account in the worker's name. These deposits constitute a fund that replaces the indemnity obligations of the employer. When workers are laid off, they receive indemnity from their own FGTS account. This eliminates the need for an employer to come up with large sums at once in the case of cutbacks or plant closings. This in turn frees employers to increase turnover in the labor force—thus keeping overall wage levels lower. Theoretically, the FGTS is optional and workers may choose, at the time of employment, to stick with the old system. In practice, however, workers are not hired if they refuse to sign the FGTS option.

The new labor movement, which came to the fore in 1977, has been devoting an increasing amount of attention to the problem of high turnover and its impact on wages. Unions have consistently denounced the FGTS for allowing a practice under which, to avoid paying wage increases, corporations fire workers just prior to the new contract date and hire lower-paid workers. The fired workers are then rehired by other corporations in the same industry to perform similar functions at lower pay, since the index is applied to a lower wage base.[3]

The importance of FGTS in making the national security state's wage-squeeze policies viable cannot be overestimated. The state's wage-control policies owe their effectiveness to the general insecurity of the job market and the new threat of mass layoffs. The combination of controlled wage-indexing and the FGTS provide an ideal cheap labor market for capital investment. Together with the positive tax and fiscal incentives in other governmental programs, this is the core of the economic development model.

FGTS has also been important for capital accumulation in its function as a source of investment loans to employers. The monthly installments paid into the fund by employers and employees go into the National Housing Bank (BNH) and are used to finance construction and other industrial projects that invest in government-approved programs. The ratio between the total amount of the FGTS that fired workers withdraw and the amount that remains on deposit for capital loans to industries provides extra incentives to investment. The FGTS has thus helped achieve capital accumulation both by lowering wages and by making available a subsidized fund for capital investment. As labor lawyer José Martins Catharino has pointed out, the FGTS should be considered not as labor legislation but rather as a financial- economic law, drafted by Roberto Campos to "eliminate job security, accumulate capital, and make Brazil a more attractive country for multinational investment."[4]

The Constitution of 1967

The new constitutional framework would have to incorporate the various measures included in the institutional acts. One problem area that had not been resolved by the first two institutional acts was the question of gubernatorial elections. According to the 1946 Constitution, such elections still had to be held in the eleven states that had not elected new governors in 1965. To resolve this problem, Institutional Act No. 3 was issued three months after the 1965 gubernatorial elections, on 5 February 1966. Its first article established that governors would thenceforth be elected indirectly, by majority vote of the state assemblies. The vote would be open and by voice. Mayors of all state capitals would be appointed by the governors; other mayors could be elected by popular secret ballot.[5]

From the point of view of the state, Institutional Act No. 3 was necessary to control the large and important states of the federation. The elections of 1965 had shown that the ruling coalition could control the rural states, particularly in the Northeast, by making efficient use of clientelistic relations. In the more advanced industrial states, with greater speed of information spread and higher levels of education and politicization, the same controls could not be applied.

The Third Institutional Act clearly spoke of the need to consolidate control at every level of political power. Its preamble justifies this goal by

Considering the imperative need to adopt measures that will ensure that the objectives of this revolution are not frustrated;
Considering the need to preserve tranquility, social and political harmony in the nation;
Considering that it is absolutely necessary to extend to the governors the indirect election method already applied to the presidency and vice-presidency;
Considering, furthermore, that it is convenient for national security to change the method of choosing the mayors of the capitals of the states.[6]

Indirect election by state assemblies provided for a great deal of control over state executives without the same cost to legitimacy that would be entailed in direct intervention. State assemblies could be kept under the control of the federal government by selective purges, if necessary. Thus, although couched in the language of legality, the new electoral process was almost equivalent to federal appointment of state governors.

Political representation was constantly limited by the cancellation of opposition electoral mandates. After it was organized as the legal opposition party, the MDB suffered further purges. In 1966 it lost seven members from Congress and thirty-eight members of state assemblies. The changing electoral legislation, coupled with constant purging of the party, fomented an intense internal debate in the MDB concerning the validity of its existence. Some members of the party argued for its dissolution as the ultimate protest against the arbitrary actions of government and as a way of demonstrating the de facto one-party character of the system.

The arbitrariness of the complementary acts and regulations became increasingly evident in mid-1966, as the government took the offensive to prepare for the coming elections. From June to August alone, the executive issued eighteen complementary acts, which regulated the conditions under which elections were to be held, the party registration of candidates, the loss of municipal mandates. It also intervened in one state and in several municipalities and further limited the powers of Congress to legislate on budgetary matters.[7] Just prior to the indirect gubernatorial elections, Complementary Act No. 19 imposed party discipline in voting, thus preventing any legislator from voting for the candidate of another party in either gubernatorial or presidential elections.[8] During the period in which Institutional Act No. 2 was in force, the president issued a total of thirty-six complementary acts.

The participation of the MDB in the 1966 congressional campaign was limited not only by the party's inability to organize itself in all of the states but also by the large-scale canceling of the registration of candidates it presented. It will be recalled that the Ineligibility Law allowed cancellation of the candidacy of anyone who was either incompatible "with the objectives of the revolution" or who could be considered to infringe some other requirement. In the state of Guanabara alone, twelve MDB candidates were denied the right to run for office on grounds of being "subversive."[9] In the state of Rio de Janeiro, the MDB had six of its main candidates and thirteen nominees challenged and threatened with *impugnação* (cancellation of registration) just before the deadline for registration. According to one analyst, "the officials of the electoral courts throughout the country set out on a violent offensive against the registration of candidates for the federal Congress and the state assemblies. Candidates were blocked even for the amazing reason of 'having once, in public, called President Castello Branco a gorilla'."[10]

The intimidation campaign was intended to weaken the MDB and to guarantee a decisive ARENA victory. It was also intended to establish a climate of crisis, which would give the government an advantage in negotiating the new constitution with an intimidated federal Congress and opposition party. The campaign thus prepared the ground for the production of a highly authoritarian constitution, meant to institutionalize the national security state.

But the rapid succession of complementary acts and decree-laws, combined with the government's attempts to limit congressional participation in drafting the constitution, occasioned rebellion rather than acquiescence on the part of Congress. The government's own ARENA party joined forces with the opposition in demanding the right to amend and draft proposals for the constitution—a demand that the government systematically refused. The conflict between the executive and the legislature reached a climax on 12 October 1966, when the president issued a decree that canceled the mandates of six federal congressmen.[11] Castello Branco had publically promised the president of the House of Representatives, ARENA congressman Adauto Lúcio Cardoso, that there would be no further rounds of *cassações*, so that Congress could freely discuss and vote on the constitutional project. Politically embarrassed by this blow to its prestige, ARENA rebelled. Congressman Cardoso refused to recognize the *cassações*, and ruled that the purged congressmen should continue to exercise their functions. In addition, he gave them the opportunity to defend themselves on the floor of the House of Representatives:

The conflict between the executive and the legislature has been definitively installed. Yesterday, Congressman Adauto Cardoso of ARENA officially stated the view of the president of the House of Representatives that the cancellation of electoral mandates should be an issue of the exclusive and "inalienable competence" of the Congress. The president of the House also made clear that he considers the six congressmen purged to be in full and rightful exercise of their prerogatives as members of Congress. . . . The response of the executive was most immediate. It sent agents of the DOPS and arrested Congressman Doutel de Andrade. . . . However, with this action, the executive brought the judiciary into the crisis, because MDB leader Viera de Melo immediately filed a writ of habeas corpus to secure the parliamentary immunity of the arrested congressman.[12]

The Executive's use of force united the two parties in support of the actions of the president of the house, and the president of the Senate publicly expressed his solidarity. For the first time, an important leader of the government party had publicly opposed what he termed the "militarization" of the executive power. Congressman Cardoso characterized his action as "the defense of a civil power, the legislative, against the coercion of a military power, the executive."[13]

The crisis produced further internal struggles in the national security state. Hard-line sectors insisted on new purges and on making an example of the perpetrators of such disobedience. For the second time in his short term in office, Castello Branco was forced to cave in: on 20 October 1966 the executive issued Complementary Act No. 23, which closed Congress for one month.[14] During the enforced recess, the president was able to legislate at will. It is significant that, once again, the preamble of the complementary act justifies an act of coercion with the language of democracy:

Considering that the federal Congress now has a small group of counterrevolutionary elements who attempt to bring tumult to the workings of the House of

Representatives and thereby harm the public order as well as the approaching congressional elections of November 15 . . . and in order to prevent the loss of prestige and authority of the legislative power of government, . . . the president decides to issue the following complementary act.[15]

With Congress closed, the government's full attention could now be turned to the coming congressional and state assembly elections. The MDB, as mentioned, was unable to participate in a number of places, and the first direct and explicit acts of prior censorship severely curtailed its political campaigning:

In the middle of all the anxiety and uncertainty, the government established a special censorship system in radio and television programs against candidates who wished to comment on certain subjects that were prohibited—including the forced recess of Congress. The situation became so serious that the electoral court judges, particularly in Rio Grande do Sul, protested that their activities had been taken over by the secretaries of security of the states.[16]

The MDB had a third, and potentially even more significant, problem: its own lack of credibility among the various opposition groups in civil society. Limitations on party organization and on the legislature itself fueled a debate—in particular within the student movement—as to the wisdom of supporting the official opposition party. Many groups did not consider the remaining unpurged members of the MDB to be representative of the opposition and urged voters to void their votes or to leave their ballots blank as a sign of protest. The *voto nulo* campaign, spearheaded by students connected to the organization Ação Popular and committed to armed struggle, began with the 1966 campaign and grew in importance in the elections of 1968 and 1970.

In the 1966 elections, ARENA candidates received 56.6 percent of valid votes for the federal Senate, as against the MDB's 43.3 percent. In the congressional and state assembly elections, the difference was larger. The impact of candidate registration cancellation, of refusal to participate in the election, and of the *cassações*, was more strongly felt: ARENA won 63.9 percent of valid House votes to the MDB's 36 percent, and it won 64.1 percent of valid State Assembly votes, to the MDB's 35.8 percent. The *voto nulo* campaign played an important role in the defeat of the official opposition party, for in the Senate elections 11.6 percent of all votes cast were blank and a further 9.3 percent were annulled. In the House elections, this percentage rose to 14.2 percent blank, 6.8 percent void, and in the State Assemblies, 12.1 percent were blank and 6.5 percent void.[17]

The actual voting process was conducted, in many places, in an atmosphere of military intimidation. Troops occupied cities in Pernambuco, Rio Grande do Norte, and Rio Grande do Sul, and they were a visible presence in most capitals. In addition, there were widespread claims of corruption and vote buying in the rural areas. Even Congressman Francelino Pereira, just re-elected for ARENA, admitted that "what happened in the last election was shameful. We never heard or had news of such widespread electoral corruption in my state. The buying of votes was visibly and openly carried out without any shame."[18]

The victory of ARENA, the closing of Congress, and the general weakening of the opposition provided the national security state with some breathing space in which to formulate the new constitution. But congressional ratification was still considered important to legitimate the document, both domestically and internationally. Institutional Act No. 4, decreed on 7 December 1966, reconvened Congress for an extraordinary session to discuss and ratify the Constitution and established the highly restrictive procedures under which this was to take place.[19] These procedures reversed the normal legislative process: the project was to be adopted as a whole, after which it could be discussed and amended during a specific time frame.

That it accepted this procedure showed the weakness of the opposition, and the Constitution was passed by a vote of 223 to 110 in the House of Representatives, and 37 to 17, with 7 abstentions in the Senate.[20] A total of 1,504 amendments were proposed, but because of lack of time, few were discussed and even fewer were incorporated into the document.[21]

The Constitution of 1967 legalized many of the exceptional measures decreed in the institutional and complementary acts. Later modified into the Constitution of 1969, it provided the basis for an institutionalized political order for the new national security state. Key sections of the Constitution of 1967 regulated the separation of powers, institutionalized the economic model, defined the concept of national security, and characterized political and individual rights.

Separation of Powers

The transfer of the legislative branch's prerogatives to the executive and restrictions placed on procedures had already considerably weakened it. The new constitution set the time limit for passage of urgent legislation introduced by the executive at forty-five days, after which it was considered automatically approved. Nonurgent legislation was considered automatically passed if not rejected within sixty days.[22] Perhaps the most important measure in the new constitution was that giving the executive the exclusive right to legislate on matters involving "national security and public finance"; Congress retained only the right to approve or reject such legislation, not to amend it.[23] All of the restrictions on the judiciary that had been instituted by Institutional Act No. 2 were incorporated into the text of the new constitution. In addition, it was stipulated that all crimes against national security be tried by military courts.[24]

The Constitution of 1967 established a state based almost exclusively on executive power. The role of the legislature was reduced to the adjustment of bills introduced by the executive. The judiciary lost the power to review the other two branches. Provisions for indirect election of the president and vice-president (mandated by Institutional Act No. 1) in the new constitution further strengthened the executive.

The relation between the states and municipalities and the federal government was also modified considerably. The new constitution gave the federal government the right to intervene in states and municipalities whenever there were "cases of grave disturbances of the public order or the threat of possible occurrence of disturbances."[25] It also gave the federal government the power to intervene in states and municipalities "that refused to adopt or comply with the economic program or the financial directives established by the federal government."[26] Finally, the National Security Council, an agency of the presidency, was given the exclusive right to decide which municipalities would be considered areas of special interest to national security. Mayors of these municipalities would be appointed, rather than elected, and they would be under direct control of the army. Approximately 107 municipalities in Brazil are currently designated national security areas.

Institutionalization of the Economic Model

I have already described the conception of economic development that is included within the Doctrine of National Security and Development. It is particularly significant that measures dealing with government economic policies were incorporated into the body of the Constitution, under Title III. The inclusion of these measures, which would normally be considered *policy* questions, was intended to force subsequent governments to pursue economic policies along the lines of those the Castello Branco government established.

One of the provisions contained in the new Constitution was aimed at removing what autonomy remained to the states in the economic sphere. All states and municipalities were to conform to a central directive plan institutionalizing a planned, mixed economy that would facilitate capital accumulation and attract multinational investment.[27] According to the new stipulations, states could not decide to nationalize foreign corporations within their jurisdiction, or even to establish state controls over the activities of multinational corporations. This was clearly intended to eliminate the possibility of a recurrence of the restrictions implemented by Leonel Brizola as governor of Rio Grande do Sul, and by Miguel Arraes as governor of Pernambuco. The section on the economic model regulated investment, the role of the state in the economy, rights of land tenure, and the rights of workers. The Brazilian economy was defined as capitalist, but with specific areas reserved for state capital. Article 157, for example, provided that the state should invest in areas that were essential for national security but that could not be efficiently developed by private enterprise.[28] This measure, along with Article 163, justified state investment in infrastructural improvements that would increase the profits of private (both national and foreign) capital.[29]

Subsoil rights was another important area discussed in the 1967 Constitution. Article 161 provided that mineral deposits, as well as potential sources of hydraulic energy, were to be considered "property that is distinctly separate from the property of the soil itself."[30] For the purpose of investment in and development of mineral deposits, the owner of the land only had the right to participate in "the results of the mining," which were defined further as "equal to the tax rate on the minerals mined." The actual mining could be undertaken only with the authorization of the federal government, by Brazilians or by "social organizations set up within the country."[31]

By 1967 Brazil's mineral resources had already been mapped. They included immense deposits of iron, bauxite, manganese, gold, uranium, aluminum, copper, and other minerals of importance in industrial development. Prior to 1964, mining corporations had enjoyed only limited access to this wealth; Hanna Mining Corporation, in particular, had been at the center of a crisis immediately preceding the fall of the Goulart government. One of the major stumbling blocks for multinational capital with respect to access to mineral deposits lay in the definition of property titles. Investment could be blocked by a landowner who refused to sell a farm plot rich in uranium, for example, or who demanded a high price for his land. The separation of subsoil mineral rights from property rights to the soil removed this obstacle. In addition, the words or by "social organizations set up within the country" allowed the government to grant exclusive mining rights to multinational corporations, as long as they formed a Brazilian subsidiary.

The one mineral that was not of immediate interest to multinational capital was petroleum. Research and development of petroleum is costly in a country that is not obviously rich in this resource. Refining and distribution of petroleum and petrochemical products, on the other hand, are profitable. Prior to the 1967 Constitution, a state monopoly, Petrobrás, conducted all research, exploration, refining, and distribution of petroleum and petroleum products. Article 162 of the new Constitution modified the previous regulations and opened up distribution and refining of petroleum and petroleum products to private enterprise. The same held true for petrochemicals.[32] Since 1967, these areas have come almost entirely under the control of multinational corporations.

Finally, the Constitution regulated wages and the labor market. Article 157 prohibited strikes in public services and in essential activities.[33] Article

158 introduced the FGTS into the text of the Constitution.[34] Finally, the legal minimum working age was reduced to twelve years, thereby institutionalizing a system of child labor, which would be important for lowering labor costs and which would bring with it significant social costs.[35]

National Security

In the text of the Constitution of 1946, the concept of national security was related to the concept of foreign aggression—defense against external forces and defense of territorial frontiers. The new Constitution changed this definition to conform to the Doctrine of Internal Security with its theory of psychological warfare and the enemy within. The threat to national security was therefore defined as a threat to *ideological* frontiers rather than *territorial* frontiers.[36] In addition, the defense of national security was to be the responsibility not only of the armed forces but also of "every individual and every juridical entity" in civil society.[37] Individuals and organizations could be held criminally responsible for failing to provide information on the activities of those whom the state considered to be part of the internal enemy. As in totalitarian states, individuals were juridically transformed into informants.

The Constitution established that the National Security Council would oversee the defense of internal security. The council was to be an agency of the presidency and was to work closely with intelligence and security organizations. It was composed of the president, all ministers of state, all members of the Armed Forces High Command, and the executive chief of staff (*chefe da casa civil*). Article 91 defined its duties as "the study of problems related to the question of national security, in collaboration with the intelligence agencies . . . and in order to prepare for national mobilization of the armed forces as well as other military operations."[38] In addition, the National Security Council was to make administrative and economic decisions in areas considered to be "of interest to national security." These included the granting of land, control of transportation and communication systems, construction of bridges, roads, and airfields, and the establishment of industries of particular importance for national security. The decision as to which areas were of particular importance for National Security was the exclusive prerogative of the council itself. The powers granted to the National Security Council made it the heart and brain of the national security state, the ultimate coordinating body within the state apparatus.

Political and Individual Rights

The restrictions on elections and on the legislature, which had been established by Institutional Acts Nos. 1 and 2, were included in the text of the 1967 Constitution. Other complementary legislation, such as the Ineligibility Law and the regulation of political parties, was also incorporated.[39]

What is particularly significant, however, is that the Bill of Rights was included in the Constitution. From the standpoint of national security doctrine, this inclusion was consistent with the permanent national objectives, which explicitly supported individual guarantees such as habeas corpus, freedom from invasion of domicile, the right to defense and trial by jury, the rights of assembly, association, and freedom of expression. The Constitution also upheld the right of legislators to parliamentary immunity, thus ruling out automatic cancellation of electoral mandates of members of opposition parties. According to the 1967 Constitution, members of Congress or of state assemblies could lose their mandates, or be tried for a crime against national security, only after permission had been given by the legislative body to which they belonged.[40] Securing the Bill of Rights was a victory for those in Congress who had fought to amend the executive's original project. The issue provoked heated floor debates, and all sectors of the opposition put pressure on the executive to include basic individual, associative, and political rights in the body of the Constitution. In arguing for their position, members of the opposition referred explicitly to the stated goal of "democracy" in the permanent national objectives, which the national security state claimed to defend.[41]

The maintenance of basic legal rights and of parliamentary immunity was to be extremely important to the political developments of the next few years. Their inclusion provided the opposition with some space in which to organize politically, to demand greater margins of participation in government decisions, and to demand fuller application of those rights.

Conclusion

The dialectic of the state and opposition began in 1965. The continuation of Operation Cleanup and the force of repression "displaced" opposition from one sector of civil society to another, rather than eliminating its causes. In 1965 the state learned to "play the electoral game" by constantly changing electoral legislation in order to retain majority control. However, the state's actions provoked changes in the opposition and an internal debate over different strategies of resistance. With the passage of Institutional Act No. 2, the opposition became divided between groups that urged preparation for armed struggle in response to the increasing violence of the state and groups that were willing to use to the fullest extent posible whatever legal institutions existed.

In the attempt to institutionalize its economic model and its structures of political control, the state made a serious effort to weaken the opposition in 1965. The federal government implemented purges and measures to intimidate and weaken political parties and Congress in order to gain time to set its program in motion prior to the transfer of power to Castello Branco's successor. In the economic sphere, the creation of the FGTS complemented wage-control policies and helped to create a favorable climate for capital investment in areas with low labor costs.

The Constitution of 1967 incorporated the most important controls embodied in the two previous institutional acts and a variety of complementary acts. These controls thus lost their exceptional character, which had been based on *revolutionary* power, and acquired the force of *constitutional* power. These measures altered the major structures of the state and institutionalized the Doctrine of National Security and Development. Although the 1967 Constitution was highly authoritarian, it reflected the basic contradictions within the system. One part of the Constitution was designed to control, to ensure the implementation of the measures mandated by the Doctrine of Internal Security to destroy the enemy within. The other part, which the opposition had succeeded in imposing in the form of the Bill of Rights, reflected the goal of restoring democracy. As the dialectic between state and opposition moved to a higher level of development in 1967 and 1968, this basic contradiction would be at the root of the institutional crisis that culminated with the passage of Institutional Act No. 5.

The institutional crisis was based on the fact that the democratic elements in the Constitution allowed the opposition some room to maneuver. It could appeal to the ultimate goals of democracy and demand greater popular participation in the decisions of government—participation restrictions in other parts of the Constitution denied. The climate of liberalization that followed the promulgation of the Constitution in March 1967 would also allow labor to reorganize and to protest the decline in wages and living conditions the government's economic measures produced. On the other hand, those sectors concerned with the quest for absolute security and with the maintenance of internal security would view such protests as evidence of Communist infiltration. They therefore applied the other parts of the Constitution—those that guaranteed national security and the defense of a specific model of development. The resulting confrontation, which reached major proportions, will be discussed in the next chapter.

5. Liberalization, Opposition, and State Crisis: Institutional Act No. 5

[handwritten notes:]
clean-p 64
→ 66 elections electoral college only [Silva]
67 "policy of relief"? → crisis
New Constitution
68 Institution Act V (total repression

The State

Marshal Arthur da Costa e Silva was elected president by a special Electoral College on 3 October 1966.[1] He took office on 15 March 1967, promising to restore normal representative political procedures and democratic rule. The president was committed to a new liberalization policy, which would slowly diffuse tensions and involve the opposition in a dialogue with the government.[2] This controlled liberalization policy, which was known as the "policy of relief" (*política de alívio*), involved a liberal interpretation of the repressive legislation contained in the 1967 Constitution. Meetings were held with opposition sectors to identify points of discord. In the labor sector, the government began to pursue an active policy of organizing trade unions and of controlling or co-opting their leadership. The government was prepared to offer limited concessions in exchange for limited support and legitimation. Discussions between government and opposition did not, however, extend to the question of restoring the balance of power, nor did they touch on wage policies and the FGTS.

The 1967-1968 liberalization remained within the bounds of the national security state as incorporated into the Constitution of 1967. The powers attributed to the executive were broad enough to make congressional approval unnecessary for measures being carried out by the new economic team. The government did approach members of the MDB with the possibility of negotiation, implying that it might be possible to make some modifications in the Constitution. But at the same time as this dialogue was beginning, military police and other agents of the repressive apparatus were fighting with demonstrators in the streets of the large cities and conductng widespread searches and arrests in the major states.

The contradiction between the language of consensus and dialogue and growing overt coercion in the streets canceled out the legitimacy gained through the promise of liberalization. Since the "politics of relief" depended on a degree of consensus impossible to reach under conditions of repression, the state moved into a situation of internal and external crisis. A shift in emphasis took place in economic policy as well. The Costa e Silva government's economic team was headed by minister of finance Delfim Netto and planning minister Hélio Beltrão. Delfim Netto soon achieved a predominant position and had virtual control over the economy. The new economic policy was primarily geared toward changing the consumption pattern of the upper middle class to promote the growth of the durable-goods sector of the economy. And although wage levels were pegged to the official inflation rate to lower production costs, tax advantages and fiscal incentives were granted to the upper stratum of the population to stimulate investment.[3]

Government policies had a clear impact on the income of the wage-earning population. A DIEESE study showed that real wages fell significantly between 1965 and 1968. In fact, 12 percent to 26 percent of the occupational categories analyzed suffered a real wage loss of more than 30 percent in the 1966-1968 period.[4] As may be seen in table 4, wage losses continued to occur, being particularly severe in 1973 and 1974.

The minimum-wage levels showed a similar downward trend in terms of purchasing power. The minimum wage is decreed by the federal government and is a basic indication of the wage level of workers. It is frequently used to indicate the purchasing power and income distribution of the population. DIEESE conducted a study of the evolution of minimum-wage levels in Brazil since 1959 and concluded that the real minimum wage after the military takeover showed a significant and constant decrease in value that was particularly pronounced after the implementation of wage-control policies. As can be seen in table 5, the 1964 minimum wage bought only 42 percent of what it could buy in 1959. There was a slight improvement in 1965 and 1966, and a further drop with the completion of the wage-control package. From 1967 on the real minimum wage fell until, by March 1976, it had reached 31 percent of its 1959 value. The decrease in purchasing power of wages occurred in spite of a sharp drop in the rate of inflation, which fell from 87.8 percent in 1964 to 20.3 percent by 1969. Thus the decrease in the real value of wages cannot be explained as the effect of inflation; it was, rather, the result of state wage-control policies.

The state's wage-control policies resulted in considerable loss of income for the wage-earning population. This factor, added to the generalized job insecurity the implementation of the FGTS caused and to the overt repression of demonstrations and protests in the streets, spurred an upsurge of opposition. Major demonstrations against the economic and social policies of the state and a rapid reorganization of opposition sectors in civil society would occur in 1967 and 1968.

The Opposition

"The opposition in Brazil is like a great forest: each tree in the forest puts down its own deep roots—but they join and intermingle underneath the ground."[5] The maturation of the economic model, combined with the repressive policies of the post-1964 governments, provided the cement for an informal alliance of various opposition sectors that began in 1967. This alliance became, in 1968, a mass social movement. Although opposition sectors organized independently, they all joined in the large demonstrations and protest marches in 1967 and 1968. Three main opposition sectors achieved enough strength and coordination to affect the political structures of the country profoundly: the student movement, the labor movement, and the Frente Ampla (Broad Front). These distinct sectors of the opposition expressed their views in demonstrations, rallies, and marches, as well as in Congress through a group of MDB deputies who had been elected in 1966. Together they exerted considerable pressure on the state and provoked an internal conflict within the government over two alternative policies: further liberalization of political, social, and economic policies; or a third and even more extensive repressive crackdown.

The Student Movement

The student movement was organized in opposition to the arbitrary firing of professors, to restrictions on university autonomy, and to limitations on student organizing. In 1967-1968, university students were protesting the broad university reform taking place under an agreement between Brazil's Ministry of Education and the United States Agency for International Development.[6] The students succeeded in setting up representative structures at the national, state, and local levels, in spite of the banning of the UNE.[7] In 1967 the UNE's twenty-ninth National Student Congress met clandestinely in São Paulo. The congress elected new officers for the organization and discussed a program.[8]

The UNE continued to enjoy the wide support of the students and succeeded in mobilizing increasingly large numbers for the various activities it sponsored. The first tactic it adopted was to hold small, quick rallies, known as "lightning rallies," to show the population that the movement existed and to avoid direct confrontation with the security forces. As the number of active militants grew, organizational tactics changed: the student movement began to hold larger marches in the streets of major cities, particularly Rio de Janeiro.[9] These were geared toward eliciting support from the broader population—the middle class, and office workers in the downtown areas.

At the same time, students continued to organize at local levels, concentrating on grievances particularly relevant to individual universities. One such local effort involved the demand to improve the food available to poorer students in a subsidized restaurant (Calabouço) in Rio de Janeiro. The government had withdrawn the restaurant's subsidies and caused it to

Table 4
Real Wage Losses over 30 Percent

Year	% of Occupational Categories with Losses over 30%
1965–1966 (base year)	—
1966–1967	12
1967–1968	26
1968–1969	21
1969–1970	17
1970–1971	9
1971–1972	7
1972–1973	11
1973	29
1974	46

Source: DIEESE, "Dez Anos de Política Salarial," p. 65.

Table 5
Evolution of Minimum Wage

Month/Year	Real Minimum Wage (1976 cruzeiros)	Index of Real Wage
January 1959	1,735.29	100
January 1960	1,204.03	69
January 1961	1,475.00	85
January 1962	1,406.38	81
January 1963	1,304.35	75
January 1964	724.14	42
January 1965	840.00	48
January 1966	849.42	49
January 1967	744.02	43
January 1968	737.88	43
January 1969	732.62	42
January 1970	724.91	42
January 1971	723.90	42
January 1972	690.96	40
January 1973	681.37	39
January 1974	623.63	36
January 1975	600.35	35
January 1976	590.49	34
March 1976	532.80	31

Source: DIEESE, Divulgação No. 1/76 (19 April 1976), p. 10.

be run as a private enterprise. With the deterioration of food quality and the increase in prices, students began to protest. They tried to negotiate for the improvement of the restaurant and demanded a meeting with government authorities. To dramatize their grievances, a small group of students staged demonstrations in front of the restaurant. On 28 March 1968, during one such small gathering, a battalion of the military police arrived and fired on the students with machine guns. Edson Luís de Lima Souto, a poor sixteen-year-old secondary school student, died instantly from gunshot wounds.[10]

The death of Edson Luís catalyzed repressed popular anger into mass actions, which took on the proportions of outright social rebellion. One thing led to another. Outraged friends carried the student's body to the state assembly of Rio de Janeiro. There it lay in state under the watchful eyes of political representatives and student leaders. Word spread quickly, and a large gathering in front of the assembly building called on the population to join in the funeral services the next day. On 29 March 1968,

At 4:30 in the afternoon, a crowd whose size can only be compared with the one that accompanied the funeral march of President Getúlio Vargas after his suicide in August 1954, gathered to follow Edson Luís de Lima Souto to his grave in the João Batista Cemetery.

Covered with the national flag, the coffin of the poor student was carried down the steps of the state legislature to the sound of voices singing the National Anthem, enhanced by the visual impact of hundreds of thousands of white handkerchiefs waving a last farewell. Flower petals rained from tops of buildings. Thousands raised black flags to demonstrate their mourning. . . .

When the body was lowered into the grave, the more than fifty thousand persons who had managed to squeeze into the cemetery grounds heard the solemn oath of thousands of young students: "In our time of mourning we shall now begin our battle."[11]

The death also provoked an emotional response in the larger population and created a climate of tension and protest in the city of Rio de Janeiro. The circumstances of his death and the general brutality of the police were the subjects of ample attention in the press and raised serious questions about the official liberalization process underway.

A funeral mass was scheduled for the morning of 4 April 1968, in the Cathedral of Rio de Janeiro (the Candelária). Approximately thirty thousand persons attended. As they left the church, mounted police violently attacked them:

The armed forces mobilized twenty thousand men to put down new student and popular demonstrations. The DOPS and the military police carried out aggressive maneuvers in the downtown area of the city. With the army, the military police, and the marines occupying strategic areas since early dawn, the events began to take place a little after twelve noon, when cavalry from the military police waited for the end of the memorial mass in the Candelária. Then they attacked the unarmed population as it left the church. Clubs and even swords were used against those who attended the Mass. . . .

Later that same afternoon, after a second memorial mass was held in the Candelária, beatings and arrests again took place. Bishop Dom José de Castro Pinto and fifteen other concelebrants of the mass held hands with the clergy present to form a large circle around the cathedral, to protect people inside and to prevent the attack by mounted police with swords in their hands.

The priests also escorted the population down the avenue in an effort to protect them from attacks, but almost in front of the *Jornal do Brasil* we witnessed close to one thousand persons being beaten by a battalion of cavalry using swords and tear gas.[12]

The violent repression at the memorial masses brought the situation to a head. The Catholic church openly joined the opposition to protest the invasion of the cathedral of Rio de Janeiro and the deliberate attack on unarmed priests and faithful during a religious service. The firm position the hierarchy took against the attack cemented an informal alliance: the church, the press, and, in general, the middle classes of the city, who had once supported the military takeover because of their fear of a Communist dictatorship, now openly supported students. The intensity of oppression and violence had begun to neutralize the effects of the liberalization.

The demonstrations grew. Other sectors of the population, now mobilized by the labor movement and the Frente Ampla, joined the protests, which had begun with the students alone. On 25 June a large and this time peaceful march was held in downtown Rio de Janeiro.[13] The military refrained from direct repression, and more than 100,000 persons gathered for an antigovernment rally in front of the cathedral. During this rally, a special committee representing the opposition groups was selected to negotiate liberalization measures with the federal government. The very composition of the "Committee of the 100,000" shows the nature of the opposition alliance: one representative of the professional sectors, two representatives of the students, one representative of the Mother's Movement for Political Amnesty, and a priest representing the Catholic church. It was a negotiating committee representing the middle classes, which were now in open opposition to the military and were fighting the police in the streets. The national security state became further isolated from civil society; the circle of power had begun to close.

Labor

Under the Costa e Silva government's "policy of relief," the Ministry of Labor began a program of "union renovation" (*renovação sindical*). The program was intended to increase the welfare function of trade unions, making union bureaucracies assume the burden of mediating between the state and the working class. The Labor Code stipulates that unions are "to collaborate with the central government." Such collaboration is ensured by the fact that, under the Labor Code, the ministry collects union dues in the form of a compulsory tax on wages and then redistributes these funds among the unions. Percentages to be spent on particular functions may be established by law. Under the new program, the percentages to be spent for dental and medical care and for continuing education programs were increased, thus forcing unions to assume social costs that the national security state no longer wanted to bear.

The renovation policy also involved the state in a union organization drive. In 1967 and 1968, 803 new urban unions were formed and 611 rural unions organized legally within the official labor structure.[14] Although some may have grown from the initiative of the labor movement, which had begun to reorganize itself in some areas, most were set up directly by the state to extend its corporative control over local unions and especially over the federations and confederations. Since the representational structure of federations gives disproportionate weight to small unions—every local has two representatives and one vote, independent of the size of its membership—it was in the interest of the national security state to organize a large number of unions, sometimes with as few as one hundred members. These "phantom unions" were to guarantee government control of the federations.

In addition to organizing phantom unions, the Ministry of Labor began to pay particular attention to the training and education of new trade union officers whom they had appointed to run the unions. The officially appointed leaders (*interventores*) had access to courses and vast resources to implement welfare programs and promote union collaboration with the state. The state machinery and the funds withheld from all salaries (whether or not the worker belonged to the union) enabled the appointed officials to increase their power and co-opt middle-level leadership. Of course, the corporative structure of the trade unions was nothing new, having remained essentially the same since the Labor Code was put in place in 1943. What is important is the way in which the national security state used existing control mechanisms effectively both to remove opposition trade union leaders from their posts and to tighten the state's direct control over the unions. This policy continues to the present.

Contrary to expectations, the liberalization policy and the trade union renovation encouraged debate and participation within the official union structure. In 1967 groups of trade union activists formed committees of the "union opposition" (*oposições sindicais*) to work within the unions to win back the electoral offices now held by government appointees. They held electoral campaigns regularly so as to imbue the corporative structures with some flexibility and legitimacy. The opposition, taking advantage of the opportunity to increase the level of awareness of the social and economic problems that affected their wages and their lives, worked within the limited space available to mobilize workers during these campaigns.

In elections held in 1967 in the Metalworkers' Union of Contagem, Minas Gerais, the contradictions of the union renovation policy became manifest. The union opposition, based on factory-level representation, organized a slate to run against the official incumbents. The opposition program included an analysis of the internal democratization of the union structure and explicitly encouraged direct rank-and-file participation in the day-to-day running of the union. The program also voiced strong criticisms of the government's wage policies and the FGTS. The opposition conducted an intensive rank-and-file campaign in all factories for a month. The head of the opposition slate, Enio Seabra, was a respected leader and a worker from Mannesman, the largest corporation in the industrial town. Just before the elections, the Regional Labor Board barred his candidacy, eliminating him from the opposition slate. Although the opposition won the elections anyway, the Ministry of Labor refused to lift the ban on Seabra's participation. Thus the victory was incomplete, but the campaign was important in that it demonstrated the limits of the union renovation program and established a climate of political and electoral organizing among the metalworkers, that contributed to the strike movements of April 1968.

The political and labor context was different in Osasco, one of the most important industrial areas of the state of São Paulo. Whereas in Contagem organizing went on strictly within the limits of the official union structure or within factory sectors, in Osasco a number of opposition groups combined: activists of the Catholic church, students in alliance with workers, political organizers in a contested municipal election in which the MDB emerged victorious, and finally, workers organized in their own factory committees. The work of the Catholic church was already of some significance in the Osasco area by 1967. The National Labor Front (Frente Nacional do Trabalho) had relatively extensive experience in organizing groups of workers in factories. Its major action, however, had been the organization of two long strikes in the Perus Factory in 1961-1962. In Osasco, the Catholic organization encouraged workers to become active in their unions and to form movements in opposition to the government-controlled directors. Other Catholic organizations linked to the Workers' Pastoral also encouraged factory-level organization of rank-and-file workers. Consistent with the prevalent Catholic social thought of the time, these networks did not propose particular programs and political platforms, but rather encouraged democratic participation in order to stimulate consciousness and autonomous decision-making among workers. The factory committees developed from this kind of perspective and activity.

The first effective factory committee was formed in Cobrasma, an automobile component manufacturer that employed around ten thousand workers at that time.[15] The Cobrasma Factory Committee was recognized by the corporation and became a legal civic association in 1965. Its officers were elected in the factory and benefited from job security, which was guaranteed under a contract negotiated between workers and management. José Ibrahim, a young worker-student at Cobrasma, was elected the first president of the Factory Committee. In 1967 he won the presidency of the Metalworkers' Union of Osasco—bringing with him the experience of the factory-committee form of organization, as well as the backing of his large, organized base in the Cobrasma rank and file. Once in the union office, José Ibrahim began to encourage the formation of other factory committees in Osasco, using Cobrasma as a model.

In the 1967 municipal elections, the student movement as a whole continued to appeal to voters to void their votes (*voto nulo*) and tried to influence the Osasco workers. One of the peculiar characteristics of Osasco was the large number of workers who were also secondary school students, studying at night in the local high school—the president of the union was one of these. This gave the student movement deep influence in the political thinking of working-class leaders in Osasco, as well as a direct organizational tie to the Metalworkers' Union. In spite of this influence, after discussing the municipal elections in assemblies, the workers rejected the call to void their votes. The trade union, as well as the students of Osasco, chose to work within the MDB, taking the position that local control of the city council and city hall constituted an important opportunity for affecting policy at a municipal level. An agreement was negotiated to the effect that, if elected, the MDB mayor would incorporate a worker and a student representative into his board of advisers and would give them power in policy development and implementation. When the MDB won a significant victory in Osasco, electing the mayor and sixteen members of the City Council (against seven for ARENA),[16] the Student Center of Osasco, as agreed, appointed a representative to work with the mayor. The Metalworkers' Union also elected a worker representative for the municipal council, and other students and workers were called in to collaborate in the administration of the city. Thus many of those who had previously worked for the election of José Ibrahim for the presidency of the Osasco Metalworkers' Union now occupied positions in the city government.

In Rio de Janeiro, the middle-class and student movement was beginning to have national repercussions: the opposition began to believe that its offensive was the beginning of the end of the national security state. Such opinions were naturally reflected in the working-class movement. Responding to the new climate nationally, trade unions organized an interunion movement against the wage laws (movimento intersindical antiarrocho, MIA). This movement was an attempt by opposition sectors to reconstruct the parallel labor organizations that had existed prior to the 1964 coup d'état.[17]

The lifespan of the MIA was limited and its effectiveness questionable, but it added to the climate of political organization and to the euphoric anticipation of major concessions from the national security state. In this political context, unexpectedly, a large strike movement began in Contagem. On 16 April 1968, seventeen hundred workers from the Belgo-Mineira factory, the largest in Contagem, took their managers hostage and declared themselves on strike.[18] Within a week fifteen thousand workers were out, and most major industries in the Contagem area were completely stopped. The workers demanded a 25 percent wage increase, whereas the official index raise decreed by the government had been only 17 percent.

The Ministry of Labor was taken by surprise. In accordance with the union renovation policy, the Metalworkers' Union in the area had a new and more active leadership. But, since the most representative leader had been purged from the ticket, the union had lost touch with its base, and it also was taken by surprise. The movement in Contagem was largely spontaneous. This, together with the fact that the demands were limited and that the Ministry had intended to raise wages up to the level of cost-of-living increases, allowed the government to adopt a conciliatory position and negotiate. Using the union as mediator, the Ministry of Labor offered a 10 percent increase for all workers in Contagem. The offer was accepted, and on 25 April the workers voted to end their strike.

The national security state moved quickly to keep other workers from following the Contagem example. On 12 June Decree-Law 5451 extended the 10 percent emergency raise to all workers.[19] At the same time, however, the decree revoked the three-year limit on the Wage Law, making the state's wage-control policies permanent.[20] This measure shows how the dialectic of state and opposition has imposed its own logic on the changing control structures in the national security state. Liberalization periods have been combined with selective repression and with adjustments to the economic model, but in its attempt to resolve contradictions and control conflict, the state has further isolated itself from civil society. The decree that made the wage policies permanent added to the general discontent among workers and fueled the strike movement in Osasco. As the political temperature went up, the example of Contagem became all the more appealing.

The Contagem strike had been largely spontaneous, and organizational efforts *followed* the outbreak of the strike. In Osasco, on the other hand, after the election of José Ibrahim to the union presidency, workers' assemblies met in factories and at union headquarters to discuss their problems, priorities, and organizational strategies. The union became the headquarters for a variety of activities aimed at raising the political awareness of the rank-and-file members in order to lay the groundwork for linking the factory committee networks to the union itself. By mid-1968, "groups of 10," or fledgling factory committees with significant rank-and-file participation, had already been organized in most factories in Osasco. Three of the five largest plants already had legal factory committees modeled on the Cobrasma prototype. These provided the base for the organization of a "strike command," which was composed of leaders elected by the factories.[21] The strike was carefully planned for November 1968.

Although the leadership was against moving up the date of the strike, a spontaneous strike action in one factory in May forced their hand and set the tone for the full-fledged movement that erupted in July. Under pressure from the rank and file, the leadership joined the movement to carefully plan strike strategy:

The rank and file told us, "You talked so much about strikes and now you are going back on your word." So we decided to go ahead and organize. The union took on the necessary tasks and planned the strike carefully.

To give you an idea of the amount of organizing done, we got in touch with the UNE and the UEE and asked them what kind of help the students could give us if a strike should be declared in Osasco within a few days. The students would organize support groups, would distribute notices and leaflets at the factory gates, and in particular would collect money for the strike support fund. They agreed to do this.

On the same day, we began to form groups to carry out a variety of tasks. Three days before the strike, we wrote the leaflet that announced the beginning of the strike movement, including a detailed description of events that had not yet taken place: "At 8:45 A.M. the Cobrasma factory stopped work and the workers occupied the factory. Workers' demands included the end of the wage control laws. At 11:15 A.M. the Granada and the Barreto Kelly corporations joined the strike, and the workers all left the plants together and marched to the union. Two hours later, Lonaflex stopped and declared its solidarity with the strike movement."

And it all happened exactly that way. We had real confidence in our work at the base, within the factories.[22]

Only one aspect of the events that followed did not go according to plan: a mistaken analysis of the political context led the labor leaders to underestimate the reaction of the national security state. It was not clear to the opposition at the time that the state could count on large reserves of coercive power nor that the military was sufficiently cohesive and prepared to use the full force of the repressive apparatus.

For Osasco, the threat of a movement organized from the bottom up was more than the government could tolerate, and, moreover, the element of surprise was not present this time. Although the union had hoped to prevent intervention by claiming that the strike was spontaneous and that the union's role was that of mediator, it was clear from the start that this was not the case. On the second day of the strike, the Ministry of Labor intervened in the union and removed all elected officials from office. José Ibrahim was persecuted, forced into hiding, and later into exile. The workers who occupied the Cobrasma plant suffered severe physical repression. A force that included 30 mounted police, 60 soldiers armed with machine guns, and two armored vehicles with heavy weapons invaded the factory. In the immediate aftermath of the invasion, 120 persons were arrested and beaten, and many were tortured. Among those arrested were two priests who worked in the factory as part of the Catholic "worker-priest" movement. Troops surrounded and occupied union headquarters. Without a place to meet, workers retired to a local church. The church was invaded, severely damaged, and everyone inside arrested. The memory of the repression of the Osasco strike remained a powerful deterrent to any attempt to break the strike laws for years to come.

With the union and its leadership gone and many members of the strike command included in a growing list of "disappeared," the movement was broken. The strike lasted for three days, with some factories continuing to resist for another two days. It ended in total defeat: none of the strike demands were met, and many of the rights that had been won previously were eliminated. The tragedy of this defeat, followed by severe repression in the entire city of Osasco, shows how far the workers were from constituting an effective movement. Support from other unions had been limited to letters of solidarity and mild attempts to convince the government not to intervene in the union.

Perhaps the most important effect of the strike was to demonstrate the weakness of a movement that had seemed so deeply rooted—stronger than it was in reality. It also proved that the national security state had at its disposal, and was prepared to use, enough coercive force to repel this kind of challenge. The experience of Osasco left scars on the labor movement, which attempted, over the next five years, to learn from it and to develop alternative organizational strategies.

The Frente Ampla

Two former state governors had played a crucial role in the 1964 conspiracy: Magalhães Pinto, then governor of Minas Gerais, and Carlos Lacerda, then governor of Guanabara. The "movement of governors," which they had spearheaded, provided the military with the legitimacy to carry out the conspiracy to overthrow an elected president. Soon after the takeover, however, both began to distance themselves from the policies of the government. As early as 1965, both Lacerda and Magalhães Pinto had begun to criticize the military government openly for its policies in relation to Congress, the judiciary, and the restriction of civilian political activity.

In 1967 Magalhães Pinto and Carlos Lacerda brought together a political movement that included a broad spectrum of political opinion. The Frente Ampla looked for its allies among traditional civilian political sectors, including conservative leadership.[23] One of those approached was former president Juscelino Kubitschek, who had had his political mandate canceled and his political rights suspended for ten years with the specific and declared intention of eliminating him from any future presidential race. His prestige was nonetheless evident in the victories of candidates he supported in the 1965 gubernatorial elections, and again in the 1966 congressional elections. Persecution of Kubitschek made him into a political martyr and increased his appeal. When the former president joined the Frente Ampla, the military government began to be seriously worried.[24]

In September 1967 the main leaders of the front met with exiled president João Goulart in Montevideo to discuss opposition activities and agree on common goals. A formal cooperation agreement, establishing the grounds for their alliance, was signed by the four leaders. This document, known as the Montevideo Pact, was the program of the Frente Ampla, which began to take on the appearance of a broad-based opposition political party. The participation of Kubitschek and Goulart gave the front legitimacy both in wider political circles and in labor and *trabalhista* sectors. The program called for redemocratization of the country, repeal of all control legislation, the end of the wage policies, and it affirmed the rights of workers, including the right to strike. Finally, the program called for immediate, free, and direct elections at all levels of political representation.

On the basis of the Montevideo Pact, widespread negotiations among politicians and trade union and student leaders began to take shape. A series of street demonstrations and rallies were planned. Although the front was not sufficiently organized to become a conduit for all dissent, broad sectors of public opinion and politicians received it enthusiastically. Its appeal was enough for Congressman Osvaldo Lima Filho, vice-president of the MDB, to remark that "in another year in this country there will only be the Frente Ampla and the government."[25]

It was particularly threatening to the national security state, insofar as it appealed to conservative members of the middle and upper classes, who had previously supported the military coup. Worse yet, it began to have an influence within the military itself, reinforcing the conviction of troop commanders that it constituted a threat that had to be met with force.[26] With student demonstrations in the streets, with growing militancy in the labor sector, and with the deepening influence of the Frente Ampla in conservative sectors and even within the military itself, the national security state decided, in early April 1968, to move decisively: it published a decree-law banning the organization.[27]

The Frente Ampla was banned as an organization and it was forbidden to hold meetings, rallies, marches, make political statements, or issue publications of any kind. The Federal Police Department (DPF) was ordered to arrest anyone who violated these prohibitions. In addition, the DPF was to seize books, magazines, periodicals, or any other written material the front produced.

The state intended to eliminate a social movement by a simple decree. But in so doing, it revealed yet another example of the contradictions between the process of liberalization and the use of repression to remove "antagonistic" sectors of the opposition from the political scene. While trying to deal with pressures from sectors dedicated to the defense of internal security, the government was still trying to discuss possible constitutional reform with the opposition, largely under the auspices of Vice-President Pedro Aleixo.[28] The contradiction between the two processes was a direct consequence of the different goals of sectors of the coalition in power, and of conceptual contradictions within the Doctrine of National Security itself: the permanent national objectives refer to democracy; the requirements of internal security make dissent intolerable. Thus it is not surprising that the state was wrenched by deep internal conflict. Within the coalition, there were groups already preparing a second coup d'état to impose a third crackdown—a situation that would bring about a confrontation between the executive and the legislature with ultimately tragic consequences.

Crisis

The Constitution of 1967 had upheld the right to parliamentary immunity. After the expiration of the time limit on the extraordinary powers given under Institutional Act No. 2, a legislator could only be tried with the approval of the House to which he or she belonged; in addition, the executive could no longer simply cancel an electoral mandate.

Congressional Crisis

Congress became a mirror of the disturbances in civil society. New opposition legislators elected in 1966 responded to the political climate and were obligated to support the growing mass protest movement among the middle class and workers. Although Congress was unable to do much legislating, most legislative questions having been transferred to the executive, it did play a role in denouncing repressive acts. Members took the floor in turn to denounce executive branch abuses and policies, thus reading these events into the congressional register. A group of around forty MDB politicians worked together on a strategy for parliamentary action that took advantage of their right to immunity: they practiced freedom of expression on the floor of Congress. According to the Congressional rules, all parties have times allocated for five-minute speeches. These times are given alternately to different members to use.[29] During one such five-minute period in mid-August, the MDB congressman from Guanabara, Márcio Moreira Alves, called on the population to boycott the Independence Day military parade and asked Brazilian women to resist the military government by refusing to date officers who remained silent in the face of repression or who actively participated in state-perpetrated violence. Although the speech went unnoticed by the press, the military chose it as the pretext for provoking a major political crisis.

The Independence Day military parade has an important psychological component as part of a strategy of intimidation. Once a year, all military hardware is on display for the population to see. By 1968 the population knew that this impressive show of force was more likely to be turned against it than against a foreign aggressor; thus the parade was to have a deterrent effect, making people fear the consequences of taking action. (It is not a coincidence that all military and totalitarian governments place such an emphasis on military parades and displays of weaponry; it is an element in a strategy of terror as a method of political and social control.) Márcio Moreira Alves's speech thus hit a sensitive point in the state's general strategy of social control. In addition, hard-line officers who were already planning a second coup d'état, which would give them a freer hand in the defense of internal security, found the speech particularly useful for their purposes. The call for a boycott of the parade, coupled with the appeal for an "Operation Lysistrata," was bound to elicit a furious emotional response in the barracks, thus preparing the ground for widespread military support for a new show of force. That such preparation was their intention is indicated by the fact that the hard-line officers made thousands of reprints of the speech and had it distributed in all the barracks in the country. Military officers reacted with outrage to what they considered a serious attack on their honor and their male dignity. The stage thus set, the military ministers who spearheaded the conspiracy lost no time: they filed a petition in the Supreme Court asking for the court-martial of Congressman Márcio Moreira Alves for having gravely offended the honor and dignity of the armed forces.[30]

Since the Constitution of 1967 was still in effect, a member of Congress could not be summarily punished for a speech made from the floor of Congress; proper procedures had to be followed. The petition was turned over to the House Judiciary Committee, which could reject it by a two-thirds vote. If the petition was not rejected in the Judiciary Committee, it went to the floor for discussion, and a vote on the question of lifting parliamentary immunity had to be taken in a joint session of the two houses of Congress. Needless to say, members of Congress had an interest in the maintenance of parliamentary immunity. The memory of the purges was sufficiently vivid for this point to be painfully clear to everyone. Thus a decision to lift the immunity of a congressman so that he could be court-martialed for treason amounted to a direct threat to all members of Congress, a fact clearly pointed out in the speeches that Márcio Moreira Alves made in his own defense.

During an agitated joint session of Congress on 12 December, with a thousand spectators in the galleries, the members of the two houses took a roll call vote. The result surprised the executive: 216 against lifting parliamentary immunity, and only 141 in favor. The 75-vote margin constituted a significant victory for those against; it also meant that many members of ARENA had joined with the MDB in defense of a common interest, thus risking their own electoral mandates by defying the party fidelity rule, which explicitly stipulated that members of Congress who crossed party lines in a vote automatically lost their mandate. All members of Congress and the spectators in the galleries burst into spontaneous applause, and many were in tears. One voice began to sing the National Anthem and was joined by others in a triumphant affirmation of civilian force; it seemed to be a moment of victory, a moment of glory.

In reality, it was a moment of defeat, one that allowed the members of the repressive apparatus a free hand in the implementation of their plan. Recent evidence indicates that Institutional Act No. 5 (AI-5) had been ready since July 1968. It was drafted in response to the growing middle-class support for the student demonstrations and to the militancy of workers demonstrated in the Contagem and Osasco strikes.[31] This point is confirmed by the speed with which the national security state acted: less than twenty-four hours after Congress voted, the text of AI-5 was published in the mass media and was repeatedly read on television and on the radio; Congress was closed indefinitely; all constitutional and individual guarantees were suspended. All over the country, the army conducted maneuvers that amounted to a veritable occupation. Opposition members of all ideological persuasions were already being arrested by the thousands.

the culmination

Institutional Act No. 5

Institutional Act No. 5 was officially decreed on 13 December 1968, one day after the congressional vote. In many ways, the text of the act repeated provisions contained in the first two institutional acts, but there was a major difference: there was no time limit on its validity. The controls and suspension of constitutional guarantees were permanent.

The powers attributed to the executive branch by AI-5 can be summarized as follows: (1) the power to close the federal Congress and state and municipal assemblies; (2) the right to cancel the electoral mandates of members of the legislative or executive branches at federal, state, and municipal levels; (3) the right to suspend political rights of citizens for ten years and the reinstitution of the "statute of the *cassados*"; (4) the right to dismiss, remove from office, transfer, or retire employees of the federal, state, and municipal bureaucracies; (5) the right to fire, dismiss, or transfer judges, and the removal of all guarantees to the judiciary with regard to job tenure, nontransferability, and the maintenance of salary levels; (6) the power to declare a state of siege without any of the impediments that had been written into the 1967 Constitution; (7) the right to confiscate private property for state use as punishment for subversion or corruption; (8) the suspension of habeas corpus in all cases of political crimes against national security; (9) trial of political crimes by military courts with no other judicial recourse; (10) the right to legislate by decree and issue any other institutional or complementary act; and finally, (11) the prohibition of any consideration by the judiciary of appeals from those charged under any provision of AI-5. All stipulations of the act were to remain in force until the president signed a decree specifically revoking it.[32]

From the time it was issued until it was finally revoked as a result of intense opposition pressure in 1979, AI-5 served as the legal justification for the punishment of more than 1,607 persons.[33] The data from the extensive research conducted by Marcus Figueiredo only go up to 1974; during the Geisel government, another 74 citizens were punished under AI-5.[34] Those prosecuted included bureaucrats, military personnel, politicians, professors, lawyers, architects, engineers, and members of the judiciary. By extending the purges to the military, the government was able to control internal dissent and eliminate the principal opposition foci within the armed forces themselves. Adding the total number of published cases of punishment under Institutional Acts 1, 2, and 5, to the published cases of arrests, suspensions, and other strong disciplinary measures, a total of 6,592 members of the armed forces suffered some form of direct coercion because of their opinions and beliefs. These data, reproduced in table 6, are incomplete in that they are based solely on published cases.

Over its ten-year life span, moreover AI-5 was used to cancel the electoral mandates of 113 federal deputies and senators, 190 members of state assemblies, 38 city council members, and 30 mayors. As can be seen from table 7, political representation must be considered to have been seriously curtailed and both quantitatively and qualitatively transformed.

Perhaps the most serious consequence of the institutional act was that it opened the way for the unbridled use of the repressive apparatus of the national security state. The restrictions on the judiciary and the abolition of habeas corpus for political crimes were crucially important in this respect. Arrests could be made without formal charges and without warrants. Together with the restrictions on the judiciary, this situation prevented opposition lawyers and others who defended political prisoners from enforcing legal guarantees. They were thus unable to prevent serious abuses of power and the violent torture of political prisoners. Furthermore, the lack of a time limit on the act's validity meant that extraordinary powers had become ordinary. The national security state was both totally centralized and isolated; the state was embodied and circumscribed in the executive. Institutional Act No. 5 gave birth to a Leviathan, which General Golbery do Couto e Silva had already predicted in his writings in the 1950s, a Hobbesian state, which absorbed all power into itself.[35]

Conclusion

Institutional Act No. 5 marks the end of the first phase of the

Table 6
Control of the Military

Branch/Rank	Type of Action		
	Expelled & Fired (A)	Put on Reserve (B)	Other* (C)
Army			
Officers	32	163	2
Sergeants & lower officers	79	174	15
Corporals & soldiers	12	0	12
Total	123	337	29
Navy			
Officers	16	12	2
Sergeants & lower officers	16	272	3
Corporals & sailors	196	167	4,707
Total	228	451	4,712
Air Force			
Officers	26	103	2
Sergeants & lower officers	241	79	6
Corporals & airmen	47	0	47
Total	314	182	17
Naval Fusiliers			
Officers	8	2	0
Sergeants & lower officers	21	22	3
Corporals & sailors	23	2	5
Total	52	26	8
Military Police			
Officers	19	10	5
Sergeants & lower officers	2	5	0
Corporals & soldiers	41	15	16
Total	62	30	21

Total military punished: 6,592

Sources: **Cols. A and B:** *Diário Oficial da União*; data from interviews and data compiled by Central Computer System of Brazilian Congress. Data gathering occurred between 1978 and 1980.
Col. C: Data based on interviews and research in *Veja, Isto E, Jornal do Brasil, Movimento, Tribuna da Imprensa, O Globo, Folha de São Paulo*, and *O Estado de São Paulo*, as well as on data gathered by the Associação Brasileira pela Defesa dos Atingidos pelos Atos Institucionais.
Notes: Actions were taken based on Institutional Acts 1, 2, and 5. The data are incomplete, as they are based only on what is published or known to political actors. This is only a sample of the extent of the repression.
*Other types of action include disciplinary arrests and suspension.

Table 7
Purges Conducted under Institutional Acts Nos. 1, 2, and 5

Branch of Government	1964–1967 Castello Branco	1967–1970 Costa e Silva & Military Junta*	1970–1973 Médici	1974–1979 Geisel	Total
National Congress	76	105	0	8	189
State assemblies	100	178	10	2	290
City councils	11	36	0	2	49
State governorships	10	0	0	0	10
Mayors	27	30	0	0	57
Total	224	349	10	12	595

Source: *Diário Oficial da União* (April 1964–December 1979).

*There is some overlap in the dates, for the Military Junta period lasted until about the end of 1969. It is significant that the largest number of purges occurred in the immediate aftermath of the enactment of Institutional Act No. 5 and in the Military Junta period.

institutionalization of the national security state, a stage of foundation building. The permanent character of the controls incorporated into AI-5 gave rise to a new period in which the economic development model could be fully implemented and the repressive apparatus could pursue absolute internal security by preventing organized dissent from the government's economic and social policies. The institutional act would thus provide the legal framework for deep structural transformations.

The contradictions within the national security state and the coalition in power were clarified in 1967-1968. A limited liberalization policy that sought to promote corporate relations of control had to be flexible enough to allow co-optation of leaders and to provide a long-term basis for state stability. This policy came into conflict with the quest for absolute internal security. The need for coercion was in turn linked to the exploitative economic and social policies of the economic development model. There is thus a constant pattern of opposition upsurge, followed by increased repression from government security forces.

Repression itself, however, was unable to eliminate the opposition altogether, as it did not deal with the underlying causes of dissent. The force employed merely *displaced* the contradiction, without resolving it. As coercion was applied to subdue one sector of the opposition, other, previously inactive, sectors of the population became engaged. As they joined in the resistance, they became, in the eyes of the national security state, part of the enemy within. The dynamic became one of escalating quantities of force needed to crush an opposition that was constantly enlarged by the adherence of new groups. It is important to remember that 1967 began with a feeble attempt by student demonstrators to call attention to their localized problems. By 1968 this movement had been joined by large numbers of people from different classes and ideological currents. The conflict had been displaced from students to the middle classes, then to the workers, and finally, through the force of repression, it involved the Catholic church. The coercive power of the state did not eliminate the original foci of the opposition; in fact, they grew stronger with the adherence of other sectors and gained legitimacy from the repercussions of their activities in Congress.

The executive-legislative crisis that ended with the closing of Congress for an undetermined period of time highlighted once more the contradiction between the state's use of the language of democracy and the practice of repression. Being forced to use its ultimate source of power—physical force—the state suffered a further loss of legitimacy. Its loss of legitimacy and its increasing isolation, in turn, gave it no alternative but to continue to escalate its use of force.

A dynamic of violence thus characterized the period that followed the passage of Institutional Act No. 5. Some sectors of the opposition took up arms, in the belief that there was no other way to fight the Leviathan. The armed struggle, in turn, strengthened those sectors within the national security state most linked to the defense of internal security. They effectively used the space provided to implant a formidable apparatus of repression and to institutionalize the strategy of control by terror. In this confrontation a brutal offensive on the part of the security forces crushed the other sectors of the opposition and much of the population that was not involved. What followed was a period of silence, of fear, of disarray, of hopelessness. It was at this point that the alternatives the Catholic church suggested and implemented provided the element crucial to the struggle for freedom to continue: hope.

Part III. The Second Stage of Institutionalization, 1969-1974

Repression

1st - Operation clean up 1969
2nd - AI 2
3rd - AI 5   1969-1974

6. Armed Struggle and the National Security State

The Political and Economic Context

Institutional Act No. 5 marked the end of the first phase of institutionalization of the national security state. Successive purges severely weakened both political parties, though the MDB suffered heavier losses. ARENA members who had voted with the MDB were summarily dismissed from their electoral posts and placed in the camp of the internal enemy. The student movement disbanded after the arrest of its top eight hundred leaders at an underground congress held in Ibiúna, São Paulo, at the end of 1968. Labor unions suffered new intervention and severe repression. In general, those sectors of the opposition that sought reform through nonviolent resistance were greatly weakened and entered a period of disarray and hopelessness.

AI-5 introduced a third cycle of repression. The first cycle, in 1964, had concentrated on purging persons politically linked to past populist governments, particularly the Goulart government. Direct physical repression was limited to workers and peasants, in a class-based strategy to eliminate resistance in those sectors. The second cycle (1965-1966), after the passage of Institutional Act No. 2, aimed at finishing the purges in the state bureaucracy and electoral offices; it did not include direct and widespread use of violence.

The third cycle was characterized by extensive purges in representative political organs, universities, information networks, and the state bureaucratic apparatus, accompanied by large-scale military maneuvers using physical violence against all classes indiscriminately. Challenges to the state from the middle classes, particularly the student movement, had convinced the forces of repression that areas of "pressure" existed among all classes. Thus the nationwide search-and-arrest campaigns spread to sections of the population that had been left untouched previously.

Congress remained closed from December 1968 to 30 October 1969, and seven state and municipal assemblies were also closed. During this time, control of the executive was firmly in the hands of those groups that emphasized internal security, that is, members of the repressive apparatus. While Congress was closed the executive issued thirteen institutional acts, forty complementary acts, and twenty decree-laws. These were oriented toward institutionalizing control of organizations in civil society. Specific controls were enacted for the press, for universities and other educational institutions, and for political participation in general. The period of congressional recess was used to the fullest to enact decree-laws regulating the economy and to provide a complete system of fiscal incentives, which facilitated the implementation of the economic development model. By the end of 1969, the legal framework for the economic miracle years was firmly in place.

In this political context, the opposition sectors that had been arguing the necessity of armed struggle gained a predominant position. The strategy of armed rebellion against the national security state had been discussed since at least 1967, but it won strong support among opposition sectors only after the violence following the enactment of AI-5. The year 1969, therefore, marked the real beginning of the urban and rural violence that would tear at the fabric of the country for the next five years. Armed struggle was most concentrated in urban areas and primarily involved organizations whose militants were drawn from the student movement. The main rural guerrilla warfare, organized by the Communist Party of Brazil (Partido Comunista do Brasil, PC do B), a split-off from the Brazilian Communist party, took place in the Araguaia region.

The prevailing theoretical perspectives on revolutionary warfare deeply influenced the students who had participated in the surge of opposition after the 1964 coup. The experience of Cuba, and of Che Guevara in Boliva, led them to support a revolutionary strategy advocated by some political parties in the underground Left. Régis Debray's book *Revolution in the Revolution?* lent a romantic note to the Cuban experience.[1] Hence the theory of *foquismo*, according to which the isolated action of a small group of committed individuals could spark revolution in Latin America, took root among the students.[2] In addition, the unlimited violence associated with AI-5 convinced many people that the dictatorship was now so firmly implanted that only force of arms could bring it down. This was the argument that finally pushed many middle-class people into armed struggle.

Political Parties and Revolutionary Strategy

Although the Catholic church remained by and large committed to nonviolence and grass-roots organizing among workers and peasants, a group that originated in Catholic social movements, Ação Popular (Popular Action, AP), had already endorsed armed struggle and *foquismo* in an underground congress held in Uruguay in 1966. The AP was particularly strong in the student movement; during the post-1964 period, it had won most of the important electoral posts in the UNE and the state organizations.

The Brazilian Communist party (PCB) advocated a peaceful road to socialism. The party program, explicit on this issue, rejected armed struggle, a position that led to major splits in the party. One of these came in 1962, leading to the formation of the PC do B, which argued the need for armed struggle.

A second major split occurred when Carlos Marighela, a member of the PCB Executive Committee, publicly broke with the party in 1967 by advocating urban guerrilla warfare as a central revolutionary strategy. Marighela founded the National Liberation Alliance (Aliança de Libertação Nacional, ALN). Unlike most other armed-struggle organizations, the ALN had substantial support among workers who had previously been militants in the Communist party. The ALN program modified Debray's *foquismo*, adapting it to a situation of urban guerrilla warfare rather than the traditional rural guerrilla warfare other parties in the underground Left promoted.[3] Except for the ALN, armed-struggle organizations intended their urban activities as a base of support for the major effort, the preparation and launching of a rural *foco* that would lead to rural guerrilla warfare. Urban actions were to secure funds and arms to send to militants who would prepare the ground in rural areas. However, because most of the organizations never reached the stage of rural activity, the armed-struggle period would be characterized mainly by urban battles. Although these groups had almost no military and strategic coordination and acted in isolation from and even in competition with each other, the theory of *foquismo* influenced all of them. They believed that small bands of armed revolutionaries, completely isolated from social movements, could spark an armed rebellion in a country of 100 million persons.

Power Struggles within the State

In August 1969, President Costa e Silva suffered a severe stroke. An intense power struggle developed over the succession. According to the 1967 Constitution, then in effect, Vice-President Pedro Aleixo should immediately succeed the president in case of death or inability to carry out the duties of the office. But Pedro Aleixo had openly opposed AI-5; thus he did not serve the purposes of the forces in control of the state.[4] A secret meeting of the Armed Forces High Command, with extraordinary powers, concluded that "the constitutional solution was not viable," and decided that the presidency would be held by a junta composed of the ministers of the army, navy, and air force.[5]

This temporary solution merely prolonged the power struggle within the military. The 1969 succession crisis gave rise to an informal process of transfer of power, a version of which is still in use. To select among the many potential military candidates, an unofficial "electoral college," composed of 104 generals, was made responsible for collecting suggestions from armed forces officers. A smaller electoral college, composed of 10 other generals, then examined the names submitted and reduced the list of to 3. A group of 7 generals made the final selection.[6] In this manner, General Emílio Garrastazú Médici was chosen to fill the office of president.

The succession crisis highlights the fragility of the national security state's efforts at institutionalization. The Constitution of 1967 was barely a year and a half old, and was already being overridden. The state lacks an automatic and regulated system for the transfer of political power; thus each instance of executive succession is a cause of crisis. The lack of acceptable constitutional mechanisms of succession brings political struggle and dissent into the military and the state itself.

The "Economic Miracle"

The period of industrial growth between 1968 and 1973 has become known as Brazil's "economic miracle." During these years, Brazil experienced double-digit growth rates (as measured by GDP), as seen in table 8. As the gross domestic product increased, the inflation rate was held down to an average of 20 percent during the period. Overall growth was largely due to the industrial sector; the agricultural sector continued to stagnate, except for a surge in 1971 caused by investment in the central plains and Amazon regions. The increase in the growth rate was due both to an increase in total foreign investment and to extensive state investment that applied funds from international lending institutions. The latter produced a dramatic jump in the foreign debt, from a total of 3.9 billion dollars in 1968 to over 12.5 billion dollars by 1973.[7]

Foreign investment was deemed of fundamental importance for Brazil's development objectives, because the greater efficiency attributed to multinational corporations was expected to fuel rapid growth. At the direction of the government's powerful economic planner, Antônio Delfim Netto, a complete system of fiscal incentives was established by decree-law. Tax deductions and even tax exemptions were established for investment in areas that the government considered crucial to the overall development plan, particularly the Amazon, the Northeast, and the central plains. Domestic interest rates were kept higher than interest rates offered by international lending institutions to encourage investors to seek outside financing. Tax subsidies were provided for export goods. Perhaps most important, tax deductions were established for capital gains, thereby spurring investment in the stock market.

The economic model the government pursued followed a tendency defined as "productivist." According to this view, an underdeveloped country

Table 8
Gross Domestic Product

Year	GDP Variation (%)
1964	2.9
1965	2.7
1966	3.8
1967	4.8
1968	11.2
1969	10.0
1970	8.8
1971	13.3
1972	11.7
1973	14.0
1974	9.8
1975	5.6
1976	9.0
1977	4.7
1978	6.0
1979	6.4
1980	8.5
1981	− 1.9
1982	0.0
1983	− 7.5*

Sources: 1964–1977: World Bank Country Study, Brazil: Human Resources Special Report (October 1979).
1980–1981: Deputado Eduardo Matarazzo Suplicy, Assembléia Legislativa de São Paulo, 6 March 1982.
1982: *Isto E* (1 January 1983), p. 52.
1983: *Folha de São Paulo* (30 November 1983), p. 7.
*Estimate based on the real fall of tax from consumer products (*Imposto de Circulação de Mercadorias*—ICM), which is one of the economic indicators.

needs to create the best possible conditions for investment, particularly foreign investment, so as to accumulate sufficient capital to reach the "take-off" stage of economic growth. Government planners argued against economists whom they described as "distributivists," because of those economists' concern with the distribution-of-income aspect of economic development.[8] The productivist position is implicit in the Doctrine of National Security and Development: growth is required to increase the overall industrial productive capacity of Brazil, to develop the interior and the Amazon so as to "plug up" paths of penetration, and to advance the ultimate objective of realizing Brazil's full potential as a world power.

Development is not geared to an immediate increase in living standard for the majority of the population, and it is not directed at the fulfillment of basic needs. In fact, as noted earlier, ESG doctrine explicitly accepts the need to sacrifice present and even *successive* generations as the price of rapid capital accumulation.[9]

Before worrying about distribution, the productivists argued, it was necessary to increase the size of the pie. For that purpose two conditions were essential: an economic climate that would win the confidence of investors, particularly foreign investors, and a sociopolitical climate of stability, something understood chiefly in terms of the absence of dissent. Mário Henrique Simonsen, one of the most influential of the productivist planners, has clearly expressed the underlying assumption:

The excellent performance and growth of the Brazilian economy in the period from 1968 to 1973—which was a higher rate than that of any other previous periods—elicits investigations into the conditions that caused this surge of economic growth. These are not only economic but also social and political conditions. Brazil was underdeveloped primarily because of a lack of political stability. This defect was successfully overcome with the military takeover of 1964, which instituted . . . a political regime that some political scientists have described as a "modernizing authoritarianism." Such a regime allows for differentiated subsystems—including political parties and interest groups—but keeps their autonomy temporarily limited.[10]

Limiting the autonomy of the subsystems was justified as necessary to allow the government to carry out economic policies that would lead to development. The policies pursued were, therefore, considered "pragmatic" and were required by a realistic technical assessment of conditions in Brazil.

Planners considered the durable-goods sector of the economy to be the most advanced, the best-suited to multinational investment and control, and thus the most critical to overall development goals. The production of durable consumer goods, ranging from automobiles to household appliances, for a limited but increasingly wealthy internal market was expected to ensure the rapid rate of industrial growth necessary for economic takeoff. Thus policies were designed to encourage investment, especially foreign investment, in such industries. The government went as far as to remove thousands of miles of railway lines (not to mention urban trolley systems) to stimulate the development of the automobile industry. Government incentives were successful in inducing an enormous increase in the overall level of foreign investment. From roughly $11.4 million in 1968, the level rose to more than $4.5 billion in 1973.[11] Of this, investment in durable consumer-goods industries was particularly significant. As we can see from table 9, foreign corporations dominated the durable-goods sector and held a high proportion of the capital-goods sector as well.[12] In the intermediate goods and nondurable consumer-goods sectors, national private capital predominated. Investment by state corporations was mainly limited to basic industry.

The emphasis on durable consumer-goods in the government's overall economic strategy necessitated, in practice, a specific pattern of income concentration. Productivist argument justified income concentration with the need to ensure a strong internal market for the products of this sector.[13] Government policies between 1960 and 1976, accordingly, sharply increased the income share of the richest members of the population and diminished that of the poorest 80 percent (see table 10). Aside from the dramatic reversal of fortunes of the richest 5 percent and the poorest 50 percent, it is important to notice that a small middle class managed to maintain and indeed to increase its income share slightly over this period. This helps to explain the relative enthusiasm that members of this group began to show for the government's economic policies.

The Médici government made extensive use of political propaganda that emphasized the economic growth of the nation and its consequent ability to fulfill its manifest destiny as a great power (O Brasil Grande). Development programs in the Amazon and the interior received a great deal of admiring attention. This, combined with the new availability of consumer goods, which the middle classes could buy through an enlarged system of consumer credit, brought a new kind of legitimacy to the national security state, a legitimacy based on continuous and accelerated economic growth. Since new prosperity was evident to the upper 20 percent of income recipients, the protests of workers were silenced or at least quieted, and, since the government effectively justified its repression by claiming that Communist terrorists were threatening the nation and the very process of economic development, there was little reason for the middle classes to risk their skins and their economic benefits by supporting the opposition. Thus, the middle classes were by and large willing to acquiesce in the repression of those years. As a consequence, the Médici government enjoyed a measure of legitimacy among elite groups that was greater than that of previous governments.

The effects of the "miracle" on the rest of the population were very different and meant not increased legitimacy for the state but rather increased reliance on violent repression. It is evident, first of all, that the productivity gains of these years were not reflected in workers' wages. Although government wage policies established (as we have seen) that the rise in the productivity of labor should be included in the calculation of the wage increase index, in reality the productivity increase was not reflected in the calculation of wages during the entire period of the economic miracle. In addition, the anticipated inflation rate (a second element of the formula for calculating increases), was consistently well below the actual inflation rate. These two crucial factors led to further reductions in the real wages of workers.

The minimum wage is a measure commonly used in Brazil to evaluate the condition of the wage-earning population. As explained earlier, the federal

Table 9
Types of Capital in Industry, 1970

Sector	Industry	Foreign		Type of Capital National-Private		State	
		No. of Firms	% of Tot. Invest.	No. of Firms	% of Tot. Invest.	No. of Firms	% of Tot. Invest.
Nondurable consumer-goods	Textile, clothing, pharmaceutical, printing, food	36	46	122	52	1	2
Durable consumer-goods	Electrical, auto parts, vehicles, electrodomestic	23	83	17	17	—	—
Capital goods	Mechanical equipment	10	56	11	44	—	—
Basic industry	Mining, steel, petroleum	10	15	27	14	5	71
Intermediate goods	Chemical, paper and cellulose, rubber, metallurgy, wood, construction materials, plastics	37	43	77	56	1	1
Total		116	38	254	36	7	26

Source: Fernando Fajnzylber, *Sistema Industrial e Exportação de Manufaturas: Análise da Experiência Brasileira*, 1971 (New York: United Nations, CEPAL, 1971).
Note: List includes 377 of the largest industrial enterprises, determined by capital plus reserves.

Table 10
Income Concentration

Economically Active Population	GNP Share per Year (%)		
	1960	1970	1976
Poorest 50%	17.71	14.91	11.60
Next-poorest 30%	27.92	22.85	21.20
Middle 15%	26.60	27.38	28.00
Richest 5%	27.69	34.86	39.00

Source: *Isto E* (9 August 1979), p. 65.

Table 11
Wage Index Differential

Year	Real Productivity Index	Index for Calculating Wage Increases	Difference
1968	6.2	2.0	4.2
1969	5.9	3.0	2.9
1970	6.4	3.5	2.9
1971	8.1	3.5	4.6
1972	7.2	3.5	3.7
1973	8.4	4.0	4.4

Source: *Ministério do Planejamento, IPEA*, Diário do Congreso Nacional of 29 September 1974, p. 3964, in Franco Montoro, *Da "Democracia" que Temos para a Democracia que Queremos* (Rio de Janeiro: Paz e Terra, 1974), p. 6.

government decrees the minimum wage, and it varies both in time and among regions. For statistical purposes, the highest minimum wage is always used for comparing income distribution and for measuring the effects of inflation and wage policies. A DIEESE study on the evolution of the minimum wage from 1959 to 1976, summarized in table 5, showed a consistent drop in the real minimum wage in Brazil. Given the reduction in the overall inflation rate, this drop must be considered a direct consequence of the government's wage squeeze, intended to increase the total rate of profit for capital accumulation. Because a high percentage of the population earns close to the minimum, analysis of the evolution of the real minimum wage in Brazil is an important tool for looking at overall income distribution. In 1970, for example, 50.2 percent of the total economically active population earned less than the minimum wage each month and another

28.6 percent earned between one and two times the minimum wage. Thus 78.8 percent of the population earned less than twice the minimum wage per month, a figure that had not significantly changed two years later in the full bloom of the miracle (table 12 shows the effect of the government's wage-compression policies during the economic miracle).

The workers' plight was compounded by the fact that the purchasing power of a minimum salary tended to decline. In 1938 the federal government had passed Decree-Law 399, which established a legal minimum amount of food considered necessary to sustain a family. This minimum was supposed to provide the basis for calculating the minimum wage level. In 1979 DIEESE published a study that compared the number of hours required to purchase this basic market basket in different years. As table 13 shows, the condition of the minimum wage earner declined by almost 50 percent over the period of the miracle. These figures also explain why the average working day in Brazil has risen to between twelve and fourteen hours.

One indication of the absolute poverty in which much of the population lived is provided by a study conducted in 1975 by the Parliamentary Investigating Committee on the overall situation of Brazilian children (Comissão Parlamentar de Inquérito do Menor, CPI do Menor). Although the committee officially estimated the number of abandoned and needy children at 15 million, it concluded that the number of children living without the *most minimal* basic needs (a condition defined as absolute poverty) approached 25 million (table 14).

Table 12
Distribution of Income, by Minimum Wage

Monthly Wage (multiples of the minimum wage)	% of Economically Active Population	
	1970	1972
Less than 1	50.2	52.5
1–2	28.6	22.8
2–3	10.2	9.8
3–7	7.1	9.4
7–10	1.7	2.3
More than 10	2.2	3.2
Total	100.0	100.0

Source: Paulo Singer, "Mais Pobres e Mais Ricos," *Opinião*, no. 116 (24 January 1975).
Note: The minimum wage in 1970 (expressed in 1976 cruzeiros) was 724.91, the equivalent of US $58.75 per month.

Table 13
Work Time Necessary to Purchase Minimum Food Ration

Year	Necessary Work Time	Index
1959	65 hours, 5 minutes	100.00
1960	81 hours, 30 minutes	125.22
1961	71 hours, 34 minutes	110.47
1962	94 hours, 48 minutes	145.66
1963	98 hours, 20 minutes	151.09
1965	88 hours, 16 minutes	135.62
1966	109 hours, 16 minutes	167.86
1967	105 hours, 16 minutes	161.74
1968	101 hours, 35 minutes	156.08
1969	110 hours, 23 minutes	169.69
1970	105 hours, 13 minutes	161.66
1971	111 hours, 47 minutes	171.75
1972	119 hours, 8 minutes	183.05
1973	147 hours, 4 minutes	225.97
1974	163 hours, 32 minutes	251.27
1975	149 hours, 40 minutes	229.96
1976	157 hours, 29 minutes	241.97
1977	141 hours, 49 minutes	217.90
1978	137 hours, 37 minutes	211.45

Source: DIEESE, Departamento Intersindical de Estatísticas e Estudos Sócio-Econômicos, offprint of *Revista do DIEESE* (April 1979).
Notes: In July 1956 and January 1959 the minimum salary reached its peak in purchasing power. If one were to calculate the minimum salary in July 1956 in 1979 currency, it would be Cr$ 4,963, three times the value of the minimum monthly wage in 1979. One can also obtain a measure of the purchasing power of the minimum salary by calculating the cost of purchasing the minimum daily essential foodstuffs for one month.

Table 14
Abandoned and Needy Children, 1975

Region	Abandoned		Needy	
	No.	% of Total	No.	% of Total
Northwest	58,284	3.1	536,142	4.0
Northeast	776,200	40.6	5,104,203	37.7
North	854,849	44.8	5,052,617	37.3
Centerwest	157,178	8.2	2,353,586	17.4
South	63,059	3.3	495,960	3.6
Total	1,909,570	100.0	13,542,508	100.0

Source: *Comissão Parlamentar de Inquérito do Menor* (Brasilia: Câmara Federal, 1975). Also published in *A Situação da Criança no Brasil* (Rio de Janeiro: Edições Muro, 1979), p. 23.

To deal with a situation of absolute poverty, a working-class family must have all family members work. This clearly has a dramatic effect on child labor rates. The Archdiocese of Rio de Janeiro sponsored a study, based on data from the government's National Household Survey of 1976 (Pesquisa Nacional por Amostragem Domiciliar, PNAD, 1976).[14] An important element of this research (summarized in table 15), was the analysis of the total number of children working either part- or full time to supplement family income. The study concluded that, in the country as a whole, 68 percent of the children studied had to work more than forty hours per week. In the state of Rio de Janeiro, 82 percent of the working children put in more than forty hours a week.

The total budget for health and education is also indicative of the low priority given to the provision of basic material needs. In 1973 the Ministry of Education (MEC) received 5.21 percent of the total national budget. That same year, at the height of the economic miracle, the Ministry of Health received only 1.09 percent of the national budget. In comparison, the Ministry of Transport, which was building the access routes for reaching the mineral deposits in the Amazon basin, got 12.54 percent, and the military ministries together received 17.96 percent.

Spending for education and health care declined steadily during the first decade of the national security state (table 16). State spending on education was concentrated in the upper grade levels, to train technicians who would run the industries and provide for the development that would turn Brazil into a world power. In addition, although the Constitution of 1967 transferred all major budgetary matters, including the collection of taxes, to the federal government, it left responsibility for primary education in the hands of the states. The resulting fiscal gap created a chaotic situation in the primary schools, a situation that not only brought about an increase in the number of children who did not attend school (see table 17), but also fueled major teachers' strikes after 1977. The high dropout rate contributed to a prevailing semiliteracy in Brazil.

Brazil's economic miracle not only failed to ease the problems of severe poverty, extreme human suffering, the deprivation of the most basic human needs of the majority of its population, in most respects, it actually intensified them. Nor was this enormous sacrifice followed by any compensating reward in the aftermath of the miracle; the process of impoverishment and income concentration has continued. The human costs entailed, it has become abundantly clear, are not to be understood as the sacrifices of a present generation for the good of future descendants, but as the ruthlessly enforced sacrifices of the majority of Brazilians for the present benefit of the small elite that keeps them in bondage.

The Dialectic of Violence

We do not believe in the possibility of a peaceful solution. There is nothing

Table 15
Child Labor, Brazil and Rio de Janeiro State, 1976
(10–14 Years of Age)

Hours per Week	No. of Urban Children	No. of Rural Children	Total no. of Children	% of Total
BRAZIL				
Up to 29	74,045	282,345	356,390	14
30–39	80,756	381,704	462,460	18
More than 40	542,641	1,171,631	1,714,272	68
Total	697,442	1,835,680	2,533,122*	100
RIO DE JANEIRO STATE				
Up to 29	3,506	1,230	4,736	9
30–39	2,824	1,690	4,514	9
More than 40	25,578	17,045	42,623	82
Total	31,908	19,965	51,873	100

Source: *Pesquisa Nacional por Amostragem Domiciliar*, Fundação IBGE. Published in *A Situação da Criança no Brasil* (Rio de Janeiro: Edições Muro, 1979), p. 24.
*Represents 18.5 percent of the total population between the ages of 10 and 14.

Table 16
National Budget Allotted to Ministries of Health and Education

Year	Ministry of Health (%)	Ministry of Education (%)
1965	—	11.07
1966	4.29	9.70
1967	3.45	8.71
1968	2.71	7.74
1969	2.59	8.69
1970	1.79	7.33
1971	1.53	6.78
1972	1.24	5.62
1973	1.09	5.21
1974	0.99	4.95

Source: Senator Franco Montoro, *Da "Democracia" que Temos para a Democracia que Queremos* (Rio de Janeiro: Paz e Terra, 1974), pp. 6–7.

Table 17
School Attendance, Brazil and Rio de Janeiro State, 1976

	Age		% of Total	
	5–9 Years	10–14 Years	5–9 Years	10–14 Years
BRAZIL				
Total no. of children	13,741,629	13,748,646		
No. out of school	8,681,958	3,856,283	63.2	28.0
RIO DE JANEIRO STATE				
Total no. of children	1,151,639	1,249,158		
No. out of school	1,086,767	154,086	94.4	12.3

Source: *Pesquisa Nacional por Amostragem Domiciliar*, 1976, Fundação IBGE, as reported in *A Situação da Criança no Brasil* (Rio de Janeiro: Edições Muro, 1979), p. 20.

artificial about the conditions of violence now existing in Brazil. They have been in existence ever since the dictatorship used force to take control. ،

Violence against violence. The only solution is what we are now doing: using violence against those who used it first to attack the people and the nation.[15]

Consolidating the Legal Framework

The organizations involved in armed struggle became increasingly audacious in 1969. In January Carlos Lamarca, an officer of the Fourth Infantry Regiment, based in Quitáuna, São Paulo, commanded a group of officers and soldiers in a raid on the regiment's arms depot. The group escaped in an army truck loaded with heavy weapons and ammunition. They were members of the clandestine Popular Revolutionary Vanguard (Vanguarda Popular Revolucionária, VPR). In June 1969, a well-organized group of armed men conducted a mass escape of political prisoners from the high-security Lemos de Brito Prison in Rio de Janeiro. Bank robberies provided financial resources for the guerrilla groups. Ambushes to acquire weapons from the military grew more frequent. To emphasize the political nature of the attacks, in August Carlos Marighela attacked the Rádio Nacional in São Paulo and read a revolutionary message over the air. On 4 September 1969, only a few days after the military junta had taken office in Brasília, the ALN and the October 8 revolutionary movement (movimento revolucionário 8 de outubro, MR-8) jointly conducted their most spectacular operation: at two o'clock in the afternoon, on a quiet street in Rio de Janeiro, a commando from the two organizations kidnapped Charles Burke Elbrick, United States ambassador to Brazil. It was the first time that a member of the diplomatic corps had been kidnapped by armed guerrillas in Latin America, and the news made headlines around the world, bringing international attention to the armed struggle in Brazil.

The kidnapping made a deep impression on the members of the military junta, confirming their theories on internal security. The state reacted in two ways: first, it began immediate negotiations with the guerrillas to meet all of their conditions, mainly because of the considerable pressure brought to bear by the U.S. government; second, on 5 September it issued Institutional Acts Nos. 13 and 14, which aimed at strengthening the legal framework of the repressive apparatus. Institutional Act No. 13 established that all political prisoners exchanged for kidnapped dignitaries were to be banished from Brazilian territory and in fact gave the executive the power to banish from Brazil for life all those considered to be "inconvenient, harmful, or dangerous to national security."[16] Institutional Act No. 14 amended the Constitution of 1967 to make death penalties, life imprisonment, and banishment applicable in cases of "adverse psychological, revolutionary, or subversive warfare" as well as in external war.[17] The definition of these kinds of warfare was left deliberately vague, as the "enemy within" was potentially any citizen. Two other important measures were enacted in the wake of the kidnapping of the U.S. ambassador: the first was the National Security Law of 29 September 1969;[18] the second was the Constitution of 1969, decreed while Congress remained closed, in the form of Amendment No. 1 of 17 October 1969.[19]

The National Security Law was a practical application of the theoretical arguments in the ideology of national security. The terms of the law are broad enough to allow the state to exercise complete discretion in determining what may constitute a crime against national security. It provides a legal framework for repression of anyone opposed to the policies of the national security state. In keeping with its orientation toward control of the enemy within, most of the articles in the National Security Law deal with prevention of strikes, control of the media and other information networks, prohibition of specific political parties, and other limits on association. The law imposes stiff prison terms for promoting strikes in essential services or public services, or among public employees.[20] Provisions with regard to the media are particularly strong in that they hold the editor, newspaper owner, or journalist responsible and criminally liable for reporting events or opinions of others who may have infringed some restrictive article. The state can also seize entire editions of magazines or newspapers, as well as close them down for violation of the National Security Law.[21] Article 16 makes it a crime punishable by six months to two years in prison "to publish news or facts slanted in such a way as to dispose the population against the constituted authorities." The National Security Law considers it a crime "to offend persons in a position of authority for political or social reasons"; to offend the honor and dignity of the president, vice-president,and a number of lesser dignitaries; to incite war, subversion, collective disobedience, animosity among the armed forces or between the armed forces and civilians; to engage in or foment class struggle; to strike in areas considered essential or in public services; to incite hatred or racial discrimination. It is also illegal to disturb legislative sessions, trials, and international conferences; to organize or reorganize a dissolved political party; and to distribute subversive propaganda by a wide variety of means. Encouraging someone to commit any of the above is also a crime.[22] With the enactment of the National Security Law of 1969, freedom of assembly, of association, and of the press, in effect, ceased to exist in Brazil.[23] The provisions of the law have constituted the main tool of political repression, and have become the foundation of state power itself.

The second important measure enacted after the kidnapping of the American ambassador was Amendment No. 1 to the 1967 Constitution. The amendment eliminated the liberal elements of the otherwise authoritarian structure of the 1967 document. The executive branch was given extraordinary powers for implementing national security policy and parts of AI-5 were incorporated into the body of the Constitution. And yet, perhaps the most significant (certainly the most extraordinary) addition to these measures came on 11 November 1971, when the government issued a decree-law enabling the executive branch to pass *secret* decree-laws, whose texts would not be published in any official register.[24] This provided a basis for the arrest of a person for infringement of a law the existence of which was completely unknown.

The post-1974 liberalization period has not revoked any of the provisions of the National Security Law, the Press Law, the Constitution of 1969, or even the Secret Decree-Law. Thus, while the latest liberalization has granted a number of concessions, the foundations of the repressive apparatus and its legal framework remain intact.

Deepening the Repressive Apparatus

The dialectic of violence between armed organizations and state repressive forces continued to spiral from 1969 to 1973. Revolutionary organizations concentrated on spectacular actions that required little coordination among groups that were ideologically fragmented and unable to unite for coherent armed actions. The guerrilla struggle began to be characterized chiefly by the kidnapping of foreign diplomats to exchange for political prisoners from the underground organizations. These were defensive, not offensive, actions.

The forces of repression decimated the ranks of the underground organizations by extensively using torture to obtain information that could lead to the arrest of others and to the dismantling of the guerrilla groups' support networks. The underground groups reacted by kidnapping three more diplomats in order to negotiate the freedom of key militants. The last of these kidnappings, that of the Swiss ambassador in December 1970, met with resistance from the national security state, which was no longer willing to make concessions. After three months of difficult negotiations, however, the ambassador was exchanged for seventy political prisoners, who were flown to Chile.

This was the last attempt to kidnap a diplomat in Brazil. General support among the population for the guerrilla organizations was limited. Estimates of total participation in the different armed-struggle organizations, based on interviews and testimony, put the total at around 6,000 for the entire period. Considering that the population of Brazil at the time was approximately 100 million, this can hardly be described as "civil war." Nonetheless, the national security state used this term to justify the most violent period of state repression in Brazil's history. The campaign included not only the institutionalization of torture as a technique of interrogation and of political control, but also the development of pacification programs and blitzes, and the implantation of a vast police network to carry out the programs of the repressive apparatus.

Pacification Programs —blitzes

Large-scale search-and-arrest operations against an unarmed population, involving large numbers of police and military personnel, were conducted in the form of blitzes: military occupation of an area in order to conduct house-to-house searches (an operation widely used by German armies of occupation during World War II). In the Brazilian version, which is still common, roadblocks are set up and houses and cars are searched. Persons without proper documentation are considered suspect and often arrested.

During the 1969-1974 period, such large-scale operations were frequent and resulted in mass arrests, beatings, and general intimidation. In spite of strict censorship, the press did manage to report that as many as five hundred persons were arrested during one such blitz.[25] Sometimes operations involving total mobilization of the army were conducted either citywide or nationally. For example, on 16 June 1969, the weekend before Nelson Rockefeller's visit to Brazil as President Nixon's emissary, up to six thousand persons were "preventively detained" in the city of Rio de Janeiro.[26] A national blitz, codenamed "Operation Birdcage," took place in the days immediately preceding the 1970 congressional elections. The press reported that over ten thousand persons had been arrested in this operation, many of them MDB candidates.[27] That campaign was clearly intended to be sufficiently intimidating to guarantee an electoral victory for ARENA.

Campaigns of terror were also carried out in the countryside. The operation in which Carlos Lamarca and his band of nine VPR rural guerrillas were encircled in the Vale da Ribeira, São Paulo, involved ten thousand soldiers, who surrounded the entire area and arrested the peasants whom they considered to be potential sympathizers.[28] Perhaps the most serious incidence of large-scale repression against an unarmed rural population took place in the region of Araguaia, between 1972 and 1975.

Some background is needed to situate the events in Araguaia in their political and economic context. In 1952 Brazil and the United States signed a mutual assistance agreement. This agreement provided for a joint military commission to prepare topographic maps and air charts of Brazil and to conduct aerial photographic surveys to provide astronomical and geological data. This survey was to be conducted in the Amazon region particularly, and would chart in detail the mineral wealth of the region.[29] Prior to the 1964 takeover, strong opposition in Congress prevented ratification of the agreement. But three months after the 1964 coup, this survey began systematically to collect data. Once it was completed and the area mapped, the region became the object of intense land speculation.

A 1968 congressional investigating committee established that over 50 million acres in the states of Bahia, Goiás, Minas Gerais, Maranhão, Pará, Amazonas, and in the territory of Amapá were under the direct control of foreign multinational corporations.[30] These corporations benefited from the system of tax incentives provided under a special program for the development of the Amazon basin. This program was coordinated by the Superintendency of Amazon Development (SUDAM) and financed by the government's Bank of the Amazon. In addition, the Médici government provided investment in needed infrastructural improvements in the area so as to allow the mining, forestry, and agribusiness projects to begin their operations. In 1970 the government began a specific program to allow access to the region's mineral wealth. Close to $150 million (US) were spent in the construction of the Transamazon and Belém-Brasília highways, which cut through the whole Amazon basin. In addition, mining companies were given a 20 percent mineral depletion allowance.[31]

The mineral deposits in the area are in the Amazon and in the Araguaia region, bordering the river from which it takes its name. Between the Araguaia and the Tocantins rivers is a large mountain chain, the Serra dos Carajás, where mineral wealth is most concentrated. In 1980, for example, what is said to be one of the world's largest gold deposits was found in these mountains. It is to be developed by a consortium of Brazilian state-owned and multinational corporations.[32] The region included in the developmental program encompasses parts of the states of Mato Grosso, Goiás, Pará, and Maranhão. Since 1969 corporations in the area have increased production of iron ore, manganese, nickel, chromite, zinc, uranium, and other minerals by more than 100 percent.[33]

The land speculation that resulted from SUDAM's development projects produced violent conflicts, however, as this region has traditionally been inhabited by Indians and peasant families engaged in subsistence farming. Corporations that gained access to land titles by decision of the National Security Council had then to rely on the state's repressive forces to evict the peasant families from the land. These conflicts have also been extended to the Indian reservations.[34]

In 1970 the PC do B was beginning to prepare a rural *foco* in this region. The underground organization moved in families and couples who began to farm and to provide technical assistance to local peasants. The entire guerrilla group never numbered more than sixty-nine militants of the PC do B. They worked with the peasants, helped them build a school, provided some health care, and gave agronomy lessons. At night they trained in the jungle.[35] They were known as the "paulistas," for they were believed to have come from the state of São Paulo. The peasants and other area residents were completely unaware of their clandestine jungle activities.[36]

The National Intelligence Service (SNI) discovered the *foco* in 1972. Immediately, the army began a veritable military occupation maneuver in the area, which involved three separate military campaigns between 1972 and 1975, and engaged a total of twenty thousand men. According to General Viana Moog, one of the commanders, "It was the biggest troop mobilization that the army has conducted. In fact, it was similar to the mobilization of the FEB [Brazilian Expeditionary Force], which fought fascism in Europe during the Second World War."[37]

The operations conducted were of a very particular nature. First of all, the entire region was declared a national security priority zone. The military set up five army headquarters, in the towns of Marabá, Itaituba, Altamira, Humaitá, and Imperatriz. Roads were built in the area to facilitate troop movements. An airport and heliport were also built near the larger towns.[38] Identification cards were distributed to the local population, and anyone without an identification card was arrested and sent to areas around the barracks, which served as prison camps. Testimony of local residents, church leaders, and even of military participants themselves indicates that torture was widely used on peasants and other inhabitants of the region.[39] Special interrogation teams were moved in because of the suspicion that the peasants were supporting the guerrillas. Dom Pedro Casaldáliga, bishop of São Félix do Araguaia, attested to the fact that repression was particularly directed against the lay pastoral agents of the Catholic church and even against the hierarchy of the church in the area: "The soldiers came and trained in the mountains of São Félix. They went from house to house in the interior regions and fell upon the population. This created a climate of authentic terror. The repression also persecuted bishops and pastoral agents, particularly the latter."[40]

Prior censorship ensured that the press did not publish accounts of army maneuvers in the region at that time. The only article published on the events in the Araguaia region appeared in *O Estado de São Paulo* in September 1972.[41] The episode remained largely unknown until 1979, when journalists were able to publish the documents and interviews collected over the previous years. Officially, the repression of the population in the Araguaia region, justified by the need to combat the "guerrilla warfare" of sixty-nine militants, is still considered a state secret. The military refuse to provide information on or an official explanation of the events that took place there.[42]

An explanation can be found, however, by looking at the events of the region within the context of the various tenets of the Doctrine of National Security and Development. First of all, the establishment of a *foco* is the epitome of the "indirect action" strategy practiced by the internal enemy and can have "multiplier effects" on the potential enemy, in this case, the Indians and peasants living in the region. Second, in geopolitical terms, the area between the Araguaia and Tocantins rivers, called the central plains region, had already been designated a vulnerable area vital for the control and development of the Amazon basin. To eliminate the vulnerability, the paths of penetration for international communism had to be plugged. In addition, the particular region in which the small PC do B *foco* was implanted was crucial to the state's economic development plans. Land speculation and mining had brought about escalation in the number of land conflicts in the region; these had to be brought under control, and the massive evacuation of peasants from the land had to be carried out efficiently. The *foco* was probably a useful justification for the military to force evacuation of the population. The region is now under permanent control of two infantry battalions, in Marabá and Imperatriz. The battalion in Marabá has fifteen hundred permanently stationed men and is armed with heavy military equipment.[43]

Military intimidation of the peasant population has not only continued but has escalated to alarming proportions. Throughout the central plains and the Amazon basin, as well as in the valley of the São Francisco River, land conflicts have become a serious social and political problem. A 1981 study by the National Conference of Brazilian Bishops concluded that between 1977 and mid-1981 there were "916 land conflicts, affecting a total of 251,891 families and involving a total of 1,972,989 persons."[44] Over the same period, some 45 rural trade union leaders and pastoral agents working with peasants being evicted from their land were murdered;[45] none of these murders have been investigated by the police.

Hence, the national security state used the *focos* to justify the implementation of a vast plan of political and social control, based on military occupation of the region, widespread troop mobilization, and violent intimidation of the population in areas of crucial economic interest. The maneuvers conducted in both Vale da Ribeira and Araguaia bear a striking resemblance to the population control maneuvers that the United States Army conducted in Vietnam under the guise of "pacification programs." This was particularly true in the Araguaia region, where large numbers of peasants were moved to prison camps surrounding the towns, where they could be kept under surveillance.

The Institutionalization of Torture

Torture is the physical abuse of prisoners which is perpetrated by employees, military or civilian, who act under the command and with the cover of higher authorities. The torture of a prisoner, perpetrated by a constituted authority, is an extremely grave fact, for all that is carried out by a collective institution ultimately must be referred to the responsibility of the Head of the organization.[46]

The period from 1969 to 1974 was one in which international religious and human rights organizations received evidence of the existence of secret torture centers in Brazil where prisoners were taken and where they sometimes disappeared.[47] Such organizations continued to receive allegations of the torture of political prisoners throughout the entire period. The International Commission of Jurists reported that at that time there were "at least 12,000 political prisoners in Brazil."[48] The victims' personal testimony is included in dossiers put together by the Organization of American States (OAS), the World Council of Churches, the United States National Council of Churches, and even the Vatican. In Brazil the testimony of hundreds of victims is on file at the Brazilian Bar Association (OAB) and in the archives of the National Conference of Brazilian Bishops. One such testimony may speak for all:

I was taken from the Tiradentes Prison to the Operação Bandeirantes (OP, army police) on February 17 at two o'clock. Captain Maurício, who, with two other policemen had come to fetch me, said, "Now you are going to intimately know the branch of Hell."
. . . When I arrived I was taken to an interrogation room. Captain Maurício's team confronted me with some people there. They wanted to know about the congress of the UNE in Ibiúna in October of 1968. . . . They took me to the *parrot's perch*. Hanging there, naked, with my feet and hands tied, I received electric shocks in the tendons of my feet and on my head. There were six torturers who were commanded by Captain Maurício. They gave me *telephone blows* and I screamed. This lasted for one hour. When I left the room my body was marked by hematoma, my face was swollen, the head expanded and painful. A soldier carried me to my cell.
. . . On Thursday three policemen woke me up at the same time as the previous day.
. . . I went to the interrogation room. A captain, surrounded by an interrogation team, began the same questions. They sat me on the *dragon's chair* and they gave shocks in the hands, feet, ears, and mouth. Two wires were attached to my hands and one to my left ear. At each electrical charge my body shook and shivered, as if the organism was about to crumble. From the shock session they took me to the parrot's perch. There I received more shocks, blows with a stick on the chest and legs. One hour later, with my body covered with blood I fainted. They untied me and brought me back to consciousness. . . . They returned to the questions and the blows, hitting my hands with wood *palmatórias*. . . . It was impossible to know which part of my body hurt more. Even if I wanted I could no longer answer the questions for I could no longer think (Frei Tito de Alencar Lima, 24-year-old Dominican monk).[49]

Frei Tito's letter is one example among thousands. Torture techniques were developed and refined in Brazil as a method of political control through a strategy of terror. Some of the more common methods include the following:

1. *The parrot's perch*: A bar from which the victim is hanged naked by the hands and feet, which are tied together. In this position, the victim undergoes electric shocks and a variety of blows. These electric shocks are administered by rudimentary machines, the leads of which are quite simply plugged into the municipal current. Where there is no current, such as in the interior, army campaign telephones are often used to provide the necessary electricity. Shocks are administered to the fingers, tongue, breasts, anus, ears, and genital organs. Sometimes the victim's body is moistened to increase the force of the shock. The blows are generally given with wet material (so no traces are left), or with clubs. Sometimes the torturers resort to direct blows with the fists or the feet.

2. *Telephone blows*: So called because they are given to both ears simultaneously. The ears are hit with the two hands, palms open. This often results in the rupture of the eardrum.

3. *The dragon's chair*: A chair covered with electric wires so as to give electric shocks to the entire body at once. It is commonly used during interrogations by both the military and the police forces.

4. *Palmatórias*: Instruments made of flat pieces of iron or wood, which are used to apply violent blows to the victim's body, particularly to the hands.[50]

Torture was institutionalized as a method of interrogation and political control. One example of the technical sophistication involved in this process is the "icebox," an entirely insulated and soundproof cage. The temperature can be electronically controlled to vary from below zero to extremely hot. A variety of sounds of differing pitches can be introduced electronically into the cell. Alternating use of bright lights and total darkness completes the setting for the psychological and physical disintegration of the prisoner. Such an elaborate mechanism requires considerable investment and could hardly be kept secret from higher authorities.

Although institutionalized torture is an efficient means for obtaining information, it is even more important as a method of political control. The widespread and institutionalized use of torture in a society has the power to create a "demonstration effect," which intimidates those who know of its existence and inhibits political participation. When combined with the force of the blitzes, the institutionalization of torture serves to deter others from any activity that might bring them into conflict with the government.

During the 1969–1974 period it was difficult to meet a Brazilian who had not come into direct or indirect contact with a torture victim or been involved in a search-and-arrest operation. Stories of institutional violence became part of everyday life. Clearly, this threat was a powerful deterrent to political practice and participation.

The deterrent effect became all the more powerful when placed in the context of the National Security Law, which allowed for preventive detention for up to twenty days.[51] During this time the prisoner was held without charges, incommunicado. Torture generally was administered during the first days, or even hours, of arrest. Because the National Security Law is so broad in its potential interpretation of what constitutes a crime against national security, and because the concepts of "arrest" and "torture" became linked in the political culture of the nation, the fear of political arrest was very great.

During this period the combined effects of economic exploitation, physical repression, political control, and strict censorship established a "culture of fear" that deterred participation in community, union, or political opposition activities. This culture of fear had three important psychological components. The first was the silence that the strict censorship of all news media and the closing of other information channels imposed on society. During this time universities were controlled, theater, culture, literature, art, music, and cinema were censored. With censors physically present on the premises and censorship regulations strictly enforced, the media were silenced and the consequences of economic or repressive government policies were not published or discussed. The population thus knew of the existence of repression and experienced the reality of institutionalized state violence, but could not voice or express its fear or protest in any public forum. This imposed silence, in turn, produced a deep sense of isolation on the part of those who were direct victims of the repression or of economic exploitation. Large sectors of the population were thus marginalized and isolated in their suffering from other segments that could potentially offer support and aid.

Finally, as a consequence of the other two characteristics of the culture of fear, there was a generalized belief that all channels of opposition were closed and that no action could have effective results. It seemed impossible to face the power of the state. A feeling of complete hopelessness prevailed and, perhaps more than anything else, maintained the climate of withdrawal from opposition activity. Nonarmed opposition groups were paralyzed in their reactions. People lost hope and withdrew into their private lives in an attempt to avoid the vengeance of the state.

The widespread use of torture and its attendant culture of fear result in contradictory political behavior: although repression angers the population and turns previously supportive groups or sectors against government authorities, the great fear of torture effectively prevents actual participation in political activities. If abuse of power is lessened, public opinion may turn against the government, but this situation may not result in active political opposition due to the deterrent effect of the culture of fear. Even during the period of liberalization, after 1976, when torture was no longer widely used on political prisoners (though it remained a reality among the working population), its power of intimidation was manifestly present. This point was dramatically demonstrated during a meeting of the Partido dos Trabalhadores (Workers' party, PT) in May of 1981. The president of the party, metalworkers' leader Luís Inácio Lula da Silva, remarked in a talk to the workers assembled there, "We must stop being afraid. What are we afraid of? Are we afraid of being arrested?" From the back of the room a worker shouted back at him, "We are afraid of being tortured! I was tortured!" There was a moment of distinct and uncomfortable silence, and then Lula responded, "Yes, my friend. We are afraid of being tortured. But we must stop being afraid of torture. There is no worse torture than to see your child crying for a plate of food or a glass of milk and to know that your salary is not sufficient for you to buy it." Although the crowd applauded, the fear nonetheless remained an almost palpable presence.[52]

One should, however, note that the effectiveness of torture as a deterrent to political participation may have long-run limitations. The fact that torture is used regularly limits its effectiveness as a tool of political control through terror. Although in the short run it has had a powerful effect, as the years go by this fear may diminish. The very fact that so many people have been tortured and have survived, both physically and emotionally, has allowed them to view it since 1981 with less panic than they experienced in 1964 or even in 1969. This was apparent in an interview I conducted with a woman worker, a union militant who had been tortured and who had witnessed the torture of her family. I asked her how she found the courage to go on with her union organizing. She reflected on the question for a moment, and answered, "Afraid of torture? Yes, I guess that I am afraid. But really, when you think of it, it is no worse than having babies. And one does have babies, and then one has other babies, doesn't one? We suffer a lot of pain for a while. But then the pain stops and you forget it."[53]

Once the pain of torture stops, what is left is anger. The reality of oppression is a stronger stimulant than fear is a deterrant. The most oppressed sectors of the population, in urban and rural areas, have suffered the strongest repression and have had the most contact with institutionalized torture. Nonetheless, it is in those sectors that we find the most vibrant alternative organizations for the defense of the rights of workers, the demand for free unions, for higher wages and better working conditions. It was among the poorest that the Catholic church's *comunidades de base* would take root. The pain of everyday oppression, in the long run, was stronger than the pain of torture.

A number of opposition militants have been brutally tortured, some of them several times. Nonetheless, they are still actively organizing against the social and political policies of the national security state. Some of the best-known leaders of peasant and working-class movements, such as Roque Aparecido da Silva, José Ibrahim, and Manoel da Conceição, were saved by international campaigns on their behalf. They lived in exile and have returned to Brazil, where they are once again active in the organization of rural or urban unions or in political parties. I interviewed a leader of an urban grass-roots movement who has been arrested and tortured thirty-two times since 1964. His fear, he commented, lessened with each arrest.

Perhaps the most serious consequence of the institutionalization of torture and the pacification programs has been the actual involvement of the armed forces in repression since 1964. There is no doubt about the active involvement of sectors of the army, particularly since the creation of the CODI-DOI networks after 1969, and in earlier phases, the navy's CENIMAR was often denounced in international documents as a center of torture. There is much less evidence of direct involvement by the air force. The center of torture seems to have become more definitively connected to the army's Operação Bandeirantes (OBAN), which was later transformed into the various CODI-DOI centers operating in the states. This was the first time in the history of Brazil that the armed forces had become so deeply involved in the torture of political prisoners and in conducting military operations for the repression of the population. This represents a serious institutional threat to the armed forces and their image, which had hitherto been linked to their role in the defense of the nation against external aggression.

There are a number of reasons for this widespread involvement. First, the Doctrine of National Security and Development had been taught to large numbers of officers, personnel, and draftees, thus preparing them to see a potential enemy in any citizen. Second, the need to apply this doctrine, in the search for absolute internal security, to a population of around 100 million, meant logistically that the armed forces would have to participate in the process of repression and torture. Finally, the personal involvement of officers in repression implicated them in the acts, thereby organically linking them to the system. As the officer becomes a cog in the machinery of repression and torture, he fears the consequences of dismantling the system and the possibility of having to answer for the crimes that he witnessed or in which he participated. Thus, involvement serves as a means of controlling the military itself.[54]

The Machinery of the Repressive Apparatus

The repressive apparatus is made up of three distinct but integrated elements: the vast political intelligence network; agencies and organizations directly responsible for carrying out repressive actions at local levels; and the armed forces apparatuses used for internal political control.

Although in principle all information is destined for the executive branch, specifically the National Security Council, in reality, the intelligence network possesses a great deal of autonomy. The National Intelligence Service (SNI) centralizes all information before it reaches the executive. This gives the SNI the power to select what information is to be made accessible to the National Security Council and the president himself. This power is the source of the SNI's ability to set itself up as a parallel source of government decisions.

The SNI was created by General Golbery do Couto e Silva and formalized by decree-law on 13 June 1964. It was already being planned during the conspiracy to overthrow the Goulart government. Although all but the administrative costs portion of the intelligence service's budget is secret, in 1981, 701 million cruzeiros (about $7 million US) were allotted for its agencies. The entire intelligence apparatus had an official budget of 1.2 billion cruzeiros, which is believed to be considerably lower than actual costs.

Directly linked to the SNI are the Divisions of Security and Intelligence (Divisão de Segurança e Informação, DSI), which are attached to all state ministries. These are charged with controlling the internal bureaucratic apparatus of the ministry and with keeping watch over the specific psychosocial area with which it is concerned. Thus, not only does a DSI have veto power over top-level and secondary-level appointments in the ministries, but its power also extends over the entire area of ministerial responsibility. The DSI in the Ministry of Education, for example, compiles dossiers on the past life of candidates for the ministerial bureaucracy as well as on the faculty and candidates for administrative positions in federal universities and other educational institutions. The same type of activity holds true for other ministries.

Also directly linked to the SNI are the Security and Intelligence Assistance departments (Assessoria de Segurança e Informação, ASI), which operate in all nonmilitary ministries, state corporations, state agencies and autarchies, as well as in companies under contract with the federal government. Each branch of the armed forces has its own information network. This apparatus consists of the Information Centers, which operate both internally and externally, and the Secret Services, with their Second Section, whose function is exclusively to control the branch to which it is organically attached.[55]

As can be seen in figure 2, each branch of the armed forces has its own Information Center (CIEX for the army, CENIMAR for the navy, and CISA for the air force). Although officially attached to the SNI, these centers exercise considerable autonomy, and there is a certain amount of rivalry in their collection of information on military personnel and civilians. This rivalry becomes particularly evident at the time of transfer of executive power, when Information Centers provide a de facto locus of political power for the military ministers, who are also usually presidential candidates.

The Secret Services of each of the three branches of the armed forces are referred to simply as the E-2 (army), the M-2 (navy), and the A-2 (air force). Their specific mission is to control the internal public by means of the departments called Second Sections. Each Secret Service is attached to a specific command. The Second Section of each Secret Service is responsible for the control of the members of all regiments, battalions, and units in the territory under the command. Although the Secret Services and Second Sections are supposed to operate internally, in fact they also carry out political surveillance and even direct the physical repression of the external public as well. This is particularly true of the navy's CENIMAR and the army's Secret Service, the latter of which is involved in direct physical repression and even torture of the population through the Center of Internal Defense Operations (Centro de Operações de Defesa Interna, CODI), and its Department of Information and Operations (Destacamento de Operações e Informações, DOI).

Up to 1967, responsibility for physical repression was left to CENIMAR

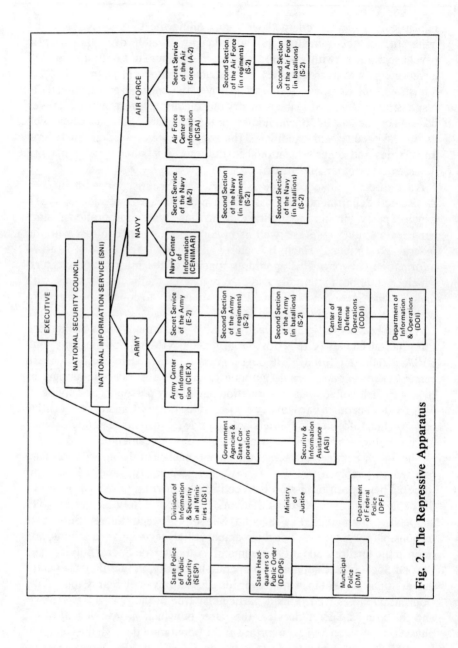

Fig. 2. The Repressive Apparatus

and the State Police of Public Security (Secretaria Estadual de Segurança Pública, SESP) in each state. The SESP coordinated the activities of the State Headquarters of Public Order (Departamento de Ordem Política e Social, DOPS or DEOPS), which in turn activated the local-level municipal police departments (DM) (see fig. 2). As the armed-struggle groups grew, the national security state designed other organisms particularly trained to obtain information. The first organization for direct violent repression was the OBAN. Financed by local and multinational industrialists, OBAN operated, in 1969, with links to the Second Army, based in São Paulo. As the dialectic of violence developed, OBAN was extended to other states, but its main activities were in Rio de Janeiro and São Paulo.[56]

The first CODI was organized in 1970 in São Paulo and was directly connected to OBAN. Eventually, the CODI and its executive branch, the DOI, were set up in other states; it is now operational in São Paulo, Rio de Janeiro, Brasília, Minas Gerais, Rio Grande do Sul, Bahia, Pernambuco, and Ceará. In international documents dealing with torture and political repression in Brazil, the organizations most often cited as practitioners of torture are the CODI-DOI, the DEOPS, and CENIMAR.

In addition to the organizations and agencies mentioned above, the executive branch of the national security state uses the Department of Federal Police (Departamento de Polícia Federal, DPF), which is directly subordinate to the Ministry of Justice. The DPF coordinates physical repression at times of national mobilization for internal security and deals particularly with censorship and control of information. The whole censorship bureaucracy is attached to it.

The military and paramilitary forces are the third important element of the official structure of the repressive apparatus. These include the three branches of the armed forces and the military police in each state. The military police force (roughly equivalent to the National Guard) was created as an independent force in each state, with independent command units answerable to state governors. Under the national security state, the military police have been subordinated to the army and have their own Second-Section divisions.[57] The state police forces, although officially independent of the army, are under the control of the secretary of public security, who is appointed with approval of the federal government and is the head of the SESP. Thus the state police forces are also considerably controlled by the federal government.

As may be seen in table 18, the paramilitary forces have dramatically increased in size, because of their importance in the day-to-day repression of demonstrations. Together, the military and paramilitary forces counted 457,550 men on active duty in 1978, with a defense budget of over $2 billion (US). These numbers, of course, do not include either the budget (partly secret) or the number of employees in the intelligence and political-information network, which constitutes the intelligence community.

Table 18

Defense Budget and Size of Military and Paramilitary Forces

Year	Size of Force Army	Navy	Air Force	Paramilitary	Defense Budget ($US)
1963	—	—	—	9,655	—
1964	—	—	—	19,275	—
1965	—	—	—	—	—
1966	200,000	45,000	35,000	10,000	214,700,000
1967	—	—	—	37,554	—
1968	—	—	—	40,049	—
1969	180,000	53,000	30,000	120,000	798,111,000
1970	120,000	44,350	30,000	120,000	—
1971	120,000	43,000	35,000	150,000	559,000,000
1972	130,000	43,050	35,000	150,000	599,700,000
1973	130,000	44,350	30,000	120,000	1,660,000,000
1974	170,000	49,500	35,000	200,000	—
1975	170,000	45,800	41,400	200,000	1,283,000,000
1976	180,000	49,000	42,800	200,000	1,548,000,000
1977	182,000	49,000	42,000	200,000	—
1978	182,750	47,000	42,800	185,000	2,088,000,000

Source: International Institute for Strategic Studies, *The Military Balance* (1963–1980/81); *Armed Forces of the World: A Reference Handbook* (1966, 1973); *The Almanac of World Military Power* (1969, 1971, 1972, 1973).
Note: Missing data were not available in any of these sources.

Changing Directions

By mid-1973 both the opposition and the state were in a position of reassessing strategies and changing directions. From the state's point of view, this period was characterized primarily by (1) an internal struggle within the civil-military coalition in power between the sectors connected to the repressive apparatus and those concerned with the long-term institutionalization of the national security state; (2) a change in the focus of legitimation from prior commitments to a return to democratic forms of government to an appeal based on economic growth and rapid development; (3) the continuing fragility and instability of the executive succession process, demonstrated in the transfer of power from Costa e Silva to the military junta, and then to President Médici; (4) the integration of the repressive apparatus and the economic model into a policy of "development with security."

By the end of 1973 the control structures of the national security state were largely in place. The second stage of institutionalization was accomplished. A shift in policy strengthened the sectors of the civil-military coalition that argued for the development of flexible mechanisms of control that would establish a long-term institutional base for the state.

By the middle of 1973 the economic miracle was beginning to encounter serious difficulties. Although economic growth remained high, the agricultural sector was stagnant at a modest 3.5 percent rate of growth. The problem created by the growing foreign debt, which in 1973 was already over $12 billion, indicated a growing bottleneck in the economic development model. In addition, the inflation rates were climbing faster than the government publicly recognized.[58] The social costs of the economic model resulted from the inequality in income distribution, and the income-concentrating policies of the economic-miracle years had reached rather alarming proportions by 1973. A study conducted by the government's statistical department, the IBGE, showed that 43.3 percent of the population earned less than the minimum wage per month and another 29 percent earned between one and two times the minimum.[59]

The continued full application of coercive power could silence social protest from the working classes. By 1973, however, the middle sectors grew restless at the first signs of deep economic trouble. The changeover to a greater reliance on the legitimation function of increased economic growth carried with it the danger of withdrawal of support at times of trouble in the economy. Debates on the social costs of the economic model were more frequently aired and the policies of the government more openly questioned.

By the middle of the year the armed revolutionary groups had been defeated and the social costs of the economic model weighed heavily, both of which increased the pressures from other sectors of the society for reforms. In addition, it was necessary to seek long-term institutionalization

very important

and to regularize the mechanisms for transfer of power. The tendency within the national security state connected to the IPES/ESG complex—the Sorbonne group—was to espouse a model of development that would be more gradual and closely connected to political flexibility. General Ernesto Geisel, the leader of this faction in 1973, reversed the governmental slogan "development with security" to provide more emphasis on a policy of institutionalization. The new goals of the state, he argued, should be development "in continuity and without immobility."[60] This model of slow liberalization should "decompress" the society by combining a renewed effort toward controlled opening with negotiations between the state and key opposition elite groups. The negotiations were meant to defuse the tensions that were building up after years of violent repression and unbalanced economic growth. In sum the group Geisel led argued for the development of new mechanisms that would enable the formation of long-lasting structures of representation as a basis for the power of the national security state.

In the general context of the state's change of direction, the opposition was also engaged in a process of reassessment and analysis. The defeated parties of the armed opposition were in disarray and reconsidering the strategy of armed struggle. As for the nonviolent sectors of the opposition, a definite change of direction was to occur. The MDB had suffered severe losses both in the congressional elections of 1970 and in the municipal elections in 1972. This weakening of the only legal opposition party was due to a combination of the effects of repression, the increase in the middle class's standard of living (which, to a greater degree, offered its support to the government), and to the continuation of the campaign for voiding of votes. Thus by 1973 the MDB was conducting an internal debate on alternative policies. Three main possibilities were considered: self-dissolution as an ultimate protest; a firm and strong opposition stance to center on demands for the end of the repression and amelioration of the distribution of income; and negotiations with the new government, which espoused controlled liberalization.

The first alternative clearly was not realistic: few members of the party were willing to commit collective political suicide. Although the third alternative could not become the sole platform of the party, lest it endanger its goal of stronger opposition, it could, nonetheless, be combined with the second. This policy of limited negotiations for the achievement of certain key concessions—in particular the return of the right of habeas corpus and the end of Institutional Act No. 5—would be one of the primary goals of the opposition party for the next period. In addition, it was felt that the party should take an aggressive opposition stance so as to break out of the paralysis of fear and isolation that its nonviolent sectors had become immersed in as a consequence of the state's strong repressive action.

The opposition party's first chance was provided by the transfer of executive power in 1973. Since both parties, under the new regulations, had the right to present candidates to the electoral college, which was to choose the next president, the MDB decided to launch a symbolic presidential campaign.[61] Ulysses Guimarães, president of the MDB, was chosen as its presidential candidate. Barbosa Lima Sobrinho, a respected journalist and president of the Brazilian Press Association, was the vice-presidential candidate. The MDB then organized a campaign in the best populist tradition of its PTB and PSD heritage. Rallies, public meetings, and civic marches were set up throughout the country in a great show of civic mobilization and political action. On 23 September 1973, at the national convention of the MDB, Ulysses Guimarães emphasized the issues that would break the silence up to then imposed on the opposition party:

The nonviability of the opposition candidacy shall be a testimony to the nation and to the world that the system is not democratic. Because, as long as the system remains, the present holders of state power shall always be in the government—an eternity of power, which would be impossible if the vote were direct, popular as well as universal, and secret. Only in the last case does the actual possibility of rotation of power become a reality. . . . It is not the candidate of the MDB who travels throughout this nation. Rather, it is the anticandidate. The anticandidate who shall denounce the antielections, imposed on us by an anti-Constitution, which is now the refuge of Institutional Act No. 5 and which submits the legislative and the judiciary branches of government to the executive power and which allows for arrest without recourse to habeas corpus, for condemnations without defense, and which violates the privacy of homes and businesses by secret listening devices, and silences all voices of dissent by imposing censorship in the press, radio, television, theater, and cinema.[62]

The purpose of the symbolic anticandidacy of the MDB was to demonstrate to the nation the gap between the language of democracy and the reality of political control. Throughout the ninety days of the anticandidacy campaign, the two anticandidates held the attention of the press and the nation. According to Barbosa Lima Sobrinho, the symbolic political impact of the campaign was significant:

When we ended our speeches during the rallies or meetings, people would applaud and, sometimes, they would shout their enthusiasm at us: "I shall vote for you!"
    At that point we would begin to explain that they in fact wold not be allowed to vote and that the presidential elections were not by direct popular vote but would be conducted by a limited electoral college whose vote was not secret and was therefore liable to power influence. The silence that would then descend on the crowd gave us an estimate of the impact of such an explanation. It was important to show the population that the process of choosing the president was not representational, not legitimate, and that they, as a people, were not allowed to actively participate in the choice.[63]

The campaign was instrumental in denying legitimacy to the indirect presidential electoral process. In addition, it achieved another crucial function: it renewed hope and decreased the paralyzing fear and isolation the repression caused. In his speeches Guimarães often confronted the issue of fear directly, encouraging people not to lose hope and to continue to strive and organize for political freedom. The slogan of the anticandidacy campaign was explitictly directed at the culture of fear and meant to counteract it by encouraging resistance: "It is necessary to navigate; it is not necessary to live" ("Navegar é preciso; viver não é preciso").

The campaign also encouraged the press to defy censorship rules and give the anticandidates widespread coverage. The opposition's encouragement gave impetus to what would become a large-scale press campaign for the end of censorship and for freedom of expression. According to an official MDB document, "The press made public the ideas of the anticandidates to the degree of increasing the total available press space for the opposition by 3,500 percent."[64]

Finally, and perhaps most important, the anticandidacy campaign awakened a repressed protest among the electorate and showed that, in fact, the official opposition party, MDB, could become an important vehicle for the organization of opposition. Participation in the party and in electoral campaigns for Congress in 1974 became thus greatly enhanced. As we shall see, the actual discontent of the voters would manifest itself in the MDB's impressive victory over the ARENA—a complete reversal of the outcomes of past elections conducted in fear and hopelessness.

In general, the changing role of the MDB was characterized by the symbolic presidential campaign of 1973. This anticandidacy marks the beginning of the stage of opposition use of the officially recognized opposition party. It was a lesson for effective engagement on the level of *formal* politics, a lesson that would be mastered in the elections of 1974, 1976, 1978, and 1982. The human rights movement, which would characterize the following years, can be considered a direct consequence of the violence of the repression unleashed by the national security state during the 1969-1974 period. The change of direction of the opposition groups involved both a critical assessment of the entire experience of armed struggle and a new commitment to nonviolent but active organization of the population levels. In the years that followed, this process would take the form of two distinct but integrated social movements: the grass-roots movements in the cities and in the countryside; and the human rights movement, which started with the defense of tortured political prisoners in the period of most severe repression.

By the end of 1973 the opposition had learned to utilize formal channels of political participation to increase the efficacy of opposition at the formal political level. In addition, it began, in alliance with the Catholic church, to organize a vast social movement at the grass-roots level for the defense of human rights and for the maintenance of basic economic and social rights. This would compose the area of opposition activity that I define as *base-related* or *grass-roots* politics, an area that would surface in the political arena, particularly after 1977.

1973, 1974 a period of hope emerges as
a result of the anti candidacy
campaigns, the moitration of
the fight for human civil, & social
rights

Part IV. The Third Stage of Institutionalization, 1974-1983

While the policy of ("liberalization") continued a there existed a parallell "illigitimate" legal system (an institution) of the national security State) who changes the laws almost daily to meet their objectives

7. The Geisel Government: Decompression

[handwritten: trying to gain legitimacy]

[handwritten: some rhetorical decompression but definitely political oppression regarding the electoral process → further institutionalization]

[handwritten: passing of repressive legislation]

Introduction

The Geisel government ushered in a third stage of state institutionalization. The first phase, encompassing the Castello Branco and Costa e Silva governments, had laid the foundations for the national security state, embodied in the authoritarian Constitution of 1967. The second stage, from 1969 to 1973, developed the economic model and the repressive apparatus, extending both the legal framework of repression and the actual machinery of coercion. During the Geisel and João Figueiredo governments planners focused on more permanent and flexible structures for long-term institutionalization of the state.

From the point of view of government planners, 1973-1974 represented a turning point. During the years of the economic miracle considerable emphasis had been placed on legitimation based on the success of the development model. With the growing difficulties now being experienced in the economic arena, the national security state became concerned with the establishment of different mechanisms to develop social and political support. A new basis for legitimacy needed to be found, one more closely connected to corporative institutions flexible enough to provide efficient clientelistic modes of support gathering. The "decompression" theory tried to provide for a decrease in social-political tension. State planners wished to build elastic representational mechanisms that could co-opt portions of the opposition.

Thus, the state's action, particularly in Geisel's first period, was aimed at the slow dismantling of the more explicit mechanisms of legal coercion symbolized in Institutional Act No. 5. In addition, the state would pay specific attention to the electoral system in order to allow sufficient flexibility for an apparently free electoral process and yet maintain a guarantee of long-term electoral strength for the government party.

Geisel's government, then, developed the "policy of decompression," also known as the policy of "distension" (*distensão*). It was a program of careful and controlled liberalization measures defined within the context of the government's slogan of "continuity without immobility" (*continuidade sem imobilidade*).[1] The "continuity" aspect translated into a policy of faithful keeping to the guidelines of the established economic development model and the theoretical precepts of the National Security Doctrine. Thus continuity maintained both the main aspects of the model and the repressive apparatus machinery. The aspect of mobility was embodied in the government's reform plan, which purported to be a movement forward in progressive liberalization for a return to democracy.

The decompression of society was to be achieved in planned stages. First there would be the partial lifting of prior censorship, followed by negotiations with the opposition to establish parameters for the handling of human rights. Second, there would be electoral reforms to increase the level of political representation. Third, the more explicitly coercive measures, including AI-5, would be revoked and other mechanisms of control incorporated into the Constitution. The overall goal of the policy of decompression was to perfect the institutionalization of the national security state and provide for more flexible political representation so as to decrease the levels of dissent and tension that had built up pressure to high levels.

The framework of the political system to be developed should constitute what President Geisel termed "relative democracy" or "strong democracy." In this model of relative democracy the state would be armed with sufficient safeguards and emergency extraordinary repressive powers in the Constitution to allow it to suspend individual rights and rule by decree whenever there was a direct threat from an organized challenge. However, the political institutions of representation would be designed with flexibility sufficient to provide for limited participation and sharing in the decision-making process. It was a program that heeded General Golbery's warning that unlimited repression in an absolute search for security would ultimately lead to an actual undermining of the national security sought. The policy of decompression and the policies that derived from the analysis were a final search for state legitimation. It was an attempt to negotiate with and incorporate some of the major demands of the elite opposition in an effort to increase the state's support base. At the same time it provided for the control of civil society by the selective application of coercive power.

The Dialectic of the Electoral System

One of the characteristics of the decompressed stage of state institutionalization was the search for increased legitimacy, gained through electoral strength. The more politically sophisticated sector of the coalition in power recognized that the maintenance of an electoral system was essential for state legitimacy and that it was necessary both to increase the legitimation elections gave by eliminating more explicit coercion from the process and to maintain exclusive control of executive posts in the states and a sufficient majority in Congress to ensure the passage of legislation required for the legal and structural reforms of the third stage of institutionalization.

The political and economic conjuncture indicated that a policy of electoral strength would meet with success. On the one hand, legitimation based on economic growth now presented increasing difficulties as the economic model ran into a bottleneck. On the other hand, the great defeat of the MDB in the 1970 congressional elections indicated to political planners that the ARENA could indeed achieve major victories in the 1974 elections. In fact, few observers doubted that the ARENA would end up with a landslide victory over the opposition in 1974.[2] In the opinion of government strategists, a freer election, with access to television and radio, and the explicit withdrawal of coercion would increase the legitimacy of the government's electoral success.

The 1974 Elections

Because of the high rate of economic growth and the support still enjoyed as a result of the economic-miracle years, the government believed that it could win the legislative elections of 1974. The MDB was given full access to television and radio and had the opportunity to conduct lively debates throughout the campaign period. At the outset, most of the MDB politicians believed that the opposition could not possibly succeed; few of the candidates even believed the party capable of organizing. This mood began to change in Rio Grande do Sul, where MDB candidate Paulo Brossard carried on heated debates with ARENA candidate Nestor Jost. By early August, the two had agreed to a televised debate, the first such experience since before AI-5 in 1968. The intense audience interest in and the political repercussions of this debate encouraged other MDB candidates to take a more aggressive political stance and use the available media. The population responded enthusiastically, and campaign volunteers flocked to the MDB. MDB militants discovered that election periods could be used for transmitting information and for political mobilization of the population. In this climate the opposition held rallies and meetings. "During the legislative period I have no instruments with which to reach the people," exclaimed MDB senator Marcos Freire. "Now, in an election period, I can speak to large numbers of them."[3]

The MDB concentrated on repression, injustice, and the inequality of the economic model. Opposition candidates spoke on radio and television about such previously taboo subjects as the National Security Law, repression, the need to revoke AI-5, and the wage-control legislation. They denounced the purchase of land by foreign multinational corporations and questioned the growing denationalization of the Brazilian economy.

Two ideas were central to the 1974 campaign. The first was expressed by the party's campaign slogan: "As long as there is one man alive, there is always hope." The second was the desire to move forward and progressively push for reforms, in a strategy that the opposition defined as "the occupation of all available political space."[4] The silence and isolation had begun to break down, and new sectors of the population could participate in formal politics.

The 1974 elections resulted in a clear victory for the opposition party. The biggest MDB victory was in the senatorial elections, where the party received four million more votes than ARENA. This was the first time that the MDB had won the largest percentage of the vote in senatorial elections since the establishment of the two parties.

Two points are immediately apparent from table 19. The first is that the percentage of valid votes for the MDB as a whole increased from the 1966 to the 1974 elections. This pattern reflects the change in the strategy of the opposition sectors, which began to give electoral support to the "official" opposition party and use it as a conduit for protest votes. The campaign for voiding votes lost much of its significance, although it still had a great deal of impact on the 1974 elections. The second point to note is that, although the opposition predominated in the 1974 senatorial elections, clientelistic patterns of vote gathering and control gave the victory to the government party in the proportionate elections for the House of Representatives and state assemblies. Even so, the MDB gained impressively at these levels as well.

The MDB significantly increased its representation in the House of Representatives: in 1970 it had won 87 seats as against 233 for ARENA; in 1974 the MDB won 161 seats, and the ARENA majority decreased to 203. In the state assemblies, the opposition won 45 of 70 seats in the state of São Paulo, 65 of 94 seats in the state of Rio de Janeiro, and complete control of the important state assemblies in Paraná and Rio Grande do Sul.[5] For most political analysts, as well as for MDB members, the opposition victory was a reversal of electoral patterns and a surprise. The elections were generally considered to have been equivalent to a plebiscite in which voters voted *against* the government, rather than *for* the opposition.

The Lei Falcão

While the MDB digested its new role as a "real" opposition party, the government's intelligence network studied the election results. The SNI's central agency conducted a detailed study, which included electoral maps, state-by-state information, voting records of each MDB and ARENA member, patterns of voter behavior, and public opinion surveys. Dossiers were compiled on all the MDB candidates, and on the elections.[6] The SNI research would be used thereafter to guide ARENA candidates, as well as to develop new measures for controlling elections.

Table 19
Federal and State Election Results, 1966–1978

	1966	%	1970	%	1974	%	1978	%
Senate								
Total no of votes	17,259,598		22,406,624		28,925,792		37,601,641	
Total no. of valid votes	13,630,743		16,123,219		24,544,678		30,770,038	
Total votes for ARENA	7,719,382	56.63	9,898,694	61.39	10,068,810	41.02	13,239,418	43.03
Total votes for MDB	5,911,361	43.37	6,224,525	38.61	14,579,372	59.40	17,530,620	56.97
Total blank votes	2,014,579	11.67	4,955,167	22.11	2,665,818	9.22	3,783,550	10.06
Total void votes	1,614,276	9.35	1,328,238	5.93	1,705,296	5.90	3,048,053	8.11
Seats won by ARENA	48		40		6		15	
Seats won by MDB	14		6		16		8	
House of Representatives								
Total no. of votes	17,285,556		22,435,521		28,981,015		37,553,882	
Total no. of valid votes	13,647,108		15,645,741		22,820,958		29,792,217	
Total votes for ARENA	8,731,638	63.98	10,867,814	69.46	11,866,482	52.00	15,024,298	50.43
Total votes for MDB	4,915,470	36.02	4,777,927	30.54	10,954,440	48.00	14,767,919	49.57
Total blank votes	2,461,523	14.24	4,690,952	20.91	4,112,973	14.19	5,042,955	13.43
Total void votes	1,176,925	6.81	2,098,828	9.35	2,047,084	7.06	2,718,710	7.24
Seats won by ARENA	277		233		161		189	
Seats won by MDB	132		87					

Table 19 (continued)

	1966	%	1970	%	1974	%	1978	%
State Assemblies								
Total no. of votes	17,260,382		22,406,624		28,867,300		37,447,839	
Total no. of valid votes	14,044,039		16,382,966		23,393,263		30,222,386	
Total votes for ARENA	9,005,278	64.12	11,442,894	69.85	12,184,240	52.08	15,410,073	50.99
Total votes for MDB	5,038,761	35.88	4,940,072	30.15	11,209,023	47.92	14,812,313	49.01
Total blank votes	2,088,927	12.10	4,129,835	18.43	3,487,546	12.08	4,632,604	12.37
Total void votes	1,127,416	6.53	1,893,823	8.45	1,986,491	6.88	2,592,849	6.92
Seats won by ARENA	0		493		457		492	
Seats won by MDB	0		208		330		353	

Sources: For 1966, Fundação IBGE, *Anuário Estatístico do Brasil*; for 1970, Tribunal Superior Eleitorial, Departamento de Imprensa Nacional, *Dados Estatísticos*, vol. 9; *Eleições Federais Estaduais Realizadas no Brasil em 1970* (Brasília, 1973); for 1974, idem, *Dados Estatísticos*, vol. 11: *Eleições Federais e Estaduais Realizadas no Brasil em 1974* (Brasília, 1977); for 1978, Márcio Moreira Alves, "As Eleições no Brasil 1978," *Revista Crítica de Ciências Sociais* (1979).

Note: Percentages for total MDB and ARENA votes are of total valid votes; for total blank and void votes, percentages are of total vote.

The study showed that access to radio and television had contributed significantly to the MDB victory in 1974 and predicted that, unless changes were made, the MDB would win a large number of new posts in the 1976 municipal elections, as well as majority control of Congress and many other state assemblies in the 1978 elections. The entire system of indirect elections to executive posts thus was in danger.

The most immediate problem was the municipal elections of November 1976. In August the Geisel government issued Decree-Law No. 6639, signed by Armando Falcão, the minister of justice. The Lei Falcão limited party use of radio and television during municipal election campaigns to a mention of the party's name and the candidate's curriculum vitae and slate register number against the background of a still photograph of the candidate.[7] Since radio and television could not be used to disseminate party platforms or the views of candidates, opposition criticism of government policies did not significantly influence the electorate. The largest newspapers in the country had a maximum circulation of 300,000 copies, reaching an estimated 20 million persons; by contrast, radio reached as many as 85 million, and television approximately 45 million, so the importance of this blackout is clear.[8] Campaign propaganda became a monotonous airing of names, numbers, curricula vitae, and still photographs of hundreds of candidates from both parties. In addition, under pressure from the Geisel government, the Superior Electoral Tribunal prohibited candidates from posting other electoral materials in public places. Thus the 1976 municipal campaign was conducted in virtual silence, and the opposition was denied the use of its main resource: debate and argumentation.

The 1976 Elections

The control of municipal posts had become increasingly important in that they were the building blocks of political power. ARENA could count on a variety of significant resources. First, the SNI study had pinpoined the most important municipalities and guided the electoral strategies of government party candidates. In addition, the entire bureaucracy of the central state and the states was put at the disposal of ARENA's electoral interests. Roads were built in municipalities under ARENA control, and in some cases, funds were cut off from municipalities under MDB control. State finances were put at the disposition of ARENA candidates. They could use official cars, gasoline, bureaucrats to work in their campaigns, mimeograph machines, office supplies. Although the candidates could not speak on television or radio, nothing could prevent governors, ministers, or the president himself from doing so on their behalf. Above all, there was the implicit and explicit threat that the liberalization policy was contingent on an ARENA victory in the municipal elections, and that an MDB victory would bring renewed repression.

The MDB did not have the financial resources to reach all the distant municipalities. In a country with over four thousand municipalities, spread over an immense territory with difficult access, the MDB conducted much of its campaign in the interior literally on the backs of donkeys or on foot.[9] It was physically unable to reach a majority of the municipalities. It seems clear that the inability to debate ARENA candidates on television and radio hurt the MDB and succeeded in curbing its growth. Silence had been reimposed, magnifying the sense of isolation and preventing the population from becoming aware of criticisms of the system.

In spite of its advantages, however, ARENA did not win with the expected landslide. The party won 15.2 million votes (about 35 percent), the MDB, 12.7 million (30 percent). ARENA's narrow victory seemed to confirm the SNI prediction that without electoral controls the MDB might have won a majority, particularly in large cities and the more industrialized states. The MDB won the mayoral elections and gained majority control of city councils in fifty-nine of the one hundred largest cities in Brazil, compared to only thirty-one in 1972. Of the fifteen cities with more than half a million inhabitants, the MDB won in 67 percent.[10]

The April Package of 1977

SNI studies after the 1976 election showed that the MDB was particularly strong in urban areas, concentrated primarily in the Center and Center-South. Analysis of the 1974 federal and state elections had confirmed the belief that opposition strongholds were in the most advanced states, in the most industrialized regions, and in the largest cities. A detailed study of the electoral map from the 1974 senatorial elections showed that the MDB had won in seventy-nine of the ninety cities with over 100,000 inhabitants; the eleven cities in which ARENA had a majority were all in the Northeast.[11]

The implications were clear: if the MDB continued to grow it would certainly win a majority in the Senate by carrying all of the large urban areas in the 1978 congressional elections. In addition, its congressional strength was likely to reduce ARENA's majority to insignificant proportions, even if it did not actually win a majority in the House. Such a situation would endanger the whole decompression plan, which had to be pushed through a government-controlled Congress.

To prepare the ground for the liberalization measures included in the decompression plan, President Geisel needed to placate hard-line sectors of the civilian-military coalition, which demanded more long-term controls over the judiciary. In particular, two significant modifications were to be established by a constitutional amendment to be presented to Congress. The first created a new body, the Conselho da Magistradura (Council of Judges), empowered to discipline judges. The second, perhaps most important for the development of the repressive apparatus, was the removal of trials of military police from the jurisdiction of the civil courts; military police officers would now be tried by special military courts composed of officers of the military police.[12] The Brazilian Bar Association (OAB) vehemently opposed these innovations, included in the judicial reform package as Constitutional Amendment No. 7, and voiced its disapproval by applying pressure on the MDB either to modify or to reject the government's proposal.[13]

Since the judicial reform had been introduced as a constitutional amendment, it required a two-thirds vote of both houses to be approved; thus the government was forced to negotiate with the MDB, whose one third in the House of Representatives could block the project. ARENA Senator Accioly Filho drafted a substitute bill, which met with MDB approval. However, the government put pressure on ARENA to reject its own member's bill and forced acceptance of the executive's original version. The situation quickly reached a stalemate and became a major political crisis. The MDB called the question on the subject and held all of its members to a vote of rejection. On 30 March 1977, the judicial reform proposal came to the floor in a joint session, as required for a constitutional amendment. The results of the voting were 241 in favor of the original proposal and 156 votes against. Because the two-thirds majority was not obtained, the package was rejected.[14] Two days later, President Geisel closed Congress for the third time since the 1964 coup d'état and used the extraordinary powers given to the executive by AI-5 to govern by decree in the interim.[15]

For the next twelve days, President Geisel carried on debates with a small number of advisers who constituted a sui generis Constituent Assembly: Minister Golbery do Couto e Silva; Geisel's private secretary, Heitor Ferreira; Senator Petrônio Portella; and then-chief of the SNI, General João Batista Figueiredo.[16] Finally, on 13 April Geisel signed Constitutional Amendment No. 7, which was nothing other than the original version of the judicial reform package just rejected by Congress. The next day he signed Constitutional Amendment No. 8, which established fiscal amendments and a series of important modifications of the 1969 Constitution with regard to elections.[17] These came to be known collectively as the "April Package" (Pacote de Abril) and established the limits of the decompression and the grounds for the continuing process of state institutionalization.

Of primary interest here are the electoral reforms introduced by Amendment No. 8.[18] Article 13 made indirect election of state governors permanent.[19] Article 39 of the 1969 Constitution was changed so that the number of seats for each state in the House of Representatives was determined not (as previously) in proportion to the number of registered voters in the state but in proportion to its total population. Because illiterates are not eligible to vote in Brazil, the previous regulation had given more representatives to states where literacy was higher, thereby favoring the MDB. The new law increased the representation of the very poor states in the North and Northeast, where illiteracy was very high and where ARENA was strongest.

Control of the Senate was particularly important for the government, because it ensured the ability to block any opposition measures initiated in either house. In the 1978 elections, the MDB only had to win seventeen of the forty-six seats up for election to control the Senate. Assuming a continuous pattern of electoral growth, the MDB should not have had much difficulty in electing those seventeen additional senators. Constitutional Amendment No. 8 changed the composition of the Senate by modifying Article 41 of the 1969 Constitution. The article had stipulated that each state was entitled to three senators with mandates of eight years. Senatorial elections were to be held every four years to elect, alternately, two thirds and then one third of the Senate. Elections were to be by direct, universal, and secret popular vote of all eligible registered voters. The April Package changed this in the following manner. The elections in which one third of the Senate was replaced would remain the same. However, in the elections in which two thirds was replaced, only one of the two available seats would be filled by direct popular vote. The other would be elected indirectly by the same Electoral College that was to choose the state governors.[20] Thus every eight years one of the senators would be chosen by an electoral college whose composition, to strengthen the government's control, had already been changed to include city council delegates.[21] The indirectly elected senators came to be known in popular political parlance as the "bionic senators." Opposition humorists invented the expression to highlight the idea that those senators were, in fact, "invincible and artificially made."

A further modification reduced the size of the Electoral College that was to choose the president. This body had been composed of all members of Congress plus delegates selected from the assemblies of each state. With control over Congress guaranteed by the measures discussed earlier, state assemblies remained a weak spot. To reduce their influence, Article 74 of the 1969 Constitution was changed to reduce the number of delegates from state assemblies from one delegate per 500,000 inhabitants to one delegate per one million inhabitants. In addition, the president's term was increased to six years.[22]

Another measure was designed to guard against mishaps such as the congressional rejection of the judicial reform package. Legislative initiatives for constitutional amendments had previously required the signatures of one third of the members of either the House of Representatives or the Senate. A modification of Article 47 of the 1969 Constitution established that a proposal for a constitutional amendment could only be introduced with the signatures of one third of *both* the House of Representatives and the Senate, rather than with one third of *either*, as previously required.[23] The MDB would be unable to fulfill the requirements, because 33 percent of the Senate was to be bionic. On the other hand, since the government was interested in having subsequent constitutional amendments passed, measures needed to be taken to guarantee that this could happen without having to negotiate with the MDB. Thus the requirement of a two-thirds majority of both houses in a joint session was reduced to an absolute majority.[24]

Finally, an important clause in the April Package extended the Lei Falcão's restrictions on use of television and radio from municipal to state and federal elections. The silence was to be expanded to all elections, thereby denying the opposition the opportunity to debate and criticize the state's policies.

But the April Package brought only mixed benefits to the national security state. Although the intricate electoral controls brought less of a loss of legitimacy than would have resulted from more explicit coercion, the closing of Congress undermined the legitimating intentions of the measures and the decompression policy itself. In addition, the creation of the indirectly elected senator lacked subtlety as a means for controlling the upper house. The opposition was adroit in pointing out the contradictions between the measures of control and the stated objectives of bringing about a democratic form of government. The publicity given to the term "bionic" subjected both the office of the indirectly elected senator and its occupant to ridicule and public rejection.

The 1978 Elections

By 1978 the MDB had become a real opposition party and had succeeded in bringing together a broad range of political opinions—from conservative to socialist—within a unified structure. The basis for unity in the party's platform was opposition to the repressive legislation and pressure for a return to democracy. The MDB denounced the April Package and demonstrated that there was a contradiction in the government's oft-repeated commitment to democracy and its denial of electoral freedom.[25]

Although the Lei Falcão had been extended to federal and state elections, the opposition party could still use radio and television in the period between campaigns. In June 1977 the MDB organized a national radio and television program in which four of the most prominent opposition leaders explained the party's program with regard to four main issues: the economic development model; workers' wages and living conditions; the April Package's arbitrary electoral reforms and controls; and political economy.[26] The day after the program was aired, a *Jornal do Brasil* survey indicated that approximately 70 percent of the population of all major cities had watched the address. Of those who watched, 69 percent expressed "complete and strong" approval of the viewpoints of the opposition party.[27]

Disgrace to Brazil

The repercussions were intense, and the Geisel government reacted violently. On 1 July the president cancelled the electoral mandate and political rights of Congressman Alencar Furtado. In addition, the government indicted the president of the party, Ulysses Guimarães, under Article 347 of the Electoral Code—a charge carrying a penalty of three months to one year in prison.[28] That same week the government brought charges against two other MDB members under the National Security Law.[29] And finally, the national security state issued yet another complementary act, which closed off the MDB's access to television and radio.[30]

The 1978 elections had a plebiscitary aspect, which was given particular emphasis in the MDB campaign. The diversity of the elements working within the party made it difficult to agree on a coherent party platform, so popular support was enlisted *in opposition* to the government.[31]

Because access to radio and television was denied the MDB candidates, the party was forced to seek support in the grass-roots networks, which were fighting for human rights, union rights, and associative or political rights. The persecution of the MDB provided it with legitimacy in the eyes of these groups, and all sectors of the opposition joined in the campaigns of the MDB candidates. In almost all states, the MDB campaign was conducted by a loose network of militants from diverse opposition groups in civil society: students, trade union organizers, party militants, church social activists, and members of the movements for political amnesty, for women's rights, and for black rights. Hence an unanticipated consequence of the extension of the Lei Falcão to the 1978 elections was to join the MDB to the grass-roots movement, bridging the gap between formal politics and grass-roots, base-related politics. The 1978 experience would provide a valuable lesson for the future, one of more effective development of links between party and grass-roots organizations (the results of the election are presented in table 19).

The MDB continued to be strongest in the senatorial races, winning almost 4.3 million more votes than the government party.[32] ARENA maintained a majority in the House of Representatives, but the difference was narrower than in previous elections. The same pattern held for state assembly elections.[33]

Because of the April Package, however, there was a significant discrepancy between popular vote and electoral outcome. In the Senate elections, in spite of the fact that it had won 56.9 percent of the valid vote, the MDB won only nine of the forty-five seats up for election in the Senate that year, whereas ARENA won the other thirty-six seats. Of those 36, 21 were won in the indirect elections of the expanded state electoral colleges. Only one such bionic senator was elected from the MDB, in Rio de Janeiro.[34] In the House of Representatives the margin of difference in the voting had been quite small: 50.4 percent for ARENA as opposed to 49.5

percent for the MDB. Because of the April Package, however, 231 congressional seats went to the government party and only 189 to the opposition. In the state assemblies, the MDB increased its representation, winning 353 seats to ARENA's 492. In general, the pattern of MDB strength in the more-developed areas and southern and central-southern states continued in the 1978 elections. ARENA maintained its strong hold over the smaller northeastern and northern states, where local bosses and bureaucracies could develop a clientelistic system of political patronage.[35]

Although the April Package damaged the credibility of the government's decompression policy, it was nonetheless successful in curbing the opposition's electoral strength. ARENA's majority in both houses of Congress was protected. This power monopoly was an essential element of decompression.

The Dialectic of Human Rights

The period of the Geisel government was characterized by the contradictions between an official liberalization policy and the lingering reality of political repression. On the one hand, the official decompression policy allowed opposition sectors more space in which to organize and greater possibility of success. On the other hand, the coordinated pressure being exerted for the improvement of living conditions, an end to press censorship, and the repeal of the major repressive legislation intensified the fears of those sectors most closely associated with the Doctrine of Internal Security. Thus, as the human rights movement grew stronger, so did the internal pressures and contradictions within the national security state with regard to policies of repression. As a consequence, the period was one of deep uncertainty, one in which on one day political action was permitted, and on the next the repressive apparatus would unleash mass search-and-arrest maneuvers. This is the context in which the activities of the Catholic church came to the fore to encourage and protect the organization of a resistance in defense of human rights.

Human Rights and the Catholic Church

I have already noted that the Catholic church was involved in the protection of political prisoners and the denunciation of state violence prior to 1974. During the period of most severe repression, from 1969 to 1973, the church moved decisively to defend those in danger or those who were victims of persecution.[36] Politically, perhaps the most significant aspect of the church's work has been its ability to bridge the gap between formal politics and grass-roots, or base-related politics. Since all church activities are organized within a formal institutional framework but descend to the level of grass-roots organization via a widespread network of committees, subcommittees, and group activities, it is the only institution that provides people with experience at both levels of political participation.

The realm of formal politics within the Catholic church is defined by the work of the National Conference of Brazilian Bishops, the organization that acts socially and politically in applying the conclusions reached in the periodic synods of bishops. Through its regional offices, committees, and organizations, the CNBB organizes the population for self-help projects and for political coordination in pressure-group tactics to challenge authorities, take direct action, or hold the state responsible for omission. This work can take the form of official CNBB documents providing evidence of human rights violations or it can involve direct grass-roots activities among the population. The CNBB is subdivided into regional offices and local diocesan branches. Each institutional level elaborates a two-year pastoral plan for religious and political working priorities. These priorities have increasingly focused on basic rights and civil-political rights, as defined in the United Nations Declaration of Human Rights.

The actual work is coordinated by the national and local pastorals, which, sociologically, are organizations for social action. Each pastoral works around a particular issue defined in its name; for example, there are land pastorals, pastorals on urban problems, on the church and the world, pastorals of the family, of the periphery, and of the slum areas of the city, of the marginalized, of migrants, of the shantytowns, of the world of work, of peasants and agricultural day laborers, of children and abandoned minors, of prisoners, of the rights of black people and Indians, and finally, of human rights in general. At the local level, each pastoral sets up its own network of groups for collective work. For example, the city of São Paulo was divided by the archdiocesan plan into fifty different sectors. Each sector has ten communities, and each community can subsequently establish its own committees and groups for the implementation of specific programs and projects. The main objective of such an organizational structure is to stimulate shared individual participation at all levels of responsibility, action, and experience.[37]

The structural organization of the Catholic church's political and social work clearly demonstrates how it bridges the gap between formal politics and grass-roots politics, for it effectively involves the population at all levels of organization and social work. In addition, the organizational format allows the church to establish a broad network of local groups, in a myriad of cell-like units involving thousands of people working in the same area. For example, the human rights pastoral might involve work in all five hundred comunidades set up in the fifty sectors of the Archdiocese of São Paulo and spread through the local-level groups in the parishes, in the neighborhoods, and in the factories.[38] This wide network of organization gives the population experience that enables it to acquire confidence in political and social participation, build self-respect and competence, and discover leaders. In addition, this myriad of organizations makes it possible to establish a mass movement around certain targeted issues quickly. This was the case, for example, with the mobilization of the cost of living movement (*movimento contra o custo da vida*), which, in 1978 in São Paulo, gathered one and a half million signatures in three months on a petition asking the federal government to freeze prices on basic foodstuffs.[39]

This organization at the base level is the source of the church's social and political influence and is also the secret of its ability to provide rapid and efficient information to the population—even during periods of strict press censorship and severe repression. In an interview with me, Cardinal Dom Paulo Evaristo Arns dubbed the Catholic church's word-of-mouth communication system in São Paulo an "Arabian telephone system." This system of communication worked so well, he commented, that if a person were arrested anywhere in his archdiocese, he would know about it in a matter of hours.[40]

Once news of an arrest arrives, the church may act in one of several ways. The CNBB or the regional conference of bishops may write an official and formal denunciation of the occurrence. The bishop or archbishop in charge may personally intercede with someone in authority and use his influence on behalf of the victim. If those two measures fail, the church may request international solidarity to protect the prisoner from further danger. Above all, the church immediately moves to inform the public, either through the press or, if that is impossible because of censorship, through the alternative communications available to it, including the grass-roots pipelines and the various parishes. These activities have been crucial in breaking down the three most important components of the culture of fear: silence, isolation of the victim from an effective aid structure, and hopelessness and lack of belief in the efficacy of any action.

From a conservative or neutral stance in the past, the Catholic hierarchy in Brazil has moved firmly to defend human rights and to oppose the state's social, political, and economic policies. When Cardinal Arns was asked if there was a church-state conflict in Brazil, he answered simply that there was in the country a church that was close to the people and a state increasingly isolated and hostile to the people. "The Catholic church," he emphasized, "cannot be considered to be a power structure—not even one that is parallel to that of the state. The Catholic church is an instrument to speak to the conscience of the people. It is the voice of those who do not have a voice."[41]

The Catholic Church and Repression in São Paulo, 1975-1976

How the Catholic church has acted as the "voice of those who do not have a voice" in moments of tension and repression was demonstrated during the

wave of political violence in Brazil in 1975-1976. During an eighteen-month period, the forces of repression conducted another national blitz, seeking out militants of the Brazilian Communist party (PCB) and the Maoist Communist Party of Brazil (PC do B). Opposition members of all ideological persuasions were arrested in this dragnet.

Amnesty International reported that over 2,000 persons were detained throughout Brazil during the period. Of those initially arrested, about 700 remained in custody, and 240 were subsequently "adopted" by Amnesty International.[42] Amnesty International also reported that, during the eighteen-month period, it received numerous allegations of torture, all substantiated by physical evidence. Thus the organization concluded that torture was still systematically practiced in Brazil. The situation was serious enough for it to launch an urgent action appeal on behalf of 200 torture victims there. In early 1975 the center of repression was in São Paulo. One of the most frequently mentioned torture centers was the Second Army headquarters, where the CODI-DOI of São Paulo operated. An extensive purge had also been conducted within the São Paulo Military Police, and suspected dissidents had been arrested and tortured. In fact, the first known death under torture during that period was of an officer in the São Paulo Military Police, Lieutenant José Ferreira de Almeida. His death was officially explained as a case of suicide by hanging while in prison.[43]

In response to the wave of repression, the Archdiocese of São Paulo became a center for humanitarian aid to the families of persons who had been arrested or had disappeared. With the encouragement of Cardinal Arns, the archdiocese set up the diocesan Justice and Peace Committee, which included some of the most respected jurists in the state. The committee was entrusted with the defense of those who were persecuted and with the initiation of civil suits against the authorities for damages in proved cases of torture. Cardinal Arns's main objective was to encourage people to resist the violent repression and not give in to feelings of despair, isolation, and hopelessness. In church services he would discuss the violence in the city, urging the people to hope and to act on that hope:

The people of São Paulo should not let themselves be crushed under the weight of the horrible things that have been happening in our state. For, when a society so clearly perceives that things cannot remain the way they are now, then civil society itself can prove that there are alternatives available, and that opportunities to change things exist.

The people should not become depressed when faced with such violence. Rather, the people should be strengthened in their resolution to fight such acts, and should take courage from the very violence and react against it as a community and as a people.[44]

In September 1975, the São Paulo security forces, led by Colonel Erasmo

Dias, launched a military operation codenamed "Operation Djakarta."
Vladimir Herzog, a news editor at São Paulo's educational television
station, TV Cultura, was one of the victims caught by the military's
repressive maneuvers. On 24 October Herzog was summoned to CODI-
DOI for questioning. He voluntarily presented himself at headquarters for
his interrogation in the Second Army division. That same afternoon, he was
dead on the premises of the São Paulo CODI-DOI. Although the official
explanation was that he had committed suicide in his cell by hanging himself
with his own necktie, his body was returned to his widow in a sealed coffin
with no further explanation. She was threatened and warned not to open the
coffin. The burial services were conducted under military guard.

Herzog had been a well-known and liked television news editor. Massive
popular anger at his death suddenly gripped the state. His widow, Clarice
Herzog, with the aid of lawyers from the Brazilian Bar Association and the
archdiocesan Justice and Peace Committee, challenged the suicide story
and filed suit against the federal government, charging it with responsibility
for the death of her husband. The case enlisted the support of journalists
across the nation. The press conducted a thorough parallel investigation,
which showed that, in fact, Vladimir Herzog had been killed under torture on
the premises of the CODI-DOI of the Second Army of São Paulo. The
Brazilian Press Association organized a petition, signed by one thousand top
Brazilian journalists, requesting an investigation into the activities of the
CODI-DOI.[45]

The day after Herzog's death Cardinal Arns officially asked for the
support of the other bishops present at the Regional Bishops' Conference in
Itaici, São Paulo. The conference issued a formal statement analyzing
repression in São Paulo and denouncing the death of Vladimir Herzog:
"There is a flagrant and open lack of respect for the human person and this is
in violation of the image of God the Creator. This violation is characterized
by arbitrary arrests and by the renewal of torture, which is sometimes
followed by the death of the prisoner." The bishops declared their complete
"solidarity with the suffering of the victims," denounced as a major human
rights violation the denial of habeas corpus, and called on Christians to show
their solidarity with the victims and families of the persecuted by "meeting
in all the cathedrals and churches of São Paulo for the religious services in
memory of those who have disappeared, those who are still suffering in
prison, and those who have died as victims of the violence."[46]

The memorial mass for Vladimir Herzog was to be held in the Cathedral
of São Paulo. The day it was to take place the city was placed under military
occupation and the square around the cathedral (the Praça da Sé) blocked
off by army troops and military police. Nonetheless, over eight thousand
persons crowded into the cathedral, and thirty thousand more filled the
square. Cardinal Arns, followed by the two rabbis who concelebrated the

religious ceremony, asked for a moment of silence for the victims of persecution and violence. Then, in the stillness caused by the presence of the surrounding military forces, the cardinal appealed to the people to remain calm and nonviolent, but to take courage, cherish their hope, and react:

This House belongs to God and to all the people who accept the path of justice and truth. Let us purify our hearts of all hatred. We shall be brothers, and we shall reject all acts of terrorism, of any kind, no matter what their origins. . . .

No one may touch a man with impunity. A human being, born from the heart of God, is to be a source of love for all other human beings. God has constantly communicated to all mankind that he who spills the blood of his fellow human being is to be cursed. . . .

Human liberty was given to us to be preserved as a priority mission, which we must all carry out together. We are all responsible for freedom. Individually and collectively, we are responsible for the life of our brother.

Thou Shalt Not Kill. Whoever kills allows himself to be judged not only by history but by the Lord. He shall not only be cursed in the memory of mankind, but shall also be damned in the judgment of God.

I appeal to justice. I appeal to your commitment. I appeal to a justice that may come to be enforced by laws, but that above all must come from the inner strength of every person who must find the courage, now, to say to himself and to others: Enough!

Enough! It is time to unite all who wish to dwell in the light that brings truth and that undermines falsehood. Hope is to be found in solidarity. . . .

At this moment, the God of hope is calling for your solidarity. The God of hope is calling on you to engage in a peaceful fight—but with a persistent and courageous fighting spirit—in the name of an entire generation that will have as its symbols the children of Vladimir Herzog, his wife, and his mother.[47]

Like the funeral and memorial service for Edson Luís in 1968, the mass in memory of Vladimir Herzog catalyzed the repressed anger of a city and an entire nation. Like the death of the student in the streets of Rio de Janeiro almost ten years before, the journalist's death under torture became a symbol for the human rights movement, which tried to end state violence. The mass reaction to Herzog's death could not, however, prevent another death under torture. Only a few months later, on 17 January 1976, a metalworker, Manoel Fiel Filho, was found dead in his cell at the São Paulo CODI-DOI. The official version was suicide by hanging, and the circumstances surrounding his death were identical to those in the cases of Lieutenant José Ferreira de Almeida and Vladimir Herzog.[48]

After the death of Manoel Fiel Filho, the Geisel government was under intense pressure to end the repression in São Paulo. The commanders of the São Paulo security forces, Second Army Commander Ednardo D'Avila and Colonel Erasmo Dias, were both hard-liners who opposed the decompression policy. It was felt that their activities in São Paulo amounted to the exercise of a parallel power, which could threaten the authority of the central executive and of the national security state itself. President Geisel acted quickly to bring the situation under control. Two days after Manoel Fiel Filho's death, the president dismissed General Ednardo D'Avila Mello, replacing him with General Dilermando Gomes Monteiro. General D'Avila Mello was transferred to the reserves.[49] Although General Monteiro, who was considered part of the "liberal" military, kept his promise to end torture in the São Paulo CODI-DOI, he could not prevent further acts of repression in São Paulo, this time directed against university students who were attempting to reorganize the outlawed UNE.

Reorganization of the UNE began in 1977, with a series of demonstrations and marches, first in São Paulo and later nationwide. The students' silent demonstrations in the streets of São Paulo met violent police repression, ordered by Colonel Erasmo Dias. On 22 September 1977 the students held a secret meeting at the Catholic University of São Paulo to elect the committee of representatives that would be charged with the underground reorganization of the UNE.[50] When the meeting ended, the students planned to hold a large, open celebration in the evening in the university auditorium. That evening, under the command of Colonel Dias, the military police invaded the Catholic University, caused physical damage to the premises estimated at over ten million cruzeiros and herded three thousand students, faculty members, and university employees into the parking lot. They were harassed, threatened, beaten, and teargassed. Five young women, students at the Catholic University, were severely burned by police chemical bombs believed to have been napalm. A total of forty-one university students were later tried under the National Security Law for collective disobedience.[51]

In addition to mobilizing the grass-roots networks, the activities of the human rights movement included initiating civil suits against the federal government. The Justice and Peace Committee of the Archdiocese of São Paulo filed three suits in the civil courts to set a legal precedent for holding the federal government responsible for repressive actions. One of these concerned the invasion of the Catholic University. It demanded payment for the damages to the university premises and made the government responsible for damages and the medical costs of the five students who had suffered burns.[52] The other two suits were brought by the families of Vladimir Herzog and Manoel Fiel Filho, with the support of the archdiocese, which provided lawyers from the Justice and Peace Committee.

In 1978 Clarice Herzog and her children won a path-breaking judicial decision: three years after the death of Vladimir Herzog, the São Paulo State Supreme Court ruled in favor of the family and held the federal government responsible for his death.[53] A decision has not yet been reached in the case of the suit filed by Manoel Fiel Filho's family. These civil suits represented another method of encouraging peaceful resistance to the violence of the state.[54]

Formal Politics

Formal politics has, up to this point, included the activities of the church as an interest-group within the sphere of human rights organizing. I have also discussed the changing role of the MDB, as the opposition learned to use the officially tolerated legal opposition party to press for further liberalization and to register a protest vote. In addition, the judicial system served as an effective medium through which to press for democratic reforms and to counter the most severe effects of state violence. The defense of political prisoners, the judiciary's restraint in judging cases, and the fact that in spite of purges and other mechanisms of control the judiciary continued to claim its independence from the executive, are all factors that contributed to forcing the government to restore some of the most important civil and judicial guarantees. The strategy of filing suits to set precedents for others and to defend against the arbitrary abuse of power was implemented under the protective umbrella of the Catholic church and of the Brazilian Bar Association. The OAB's activities in the judicial sphere were important in helping to neutralize the three elements in the culture of fear: the defense of political prisoners countered both isolation and hopelessness; the association's education campaigns were effective tools against the silence that had been imposed.

The Brazilian Bar Association

Under the national security state, large numbers of lawyers moved into the opposition for two reasons primarily. The first was that the state, to justify its activities, had established a parallel structure of extraordinary laws, which were enacted and revoked by simple executive decree. The OAB has termed this parallel system the "illegitimate legal system"; it continues to exist side by side with the traditional body of law the Constitution supports. The existence of this dual structure, furthermore, has made it difficult for lawyers to function professionally. As lawyer Antônio Modesto da Silveira put it, "A lawyer had to wake up and read the *Diário Oficial da União* before he could get up and go to work to see if there had been any new laws promulgated during the night or any others revoked by decree."[55] There were so many laws, regulations, decrees regulating or revoking other laws, that the life of a lawyer became "a legal nightmare."[56] In addition, lawyers who defended political prisoners or dared to investigate the activities of the repressive apparatus often became targets of repression themselves. As a result, they began to use their professional association to press the federal government to return to a state of law and revoke the parallel structure.

The Brazilian Bar Association is particularly suited for the role of defender of human and legal rights. As the first professional association created in Brazil (1930), the OAB derives legitimacy and authority from its history. Furthermore, it differs in one crucial aspect from other professional associations: it is completely autonomous. Its autonomy, which derives from its function as defender of judicial harmony and the Constitution, is guaranteed by a special statute:

The Ordem dos Advogados do Brasil is a part of the indirect administration, as an autarchy, but it has specific "sui generis" organization, which is embodied in its perfect and integral decentralization. This aims to protect the dignity and the independence of the *ordem*, for its main mission is not limited to the activities in administration but rather is meant to defend the juridical harmony and the federal Constitution. The Ordem dos Advogados do Brasil is protected by a specific piece of legislation (Law No. 4215, article 139), which determines that "regulations and legal dispositions that refer to autarchies and other self-governing agencies of the state shall not be applied to the Ordem dos Advogados do Brasil."[57]

Thus, the OAB is not a professional association limited to the concern with and defense of the interests of the membership. It is a legal body whose mission is the overseeing of the application of the Constitution. All lawyers go through a training period with the OAB and must be affiliated with the organization in order to practice. The influence that the association derives from this supervisory position gave it the necessary independence and authority to play a crucial role in limiting abuse of power and protecting the independence of the judiciary, in spite of the state's attempts to institute controls, purges, and other limitations on that independence.[58] The OAB's work was particularly important in the establishment of the boundaries between the legitimate juridical framework—defined as those laws enacted by Congress and in accordance with a constitution—and an illegitimate, parallel juridical system—defined by the body of laws passed by force of the executive after 1964 without the approval of Congress as laws of exception; the defense of human rights and the demand for a repeal of repressive legislation; and public education on legal issues and public or civic rights.

The first stage of the opposition work of the OAB concentrated on the defense of political prisoners and denunciation of arbitrary arrests and torture. With the Fifth National Conference of the OAB, in 1974, the list of concerns was broadened to include a general defense of human rights. Hence the OAB moved in the same direction as other sectors of the opposition to enforce respect for political, civil, social, and economic rights. The work of educating the public was carried out in published interviews with the officers and members of the OAB and by reprinting and widely distributing OAB-promoted studies. In 1976 the OAB began to pay greater attention to the question of its own autonomy and independence from the state. Geisel's government had begun the sweeping juridical reforms that included the judiciary reform amendment establishing new controls over judges in a manner unacceptable to the Bar Association. With the Seventh National Conference of the OAB, in May of 1978, a synthesis of all the above concerns was developed.[59]

In addition to concerns over legal and civil guarantees the OAB published the *Declaration of Brazilian Lawyers*, a document that established a new, aggressive phase of Bar Association opposition activities. The new president of the OAB, Dr. Raymundo Faoro, became a leading spokesman of opposition views and applied considerable pressure on the state to revoke AI-5 and, above all, to reinstate habeas corpus for political crimes. For the next period the OAB would concentrate almost exclusively on these two issues.

Perhaps, however, the most politically important contribution of the OAB has been its questioning of the legitimacy of the legal framework of the national security state. The Bar Association and respected jurists established a distinction between a "state of law"—defined by a system regulated by a legitimate legal framework—and a "state of exception"— defined as an illegitimate legal framework. The definitions of and the insistence on this distinction denied the national security state the legitimation it had sought by constantly enacting decree-laws, institutional acts, and complementary acts, for, according to spokesmen of the OAB, there could be no legitimation in a system regulated by illegitimate laws:

We affirm that there is a *legitimate juridical order* and an *illegitimate juridical order*. An order that is imposed by force, from the top down, is an illegitimate order. It is illegitimate because its very origin is illegitimate. Only a legal order that is born and rooted in the people through the legislative representatives freely elected may be considered to be a legitimate juridical order. . . . We warn that the exercise of constituent power by any authority other than the authority of the people as represented in their freely elected Constituent Assembly is, in any democratic state, an unlawful encroachment of political power. As lawyers we vehemently deny the possibility of any coexistence—within a single country—of two constitutional orders: one legitimate and the other illegitimate. . . . We proclaim that the legitimate state is the *state of law*. This is the constitutional state, based on the legitimate order that comes from the people in a free Constituent Assembly. The other states are those where the executive power has taken on a constituent power. These are the states that are obsessed by their own security, their own survival and continuity. They are the oppressor states. They are what we have termed the *states of exception*.[60]

The Brazilian Press Association

The control of the press, of radio, and of television has been extremely important in the overall logic of the national security state. One of the needs of a repressive state is to limit the flow of information available to the population, hide abuses of power, and impose a silence that will not only limit opposition but also increase the sense of isolation and fear necessary for the proper impact of a strategy of rule through terror. Hence, censorship has been widely used to keep large sectors of the population uninformed and, therefore, unable to participate politically in effective ways. Censorship in Brazil has been carried out in two forms: a priori censorship, in which orders are transmitted to the media directly by the police network of the repressive apparatus, thereby prohibiting the publication or airing of certain subjects, events, or opinions: and a posteriori censorship, which involves the prohibition of the sale of newspapers, magazines, or the transmission of taped programs on television or radio.[61]

A priori censorship (*censura prévia*) is achieved in a variety of ways. A censor (usually from the Ministry of Justice) may be physically present on the premises of the medium and oversee all materials, read, edit, and cut out any parts considered offensive. Publishers, newspapers, magazines, and the like may be forced to send all finished materials—text of books, stories, newspaper articles, facts, illustrations, films, tapes, photographs—to a government department (usually within the Ministry of Justice or in the Federal Police Department), in the same city or even in Brasília itself. The material that is not approved, or "liberated" (*liberado*), cannot be published or aired. This process, needless to say, involves considerable financial burdens for the corporations involved and has caused, at times, the economic death of an enterprise that is particularly targeted by the government. This was the case, for example, of the venerable newspaper *Correio da Manhã*, and of the weekly newspaper *Opinião*, which were killed economically by a campaign organized by the government in retaliation for their strong opposition stance.[62] Other legal restraints include the possibility of criminal indictment of journalists, editors, or even owners of newspapers.[63] These controls are contained in the National Security Law and in a special piece of legislation known as the Press Law (Lei de Imprensa).[64] These laws prohibit the publication of material deemed subversive, offensive, slanted, or threatening to the interests of national security or to the constituted authorities. Journalists, editors, and owners are held personally liable for the news in their medium. Many have in fact been indicted and arrested for a variety of infringements of the censorship laws.

A posteriori censorship also takes different forms. The entire edition of a printed medium may be seized or a program prohibited from the air. The systematic implementation of such control always means the economic death of the company. The government may also close down operations either temporarily or permanently after disobedience of an a priori order has been established. Part of an edition or a program may be seized or "requisitioned" by the federal government for examination in Brasília. Indictment, arrest, and other punishments may occur even after the material has undergone prior censorship and passed the test of the physically present censor. The text may irritate a member of the federal government, who will then file an a posteriori petition against the responsible publisher or the journalist, editor, or owner. Of course, these direct forms of censorship are considerably reinforced by the self-censorship generated by fear of retaliation.

Largely because of a widespread press campaign against prior censorship a progressive easing of direct censorship in the written media became part of the controlled liberalization campaign after 1976. Censors were eventually removed from two of the country's major newspapers, *O Estado de São Paulo* and the *Folha de São Paulo*. At first, they remained in all other newspapers, but were gradually removed from even the smaller opposition papers and the Catholic church's papers.

In 1977 Press Secretary Toledo Camargo established the government's new policy: the written media would not be subjected to direct censorship, although the controls in the National Security Law were to remain active. Radio and television, however, would still be subject to both a priori and a posteriori forms of censorship.[65] In a country in which 40 percent of the population is still, in effect, illiterate, and in which, of the literate population, only a small number can afford to purchase written media, it is clear that radio and television are much more politically significant.

Not only did prior and direct forms of censorship remain active for radio and television, but the period of liberalization would see other forms of control of information (related to electoral and party program propaganda) imposed on the broadcast media. In addition, other underground and clandestine forms of intimidation developed in the form of direct terrorist bomb attacks on the premises of newspapers and newspapers stands.

Theater, literature, cinema, and music are all considered important transmitters of "psychological warfare" and have, therefore, been subjected to censorship. Plays and theater are subject both to a priori censorship—with censors reading and cutting out material considered undesirable—and a posteriori censorship. Censors must be present at performances and may suspend or close down a play any time they feel it is not conforming to the censored text. All cultural performances, including concerts, must provide the censorship bureaucracy with four free tickets so that censors can attend the show and testify to its conformity with established regulations. Songs, likewise, must be cleared by the federal police prior to presentation in a performance, show, or recording. If the Federal Police Department does not approve the words of the song, it can no longer be sung: the words are censored, and only the music can be played.[66] The same rules apply to literature, art, and cinema—particularly cinema, which is considered the most dangerous medium of psychological propaganda. Entire books and works of literature have been prohibited from publication in Brazil, some for as long as ten years.

In 1977, in the midst of the controlled liberalization program, the strictness of censorship was diminished, but an additional control on information was introduced. Minister of Justice Armando Falcão passed a decree-law establishing that books, magazines, newspapers, or journals received from foreign countries must also be subjected to censorship.[67] In short, cultural expression of any form has been identified with the activities of the internal enemy and is automatically considered suspect.

The Brazilian Press Association (Associação Brasileira de Imprensa, ABI), founded in 1931, resulted from a fusion of all press associations then in existence in the country. It speaks for the profession as a whole—for the press enterprises as well as for individual journalists, editors, and newspaper owners. The association is governed by an Administrative Council of forty-five members elected by the membership, a structure that allows both flexibility and participation in its decisions. Although the ABI does not enjoy any legal guarantee of autonomy vis à vis the state, it does in practice act as an independent institution in relation to the authorities of the national security state. Like their counterparts in the legal profession, journalists in Brazil pride themselves on a legacy of political participation in the movement for the abolition of slavery, for the independence of Brazil, for the installation of the Republic, and, above all, in the constant defense of freedom of expression during the period of the Estado Novo. The ABI was built on the foundations of this liberal tradition.

During the first phase of institutionalization of the national security state, the role of the ABI was limited to the coordination of activities of journalists, the defense of threatened professionals, and the promotion of educational debates, conferences, and study sessions. Since the press was not subjected to direct prior censorship until 1969, the role of the ABI was basically educational:

During that time in the ABI, we organized conferences, meetings, and courses on some of the basic aspects and issues that concerned not only journalists but society at large. I believe that one of the most important roles that the ABI played in that period was the printing and dissemination of the United Nations Declaration of Human Rights. We prepared several editions within the Press Association, for it was fundamental that all should know them. People talked a lot about human rights, but few really knew the U.N. Declaration.

We were a great university in which people could openly discuss matters of elections, controls, representation, and freedom of expression. The ABI was a center for debate and freedom to express different viewpoints.[68]

During that period of the Castello Branco government, the press played an important role in uncovering, proving, and campaigning against torture of political prisoners. As we have seen, the *Correio da Manhã* spearheaded this movement and effectively forced the government to end the consistent and systematic torture of political prisoners temporarily.

With the enactment of AI-5, the press was smothered by prior censorship and stringent controls. Reaction took two forms: first, the creation of innumerable small, alternative weekly newspapers or tabloids, which criticized the government's repressive or economic policies more freely; second, the slow articulation of symbolic campaigns of resistance to censorship itself. The smaller press, with a much smaller investment, could afford to take a more aggressive opposition stance. The censorship of small opposition papers, such as *Opinião*, was at times particularly severe, but this very severity encouraged resistance and organization to secure freedom of expression. The symbolic campaign was conducted either by printing information in an oblique and disguised manner—so that the reader could read between the lines—or directly by providing evidence of censorship. Newspapers and magazines utilized a variety of techniques for shocking the public with the extent of prior censorship and the number of lines or articles cut from their pages by the censors. In some there would simply be an empty square where the censored lines had been cut. Others would print a black square with an advertisement urging people to read and support the paper or magazine. One of the most imaginative campaigns was conducted by the large conservative newspaper *O Estado de São Paulo*, which alternated poems with recipes or photographs of animals wherever lines or parts of articles were cut by the censors.

The ABI continued its educational role; in addition, it provided an umbrella for the organization of numerous committees and groups working to counter censorship in the press, radio, television, theater, cinema, art, music, and literature. With the force and authority of its tradition, the ABI could provide legitimacy for the work of a variety of groups that could not survive outside of its protection. Hence, after 1969 the ABI increasingly became a forum for the expression of dissent against controls on opinion and thought. As such, the ABI served to coordinate the activities of opposition groups concerned with freedom of expression and to channel their activities into the realm of formal politics so as to provide direct pressure on the state. The combined pressure of the activities of the association and the symbolic campaign of the major newspapers forced President Geisel to eliminate direct censorship of the large newspapers in 1975 and, in 1978, direct prior censorship of the smaller, more aggressive opposition press.

With the lifting of prior, physical censorship, the press took on a major role in enlarging the timid liberalization process. Major articles criticizing the economic model and denouncing the corruption of high government officials appeared in the larger media. Most important, however, was the breaking down of the culture of fear by eliminating the silence: whenever cases of torture were reported, the press gave them widespread coverage, demanding investigations and an end to the violence.

State Reforms and Dialogue with the Opposition

The pressure of combined elite groups in the realm of formal politics

forced the state to engage in a political dialogue with prominent figures of
the organized opposition. By 1978 Geisel's government began a series of
meetings with the leaders of the MDB, the OAB, the ABI, and
representatives of the CNBB. In these meetings, an effort was made to
identify the most crucial issues.[69] The resulting reform package, prepared by
the government and introduced in the form of Constitutional Amendment
No. 11, contained some significant improvements.[70]

Article 182 of the Constitution of 1969 was repealed. This effectively
eliminated AI-5 and all the subsequent complementary acts and legislation
designed to complete it.[71] The repeal of Article 182 allowed for the
restoration of the most fundamental legal rights: the right of habeas corpus
for political crimes and the right not to be arrested without a charge or
warrant. It also restored the three essential guarantees of judicial
independence: the guarantee of job tenure, and guarantees that judges
would neither be transferred nor have their salaries reduced as a result of
their decisions.

A second change was the elimination of some of the extraordinary powers
of the executive branch over the legislature. The executive lost the power to
suspend or close down Congress and the state assemblies. It also lost the
power to cancel the electoral mandates of political representatives by
decree, without recourse to defense or appeal.

Under the new regulations, an accused representative must be tried by the
Federal Supreme Court. Prior approval of the house to which he or she
belongs is not required—a measure clearly aimed at avoiding the kind of
confrontation that had developed in the case of Congressman Márcio
Moreira Alves in 1968. Since this was not a restoration of full parliamentary
immunity (the legislative branch was still subject to the power of the other
two branches), the opposition considered it only a partial victory.

For the most part, Amendment No. 11 brought about a *status quo ante*,
returning to many of the provisions that had been included in the
Constitution of 1967 prior to AI-5. However, one new mechanism of
control was a series of measures labeled "emergency safeguards." These
provided the basis for a new form of strong regime, and for the more long-
term institutionalization of the national security state. The safeguards were
intended to supplement the constitutional provisions for declaring a state of
siege, giving the executive the power to exercise extraordinary powers "in
case of external war, of danger to the existence of the state, or in cases of
internal upheaval." Such a "state of emergency" could be applied, without
approval of Congress, for a ninety-day period and could be extended for an
equal period.[72] The executive was also empowered to determine which areas
of the country were to be affected by the state of emergency. Whereas the
precise regulations to apply to these areas were to be set at the time a state of
emergency was declared, the following were specified in the amendment

itself: (1) the power to appoint governors and all other administrative personnel in areas under a state of emergency; (2) exclusive power to oversee the maintenance of social control and to decree other measures believed necessary for this end; (3) the requirement that citizens in the affected areas have a fixed residence; (4) permission for the government to take over buildings for the purpose of temporary housing of prisoners; (5) suspension of legal guarantees, and blanket permission for authorities to engage in search-and-arrest maneuvers in private residences and elsewhere; (6) automatic suspension of freedom of association and assembly; (7) explicit authorization for censorship of the press, of correspondence, of telecommunications, and of all cultural activities; (8) the immediate suspension of all job tenure guarantees; (9) permission for the takeover of property, state corporations, and private corporations under government contract.[73]

The state of emergency powers included in the reform package reproduced many of those in the repealed institutional acts. The state of emergency in reality authorized temporally limited and sectorially specific cleanup operations for the repression of ′dissent and opposition. The safeguards, according to the government, were necessary to defend the national security state from threats to its security, and thus the reform package continued to reflect national security doctrine. The Bar Association severely criticized the safeguards, and the opposition accused the government of attempting to disguise an "illegitimate legality" within a constitutional framework, thereby giving the appearance of a more "legitimate legality," all the while reserving for itself sweeping powers of political control and repression. The negative reactions from all sectors of the opposition and the press were strong enough to indicate that the universe of demands from civil society had far surpassed the limitations set by the ideology of national security and development.[74]

Nonetheless, the reform package and the end of AI-5 were to be crucial for the negotiated liberalization. They would open political space and allow links to form between formal and base-related politics. They were thus a compromise for both sides.

Conclusion

The opposition in 1973 was generally demobilized and weak. In the 1974-1979 period, the situation reversed partially, though it remained contradictory and uncertain. Large sectors of elite groups moved into the opposition and engaged in pressure-group tactics to force the state to liberalize. In spite of the fear of renewed repression, particularly in São Paulo, the middle and upper classes predominated in both the organization and strengthening of civil society and in negotiations with the state over concrete steps to be taken in the liberalization process. In addition, the opposition organized vertically, using the existing corporative and associative structures. The OAB and the ABI played crucial roles in expressing the opinions of key elite sectors and in providing the institutional framework for further organization. Through the activities of its top echelon and through the CNBB, the Catholic church became an active part of civil society and pressured the state for further liberalization.

Some immediate questions come to mind. Why did elite sectors in civil society withdraw their support from the state and move so firmly in the direction of organized and effective political resistance? Which opposition groups were most important during this period in forcing liberalization? Finally, how did these sectors organize, and which channels were most effective in building pressure and establishing links between the different groups in civil society?

The answer to the first question requires consideration of three factors. First, key elite groups felt threatened professionally by the continuation of the tight repressive controls and the centralization of power. Second, these groups also felt themselves to be threatened personally by the violence of the repression. Finally, these groups came to view the authoritarian state itself as unnecessary for the protection of their own interests and, indeed, as more of a hindrance than a support.

Professionally speaking, lawyers encountered difficulties in the quagmire of dual legality, the chaos of hundreds of decree-laws, institutional acts, and complementary acts. Journalists and news editors could not function professionally under the tight system of prior censorship, which had been added to the press controls established in the Press Law and National Security Law. Newspaper and communications media owners were similarly constrained. Censorship had damaging effects on communications firms and imposed a financial burden that was unbearable for most. The written press in particular lost considerable investments with the periodic seizure and prohibition of entire editions, with the heavy penalties for infringements of censorship regulations, or through the state's vengeance against enterprises it considered too independent-minded. Some succumbed, notably, *Correio da Manhã* and *Opinião*. The same censorship provisions meant that writers, artists, actors, musicians, and other members of the intellectual elite suffered professionally. Publishers had to submit books to the censors and could find themselves prohibited from marketing a book for years after the initial investment had already been made. All sectors censorship affected organized within the general umbrella of the ABI and around the unifying theme, "freedom of expression."

Some important industrialists and capital owners also began to believe that their economic and professional interests were threatened. The 1976-1977 period saw the emergence of an outspoken group of business executives in key industries of the national private sector. Although these executives were often in partnership with both the state and the multinational corporations, they no longer believed that a highly centralized state was essential to their economic interests. On the contrary, they began to see the state as isolated, and themselves, as a class, excluded from full access to the decision-making apparatus that affected their economic survival. The Planning Ministry, which issued hundreds of economic decrees, counterdecrees, regulations, and plans, was often inaccessible to the private sector. Decisions made by isolated bureaucrats sometimes had disastrous effects on the economic health of a corporation. Furthermore, as I have pointed out, this period saw the end of the "miracle" and sharply intensified doubts about the path the centralized technocratic apparatus of the state was following.

The violence of repression was a personal threat to all members of civil society. I have analyzed the nature of the repressive system, the interpenetration of the intelligence network and the agents of physical repression at all levels of civil society, and the fine line that separated what the repressive apparatus considered to be "tolerable and responsible opposition" and "pressure and contesting opposition." Those in charge of this apparatus were guided by the theory of internal security, with its emphasis on the "enemy within." This internal enemy was, potentially, anywhere, in all classes and all sectors of political and civil society. Membership in a key elite group was no longer a protection, and after the enactment of Institutional Act No. 5, the violence of repression severely affected middle and upper classes. Attacks on middle- and upper-class university students in the streets of São Paulo in 1977 and the death under torture of an important journalist showed all groups that repression was not necessarily class-selective. In recognition of this, elite sectors moved to at least place clearer limits on the pervasive power of the repressive apparatus. At this point, the OAB, the ABI, and the CNBB, with the support of the top of the Catholic church's hierarchy, joined together in the defense of civil, political, legal, and human rights.

The national security state during this period was thus threatened by the loss of support from key elite sectors and by serious internal divisions in both military and civilian ranks. The transfer of power from President Geisel to his successor created the most severe crisis in its history. Without a mechanism for conflict resolution, the state's underlying institutional fragility was laid bare in yet another of its periodic power struggles.[75] Three main currents within the military fought over the executive post. General Sylvio Frota, army minister of the Geisel government, declared his candidacy in 1977. Frota was a hard-liner, connected to the army's security apparatus, the Army Intelligence Center (Centro de Informações do Exército, CIEX). General João Batista Figueiredo, chief of the SNI, was

Geisel's choice as successor and the secret "official" candidate. The struggle between the two candidates spilled over into the intelligence community, as each exploited his own power base.[76] In fact, the succession struggle between Frota and Figueiredo indicated the existence of a deeper power struggle within the framework of the state repressive apparatus itself.[77] We should remember that the intelligence community had been the de facto source of state power since the founding of the national security state.

Frota made no secret of this dispute and utilized the extensive CIEX network to build his own base in the campaign for president and, eventually, in conspiring to overthrow the Geisel government. Geisel's group, on the other hand, used the equally extensive SNI network to uncover and counter the conspiratorial plans of the army minister and to bring about his dismissal.[78] In addition, the nationalist and democratic sectors of the military supported the candidacy of General Euler Bentes Monteiro. A liberal-minded military officer, General Bentes Monteiro was officially sponsored by the MDB. Thus, for the first time, the conflicts between the main forces within the military became an open battle, and sectors within the military sought the official support of the key elite opposition groups.[79]

The national security state became torn by contradictions and power struggles within its own ranks. It was thus limited in its ability to react to the challenge coming from the elite opposition sectors engaged in formal political organization. Because of this factor the liberalization measures may have gone beyond original plans, but, nonetheless, the policies of the stage of decompression did not pose a serious danger to the national security state. The period of decompression, by and large, remained bounded by the Doctrine of National Security and Development and signified in particular a further cycle of liberalization rather than a transition period to democracy.

For the opposition, the Geisel period was one of intense learning characterized by renewed involvement at the level of formal politics in an attempt to shed the paralyzing effects of government intimidation. In its dialectical relation with the state, the opposition began to find ways to break down the three fundamental elements of the culture of fear. The combined action of the groups pressuring the state to lift censorship effectively joined with elite political leadership in the MDB to broaden the field of freedom of expression. Their success allowed the media to play an important role. The silence then imposed on society was slowly lifted, and the press published debates on the economic questions and denounced cases of abuse of power or state violence. With the breaking of silence, civil society responded, and people tended to take recourse to the new public forum to voice protests against government brutality. The Catholic church and the OAB's efforts to secure legal and civil guarantees, in time allowed the population to lose its sense of isolation. There were available channels and organizations set up and ready to offer effective aid and support to victims of state violence. Lawyers defended political prisoners and won important victories. The Catholic church legitimized the struggle for human rights and brought its strong moral legitimacy to bear on the state in defense of those persecuted. Finally, and most important, the activities of all the groups in civil society began to break down the deep feeling of hopelessness. With political channels available, organized and legitimate groups in civil society ready to come to a victim's defense, and a great deal of publicity offered, there was no longer a feeling that any action was bound to meet with failure. Small victories increased hope and brought people together in a common cause, further reducing the sense of isolation and hopelessness. The cycle of the culture of fear was broken. Hope resulted from the collectivity and the general support opposition members felt.

Activity in the realm of formal politics—defined here as the efficient use of institutional channels and existing networks—was one of the most important ways of breaking through the barrier of the culture of fear. First, different sectors of the opposition learned to use the official opposition party—the MDB. Second, the opposition used all available channels to increase pressure in defense of human rights so as to inhibit the institutionalized use of state violence. Third, the opposition learned to use corporate and associative organizations. By concentrating on freedom of expression, the Brazilian Press Association countered the silence. By defending those who were persecuted, tortured, kidnapped, or deprived of their rights, the Brazilian Bar Association countered the fear of isolation. Their collective activity allowed the population to hope and enforced respect for individual and collective rights. In time, hope itself allowed for the organization of more effective action by encouraging other sectors— particularly in the working population—to join and strengthen the opposition.

8. The *Abertura* Period

The government of General João Batista Figueiredo officially initiated a policy of *abertura*, or political opening. This policy continued the third stage of institutionalization of the national security state, begun with President Geisel's decompression policy in 1974. During his term in office, President Figueiredo broadened the liberalization policy while remaining within the parameters of "strong democracy" set forth under Geisel. Like the decompression policy, the *abertura* encompassed a series of planned stages of liberalization, carefully monitored by state political strategists. Enough political space was to be opened up to pacify the elite opposition, in the hope that this would provide the national security state with greater stability and wider support. On the other hand, the parameters of strong democracy were defined in such a way as to limit the participation of hitherto excluded sectors of the population and allow the state to determine what constituted acceptable or intolerable opposition. Groups linked to working-class and peasant social movements, whether secular or church-related, met with continuous and systematic repression. Other sectors, not believed to be sufficiently organized to constitute an "antagonism" or "pressure," as defined in the Doctrine of National Security and Development, were offered the chance to reorganize and to participate in government decisions. This was General Figueiredo's "extended hand" policy.

The elite sectors of the opposition (the CNBB, the OAB, the ABI, and the groups organized in the MDB) played a crucial role during both the Geisel and Figueiredo governments. They opened up political space by confronting the state from their positions of authority in civil society and by challenging the legitimacy that the national security state was trying to assume. Elite opposition also served to block attempts to reinstate coercive measures. At the level of formal politics, their demands included the dismantling of the repressive apparatus, the drafting of a new constitution, and the modification of the economic model. It is important to note that the liberal sectors of the national bourgeoisie joined in the last by demanding more participation in the formulation of economic policy.

A significant aspect of this period was the emergence of a popular movement composed of an alliance between the church-related *comunidades de base*, the secular grass-roots groups, and the new labor movement in the countryside and the urban areas. Activities at the level of formal politics widened the maneuverability margin available to all opposition groups. The end of Institutional Act No. 5 opened up new legal possibilities for grass-roots organization, and the popular movement was to play a key role in the political process.

The Grass-Roots Movements

Secular Grass-Roots Organizations

There are two kinds of grass-roots movement in Brazil: secular, and those related to the Catholic church. Secular grass-roots organizations are civic associations, autonomous from the state in both their administration and financing. Data on existing associations in São Paulo, for example, indicate that 96 percent are registered civic associations with no links to municipal or state administrations.[1] These organizations have a variety of names: neighborhood associations (*associações de moradores de bairros*); societies or associations of friends of the district (*sociedades* or *associações de amigos do bairro*, SABs or AABs); associations of the *favelas* (*associações de moradores de favelas*); or even simply community associations (*associações comunitárias*).

Data are not available on the number of neighborhood organizations nationally, but we can come to some appreciation of the scale of the neighborhood movements by looking at the data that do exist. In Rio de Janeiro, for example, the Federation of *Favela* Associations (Federação das Associações de Favelas do Rio de Janeiro, FAFERJ) coordinates at least 110 *favela* associations. In the poor district on the outskirts of greater Rio de Janeiro, the Baixada Fluminense, there are over 350 neighborhood associations, about 80 of which are formally coordinated by the Movement of Friends of the District of Nova Iguaçu (Movimento de Amigos do Bairro de Nova Iguaçú).[2] The Federation of Associations of Residents of the State of Rio de Janeiro (FAMERJ) has at least 40 different associations affiliated with it.[3] According to the Coordinating Council of the Societies of Friends of the city of São Paulo (Conselho de Coordenação das Sociedades de Amigos do Bairro de São Paulo), there are 1,300 societies of friends of the district (SABs) in the state of São Paulo. Approximately 800 of these are located in greater São Paulo, and 500 are in the city of São Paulo itself.[4]

Neighborhood organizations grew rapidly during Figueiredo's period of liberalization. The blocking action of the elite opposition groups provided space for maneuvering and organizing at the base. In 1978 President Geisel was forced to devote most of the state's attention to negotiations over the reform package with the OAB, CNBB, and the ABI and to trying to block the measures that the MDB introduced in Congress to broaden civil and political liberties. In addition, the national security state was torn by an internal power struggle, with General Sylvio Frota's attempted coup d'état and the challenge presented by the candidacy of General Euler Bentes Monteiro. In the context of a broader political opposition, the grass-roots movements mushroomed. In 1980, for example, it was reported that in the state of Rio de Janeiro alone, a new neighborhood organization was founded every week.[5] A similar pattern developed in the states of Rio Grande do Sul, Minas Gerais, Pernambuco, Bahia, Maranhão, Amazonas, Pará, Goiás, Espírito Santo, Santa Catarina, and Paraná.

Secular grass-roots organizations in the neighborhoods are primarily located in poor, peripheral, urban districts. Most of them began during the years of populist politics, sometimes directly stimulated by politicians looking to organize electoral committees. In São Paulo, for example, there were SABs as early as 1945-1946, but their main organizational period came with the advent of Janismo in São Paulo in 1953.[6] Thus they originated in clientelistic mediation functions.

The neighborhood and *favela* associations mobilize the population for pressure-group political activities. They were born in a period of rapid capitalist industrialization, with capital concentration in the cities and a high incidence of migration from rural to urban areas. Their rapid growth and increasingly aggressive demands for social, political, and economic participation in government decision-making (at local, state, and federal levels) is a direct result of the highly unequal distribution of income and the high rate of exploitation of the working population (concentrated in the poor, peripheral areas of cities, or in the *favelas*). The neighborhood and *favela* associations tend to create central coordinating bodies in the form of federations or confederations. These link networks at the municipal, state, and regional levels, allowing for the formation of mass-based social movements to press for specific improvements of interest to all (such as a freeze of food prices, legal access to urban land, improvements in sewage and health facilities, day care centers, and education).

Although clientelistic functions persist among many neighborhood associations, there is a growing tendency toward autonomy and base-related modes of political action. Evidence of this increasing independence can be found in their refusal to comply with regulations established by the administrative authorities.[7]

The structure of the associations active in the opposition is usually highly democratic, often with intermediate levels of representation—elected councils of residents of one (sometimes two) neighborhood streets—which have significant participation and influence. In the opinion of César Campos, president of FAMERJ, internal democracy helps prevent any particular group from gaining control over the organization and keeps it from serving the interests of a particular political or corporative organization.[8] In many of these associations, in fact, the street councils elected by residents of each street have veto power over the decisions of the association's board of directors.

In areas where an association does not exist, the grass-roots opposition has attempted to form one. Whenever the association is in the hands of directors connected to the government or tied to clientelistic patterns of political behavior, an opposition group may organize within it and run for office. The strategy consistently has been to increase the levels of political activity of the organization itself and to encourage participation by the membership.[9]

Neighborhood and *favela* associations concentrate much of their work on mobilizing the population to achieve improvements in the neighborhood. They see governmental structures as ultimately responsible for the conditions in their immedite neighborhoods and thus pressure state and local authorities to solve problems that are understood as the proper concern of government: housing, sewage disposal, water, schools, garbage collection, electricity, street paving, day care centers, and urban street cleaning.[10] To achieve such goals, associations use a variety of techniques: petitions, meetings, public rallies and assemblies, marches on city hall, sit-ins in administrative offices, and even—in extreme cases—setting up street barricades until demands are met.[11] The associative role of the organizations may include collective self-help projects that mobilize the entire neighborhood. Thus many associations have set up their own day care centers, health clinics, community centers, mothers' clubs, film clubs, and organized courses and recreation activities. Actual work is often carried out by the collective labor of the community, in projects known as *mutirões*.[12]

During the period of the national security state, the neighborhood and *favela* associations have played a crucial role in the organization of the poor. From their local organizations, the population has learned to coordinate larger, statewide or national campaigns to pressure the government. One example was the cost of living movement, which by 1978 was strong enough to call for the government to freeze prices on basic foods (it collected 1.5 million signatures in support of its demands).[13]

Whereas such movements are generally initiated by the grass-roots associations and federations, sometimes the federal or state government takes an action that sets off a major campaign, mobilizing large numbers of local residents. This was the case, for example, in Nova Iguaçú in 1979. The National Housing Bank (BNH) began a forced eviction of sixteen thousand families from twenty-three huge, low-cost housing developments that it owned in Nova Iguaçú, Rio de Janeiro. The residents were extremely poor, living on wages that increased once per year at below-inflation rates, and they could no longer make the mortgage payments. The mortgage payments were set by the bank and were raised periodically at inflation or higher-than-inflation rates. BNH officials claimed that the majority of residents were either in default, or were invaders who had no legal right to the property, regardless of payments they had made to the financial institution.

Each of the twenty-three housing complexes had its own residents' association, and these were coordinated by the Movement of Friends of the District of Nova Iguaçú (MAB).[14] The associations conducted a detailed survey and discovered that, besides those who could not meet the increasing mortgage payments, there were some residents who continued to pay without ever having received a legal title to their apartments. Some had purchased titles they believed to be legal years before.[15] When the BNH refused to consider their cases, the MAB organized a series of meetings, assemblies, rallies, marches, and petitions to build enough support among the population to back the demand for negotiations. The federal government was forced to intervene and order the National Housing Bank to negotiate new terms of payment and the matter of property titles. The local associations and the MAB elected a negotiating committee composed of representatives of the associations, of the MAB, and the bishop of Nova Iguaçú, Dom Adriano Hipólito. The negotiations lasted for a number of months and demands were eventually satisfactorily resolved.[16]

Church-related Grass-Roots Organizations

According to theologians of the Brazilian Catholic church, the base "is understood as that part of the population in a society that is deprived of the right to power, to property, and to knowledge."[17] At a socioeconomic level, those in the base produce society's riches, but can participate neither in the organization nor in the distribution of their own work and products. At a political level, they have no say in the decisions of the state that directly affect their lives. The culture in which they are immersed is meant to protect the privileges of those who deprive them of their rights. The church's preferential option for the poor (the base) has the fundamental goal of liberating this segment of society, restoring to the poor the rights that are naturally theirs. The Catholic church is working to restore to the base the rights to know, to own, and to participate in political life in decisions about the nation and the work place that affect the organization and distribution of the products the poor create.[18]

In addition to the Catholic church's grass-roots work, which is institutionally channelled through the CNBB and the different pastorals mentioned earlier, there has been a growing movement among the laity of the church: the basic Christian communities (*comunidades eclesiais de base*, CEBs). The CEBs are small groups of local people who organize around an urban or rural parish. Many, in fact, are organized in remote areas where the population does not have access to a chapel or to regular religious services. A CEB is usually initiated by pastoral agents, community organizers (*animadores de comunidade*), or, more traditionally, deacons, priests, or members of religious orders. The nontraditional lay agents may perform many of the religious functions and services that would otherwise not be available to the population on a regular basis because of the shortage of priests.[19]

Some authors place the origins of the CEB in the experience of the groups organized in the *movimento de educação de base* in the Diocese of Natal in 1960.[20] Others trace them back even farther, to the missionary work of the Diocese of Barra do Paraí in Rio de Janeiro in 1956. There is, however, general agreement that extensive organization of the CEBs began in the period after the violent repression of 1969. In 1975 a national meeting of basic Christian communities was held in Vitória, Espírito Santo, to evaluate the experiences of the CEBs and coordinate plans for future growth. At that time it was established that some fifty thousand *comunidades de base* already existed throughout Brazil.[21] In 1981 that number was estimated at around eighty thousand, mainly in rural areas and in the poor peripheries of the cities.[22] These CEBs had the dual function of leading religious services and Gospel study, and of organizing liberating work and communitarian action.

A CNBB study defined the characteristics of a CEB:

1. *Comunidade:* They must be primary social groups, in which the members have personal knowledge of each other and a personal relationship. They must, in addition, have common objectives and interests. The number must be limited so as to enable personal relationships to develop.
2. *Base:* They must be formed by the people and be born from the people, wherever they live, work, meet, and relate to each other. The criteria are varied: geographical, professional, residential, etc.
3. *Eclesial:* They must include (a) an open reception of the Word of God—which is the starting point of conversion; (b) conversion, which is to be further translated into (1) an open relationship with oneself as a person; (2) an open relation to others; (3) an open relation with the surrounding social reality. They are to be the leaven of the masses, the embodiment of a personal, vibrant, alive, liberating, and prophetic church. (4) They must have communion with the visible church, local, particular, and universal. (5) They must be a celebration of the life of Christ, through the sacraments, prayers, liturgy, etc.[23]

The CNBB study noted that the CEBs are most often born from the concrete experiences of the community itself. They are the "church that is born from the people" in response to personal relationships; meetings to pray, celebrate the liturgy or sacraments; an understanding of the deeper meaning of the Gospel and its message to the concrete existence of the community and the world; reflection on the social and economic reality, using the pedagogical method of "seeing, judging, and acting"; concrete organization of action, with the distribution of tasks and services to individual members; the carrying out of activities in a communitarian manner, to benefit the community as a whole collective engagement in an evangelical action.

Most studies of the CEB's organizational structure conclude that it undergoes distinct stages in the growth of critical consciousness, as summarized in figure 3. Each step in the development of a CEB is carefully thought out so as to maximize the participation of each individual. The main organizational characteristic is the care taken in studying the problems, acting on the results of the analysis, reflecting on the action, and increasing the integration of all members, thereby enhancing the democratic participation with nuclei and in the *comunidade* itself. Division into nuclei facilitates personal and group dynamics, allowing for greater freedom of expression, participation in discussion, and learning. Persons who have been denied the right to participate become less afraid to speak out and make themselves heard; they acquire experience in exchanging opinions, in evaluating work, in the actual planning, organization, and carrying out of activities and self-help projects, and in the sharing of responsibilities. Only after this do they meet to elect a central coordinating body, a Council of the Community, and thereafter engage in more collective assemblies and work. The development of the CEBs follow different rhythms of critical consciousness, depending on the level of confidence each member feels.

The CEB's chief concerns are related to the experiences of the community itself. The questionnaire that was used to prepare for the regional meetings of the CEBs (in preparation for the fourth national meeting of the basic Christian communities in São Paulo) shows some of the areas in which the CEBs are working. The questionnaire was divided into six areas, with questions to be discussed by the different CEBs prior to the regional preparatory meeting. The questions for debate were the following:

1. *The reality in which the CEB is immersed*
Questions to reflect upon: Where do you live? In the city or the countryside? Where do you work? In the fields, factory, self-employed, migrant worker, etc. . . . How much do most of you earn? Are there jobs for all? Are there enough schools? Until what grade do people study? Are there many who cannot read and write? Do people own the place where they live? Do they have a title for their land or their home? What are the biggest housing problems? Are there many sick people? Are there any hospitals? Can you afford medicines?

2. *The organization of your CEB*
Questions to reflect upon: How is your community organized (in teams, groups, etc.)? Is there a coordinating body in the community? How does it work? How was it elected and do you think it is working? Do you have enough meetings in your CEB? How are community decisions made? Are they made with enough participation by all members? How much do the women in your community participate? How is the religious liturgy celebration organized? Are there priests and nuns? What do they do in the community?

Fig. 3. Stages in the Growth of a CEB

I. PREPARATION: 1. Knowledge of community. 2. Reflection on concrete situation in discussion with community *pastorais*, work groups and teams. 3. Motivation of group members for community work. 4. Choice of "community stimulators" (*animadores comunitários*). 5. Training of team and development of program. 6. Formation of the community.

↓

II. TRAINING: 1. Training of leaders and community stimulators. 2. Group dynamics. 3. Community work. 4. Methodology and stages for development of community work. 5. Self-help projects. 6. Community pastoral. 7. Basic community.

↓

III. FORMATION OF NUCLEI: 1. Observation of area. 2. Study of nuclei or basic communities. 3. Division of area into three or four nuclei. 4. Discovery of "poles of attraction." 5. Formation of "stimulation" team and coordination of nuclei.

↓

IV. SELECTION OF NUCLEUS LEADERS: 1. Choice of leaders. 2. Personal invitation. 3. Motivation for work. 4. Global and participative work. 5. First meeting of nucleus. 6. Central meeting of various community nuclei.

↓

V. MEETING OF NUCLEUS: 1. First meeting of nucleus. 2. Presentation of work and function of group. 3. Invitation to more leaders; intensive training of groups. 4. Establishment of priorities and programming of activities, after studying problems and needs, and with participation of all members.

↓

VI. IMPLANTATION: 1. Implantation of communitarian work. 2. Reflection on and study of effectiveness. 3. Participation. 4. Integration of other community resources. 5. Projects and programs for the different sectors of central coordination. 6. Self-help projects.

↓

VII. STRUCTURE: 1. Autonomy of basic communities. 2. Consolidation of leadership. 3. Stimulation in each nucleus and communitarian coordination. 4. Election of Council of the Community. 5. General meeting of all nuclei to discuss and debate the pastoral plan; work, services, programs; cult services; activities and teams.

↓

VIII. INTEGRATION OF COMMUNITY AND EVALUATION: 1. Integration in nucleus. 2. Contacts with other groups. 3. Common services. 4. Participation in common activity. 5. Interchange of different nuclei. 6. Common programming of community projects. 7. Community assemblies.

Source: Mariano Baraglia, *Evolução das Comunidades Eclesiais de Base* (Rio de Janeiro: Vozes, 1974), p. 69.

3. *In the face of oppression, what does your CEB do?*
Questions to reflect upon: Under what kinds of oppression do the people suffer? Why do these oppressions exist? In the face of the injustice to which the people are submitted, is the community doing anything? What? What difficulties did your community find in organizing? How did it overcome such difficulties?

4. *Does the community have a connection to other CEBs?*
What is this connection? Do you meet together? For what? Are there actions that you do together?

5. *Does the CEB participate in or organize with other groups?*
Questions to reflect upon: Which groups do you work with? (*favela*, neighborhood associations, popular movements, the cost of living movement, trade unions, political parties, the many pastorals, such as the land pastoral, the CIMI, or which others?) Is this connection helpful, or does it make your work more difficult? Why?[24]

Such questions are discussed in the nuclei, then in the general meetings of the different nuclei, and finally are brought to a general assembly of the local CEBs. When a consensus is reached, each CEB drafts a report to be read, studied, and debated further at the preparatory meetings. The CEB delegates who are elected to go to the national meeting later analyze and discuss all of the documents. Finally, the results are taken back to the base for evaluation, reflection, and more discussion as to the best manner of coordinating and acting. In this way, the "see, judge, act" method becomes an intrinsic part of the very life and organic structure of the CEBs and allows for a maximum of flexibility and individual participation in the thinking about, discussion, evaluation, and implementation of all decisions and projects.

Over the last few years, the development of the CEBs has followed certain stages of political growth. All of these are interwoven in a dialectical process of rising political consciousness. According to national coordinator Frei Betto, the first stage is the establishment of the *comunidade* itself. This stage is particularly centered around religious motivation and the search in the Gospel for directives for life. The second stage is reached with the participation of CEB members in popular movements, side by side with people who may not share their faith but who share their concern for the oppressed and persecuted. The third stage is the actual strengthening of the working-class movement itself. Frei Betto considers this to be the stage that involves the most direct political consciousness, when members of the CEBs in the cities and rural areas participate in the opposition within trade unions to win union elections and in neighborhood organizations. A fourth stage was reached with the Party Reform Bill of 1979, when political debate and action within the new political parties began to take place.[25]

The political and social importance of the CEBs lies in their capacity to awaken the critical consciousness of the condition of oppression and to stimulate self-respect, hope, and thus effective action for change. The consciousness-raising role of the CEBs has contributed to a significant increase in the strength of the popular grass-roots movements. They perform two important functions in the overall social movement: they encourage effective organization, and they bring a deep commitment to internal democratic participation. In the CEB the value of each human being is brought out in such a manner that his or her potential as an agent of historical change becomes enhanced.

Thus the *comunidades de base* have been the schools and the seedbeds of participatory democracy. The experience of collective and democratic leadership gained in the communities is transmitted to the larger social movements through the activities of CEB members. In this way, they have influenced the behavior and structures of neighborhood associations, rural unions, trade unions, and even the opposition political parties. Their concern with participatory democracy within their organizations, their effort to decentralize, to share responsibility, and to emphasize the individual's importance as a participant, are some of the organization's main characteristics and have been, perhaps, their most valuable contribution to Brazilian social movements.

Grass-roots activities, both secular and church-related, have been fundamental in denying legitimacy to the national security state and in structuring the resistance to unjust social policies. Eventually, the democratic nature of the organizations themselves began to demonstrate an alternative to the model presented by the third stage of institutionalization of the national security state.

The New Union Movement and the Strikes of 1978, 1979, 1980

Two major factors condition the activity of the urban and rural union movement in Brazil: the controls set out in the Labor Code, and the code's immersion in the context of the national security state.

Union Structure and the Labor Code

The Brazilian Labor Code, Section V of the Consolidated Labor Laws (Consolidação das Leis do Trabalho), tightly regulates the formation, registration, and functioning of labor unions.[26] Mussolini's Fascist legislation, particularly the Carta del Lavoro, inspired the code. Passed in 1943 in a period of dictatorship, the Brazilian Labor Code remained unchanged throughout the years of progressive redemocratization. The structure of the labor unions served the state's interests by maintaining control over workers, no matter what the ideology of those in power. During the more liberal democratic governments, which depended on popular vote, the most severe restrictions and penalties were not applied; however, these measures were never eliminated.[27] The military left the Labor Code largely intact, making a few minor changes to increase its overall effectiveness for the purposes of the national security state.

Unions are organized in a pyramidal structure, to prevent horizontal organization across occupational categories. The Labor Code explicitly prohibits the formation of coordinating bodies among unions at the local level. Thus a metalworkers' local may not coordinate activities (formally and legally) with bank workers, urban transport workers, or any other category of union. It may meet only with other members of its own job category and at the federation level. Only at the top, through the confederation, do all job categories in the same sector of the economy meet in a formal sense. Figure 4 shows the pyramidal structure of the unions, and figure 5 shows the impediments to horizontal organization. Horizontal connections between job categories are not legally allowed. The vertical organizational structure is geared to ensure as much centralization as possible at the federation and confederation levels.

The Ministry of Labor can use other than structural controls to regulate union activities. First, the state, by decision of the ministry, has the right to intervene directly in a union to remove and replace elected officials. Second, any union officer so removed is permanently ineligible for union office. For this reason, the president of the metalworkers' union of São Bernardo do Campo and Diadema, Luís Inácio Lula da Silva, has called this provision the "AI-5 of the workers."[28] Third, the government has the final say over legal recognition of trade unions and can itself set up trade unions—the "phantom" unions. In addition, the government's right to cancel the recognition of and dissolve trade unions has been an impediment to free trade-union activity.

The budgetary regulations established by the Ministry of Labor are another important means of controlling unions. The budget of each union comes from an automatic wage deduction assessed against all Brazilian workers (whether unionized or not) equivalent to one day's pay per year. This fund, known as the "union tax" (*imposto sindical*), is deducted from paychecks by the corporations and is transferred directly to the federal government. It is redistributed through government institutions and the Bank of Brazil to confederations, federations, and local unions, with the two higher levels having discretion over how the locals will receive their share of the budget. In addition, the unions must draw up a detailed "spending report" on how they will utilize their funds. The Labor Code itself specifies certain kinds of allocations, including percentages that must be spent for medical care, dental care, cooperatives, and continuing education programs for members of local unions. Spending for political participation, political campaigns, or political parties is prohibited by law. Use of any kind of union money for strike funds is also prohibited by law.[29] In fact, unions have been

Fig. 4. The Labor Union Pyramid

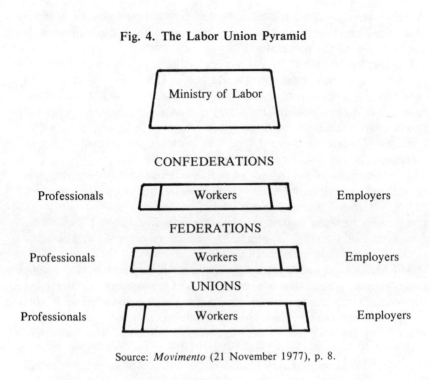

Source: *Movimento* (21 November 1977), p. 8.

Fig. 5. Impediments to Horizontal Trade-Union Organization
CONFEDERATION

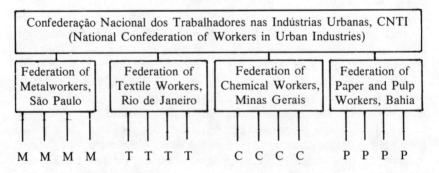

Notes: The confederation, the federations, and the particular local unions are examples that indicate the nature of the legal representational ties. The letters at the local-union level symbolize the particular local union of the category.

transformed into social welfare organizations that perform the functions of a welfare state and release the central government from social obligations to a large extent. At the same time, the burden of such a role prevents unions from fulfilling their inherent function, that of representing the economic interests of workers.

Perhaps an even greater restriction on freedom of organization is the legal stipulation that all unions must deposit all of their income—from the wage tax, from union dues, grants, benefits, or any other source—into one particular bank account in the Caixa Econômica, a government financial institution. The government can freeze this account whenever it sees fit, for example, when the Ministry of Labor decides that some of the budgetary rules or percentages have been violated during a strike that is considered illegal.

A fifth important mechanism for controlling labor unions is the legal prohibition from affiliation with international trade-union organizations without prior government approval. Thus, since 1964 it has been difficult for opposition unions to affiliate with international union networks that could have provided support and aid.

To what extent have the military governments since 1964 used these controls? The data in table 20 show the number of confederations, federations, and local unions in Brazil from 1964 to 1979. These include professional and employers' organizations and urban and rural workers' unions. All are part of the pyramidal structure tied to the national security state through the Ministry of Labor (see fig. 4). The number of confederations and federations has remained relatively stable during the years of the national security state; however, the total number of local workers' unions has oscillated according to how many unions were formed or dissolved by a governmental decree. The urban employers' unions, on the other hand, have remained much more stable over the same period of time. I found no case of direct state intervention in an employers' organization to dismiss officers or dissolve a union on political grounds. The same comments apply to the data on total union membership from 1964 to 1979 (table 21). The chaotic situation in the countryside prevented compilation of membership data until 1974, when the Confederation of Workers in Agriculture (CONTAG) began to gather systematic information independent of government statistics.

Table 22 presents data on the number of acts of interference in trade unions by the government between 1964 and 1979. In compiling these data, I paid particular attention to urban and rural labor unions as well as to professional white-collar organizations. The data on interference in trade unions refer to local, federation, and confederation levels. Interference refers not only to direct intervention, but also to the extension of intervention beyond the ninety days stipulated in the Labor Code whenever

Table 20
Confederations, Federations, and Trade Unions

	Number							
	1964	1965	1966	1967	1968	1969	1970	1971
CONFEDERATIONS								
Workers'	7	7	7	8	8	8	8	8
Employers'	4	4	4	4	4	4	4	4
Professionals'	1	1	1	1	1	1	1	1
Total	12	12	12	13	13	13	13	13
FEDERATIONS								
Workers'	107	107	118	119	119	122	123	128
Employers'	63	63	74	78	83	87	88	87
Professionals'	4	4	5	6	6	6	6	6
Total	174	174	197	203	208	215	217	221
URBAN TRADE UNIONS								
Workers'	1,948	1,149	1,158	1,137	1,991	1,987	1,991	1,989
Employers'	1,119	1,170	1,235	1,222	1,186	1,181	1,190	1,215
Professionals'	120	124	129	129	114	111	112	123
Total	3,187	2,443	2,522	2,488	3,291	3,279	3,293	3,327
RURAL TRADE UNIONS								
Workers'	*	*	294	381	845	1,225	1,268	1,290
Employers'	*	*	449	478	625	745	829	995
Total	*	*	743	859	1,470	1,970	2,097	2,285

CONFEDERATIONS								
Workers'	8	8	8	8	8	8	8	8
Employers'	4	4	4	4	4	4	4	4
Professionals'*	1	1	1	1	1	1	1	1
Total	13	13	13	13	13	13	13	13
FEDERATIONS								
Workers'	134	139	137	139	139	137	138	138
Employers'	87	87	88	86	88	86	86	86
Professionals'	5	6	6	7	9	7	7	7
Total	226	232	231	232	236	230	231	231
URBAN TRADE UNIONS								
Workers'	1,940	1,956	1,949	1,958	1,964	1,975	1,734	1,947
Employers'	1,216	1,235	1,253	1,275	1,296	1,317	1,310	1,310
Professionals'	111	125	130	132	136	141	155	147
Total	3,267	3,316	3,332	3,365	3,396	3,433	3,199	3,404
RURAL TRADE UNIONS								
Workers'	1,154	1,346	1,519	1,669	1,745	1,826	1,868	2,023
Employers'	1,365	1,389	1,406	1,445	1,485	1,510	1,367	1,449
Total	2,519	2,735	2,925	3,114	3,230	3,336	3,235	3,472

Sources: For urban unions, Fundação Instituto Brasileiro de Geografia e Estatística (IBGE), *Anuário Estatístico do Brasil* (for 1964 to 1979); for rural unions, Coordenadoria de Informática, *Inquérito Estatístico Sindical* (Brasília: Câmara Federal).
*No data available.

Table 21
Trade Union Membership

Type of Union	No. of Members							
	1964	1965	1966	1967	1968	1969	1970	1971
Urban								
Workers'	1,448,151	1,602,021	1,628,202	1,740,377	1,873,898	1,952,752	2,132,086	2,317,775
Employers'	119,314	161,759	173,217	192,381	191,452	211,478	235,118	257,197
Professionals'	49,195	50,913	54,949	58,897	66,098	68,172	72,989	92,867
Total	1,616,660	1,814,693	1,856,368	1,991,655	2,131,448	2,232,402	2,440,193	2,667,839
Rural								
Workers'	*	*	*	*	*	*	*	*
Employers'	*	*	*	*	*	*	*	*
Total	*	*	*	*	*	*	*	*

Type of Union	1972	1973	1974	1975	1976	1977	1978	1979
Urban								
Workers'	2,488,208	2,720,055	2,930,672	*	3,224,425	3,509,915	4,271,450	5,139,566
Employers'	280,339	304,962	320,310	*	340,579	359,205	415,550	455,468
Professionals'	99,043	102,890	109,441	*	118,866	125,241	147,307	157,728
Total	2,867,590	3,127,907	3,360,423	*	3,683,870	3,994,361	4,834,307	5,752,762
Rural								
Workers'	*	*	3,008,943	*	3,425,995	4,033,122	4,568,412	5,098,522
Employers'	*	*	496,396	*	555,373	573,303	619,427	678,125
Total	*	*	3,505,339	*	3,981,368	4,606,425	5,187,839	5,776,647

Sources: For 1964–1968, Fundação IBGE, *Anuário Estatístico do Brasil*, 1965–1969; for 1969–1973, ibid, 1970–1974; for 1974–1979, ibid, 1975–1980; for rural unions, Confederação dos Trabalhadores na Agricultura (CONTAG), and Coordenadoria de Informática da Câmara Federal, Brasília.
*data not available.

Table 22

Direct Government Interference in Trade Unions

Type of Interference	1964	1965	1966	1967	1968	1969	1970	1971	Total
				Number of Occurrences					
Intervention	452	358	26	72	57	34	46	12	1,057
Removal from office of leader	3	6	3	4	2	1	18	3	40
Cancellation of election	1	3	6	6	2	3	3	0	24
Dissolution of union	1	7	5	64	50	53	21	10	211
Total	457	374	40	146	111	91	88	25	1,332

Table 22 (continued)

Type of Interference	Number of Occurrences								
	1972	1973	1974	1975	1976	1977	1978	1979	Total
Intervention	24	25	12	27	20	6	18	13	145
Removal from office of leader	1	8	4	1	0	0	0	24	38
Cancellation of election	1	0	0	0	1	2	2	1	7
Dissolution of union	16	4	0	1	8	2	2	10	43
Total	42	37	16	29	29	10	22	48	233

Source: *Diário Oficial da União*, daily issues from 1964 to the end of 1979.
Notes: Intervention is here defined as a governmental act based on the Labor Code (Consolidation of Labor Laws) that either directly intervenes in a union, removing the elected officials from office and appointing governmental administrators, or that officially extends the period of intervention decreed by a local regional labor delegate.
Removal from office is an official act of the Ministry of Labor and most frequently means the removal of one, two, or three members of a board of directors. In only twenty-five cases did the ministry remove all of the members of a board of directors.
Interference in elections can take the form of annulling the results of an election or prohibiting the candidacy of one or more persons on political grounds. I have counted only those cases of trade union dissolution justified by at least one of four reasons: (a) the trade union did not present its budget to the Ministry of Labor; (b) the leadership was disappeared or the regional labor delegate declared the directorate vacant; (c) the union did not conform to the "unified statute" required by the Labor Code; (d) to break up the profession or include the union in another trade union.

a decision to intervene regulated a de facto action either of the regional labor authorities or of a military commander. Intervention was extended beyond the legal limit only in 1964, when troops occupied a union later declared under intervention. Furthermore, in 1964 intervention was not always justified by the relevant articles in the Labor Code, but was often carried out for two other reasons: because the union officers could not be found and thus were considered to have "disappeared" and vacated their posts; or because the union was being occupied by troops and clearly required government intervention to restore its proper activities. These justifications were published in the preambles of the intervention decrees and show the extent of violent repression in the labor unions.

The New Union Movement

The new union movement, which emerged as a major political force in 1977, is the result of years of struggle to regain control of unions under intervention, to organize others, to activate the phantom unions, and to strengthen organization at the base in the factories, on the farms, and in other work places. By 1977 this movement had built up enough strength and political consciousness to have a real impact on the state and to begin to push for structural transformations.

The new union movement should be considered part of the democratic opposition as a whole. Its platform of demands demonstrates its political commitment to democracy and freedom of organization. The movement's demands include (1) the abolition of repressive legislation and return to democratic forms of government; (2) direct popular elections for all levels of political representation; (3) participation of representatives of the working population in the management of special funds set up for social programs such as the PIS-PASEP (Programa de Integração Social-Programa de Ação e Serviço em Produção), the FGTS, and the National Housing Bank; (4) the abolition of the wage-control policies and recognition of the right to engage in collective bargaining; (5) the right to strike; (6) the right to organize unions without state interference (union autonomy) and thus modification of the Labor Code to eliminate the controls established in Section V. The implication of the unions' demands, taken together, is that the national security state itself must be eliminated and the economic development model transformed to provide for popular participation in political, economic, and social decisions of government.

The rural unions have grown the most under the national security state and have, by and large, been most successfully organized by the opposition. This organizing has been carried out in close association with the Catholic church's organizations for defense of landless peasants and the rights of squatters (*posseiros*) to their land, and with the rural *comunidades de base*. The rural union organizers have been more successful than their urban counterparts in functioning democratically within the official union structure. Unlike the urban federations, many rural union-federations have fought vigorously in defense of farm workers' rights and for the right to land.

The most significant difference, however, is that rural organizers have won control of their confederation, CONTAG. José Francisco da Silva was elected president of CONTAG in 1968, and was re-elected in 1971, 1974, 1977, and again in 1980. Under his leadership, CONTAG has encouraged the organization of representative federations and local rural unions all over Brazil. National meetings have been held to establish priorities. The Third National Congress of agricultural workers took place in May 1979, marked by a decision to continue to defend the individual rural worker and teach the principles of free trade-unionism, but the congress emphasized especially the reinforcement of all forms of collective organization in the countryside. This new role reflects the increase in land conflicts, the move among landless peasants to gain rights to land, among squatters for the right to retain their land, and among migrant farm workers (*bóias-frias*) to achieve regular work benefits and health guarantees.

In 1980 CONTAG officially represented 21 federations of rural workers, one territorial branch (in Rondônia), and 2,500 rural locals. Total membership reached over 6.8 million, out of a rural population of 11.5 million that fell within the category eligible for union membership.[30] As may be seen in table 21, in 1978 Brazil's urban industrial workers' unions counted 4,271,450 members. White-collar professional unions counted some 146,300 members. Because they are not allowed to form trade unions, government employees and civil servants have separate associations, which are not always legally recognized. Thus, including urban industrial workers, white-collar professionals, and rural or agricultural workers, in 1978 there were over 11,316,000 unionized workers out of an economically active population estimated at approximately 40 million.[31]

Not all of these are active in the new union movement. Its strength can be approximated by considering the unions present at the First Conference of the Working Class (Primeira Conferência das Classes Trabalhadoras, CONCLAT), held in São Paulo in August 1981 to discuss concerns, draft a common program of action and a list of specific demands, and, above all, elect an executive committee to organize a second national conference to be held in 1982 or 1983 in preparation for the development of a central union organization, autonomous from the Labor Code framework. A total of 1,126 unions were represented at the first CONCLAT, of which 384 were rural unions and 480 were urban.[32] There were more than 5,247 delegates, indicating the active participation of approximately 24 percent of Brazilian workers' unions in the new union movement. The government's "official" trade union structure boycotted the meeting.

The resurgence of the labor movement dates from two events of great symbolic importance. In August 1977 the government made the startling admission that official inflation statistics for 1973 and 1974 had been manipulated. Since these statistics are the basis for the calculation of wage increases, the result had been a 34.1 percent real wage loss for workers during the period. The São Bernardo do Campo Metalworkers' Union organized a campaign to force the government to pay back wages to make up the loss. The "campaign of the 34.1 percent" brought together a number of groups in an ongoing alliance.[33] It was also important in arousing public opinion and as a symbolic test of the effectiveness of the union's organizational structure. Thus it helped to lay the foundation for the strikes that would follow in 1978, 1979, and 1980.[34]

The other key event was the Congress of Industrial Workers held in Rio de Janeiro and controlled by the government through the National Confederation of Workers in Industry (CNTI).[35] This meeting brought the conflict between officials of government-approved unions (the *pelegos*)[36] and the emerging leadership out into the open. The conference also provided a meeting place for the different opposition unions. The discussions that took place there gave rise to the first document to state the principles of the new urban union movement, the "Carta de Princípios."[37]

The document summarized the movement's concerns as follows:

National Problems: (a) the right to elect political representatives by direct popular vote, including senators, governors, and the president; (b) repeal of the legislation of exception; (c) guarantees of freedom of the press and of expression; (d) freedom of association without restrictions or controls; (e) repeal of the emergency measures and the safeguards [that give temporary extra powers to the president]; (f) political amnesty; (g) respect for human rights; (h) return to a state of law.

National Development Policy: (a) the end of the wage-squeeze policies, with a redistribution of income and a just wage to be freely negotiated in collective bargaining with employers; (b) agrarian reform; (c) control of the activities of multinational corporations; (d) adoption of regional development policies with emphasis on labor-intensive investments; (e) minimum-wage levels high enough to support a worker and his or her family.

Trade Union Activity and Organization: (a) modification of the Labor Code to provide for union autonomy from state control; (b) the right to strike and the repeal of all restrictive legislation; (c) the right to collective bargaining and the end of the individual contracting of workers; (d) recognition of union shop stewards for shop floor representation, with guarantee of job security; (e) freedom to associate with international trade-union organizations without government authorization.[38]

With the metalworkers' strike of 1978, the labor movement emerged as a major power in the political arena. By Brazilian standards, the metalworkers were among the best-paid workers in the country in 1978. The hourly wage of an autoworker in Brazil, however, was the equivalent of 60 cents (US), as opposed to $8.65 in the United States and Canada (see table 23). The

Table 23
Hourly Wage in Automobile Industry, 1978
(U.S. Dollars)

United States	$8.65
Sweden	6.20
West Germany	5.65
Japan	4.30
France	3.50
England	3.45
Italy	2.90
Mexico	2.05
Venezuela	1.60
Peru	1.50
Colombia	.80
South Korea	.80
Brazil	.60
Argentina	.55
Philippines	.35

Source: *Movimento* (31 July 1978), p. 11; data from International Metalworkers' Federation.

metalworkers of São Paulo Bernardo do Campo and Diadema knew that they were in a privileged position in Brazil's productive system and were keenly aware of their power to "bring the system to a halt." They did not, however, behave like a "labor aristocracy" and felt a deep responsibility to use their advantage for the benefit of others.[39]

Because of their strategic position in the productive system, they could take initiatives that other unions could not. In São Bernardo do Campo, workers had been discussing the Labor Code, the strike law, wage policies, and possible forms of opposition for a number of years and had come to three principal conclusions with regard to past opposition strategies. First, the 1968 Osasco and Contagem strikes had failed primarily because organization, consciousness, and, thus, degree of participation, were not well enough developed to force a negotiation. Second, nothing in the strike laws indicated that workers who went to work but did not turn on their machines were legally on strike. Finally, metalworkers were not included in the list of categories considered "essential" and thus specifically prohibited from striking under the National Security Law. These observations shaped the action that was taken.

After ten years of apparent quiescence, 100 workers at Saab-Scania, a producer of buses and trucks in São Bernardo do Campo, went to work, punched in, sat down in front of their machines, and crossed their arms. Within a week, all 1,800 Saab-Scania workers and workers from 23 other corporations had joined the strike. By the second week, 77,950 workers were on strike in Santo André, São Bernardo, São Caetano, and Diadema— the ABCD region, the industrial heart of Brazil. In every instance, the workers punched their cards, sat in front of their machines, and crossed their arms in silence. Their demands included a 20 percent raise over the government's official index, and the right of their union to bargain directly with management.

Caught by surprise, the military government was temporarily stunned into inaction. The employers, on the other hand, were suffering heavy losses every day the strike continued, so they began a de facto collective bargaining process, out of which came a settlement. On 31 May the Metalworkers' Union of São Bernardo do Campo and Diadema signed an agreement with the employers' representatives for staggered wage increases, which, by February 1979, would add up to 24.5 percent more than the wages of April 1978.[40]

In subsequent debate and analysis of the strike, workers drew several lessons. The wage policy had been broken de facto, by actions that the national security state could not stop. The old union demand, to have readjustments every three months in order to have salaries keep pace with inflation, was becoming a reality with the staggered raises. The strike movement had proved that the strike legislation could be bypassed by strong, united action by workers and that such a movement could force the government to consider their demands. Finally, workers found that they were able to force corporations to negotiate and carry on independent collective bargaining.[41]

According to Luís Inácio Lula da Silva, what had happened was the consequence of the mature organization of a class from the base. The union's role was to coordinate the proposals that came from the workers themselves. The workers had discovered that it was much easier to negotiate when "the machines had stopped" and intended to recover their main bargaining weapon—the strike:

We cannot consider what happened to have been abnormal. The strike was perfectly normal. It was a manifestation of the working class, which only wanted to show that it does in fact exist, and is a living part of the nation. As such, it must be respected and considered.

The strike was legitimate. Perhaps, from lack of habit, many people believed that the strike was abnormal, fantastic. In reality, it was only the legitimate use of a bargaining weapon of a class. The fact that it was judged illegal has no validity, for the worker made strikes legal from the moment that so many practiced their real human right.[42]

Other industrial workers were quick to follow the lead of São Bernardo. Over a nine-week period, 245,935 workers were on strike in the State of São Paulo in nine different cities (see table 24). From the São Paulo

Table 24
Metalworkers' Strikes, São Paulo, 12 May–13 July 1978

Week	No. Factories Going on Strike	No. Workers Going on Strike	No. Towns Affected*	Total Workers on Strike
1	24	60,500	3	60,500
2	12	17,450	3	77,950
3	21	17,990	5	95,940
4	27	29,470	9	125,410
5	38	39,694	9	165,104
6	32	22,967	9	188,071
7	17	23,441	9	211,512
8	21	19,803	9	231,315
9	21	14,620	9	245,935

Source: *Movimento* (19 June 1982), p. 8, and (17 July 1978), p. 15; *O Estado de São Paulo; Folha de São Paulo; Jornal do Brasil.*

*First and second weeks, Santo André, São Bernardo, São Caetano; third week, São Paulo, Osasco; fourth week to ninth, Jandira, Taboão da Serra, Cotia, Campinas.

metalworkers, the movement spread to other states and to other job categories.

It is important to note that middle-class and white-collar workers suffered from the same wage-squeeze policies as did blue-collar workers. For example, in 1978 teachers in the prosperous states of São Paulo and Paraná earned the equivalent of $226 (US) per month. Doctors fared no better: as health care employees of the state medical system and private clinics contracted to the state, they earned around $300 (US) per month.[43] Bank workers were also in a difficult situation: in 1978, 57 percent of them earned around $187 per month.[44] Hence, white-collar workers began to organize in unions and associations and to strike for collective bargaining and better working conditions. As we can see from table 25, by the end of the year there had been a total of 539,037 workers out on strike—including middle-class, white-collar, blue-collar, and agricultural workers.

An analysis of the demands of the strikes, their results, and the government reaction to them (see table A-9, Appendix, for details) leads to the conclusion that strikers were primarily concerned with improving their wage levels. Most strikes won less than the workers had initially demanded but still achieved some improvement. In most cases, faced with a growing number of strikers from different social classes and caught by surprise, the

Table 25
Strikes in 1978

Sector	No. Strikes	No. Strikers
Metallurgical	5	357,043
Port	1	1,200
Urban transport	1	170
Tobacco	1	400
Glass	1	450
Ceramics	1	2,000
Textiles	1	5,390
Chemical	1	2,750
Banks	1	10,000
Health	1	7,500
Primary & secondary teaching	3	138,634
University teaching	1	800
Medicine (doctors & residents)	5	11,500
Rural	1	1,200
Total	24	539,037

Sources: *O Globo; Jornal do Brasil; Folha de São Paulo; Ultima Hora; Movimento; Veja; Isto E; Em Tiempo; ABCD Jornol;* and union newspapers and pamphlets.
Note: The following states were involved: São Paulo, Minas Gerais, Rio de Janeiro, Bahia, Paraná, Rio Grande do Sul, and Brasília (Distrito Federal). The actual number of factories on strike is of course much greater than the number of strikes. In Brazil, a union calls a strike for its entire territory, which can involve up to thirteen thousand factories (as in São Paulo).

government adopted a neutral stance and chose not to interfere in the negotiations. Police did, however, break up picket lines. In some cases, as with the Santos port workers, the slowdown never got off the ground. The dockworkers were in the "essential" category and met with the most severe military repression of the year. In the case of public employees (health workers and primary and secondary school teachers), the government reacted with immediate and severe coercion. The state's repressive forces threatened the employees and threatened to intervene in their unions or associations. However, no union interventions were in fact carried out as a result of the 1978 strikes.

The bank workers were singled out for special treatment. Not only was their strike severely repressed, but they were made the target of a new piece of strike-control legislation. On 4 August 1978 the Geisel government issued Decree-Law No. 1632, which included bank workers in the "essential" category. The law also raised the penalties for infringement of the prohibition on strikes in essential activities to include a thirty-day suspension, which could be followed by dismissal with just cause, meaning the total loss of social security rights for the workers dismissed. These penalties were to be applied in addition to indictment under the National Security Law, which could carry a sentence of up to twenty years in prison.[45]

During the 1978 strikes, the São Bernardo and Diadema Metalworkers' Union emerged as a clear leader in the overall labor movement. But as the year ended, it became clear that the in-factory strikes would no longer be tolerated:

The bosses were now ready for these. . . . In São Paulo, by November 1978 the bosses knew that they had to fight the strikes and they came up with a clear orientation: if workers stopped work inside the factory, no meals were served and a lockout was set up in order to force them out onto the streets. Once in the streets, the police can be called to resolve a disturbance. So in São Paulo after 1978 we could no longer use the strategy of strikes inside the factory.[46]

The employers carried out their plans. In 1979 strikers were forced out onto the streets, so workers had to organize picket lines and confront the police there. A new format of organization and preparation for strikes developed with the 1979 strike of the metalworkers of São Bernardo and Diadema.

Before the 1979 metalworkers' strike in São Bernardo, large assemblies of workers were held in the local soccer stadium, Vila Euclides. At these meetings, general strategy for the strike was discussed and votes were taken to guarantee the metalworkers' participation in the movement. Once the actual strike was called, the metalworkers lost important institutional support, when the government intervened in the three largest unions involved in the strike movement, those of São Bernardo, Santo André, and São Caetano. The Catholic church offered the Cathedral of São Bernardo do Campo as a temporary, unofficial union headquarters. However, the combination of attacks on the picket lines and the lack of adequate institutional infrastructure discouraged many workers. Slowly, more and more of them returned to work. A vote was taken to establish a forty-five-day truce for negotiations, at the end of which an agreement for a 63 percent wage increase was signed. The government then restored the unions to the elected leadership.

This strike generated one of the largest strike waves in Brazilian history. As can be seen in the summary in table 26, over three million workers participated in strike actions that reached fifteen of the twenty-three states. The range of demands, events, and government reactions is presented in table A-10 of the Appendix.

The scope of the workers' demands had expanded significantly. Virtually all categories remained interested primarily in improved wages and working conditions; in addition, however, some groups showed interest in pressuring Congress for approval of regulatory legislation. The teachers, for example,

Table 26
Strikes in 1979

Sector	No. Strikes	No. Strikers
Metallurgical	27	958,435
Urban transport	19	443,160
Construction	8	303,000
Wheat mills	1	1,500
Textiles	2	3,350
Baking	1	500
Food industry	1	1,500
Clubs	1	3,000
Ceramics	1	1,050
Grave digging	1	1,000
Gasoline	1	3,000
Gas	1	8,000
Paper and cardboard	1	2,000
Garbage collection	4	10,000
Mining	4	34,600
Electric	1	10,000
Commercial establishments	1	40,000
Health	1	10,000
Banks	4	105,000
Security	3	20,000
Primary and secondary teaching	16	752,000
University teaching	4	14,139
Public employees	5	387,998
Medicine (doctors)	1	2,400
Journalism	1	1,500
Rural	3	90,162
Total	113	3,207,994

Sources: *O Globo; Jornal do Brasil; Folha de São Paulo; O Estado de São Paulo; Ultima Hora; Movimento; Veja; Isto E; Em Tempo, ABCD Jornal*, and union newspapers.
Note: The strikes involved the following states: São Paulo, Rio de Janeiro, Bahia, Pernambuco, Paraíba, Espírito Santo, Paraná, Santa Catarina, Minas Gerais, Goiás, Mato Grosso, Ceará, Rio Grande do Norte, Rio Grande do Sul, and Brasília (Distrito Federal).

continued to demand approval of the Teachers' Statute, a proposed law under consideration in Congress to regulate the profession and provide increased benefits and promotion plans.

Doctors wanted to come under the general labor legislation so that they could receive benefits and work under regular contract. Fiat workers struck against layoffs and later called a second strike to force the corporation to rehire one of their main section leaders as well as to guarantee job security for the factory committee. Such demands meant that the workers were increasingly coming up against the limitations of the Labor Code. Questions of job security, job guarantees for members of factory committees, and the right to have shop floor union representation were all direct challenges to the labor laws. Although most employers were willing to discuss wage levels and working conditions, in no case were they willing to negotiate matters of union representation or job security.

The employer's inflexibility on these questions was reflected in their actions. Conditions for organizing workers became increasingly difficult in 1979, as employers used discretionary firings of labor leaders to weaken workers' organizations. This was particularly true in the automobile industry, where, by 1979, the employee turnover rate in the industry in São Paulo had reached alarming proportions. Employers also used dismissals to manipulate wage levels: large numbers of workers would be fired before a new contract was to come into effect and new workers hired at a lower starting salary.

Union leaders had frequently denounced such practices in the past. DIEESE research (see figs. 6 and 7) shows that in 1979, almost 75 percent of workers who left their jobs were dismissed and had not left voluntarily, as the corporations had claimed. This explains why job security and the FGTS had become such a central question for workers. As Lula pointed out, there was no point in negotiating better contracts with higher indexes for the workers as long as the corporations could circumvent any agreement simply by increasing turnover in the work force. A worker dismissed by Ford would be hired by Volkswagen or another automobile company to do the same job he or she had done at Ford, but at a lower wage.

Throughout 1979 increased levels of repression were applied against striking teachers and bank workers in particular. The Ministry of Labor intervened in the bank workers' unions in the cities of Rio de Janeiro, São Paulo, and Porto Alegre and removed some of the elected officers of twenty-four other bank workers' unions, particularly in the states of Rio Grande do Sul and Minas Gerais. The president of the Porto Alegre bank workers' union, Olívio Dutra, was imprisoned for over two weeks. The teachers faced the military police and had their association in the state of Rio de Janiero permanently closed down.

In September 1979 the metalworkers of São Paulo voted to call a strike in spite of the opposition of the union president, Joaquim dos Santos Andrade. The strike engendered the most severe government reaction, including the employment of troops to break up picket lines, invasion of local churches to dissolve support meetings, and harassment of striking workers in their own neighborhoods. A confrontation between the military police and strikers at a factory gate resulted in the shooting death of Santos Dias da Silva, one of

Fig. 6. Dismissals and Voluntary Resignations
(Percentage of Year's Total)

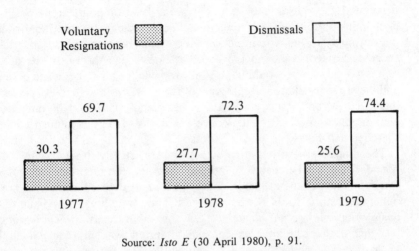

Source: *Isto E* (30 April 1980), p. 91.

Fig. 7. Dismissals and Voluntary Resignations, City of São Paulo

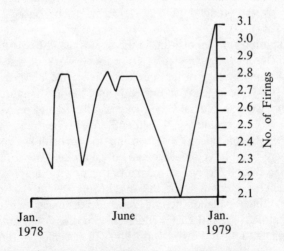

Source: DIEESE. Published in *Veja* (25 July 1979), pp. 100-101.

Note: The relation between the dismissals and voluntary resignations shows how many people were fired by corporations for each person who left voluntarily.

the top Catholic lay union organizers. His death strengthened the Catholic church's position in support of workers' rights and against the violence of the state.

From the point of view of the national security state, 1979 defined the limits of the policy of *abertura*. At the same time as the government negotiated the question of political amnesty with political parties and civilian institutions of the elite sectors, it made it clear that the liberalization did not apply to the working class. Repression became refined and class-specific. Strikes would no longer be tolerated, and the full force of the repressive apparatus would be used to stop challenges to the wage policies and the strike legislation. Repression of the *posseiros* and landless peasants increased in rural areas where there were land conflicts. Claiming to be eliminating criminal elements, police and death squadrons intensified their searches and blitzes in poor districts.

The limits of "strong democracy" were clearly traced within the boundaries of the Doctrine of National Security: certain organized sectors, which challenged the model of development and stressed basic needs over manifest destiny, could not be tolerated. They were pressure points, to be dealt with as internal enemies. On the other hand, the government recognized that the buildup in social tension was in fact potentially explosive. The collective and sometimes violent nature of some of the strikes had frightened state planners, so the government passed Law No. 6708, which provided that wage adjustments, based on the consumer price index would take place every six months, rather than once a year. In addition, unions would now be allowed to engage in direct negotiations with employers over an added percentage raise, to be based on calculated "productivity rates."[47]

The most important innovation in the new wage law was the differential raise for different wage brackets. Only those workers who earned three times the minimum wage or less could receive wage increases greater than the cost of living increase. Workers who earned more than three to ten times the minimum wage would have their wages adjusted on a par with the cost of living index. The remaining 4 percent of wage earners would receive progressively lower raises.[48] According to opposition economists, this supposedly redistributive measure had only a limited "Robin Hood" effect. Since the legislation did not affect capital or profit rates, it amounted to a redistribution of income from the middle classes to the lower classes, without affecting the higher income groups, so the measure backfired in that it spurred already-dissatisfied middle-class professional categories on to further organization and strikes in 1980. In the short run, however, the measure did reduce the tension among the lowest paid workers and contributed to a reduction in the number of strikes by these workers in 1980.

For the opposition as a whole 1979 was a decisive year. First, the working class discovered its power. In the process of supporting the strikers, moreover, a functioning network of alliances was established among grassroots organizations, social-movement organizations linked to the church (including the CEBs), and the labor unions. To this was added the role of the elite opposition in defending the strikers and pressuring the government to return unions to elected officials. In addition, the Catholic church gave decisive support to the ABCD metalworkers in April and May 1979, to the point of allowing them to use the cathedral as temporary union headquarters. In September 1979, Catholic militants of the base and of the union opposition essentially organized and coordinated the São Paulo metalworkers' strike, against the explicit wishes of metalworkers' president. Workers' meetings were held in hundreds of small parishes across the city.

Some of the lingering problem areas for the labor movement were also highlighted in 1979. First, strikes that had been organized with union support had been much too dependent on the top union leadership. There was a need to develop intermediate levels of leadership and alternative strike commands. Second, most strikes had been organized against the wishes of *pelego* union officers or had resulted from spontaneous revolts, which occasionally turned into violent riots and street battles with the police. These strikes did not necessarily imply any political consciousness on the part of the workers involved. Essentially, they represented an explosion of tensions caused by the low wages and extremely exploitative conditions to which workers had been subjected for fifteen years. These strikes lacked effective leadership and an organizational network. In many cases, after a spontaneous strike had broken out, the small group of "authentic" union leaders would be called in to help set up emergency organizational structures and conduct on-the-spot leadership training. For example, when a construction workers' strike in Belo Horizonte became violent, and the *pelego* union president was physically expelled by the workers, Lula, Jacó Bittar, Olívio Dutra, and other union leaders from different states quicky had to set up an alternative organizational structure.

From discussions of the experiences of 1979, workers concluded that stronger connections had to be developed between leadership and rank-and-file. Reliance on individual union leaders, like Lula in São Bernardo do Campo, weakened overall coordination, thereby making it possible to dismantle the movement by arresting a few leaders.[49] Because of this, in 1979 the São Bernardo do Campo Metalworkers' Union began to train middle-level leadership and strike committee personnel and work to raise the consciousness of the workers so that the next phase could proceed without excessive dependence on the primary leadership.

Job security and the right to shop floor union representation became top priorities for the metalworkers. In preparation for further action, the Metalworker's Union of São Bernardo do Campo organized meetings by factory, assemblies in the factory and at union headquarters, study sessions, and debates, to arrive at a consensus on major issues and to elect representatives of various intermediate organization levels. The organizational structure of the Metalworkers' Union of São Bernardo do Campo and Diadema that was set up in 1979 and that would lead the 1980 strike, is presented in figure 8.

When negotiations broke down on 30 March 1980 and the metalworkers of the ABCD region once again decided to strike, the new organizational strategy was applied. The middle-level leadership—the Committee of 450 and the Wage and Mobilization Committee—ran the strike and organized the structures necessary for the next six weeks. This was to ensure that, even with government intervention in the union and arrest of its leadership, the movement would continue.

As in 1979, the metalworkers from São Bernardo and neighboring towns met in the soccer stadium to discuss the strike and vote on questions of planning and implementation. When military troops surrounded and occupied both the stadium and union headquarters, the church again offered facilities for meetings. As in 1979, the São Bernardo union headquarters moved to the backyard of the Cathedral of São Bernardo do Campo. But this time the reaction of the national security state was quick and decisive: the decision to move in with the full force of the repressive apparatus had already been made. This was not to be treated as a strike for better wages, working conditions, and freedom of union organization, for the government had already labeled the metalworkers a pressure point—a segment of the internal enemy that had to be destroyed. The government actually prohibited firms from negotiating with the strikers and threatened corporations that defied the order with the withdrawal of government credit and tax benefits.

The 1980 metalworkers' strike disclosed the limits of the political opening. Organized popular pressure for participation in government decisions was not to be tolerated when it constituted a threat to the economic development model. A society defined within the strict boundaries of the Doctrine of National Security and Development is one in which any strong manifestation of social and economic grievances is an unacceptable pressure, when it comes from working-class sectors. The more organized the action, and the more popular support it receives, the more it is treated as a threat that must be crushed. Consistent with this doctrine, São Paulo was placed under the command of the Second Army Division, whose commanding general became a virtual governor-administrator. Although a state of emergency was not declared, the effect was the same. Troops occupied the cities affected by the strike, including a large part of greater São Paulo. Maneuvers were carried out by the state police, the military police, and the army, under the command of the Second Army.

The procedures followed the guidelines outlined in the ESG and ECEME

Fig. 8. Organizational Structure of Metalworkers of São Bernardo do Campo and Diadema

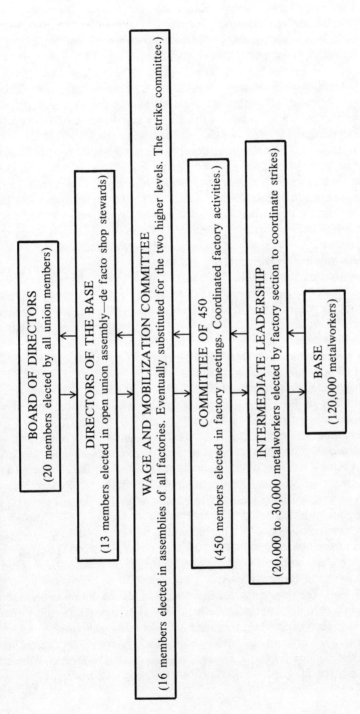

BOARD OF DIRECTORS
(20 members elected by all union members)

DIRECTORS OF THE BASE
(13 members elected in open union assembly—de facto shop stewards)

WAGE AND MOBILIZATION COMMITTEE
(16 members elected in assemblies of all factories. Eventually substituted for the two higher levels. The strike committee.)

COMMITTEE OF 450
(450 members elected in factory meetings. Coordinated factory activities.)

INTERMEDIATE LEADERSHIP
(20,000 to 30,000 metalworkers elected by factory section to coordinate strikes)

BASE
(120,000 metalworkers)

Source: *CooJornal* (June 1980), p. 21.
Note: Arrows indicate information flow, interconnections, and leadership.

training manuals: total army mobilization, occupation of strategic sites, joint attacks on crowds and seizure of top leadership—a veritable kidnapping operation—wherever leaders could be found. Strike leaders were pulled out of meetings in the churches, dragged from the car of the mayor of São Bernardo, and taken from the automobiles of opposition federal deputies and senators who came to São Bernardo to afford a measure of protection with their own parliamentary immunity. Church lawyers such as the president of the Justice and Peace Committee of the Archdiocese of São Paulo, José Carlos Dias, and jurist Dalmo Dallari, were also arrested without warrants. In the blitz against the striking metalworkers, the military employed heavy weapons, armored vehicles, and army helicopters to support infantry troops and military police. Strike leaders were kept in prison and for a while were even held incommunicado. Worker resistance that emphasized nonviolence was organized.[50] Their actions contrasted sharply with the violence of the state, further undermining the legitimacy of the government's action and discrediting the state's argument that the movement was inherently subversive.

The Catholic church publicly supported the workers' claim that the strike was legitimate and challenged the legitimacy of the state's laws of exception. By 1980 the church was deeply committed to the metalworkers. The hierarchy, represented by Cardinal Arns and Bishops Mauro Morelli and Claudio Hummes, considered the workers' basic demands legitimate. Their actions were reinforced by the CNBB's expressions of solidarity in the name of the bishops' conference as a whole.

With the encouragement of the Catholic hierarchy, militants in the *comunidades de base* and the various grass-roots pastorals worked with other opposition groups—including opposition federal deputies and senators, members of the Brazilian Bar Association, and other organizations—to coordinate a vast support network. A strike fund was established, with volunteers working to collect material support for families of strikers. The network's headquarters was in the Cathedral of São Bernardo do Campo. There, workers, Catholic militants, and other volunteers wrapped food in packages calculated to support a family for one week. Money and food collected throughout Brazil were sent to São Paulo, and in this way, the strike fund was able to distribute an estimated six tons of food per week over the six-week period of the strike. Although this effort reached only some 15 percent of the affected families, it was crucial for the maintenance of the strike. Even more important, it cemented the alliance of opposition sectors in support of the labor movement.[51] The effectiveness of this alliance between secular and church-related grass-roots organizations was also evident in the blockades set up in all neighborhoods to stop "scabs" from leaving their homes for the factories. These blockades made it possible for a strike of some 200,000 workers to be conducted without picket lines.

Throughout 1980 the alliance of the grass-roots organizations, the church, the labor movements, and opposition sectors engaged in formal politics became more firmly established. Its importance was demonstrated during strikes such as those of primary and secondary school teachers in the Northeast and in Minas Gerais, and especially in the sugarcane plantation workers' strike in Pernambuco. The latter involved around 240,000 sugarcane workers spread over hundreds of local farms in different parts of the state and thus particularly vulnerable to threats of dismissal and repression. The difficulties in organizing such a large number of rural workers made it necessary to form a coalition of forty-two different rural unions and the church's rural *comunidades de base* and the land pastoral, which was responsible for planning. The network proved its efficiency, as the strike began and ended on the day and at the hour that it had determined.[52]

In 1980 there was a sharp drop in the overall number of workers on strike (see table 27). This drop was due to a combination of the effects of violent repression and the fear that the growing recession would lead to unemployment, a fear aggravated by the corporations' practice of firing striking workers and made more effective by the fact that the new wage policy of 1979 slightly diminished the desperation of workers who were employed. On the other hand, there was an increase in the number of strikes in middle-class (i.e., professional) sectors for better salaries and improved conditions.

The 1980 strikes had a distinctive character: they were more carefully organized and less spontaneous, and there was more extensive participation of the membership in the decisions affecting the movement; and, they were generally less strictly concerned with economic questions and took on a definite political importance. Demands for job security guarantees, for shop floor union representation, for the enforcement of legal rights and previous contracts, and for worker control of government funds became increasingly common (see table A-11, Appendix, for details).

The participants' level of political consciousness was demonstrated by their insistence on democratization of the work process. Workers asked for the right to elect the section chief, run safety committees, and organize factory committees. Luís Inácio Lula da Silva stated part of the reason for such change:

In 1980 we understood that it was not enough to ask for a 10 percent raise. It was clear that it was not a question of getting 10 or 20 percent more. That will not solve the problem of the workers. So we demanded improvements that were noneconomic: for example, job security, a reduction of the work week. We wanted to control the process of choosing the section heads and have the right to free access by union officials to the plants. In 1980 the last issue of concern to workers was the actual percentage raise in their salaries. What had been the most important point of discussion was the least important by 1980.[53]

Table 27
Strikes in 1980

Sector	No. of Strikes[a]	No. of Strikers
Metallurgical[b]	2	244,500
Port	1	12,500
Oil and refinery	1	2,000
Construction	1	10,000
Primary and secondary teaching[c]	3	110,000
University teaching[d]	26	39,200
Medicine (residents)[e]	15	6,500
Rural[f]	1	240,000
Total	50	664,700

Sources: *O Globo; Jornal do Brasil; Folha de São Paulo; Ultima Hora; Movimento; Veja; Isto E; Em Tempo; ABCD Jornal*; union newspapers and leaflets.

Notes: [a]I have counted as one a strike action called by a union either for a general strike or for a particular establishment or factory. Thus, the metallurgical strike of the ABCD region has been counted as one, although it affected a large area and a number of factories. On the other hand, the doctors' strikes were individually called by different unions and thus counted individually.
[b]General strike in ABCD region in São Paulo; involved three towns and approximately 150 corporations.
[c]General strikes of primary and secondary teachers in three states; affected most schools in all the municipalities in the states.
[d]The strike in Rio de Janeiro affected five universities. The general strike of university professors of federal universities affected nineteen universities in fifteen plus eight other learning establishments connected to the Ministry of Education.
[e]Affected fifteen states and most of the state hospitals in each state.
[f]Strike of sugar plantation workers primarily in the state of Pernambuco; organized by a coalition of forty-two rural unions, the *pastoral da terra* and the rural *comunidades de base*.

Finally, workers were becoming increasingly concerned with political organization and with the strengthening of opposition political parties. The question of union freedom was understood to be linked to the problem of political participation in the decisions of government.

The period that followed the great strikes of 1978, 1979, and 1980 would be primarily characterized by participation in the building of political parties and in the search for alternative in-plant organization. The unions became concerned with democratization of the work place and engaged in negotiations for the establishment of factory committees. Growing unemployment switched the emphasis from strikes for wages to actions geared at ensuring job security. The limited strike actions that occurred in 1981 and 1982 were meant to force companies to rehire fired employees.

In 1981 and 1982 the deep recession in Brazil's economy affected the labor union movement's ability to organize. Growing unemployment made it primordial for unions to find alternatives for the organization of the unemployed and to guarantee job security. Hence, unions placed increasing emphasis on in-plant union representation, through factory committees and shop stewards, to establish influence in the hiring and layoff criteria as well as to present alternative policies for increasing the level of employment. To raise job availability unions proposed a shortened work week, which would allow corporations affected by the economic slowdown to keep workers rather than lay off large numbers. Strike actions became closely issue-connected and were called by workers as a means of enforcing specific demands that management refused to negotiate. As an example, strikes in 1981 and 1982 were called to reinforce a demand for an end to layoffs and to effect the rehiring of laid-off workers. The major strike of 1981 involved nine thousand workers of the Ford plant in São Bernardo do Campo. That strike was called to pressure management to negotiate a factory committee with the union. Taking advantage of a visit of Ford executives to the plant, the workers closed the premises and occupied the factory until management agreed to talk about the free election of a factory representative committee.

The success of the formal agreement that set up the Ford Factory Committee, in turn, led to similar actions and negotiations for factory committees in other plants in São Bernardo do Campo and Diadema. In December of 1982 the election of the Volkswagen Factory Committee marked a major advance for the Brazilian labor movement. The Volkswagen plant in São Bernardo, with thirty thousand workers, is the largest in the country. Nine thousand workers, or 89 percent of signed union members, voted to choose a seventeen-person committee composed of three representatives of the office staff and fourteen of production-line workers. The new agreement replaced a statute that the company had imposed on the workers at the end of 1980. At that time the union executive committee, headed by Lula, was on trial under the national security laws for participation in the 1980 strike, and the Ministry of Labor was running the union. Volkswagen took advantage of the situation to undermine the union's influence by holding elections for a factory committee controlled by management. The vast majority of the workers boycotted the elections and the committee that was elected. In the new agreement the company promised to allow union activity within the factory and union representation on the floor.

The process of direct labor-management bargaining gained new impetus, and unions directly negotiated such contract issues as length of working day, criteria for hiring and firing, production rate, and in-plant representation in the form of factory committees and shop stewards. It is perhaps in the post-1980 period that unions have most advanced in actual achievement of goals and major union organizational matters. Although officially shop floor representation is still considered illegal, in practice major corporations have come to direct agreement with the unions to establish freely elected representation and allow circulation and union organization within the factory. Direct bargaining between labor and management has become established as a parallel system of negotiation outside of the government-controlled labor court system. In reality, major rights for independent union organization and improved labor conditions have been won.

The *Abertura*'s Controlled Liberalization

According to General Golbery, at that time the chief policy ideologue of the national security state, by 1980 the state had three primary areas of concern. The first was the tendency for all decisions, both administrative and political, to be centralized in the executive. The bureaucratic entanglements that such a situation produced had become a growing problem for the state: given such centralization, unimportant matters automatically became state concerns. "We marched, unconsciously, toward maximum centralization, side by side with maximum inefficiency, in a process of concentration that could—in its extreme—be compared with the phenomenon of 'black holes,' which have been detected by modern astronomy, and where even the light of the star itself cannot escape the growing gravitational force."[54] To solve the problem it was necessary to decentralize and share decision-making power not only with states and municipalities but with other groups in civil society.

The extreme centralization of the intelligence networks and security forces, caused by a "rigidity in the system of social control," provoked this process. Centralization threatened a rupture of the "social structure, which became subjected to intolerable pressures, caught, as it were, in the limits of centralization-decentralization of the state."[55] The pressure building up in the social structure endangered the credibility of the state; thus, the liberalization policy had to be carried forward and more flexible forms of social control developed. On the other hand, Golbery continued to emphasize the limits of "strong democracy." He did not favor the inclusion of previously excluded sectors, whose participation would require structural modification of the state and of the economic model.[56] A solution required the development of mechanisms that were flexible enough to co-opt the organized elite sectors of the opposition but sufficiently coercive to curb "permissiveness" with regard to the growing social movement.

Golbery considered the second obstacle to the state's successful institutionalization to be the bipolar nature of the government-opposition confrontation. By definition, the groups in power were considered by the voters to be "government." The rest was the opposition. Whereas the opposition clearly contained extremely heterogeneous currents, the bipolar character of the highly centralized state neutralized those differences. The solution, which was aimed at disarticulating the opposition system, was a plural political party system.[57] General Golbery recognized that the MDB was a conglomerate of diverse opposition groups whose only available political channel was the single legal opposition party. It was in the long-term interests of the national security state to disaggregate these organizations; this could be accomplished by ending the MDB.

Failure to come to terms with all these questions, Golbery warned, would eventually risk the end of the entire system.[58] What was needed was a careful master plan for a political opening of the system sufficient to allow steam to escape from the "pressure cooker." This plan, devised by government planners, followed a carefully established timetable.[59]

Political Amnesty

The first step toward the release of social pressure was the granting of partial political amnesty in 1979. This measure was to allow the venting of political opinion while disarticulating a vast social movement, which had been built around the issue of amnesty for prisoners of conscience. Political amnesty had been an opposition demand ever since Institutional Act No. 1. The movement around the demand had grown such that by 1978 the national security state could no longer ignore it.[60] The amnesty movement had fostered debates, organized marches, demonstrations, rallies, and had lobbied in Congress for a bill that would grant amnesty to all prisoners and to anyone who had been purged under any of the three principal institutional acts and their successors. The fact that the acts themselves were in the process of being revoked made it difficult for the state to avoid granting amnesty.

The Amnesty Bill of 1979 was the product of intense negotiations with the opposition. What emerged was a distinct compromise between opposition pressure and military hard-line sentiment.[61] On the one hand, the bill did not grant amnesty to those who had been involved in the armed struggle and were charged with what the government defined as "blood crimes." Neither did it immediately free those political prisoners who had been sentenced under the National Security Law for attempting to reorganize an illegal party. Members of the armed forces who had been purged for political reasons would not be allowed to return to the service, but would receive full retirement pay instead of partial pensions. Public employees, diplomatic personnel, university professors, and members of the judiciary would be allowed to return to their jobs pending the decision of a special investigation committee. More seriously, the Amnesty Bill of 1979 included a blanket pardon for members of the repressive apparatus who had been involved in torture. This provision was a clear victory for the hard-line sectors: it eliminated the possibility of criminal indictment of those accused of torture and would inhibit investigation into the activities of the repressive apparatus.

In spite of these limitations, however, the Amnesty Bill of 1979 represented a real gain insofar as it allowed all exiles to return to the country and all political leaders to regain their political rights. The Ineligibility Law was modified to allow those who had been granted political amnesty to run for political office. The leadership that had been removed from the political process was consequently able to participate again in politics. In addition, in the long run, all political prisoners were released after individual consideration of their cases. It should be stressed, however, that the bill was retroactive; it did not eliminate trials under the National Security Law and the real possibility of new prisoners of conscience.

The Party Reform Bill of 1979 and New Political Parties

The party system created by the Second Institutional Act had been intended to ensure a smoothly functioning, cooperative relationship between the military rulers, a government party, and a "loyal opposition." Since both government (ARENA) and opposition (MDB) parties were created by the state, such "cooperation" was at the outset easily achieved: the legislature was composed, as a popular saying put it, of a "Yes" party and a "Yes, Sir" party.

With the passage of time, however, the MDB increasingly brought together and expressed real currents of dissent and resistance to state policies. By 1979 the civilian-military coalition in power perceived in the electoral growth of the MDB a substantial threat. Studies by the SNI and other governmental agencies indicated that, in spite of the new electoral regulations, it was likely that the opposition would win control of Congress, the state assemblies, and even many of the municipal governments in the next elections. Hence it had become necessary, as General Golbery explicitly acknowledged, to attempt to divide and fragment the opposition and to control more carefully the organization of political parties. It was, moreover, important to move quickly to reshape the party system while the government still held a majority in Congress. The Party Reform Bill of 1979, passed over the loud protests of the MDB, must thus be seen as part of the master plan to which Golbery referred in his speech to the ESG.[62] The provisions of this bill redefined the landscape of formal politics and revealed quite clearly the major goal of the state: to assure government control of the opposition without sacrificing the legitimation advantages of "free" elections.

The Party Reform Bill abolished the MDB and ARENA.[63] It was expected (correctly) that members of the government party could, with relative ease, be kept together to form a new party and would, moreover, see electoral advantage in the change of name. Thus members of the old ARENA were able to shed their identification with unpopular state policies and immediately reform as the Partido Democrático Social (PDS, Social

Democratic party). Members of the MDB, in contrast, had strong reasons to maintain their identity as a growing and unified movement. Hence the announcement of the government's intention to abolish the parties was met by widespread resolve to see the MDB "reborn like the phoenix from its ashes" on the very day after its forced extinction. To make this more difficult, the government endeavored to force a change of name by stipulating in the bill that names that did not include the word *party* were prohibited.[64] Predictably, the opposition responded to this provision by merely attaching the word *party* to their old name, becoming the Partido do Movimento Democrático Brasileiro (PMDB, Party of the Brazilian Democratic Movement). Continuity was further emphasized by printing the *P* in light colors and the *MDB* in dark, contrasting colors in all party publications.

Whereas the Party Reform Bill attempted to divide and fragment the political expression of the more conservative sectors of the broad opposition alliance, it sought to exclude altogether the more radical voice of the new popular movement. Already, trade union leaders and members of grass-roots organizations and of *comunidades de base* had taken steps toward the creation of a Partido dos Trabalhadores (PT, Workers' party). The Party Reform Bill sought to stop this by prohibiting "the use of a term that elicits an affiliation by appealing to religious beliefs or feelings of class or race."[65] It was hoped that the Supreme Electoral Tribunal would refuse to register the Workers' party on the grounds that it was class-based, but the PT managed to argue successfully that its membership included peasants and members of the middle class as well as workers, and that its appeal was based on its program rather than on class affiliation.

More generally, the Party Reform Bill of 1979 introduced a series of complex regulations that had to be followed by a political association in order to be registered as a political party. The first stipulation required a party to hold regional conventions in at least nine states, and municipal conventions in at least one fifth of the total municipalities in each of the nine states.[66] In addition, the municipal conventions could be held only in municipalities where a minimum number of members were already affiliated to the party. This minimum number was calculated according to a complex formula that favored small municipalities.[67] This last requirement was intended to favor the party that replaced ARENA, for it would have access to federal and state bureaucracies and profit from local bosses and clientelistic relations to organize the required number of municipalities quickly in those states with large numbers of small towns. On the other hand, the states with large municipalities, the traditional stronghold of the opposition, would be more difficult to organize because of larger minimum membership requirements. All of these stipulations had to be fulfilled within twelve months of the enactment of the bill.

Once a party succeeded in being temporarily registered, it must receive 5 percent of the votes in the next congressional election, with at least 3 percent in each of nine states. If the party failed to distribute its votes properly, for example, if it received more than 5 percent of the votes, but lacked the minimum 3 percent in all of the nine states, it would automatically lose all of its congressional and state assembly representation, and the votes cast for it would be considered void.[68] Only after the elections that were scheduled for November 1982 would parties be legally recognized for permanent registration.

In addition, Article 19 of the Party Reform Bill specifically prohibited coalitions between parties for elections to the House of Representatives, the state assemblies, and the municipal chambers. At that time, nothing was said about the possibility of party alliances for the gubernatorial and senatorial elections.[69]

The difficulties placed in the way of registering a political party forced the various opposition sectors to engage actively in party organization at both the formal and grass-roots levels, an activity that involved the efforts of thousands of party militants over the next two years. The initiative of the state in dissolving the MDB and ARENA while erecting obstacles to the organization of new parties threw the opposition into considerable disarray. The years after the Party Reform Bill of 1979 would be marked by internal discussion and debate on the best path to follow. Major opposition sectors defended the "democratic front" alliance, arguing that the sole alternative was to remain together in the one political party, which had been born "like the phoenix" from the extinct MDB. More conservative sectors of the opposition, however, viewed with interest the new possibility of acting as a transition government. The military government carefully wooed these sectors with the offer to negotiate a "new social pact" and allow the formation of transition conservative civilian governments. Hence, these sectors wished to separate from more liberal or leftist members of the opposition so that they could guarantee their ideological clearance by the hard-line sectors of the military—a clearance that would be necessary if they were to play an important transition role in government. Finally, working-class sectors of the opposition saw a new opportunity to build a grass-roots party more identified with labor and class concerns and open to the participation of workers. The debate deepened, with opposition members seeking to form ideologically defined political parties to tie together the levels of formal and informal politics and bring the grass-roots into the discussion of political alternatives, party organization, party program, and representative mechanisms of internal party democracy.

The Party Reform Bill may have backfired insofar as it accomplished the very politicization of the associations, unions, and other organizations of civil society that General Golbery had specifically wanted to "drive back into their formal roles" and out of politics. The attempt to prevent and control political activity unleashed new opposition energy in ways that the state had neither expected nor intended. The depth of the political-alternatives debate and the effort required to reorganize new political parties after the forced extinction of the MDB and ARENA brought to the grass-roots the discussion of political party organization. The labor unions, peasant organizations, neighborhood associations, and the *comunidades de base* all increasingly participated in the political debates to determine strategy and party alternatives. Far from being removed from politics, therefore, these civil organizations were immersed in it: they were politicized and became actually involved in the work of reorganizing party structures.

On the other hand, the differentiation of positions and the ideological fragmentation of the opposition into different political parties gave the national security state space so that it could retain the initiative in the political arena. While the opposition became entangled in the debates and distracted by the practical work of fulfilling the legal requirements to organize a political party, the state prepared new legislation that would ensure the electoral strength of its support party, the PDS. The disarray of the opposition in the wake of the dissolution of the political parties gave the state sufficient time to elaborate policies that would maintain majority control in Congress and, particularly, in the Electoral College, which was to choose President Figueiredo's successor in 1985.

For the opposition the difficulty with the birth of the political parties lay in the dilemma presented by such a political conjuncture. Whereas, on the one hand, the state held the trump cards by being able to impose other electoral or party modifications to suit its purposes, on the other, the opposition clearly perceived a need to build political parties sufficiently well established to express the will of different classes and to channel demands for the transformation of the political and economic model. These opposition parties should benefit from specific programs so as to elicit the participation and support of increased numbers of people. Hence, although the division into different parties was recognized as a danger, which could weaken the electoral position of the opposition as a whole and allow the PDS to achieve victories in certain states, nonetheless it was still argued by many that there was a pressing need to build political parties that could politically organize the different concerns expressed by the grass-roots movements, the labor unions, and the peasant organizations.

For the most part, the opposition took into account the two different angles of the dilemma. As may be seen in table 28, by October of 1980 all political parties had succeeded in meeting the requirements for temporary registration.[70] As some of its members had predicted, the PMDB did "rise from the ashes like a phoenix" and was successful in organizing almost as

Table 28

Directorates Formed by Political Parties by October 1980, Compared to ARENA and MDB

State	No. of Directorates								No. of Municipalities	20% of Municipalities[a]
	ARENA	MDB	PDS	PMDB	PP	PDT	PTB	PT		
Acre	12	6	—	10	—	—	—	3	12	3
Alagoas	94	40	26	37	—	—	19	—	94	19
Amazonas	44	27	43	—	—	—	11	—	44	9
Bahia	336	222	310	102	97	—	—	—	336	68
Ceará	141	119	136	77	33	—	—	31	141	29
Espírito Santo	53	53	53	51	—	18	14	14	53	11
Goiás	223	221	218	211	—	—	—	46	223	45
Maranhão	130	119	42	34	—	30	—	30	130	26
Mato Grosso	93	84	54	33	26	14	8	—	38	8
Mato Grosso do Sul[b]	—	—	64	51	—	16	11	17	55	11
Minas Gerais	722	420	149	166	150	—	—	199	722	145
Paraná	83	42	78	43	20	20	18	—	83	17
Paraíba	171	116	119	80	65	—	—	—	171	35
Pará	290	289	302	207	64	61	65	—	291	59
Pernambuco	164	102	137	101	—	45	44	—	164	33
Piauí	114	49	102	41	59	—	—	25	114	23
Rio de Janeiro	63	64	59	40	43	23	16	11	64	13
Rio Grande do Norte	150	131	120	30	55	—	—	29	150	30
Rio Grande do Sul	232	232	227	216	47	145	—	45	232	47
Santa Catarina	197	177	195	150	—	143	—	45	197	40

São Paulo	571	418	560	410	194	43	128	130	571	115
Sergipe	74	48	72	37	16	—	—	—	74	15
Total	3,957	3,066	2,979	2,127	869	558	334	625	3,959	792

Source: *Movimento* (3–9 November 1980), p. 4.

Notes: Territories were not included because they are of little electoral import. Temporary registration for each small party was based on the number of provisional committees; zonal temporary committees in big cities were not included.

[a] Refers to minimum number of directorates a party must form in each state to obtain registration.

[b] Directorates of ARENA and MDB in present states of Mato Grosso do Sul and Mato Grosso do Norte have been combined because Mato Grosso was a single state before 1980.

many regional and municipal offices in one year as the old MDB had been able to do in fourteen years. It had fulfilled the legal requirements in almost all states by October of 1980 and was established as the largest of the opposition parties and the official inheritor of the majority of the members of the old MDB and of its physical property. The PMDB thus gathered under a single banner groups that ranged from capital owners to labor unions of the new union movement to peasants.

Ideologically, the membership of the PMDB was diverse. It included former members of the military governments as well as those who had participated in armed struggle. It had the support of conservatives and of clandestine leftist parties such as the Movimento Revolucionário 8 de Outubro (MR-8, October 8 Revolutionary Movement), the Partido Comunista do Brasil (PC do B, Communist Party of Brazil), and the Partido Comunista Brasileiro (PCB, Brazilian Communist party). The purpose of such a broad-based alliance, the democratic front, was to defeat the official party, the PDS, in the general elections of 15 November 1982. The PMDB remained in a strategic position always to respond immediately to the individual political initiatives of the government.

The Partido Popular (PP, Popular party) was formed by conservative members of the old MDB who believed in their potential role as a transition civilian government within the context of the *abertura* policy of controlled liberalization. Composed primarily of capital owners and members of the financial sectors, the PP could count on considerable economic support and sufficient political clout to force negotiation and sharing of power. By October 1980 the PP had established its influence and fulfilled the legal requirements for organization in thirteen states. It represented specifically capital owners who intended to increase their voice in the process of government decision-making.

By October 1980 the Partido Trabalhista Brasileiro (Brazilian Labor party, PTB) had organized 20 percent of the municipalities in ten states. It succeeded in joining three important currents of political power: the populist labor politics of Getúlio Vargas, represented by the party's president, Ivete Vargas, a niece of the former president; the São Paulo-based strength of Janismo, a political movement led by former president Jânio Quadros; and the conservative legacy of former governor of Rio de Janeiro Carlos Lacerda. Hence, the union of *trabalhista* labor currents with Janismo in São Paulo and Lacerdismo in Rio de Janeiro would allow the party to show significant strength in the political arena. Its strong opposition language was balanced by a de facto base of practical negotiation, which allowed members of the PTB to vote sometimes with the opposition and sometimes with the government. As such, the party played a pivotal role in the balancing of political negotiation between the state and the opposition.

The Partido Democrático Trabalhista (PDT, Democratic Labor party)

PMDB – broadest based support
PP – financial sector, supp in plenary(?)view
PDT – Labor, Socialism
The *Abertura* Period   219

had organized 20 percent of the municipalities of eleven states by October 1980. Originally formed by exiled members of the opposition led by former governor of Rio Grande do Sul Leonel Brizola, the PDT resulted from the split of the PTB when Ivete Vargas won a suit in the Superior Electoral Tribunal that gave her the right to use the PTB acronym. The PDT attempted to revive a leftist labor-political current and reorganize the remnants of the *trabalhista* heritage of deposed president João Goulart. Of social democratic political makeup the PDT included a small socialist wing, which influenced the final composition of its program. The PDT maintained a strongly centralized organizational format, with top leadership making decisions. Its program aimed at forming a socialist party and emphasized, in particular, the rights of black and Indian minorities as well as minor children.

The Partido dos Trabalhadores (PT, Workers' party) by October 1980 fulfilled the legal requirements in 20 percent of the municipalities in thirteen states. By the end of the following year the PT had achieved the minimum level of organization in one fifth of the municipalities in nineteen states and had a total party membership of close to half a million, making it the third-largest opposition party. The PT was born out of the strikes of 1978, 1979, and 1980, in close alliance with the grass-roots movements in the rural and urban areas and with the social work of progressive Catholics. The idea of forming a party that could channel the demands of various popular movements was discussed in 1979, when the government intervened in the labor union of São Bernardo do Campo and in various bank workers' unions. The intervention highlighted the need to achieve strength in political representation to influence the modification of the Labor Code. More strictly class-based than the other opposition parties, the PT gathered a variety of social movements, members of secular neighborhood councils, *comunidades de base*, peasant and union activists. It also counted on the support of opposition intellectuals and part of the student movement. Perhaps due to the influence of Catholic organizers, the PT followed an organizational format that closely resembled that of the *comunidades de base*. It was composed of cell units organized at the base level—the *núcleos*—charged with the organization and running of the party. Local directorates were formed by members of each *núcleo* in the area. The different directorates then chose a regional coordinating board to form a state committee. All the directorate delegates would participate in a great many informal conventions (both regional and national) to decide matters of interest to all. By this process both the program and electoral platforms of the party could reflect issues that had been discussed in thousands of *núcleos* throughout the country, then voted on in sectoral, regional, and national party conventions. Hence, the PT was the only opposition party to devise a system of essentially parallel organization: on the one hand, it carefully followed all the legal intricacies required in the Party Reform Bill so that it could exist as a recognized party; on the other, administrative and internal policy matters were discussed in the preconventions held prior to the legally required conventions. While fulfilling the organizational stipulations handed down from the top the PT succeeded in eliciting strong participation from the membership at the informal local, state, and national meetings. It emphasized critical consciousness and participation.

The PT defined its function as instrumentalizing the demands of the disenfranchised. It tried to increase the opportunity for political participation to allow the active engagement of persons who had never participated in politics at the formal level. Its intent was to channel demands in order to acquire national political force and increase political representation and power. It did not, however, intend to absorb the actual organizations of the popular movement, as its president, Luís Inácio Lula da Silva, emphasized:

We do not need to have a different way of organizing the base in the parties, in the unions, in the mass movement, or in the church. What we do need is to develop a clear differentiation between the actual institutions. The PT has its own program, its own documents and ideas. The PT does not intend to take over the work of the church or of the union movement. The PT does not want to transform the basic communities, the neighborhood organizations, the youth groups, or the unions. It does not want to turn them into political party committees. What the PT intends to do is to channel all the organizations so as to acquire a national significance. . . . . In terms of actual organization, each sector of society needs to be organized; the church and the basic communities have a specific role to play. The unions and neighborhood organizations also. And the political party has its own role, that of joining them at regional and national levels.[71]

Of all the opposition parties, the PT was perhaps the newest in terms of organization and encouragement of new political participation. All other parties were rooted in traditional political currents and benefited from both experience and past organizational machinery. On the other hand, the PT suffered from a politically inexperienced membership—more accustomed to grass-roots or labor-union militancy than to political party formation— and from a serious lack of financial support and resources. Without the inherited physical and property rights, which the PMDB had, and without the support of economically powerful social groups, which the PP, the PTB, and the PDT had, the Workers' party was limited in its ability to organize. It reserved for itself, therefore, the primordial role of becoming a civic education school where citizens could learn to participate freely and engage in formal political party organization.

The Elections of 15 November 1982
Throughout 1981 the negotiations for a liberalization of policy continued. Elections for all posts were scheduled for 15 November 1982. All legally

recognized parties were to run candidates for city council, mayor (except in state capitals and municipalities considered of interest to national security, which remained within the indirect election system), state assembly, governor, Congress, and the Senate. The elections were to be held by direct and secret universal ballot. It was anticipated that these would be the most important elections in recent Brazilian history: 55 million voters would go to the polls to choose nearly 400,000 candidates.

For the purposes of legitimacy and permanent insitutionalization it was important that these elections take place with maximum freedom. On the other hand, the *abertura* policy remained on the course set by the master plan of controlled liberalization. It was fundamental that the national security state maintain its control over the Senate—control was guaranteed by the bionic senators—and over the Electoral College, which was to choose President Figueiredo's successor. The Electoral College was to be composed of members of Congress plus delegates from state assemblies and municipal chambers. The PDS's municipal strength was to guarantee the government's hold over the members of the 1985 Presidential Electoral College so that there would be room for negotiation with elite opposition sectors for a sharing of power in other posts. In addition, the general elections were to increase the legitimacy of the state and become an instrument for long-term stability.

The smooth progress of the planned *abertura* policy, however, had been interrupted by a series of activities on the part of hard-line military sectors, which opposed the liberalization policies. In 1976 ten bombings shocked the country. A right-wing clandestine organization, the Aliança Anti-Comunista do Brasil (AAB, Brazilian Anti-Communist Alliance) claimed responsibility for all of them. In the case of the bombing of the research institute, CEBRAP, in São Paulo, there was strong evidence of involvement of members of the repressive apparatus. That same year the bishop of Nova Iguaçú (Rio de Janeiro), Dom Adriano Hipólito, was kidnapped. Those responsible were later found to have been members of the local military staff. In 1977 right-wing underground groups were responsible for another six bombings. In 1978 terrorist activities mounted, with a total of fifteen bombs exploding throughout the country, but aimed particularly against members of the political amnesty movement in Minas Gerais. In 1979 a bomb destroyed the opposition paper *Em Tempo* in Minas Gerais and another exploded in the car of João Pires de Vasconcelos, president of the Metalworkers' Union of João Monlevade, Minas Gerais. In December 1979, a bomb exploded under the main altar of the Cathedral of Nova Iguaçú, and Bishop Dom Adriano Hipólito was again a victim of threats.[72] In 1980, however, there was a dramatic rise in terrorist attacks. The year ended with a total of forty-six acts of violence from right-wing sectors. These included the kidnapping and knifing of jurist Dalmo Dallari, a member of the archdiocesan Justice and Peace Committee of São Paulo and an active oppositionist. There were several bomb attacks in the city of Rio de Janeiro. In September 1980, a letter bomb, addressed to the president of the OAB, Dr. Eduardo Seabra Fagundes, exploded and killed his secretary, Lyda Monteiro da Silva. That same day a bomb destroyed the offices of city councilor Antônio Carlos de Carvalho in the municipal chamber of Rio de Janeiro.[73] In early 1981 two other bomb attacks in Rio de Janeiro focused military dissent: in April a bomb destroyed a room in the house of PMDB congressman Marcelo Cerqueira; that same month another bomb wrecked the opposition press *Gráfica Americana*, whose owner had just published his personal account of imprisonment and torture.[74] The underground right-wing attacks culminated with the bombs that exploded in the convention center of Rio de Janeiro, Riocentro, during the night of 30 April 1981. There were at least two bombs involved in that incident, although early evidence indicated the presence of undetonated bombs. The first exploded inside a car occupied by an army sergeant and a captain, both of whom were later revealed to have been there under direct orders of the Command of the First Army and to work for Rio de Janeiro's CODI-DOI. The first bomb apparently exploded accidentally, for it was on the sergeant's lap. It killed him instantly and seriously injured the driver. The second bomb exploded shortly afterwards and cut off the power in the Riocentro concert hall, where twenty thousand young people were listening to a concert by opposition performers.[75]

The bombings of Riocentro highlighted certain important aspects of the complex political conjuncture. They demonstrated the direct involvement of the official structures of the repressive apparatus in acts of terrorism. They strongly divided the military between those who were directly connected to physical repression—and hence opposed liberalization out of fear of possible prosecution and trial for past activities—and those who were increasingly worried about the bad image of the armed forces as an institution. This split was reflected in an investigation, which followed a dramatic, bouncing trajectory and eventually was shelved. This led directly to a deep crisis within the state and the resignation of General Golbery do Couto e Silva, who publicly announced that he could not remain in a government that was incapable of controlling the parallel forces of the repressive apparatus. Finally, the events of Riocentro demonstrated that the intelligence community remained an important locus of real power vis-à-vis that of the executive. Negotiation between the two opposing factions of the national security state resulted in a compromise: those responsible for the terrorist bomb attacks would not be prosecuted and tried; in exchange, the hard-line sectors would accept electoral policy and would cease to object to elections in November of 1982.

With the resolution of the crisis, the master plan could proceed. On 25

November 1981, President Figueiredo announced the electoral reforms, which were to be included in a project introduced in Congress under the *decurso de prazo* procedures. It was also decided that the government would instruct the leadership of the PDS to "close question" on the voting of this new electoral reform package.[76]

The electoral package was tailored to ensure a PDS victory in the general elections of many states because a SNI study indicated that the PDS would win the gubernatorial elections of 1982 in only four states: Alagoas, Sergipe, Bahia, and Maranhão. Under the Doctrine of National Security and Development this was an intolerable situation for it required alternation of power with the opposition parties—which the sectors connected to the intelligence community would not tolerate. The reforms prohibited the formation of coalitions for the purpose of electing governors. A provision required that each party field candidates for all offices being contested in a given municipality. Should a party fail to comply, it would be barred altogether from the ballot in that municipality. This provision forced opposition parties—which were involved in advanced negotiations for coalitions for governorships—to run their own candidates in municipal races and thus compete with each other.

The reform package further provided for a system whereby the voter would be forced to vote a straight ticket—from city council up to governor. A cross-vote would be considered void. This provision, termed *voto vinculado* (tied-vote ballot), further emphasized the division of the opposition.

In addition, the package included a regulation that prohibited a candidate from withdrawing from a race unless the party issued a general withdrawal. This provision would make it difficult for opposition candidates to withdraw just before an election and pledge support to another opposition candidate.[77] The package thus reversed electoral expectations, for the PDS—much stronger at the municipal level—would probably benefit from the tied-vote regulation and, of course, take advantage of the forced split of opposition votes.

The electoral reform package considerably strengthened the position of the PDS in state assemblies, municipal chambers, and Congress. It was hoped that the administrative power of the state could enforce established clientele relationships and induce voters to choose candidates for local office first. The tied-vote provision would, in turn, force voters to choose other candidates from the same party, hence strengthening the PDS's position in the senatorial and gubernatorial races.

The provisions were insufficient, however, to guarantee complete control of the House of Representatives. Even though the government could maintain its majority in the Senate (because of the bionic senators), the possibility of an opposition majority in the House, nonetheless, was real, because President Geisel had changed the procedure for modifying the Constitution. It will be recalled that, because of short-term interests, the executive had included a provision in the April Package of 1977 that required only a simple majority in Congress to modify the Constitution. This measure now threatened to backfire and allow the opposition to change other constitutional provisions by simple majority vote. Hence, President Figueiredo introduced a second piece of legislation under the *decurso de prazo* procedure. The main provision in the new bill required a two-thirds majority in the House of Representatives for any change in the Constitution.[78] The measure was clearly a preemptive move to prevent opposition parties from pushing through any modifications if they were victorious in the November 1982 elections. It was a skillful attempt to freeze the *abertura* at the present, limited stage so that even if the PDS emerged the loser in the elections the rulers would not lose control of government. To lessen the bitterness of the pill, the package included a provision that postponed implementation of Article 16 until the 1986 elections.

How did the opposition react? The quick measures of the executive indicated clearly that the state still held the initiative. For the opposition, the debate as to the best course to follow deepened. The leadership of the Popular party strongly denounced the measures as a distinct step backwards, a step that would make the party's planned role as a transition civilian government impossible. The PP, representing the interests of national business sectors, could certainly not carry sufficient voting weight by itself to exist after the elections. In retaliation, it voted in a national convention to dissolve itself and merge with the PMDB. It was felt that this action would strengthen the overall chances of regaining the political power threatened by the tied-vote regulations. The smaller parties—PTB, PDT, and PT—were unwilling to dissolve and lose their potential for independent political action so ran independent slates for all posts. Of the three, only the PT, however, was able to field a slate of candidates in all municipalities.

The tied-vote regulations and the merger of the PP with the PMDB returned the political field to basically a two-party system. The PMDB and the PP had been, respectively, the first- and second-largest opposition parties. Their merger greatly increased the opposition's overall electoral strength by rejoining the PP's conservative element to the liberal-Left coalition prevalent in the PMDB. The smaller parties lost much of their national potential, for the tied-vote requirement localized the elections so much that voters tended to disregard potential politically effective candidates for top posts. By being forced to vote a straight ticket, the electorate tended to manifest a preference for known local candidates and to choose between one of the two larger parties, the new PMDB or the PDS. In addition, the campaign that the PMDB waged to urge voters to choose the one opposition party that had sufficient local support to defeat the PDS strengthened the plebiscital nature of the general campaign. The PMDB called on opposition members to vote "usefully"; a useful vote would be that given not necessarily to the best party or candidate but to that which was most likely to defeat the PDS.

The PDT conducted a strong campaign mainly in the states of Rio de Janeiro and Rio Grande do Sul. The PTB was politically influential in São Paulo, with the candidacy of former president Jânio Quadros for governor, and in Rio de Janeiro, where it absorbed the influence of Lacerdismo. The PT campaigned nationally, concentrating on salary, health, education, and housing issues, and on organizational rights of the working population. Perhaps the most significant aspect of the PT campaign was its ability to open the political process to marginalized sectors of the population who had never before been active in political organizations and parties. Unlike the PTB and the PDT, the PT organized active campaigns in all states except Alagoas. District residents set up and organized local rallies, for the PT concentrated on politicizing workers to emphasize the importance of achieving a voice in government.

The PDS relied on the strength of administrative and executive power not only to finance propaganda, billboards, television and radio spots, but especially to coordinate exchanges that reinforced clientelistic patterns of voter behavior. Public money, administrative facilities, printing services, gasoline, cars, and airplanes were used openly to facilitate the campaigns of all PDS candidates. In addition, the PDS used an effective strategy for gaining actual voter support: regular administrative responsibilities of government became the material basis for the professional propaganda of candidates who personally claimed credit for accomplishments. In many cases PDS candidates elicited a formal pledge of campaign support in exchange for the installation of water and sewage systems, day-care facilities, public schools, health clinics, and road paving. Rural labor leader Vitorino Agapito, of São Lourenço da Mata in Pernambuco, described the methods PDS candidates used in the drought-stricken region:

The PDS would send in a water truck to the area, where there had been no rain for four years. Once the work of providing temporary water was done, they would obtain a formal pledge for a certain number of votes in that one electoral district. After the elections, in exchange for the fulfilled agreement, it was promised that other water trucks would follow.[79]

This strategy proved to be the strength of PDS municipal support in many of the poor areas of the country. With the tied-vote regulation a voter had to vote a party slate, which reinforced the PDS's strength in the elections for higher offices, including senator and governor. Administrative power was thus used not only to finance the campaigns of the PDS candidates but principally to reinforce close clientele ties with the population.

Opposition members alleged that another effective vote-getting strategy of the PDS involved intimidation of poor voters. According to reports from the Northeast region, the PDS, by a practice termed *voto formiguinha* ("ant vote"), directly controlled votes in the rural regions.[80] Under Brazilian law all votes, to be considered valid, must be written on a ballot that is signed on the back by a judge who presides over each polling area. This measure is meant to ensure that false votes are not counted and that the secret ballot is respected. This stipulation, was allegedly circumvented by the PDS in the following manner. Local bosses transported their workers to the polling area and supervised the voting. Under threat of loss of employment workers were made to comply with certain requirements. The first voter in line received an exact copy of the legal ballot, but already filled in with the names of PDS candidates. This ballot, of course, had no signature on it and would thus be invalidated. The worker deposited it in the box and returned to the boss the legal ballot, received from the judge on entering the polling area. Although the first vote was sacrificed, the technique worked, for all other voters received two ballots: a signed ballot (passed along by the previous voter) was filled in by the boss and had to be deposited in the ballot box; a second ballot (which the voter received from the election judge on entering the polling area) had to be returned to the political boss as soon as the voter left the polls.

The opposition alleged that the system eliminated the secret ballot and forced voters to comply with the political choices of bosses under penalty of loss of job or position. When combined with the administrative enforcement of clientelistic patterns or voter behavior, this strategy enabled the PDS to increase support in working districts. The ant-vote strategy guaranteed strength in captive-voter regions of the interior; the second strategy allowed the PDS to influence voters in more sophisticated urban working districts.

The dynamics of a difficult and extremely competitive electoral campaign in which different parties participated considerably raised the level of debate and politicized the electoral process. As early as May of 1982 major debates between candidates for all posts, particularly for the major Senate and gubernatorial positions, were held on radio and television. Party programs and alternative political solutions to social and economic problems were discussed and confronted, for the first time since 1974, in a process crucial to the critical education of the electorate.

The televised debates proved harmful to the PDS candidates, who could not get off the defensive under fire of opposition candidates. Hence, in early August 1982, the military government broke off the negotiations for the repeal of the strict electoral propaganda control legislation, the Lei Falcão. Because of the important role that television and radio could play in the education of the electorate, the government decided that the Lei Falcão should remain in effect. All political debates and discussion of party platforms were prohibited on radio and television for the two months immediately preceding the elections. Candidates were, once more, forced into silence and could merely display their names and curricula vitae with a still photograph. The measure had an extremely prejudicial effect on the electoral strength of the opposition candidates and limited their maneuvering space by preventing open discussion of alternatives. With their limited resources and organizational potential, the PDT and the PT particularly were hurt.

The preliminary results of the general elections of 15 November 1982 show the effectiveness of the controls. First of all, the 1977 reform, the April Package, gave greater representational weight to the Northeast.[81] The proportionate difference in the number of seats assigned the Northeast by the April Package allowed the government to gain a greater number of seats in the House than would have been the case prior to the 1977 modifications. This became significant for the government because, in spite of the changes introduced in the 1981 electoral legislation, the opposition jointly won a majority of the House of Representatives in the 1982 elections. For the opposition parties the elections in fact represented a major advance. Together, they gained control of the governorships of over 60 percent of Brazil's territory, within an area in which 58 percent of the population lives (tables 29 and 30 summarize the elections).[82] In a study published in the *Folha de São Paulo*, Helival Rios showed that the ten states in which the opposition won the governorship represent 75.2 percent of the total consumer taxes (ICM—Imposto de Circulação de Mercadorias, Tax on Circulation of Merchandise) and 70.5 percent of all federal taxes.[83]

The gubernatorial results contained some surprises, including the unexpected PDS victories in the key states of Pernambuco and Rio Grande do Sul, where the opposition had been expected to win. In Rio Grande do Sul the PDS victory was the consequence of a strong split between the opposition vote. Hence, in a state that had been a traditional opposition stronghold, the government was able to savor its most important electoral success. In Pernambuco a tight race between the PMDB and the PDS ended with a PDS victory that reversed all expectations. According to Senator Marcos Freire, the PMDB gubernatorial candidate in Pernambuco, the defeat was due to a combination of factors: the PMDB suffered from extreme internal divisions, which weakened the party in the face of a united PDS; in addition, the ant vote and especially the clientele arrangements in the drought-stricken interior regions allowed the PDS to obtain a position in poor areas sufficiently advantageous to offset the opposition's victory in the major cities.[84]

In both Rio Grande do Sul and Pernambuco the PMDB also blamed the defeat on corruption during vote counting. In Rio Grande do Sul, Pedro Simon, the PMDB gubernatorial candidate, filed a suit against the PDS for

Table 29
Congressional Election Results, 15 November 1982

| Party | No. of Seats Won | |
	House of Representatives	Senate
PDS	235	46
PMDB	200	21
PDT	23	1
PTB	13	1
PT	8	0

Table 30
Gubernatorial Election Results, 15 November 1982

Party	No. of States Won	No. Votes Received	No. of Reg- istered Voters	Population	Territory (sq. km)	Territorial % of GNP
PDS	12	7,807,696	22,225,818	47,425,296	2,810,207	23.90
PMDB	9	11,612,702	30,134,704	58,400,155	5,037,937	58.22
PDT	1	1,416,630	6,292,265	11,297,962	44,268	16.68

Source: *Folha de São Paulo* (27 November 1982), p. 1.
Notes: The PDS won States of Maranhão, Ceará, Rio Grande do Norte, Paraíba, Pernambuco, Piauí, Alagoas, Sergipe, Bahia, Mato Grosso, Rio Grande do Sul, and Santa Catarina; the PMDB won São Paulo, Minas Gerais, Espírito Santo, Mato Grosso do Sul, Paraná, Goiás, Pará, Amazonas, and Acre; the PDT won the State of Rio de Janeiro.

fraud and asked the regional courts for a formal recount of large numbers of districts after campaign workers found almost two thousand legally signed ballots thrown in a sewage drain.[85]

Perhaps, however, the biggest surprise of the 1982 elections occurred in Rio de Janeiro, where the PDT's candidate for governor, Leonel Brizola, won by a more than 200,000 vote margin. The local political situation allowed Brizola to win in spite of the PDT's lack of organizational strength. In Rio de Janeiro, the PP was composed of members of a political machinery controlled by Governor Chagas Freitas. The administration had been prone to corruption and alleged involvement in gambling activities; the merger of the PP and the PMDB, therefore, had the effect of tainting the PMDB with the unresolved administrative problems of the PP. The population of Rio de Janeiro reacted negatively both to the federal and to the state governments. In the vacuum of opposition leadership, Brizola gained support as a possible alternative. It should also be noted that the national

Table 31
1982 Election Results
(Percentage of Total Valid Votes)

Party	House of Representatives	Senate	State Governments	Electoral College for President
PMDB	43.0	43.7	44.0	39.5
PDT	5.8	5.9	6.1	2.0
PTB	4.4	4.6	4.7	4.3
PT	3.6	3.7	3.7	1.3
Total	56.8	57.9	58.5	47.1
Blank votes	10.9	10.2	8.3	—
Void votes	4.2	3.3	3.0	—
Total No. Valid Votes	48,455,879	48,746,803	48,188,956	695

Source: Luiz Carlos Bresser Pereira, "Os limites tecnoburocráticos-burgueses da abertura brasileira." Paper presented at XI International Congress of the Latin American Studies Association, Mexico City, 29 September–1 October 1983.

campaign that the PMDB waged in favor of the "useful" vote backfired in Rio de Janeiro, where it convinced voters that Brizola's candidacy was in fact the most useful alternative.

The tensions of November's election were also most felt in Rio de Janeiro, where the hard-line sectors of the military were most active. The victory of Leonel Brizola, former exile and considered by the hard-line military one of the state's most dangerous enemies, again brought to the surface the deep resentments expressed by past terrorist bombings. The process of vote counting in Rio de Janeiro was interrupted by the discovery of serious fraud. Some members of the SNI and hard-line military personnel, including Colonel Job Lorena, who had been involved in the Riocentro incident, elaborated a conspiracy to negate Brizola's victory. A computer firm that had been hired by the electoral courts to aid in the processing of election data was utilized to transfer some 15 percent of the votes cast for Brizola to blank and void votes and then some of the latter to the PDS. The computer fraud forced the intervention of the Regional Electoral Tribunal, which suspended all vote counting and ordered an official court investigation.[86] A recount gave Brizola the victory.

Once the fraud failed, the officers planned a military uprising to void the elections altogether and keep the elected governors from taking office. The hard-line officers planned to take over the Rio de Janeiro radio stations on the night of November 27 and issue a "proclamation calling for the return to the genuine spirit of the 1964 revolution." All members of Brizola's party would then be arrested, and the officers would lead a general military uprising in army units throughout the country.[87] The quick and decisive action of President João Figueiredo and Army Minister Valter Pires foiled the conspiracy, but the events, coming from the same sectors involved in the bomb attacks against opposition groups, indicate the seriousness of the refusal of many hard-line military to accept the liberalization policy. This resistance introduces a further aspect to the complex political negotiations of the *abertura* period and is one of the remaining signs of the de facto power still held by the repressive apparatus.

1983: Brazil Goes to the International Monetary Fund

The victory of the opposition parties in the most industrial states coupled with their new strength in Congress was counterbalanced in 1983 by the growing social and economic crisis. A political stalemate between the opposition forces and the central power of the federal government led to an increasingly rapid development of the dialectic between the state and the opposition.

At the end of October 1982, the National Monetary Council (Conselho Monetário Nacional, CMN) drafted the goals the government intended to pursue during 1983 to enable the country to lower the deficit in the balance of payments. To achieve the programmed goals the government intended to raise the level of exports to the developed nations—counting on the economic recuperation of the developed economies—as well as lower the cost of servicing the debt through the expectation of lower interest rates charged by international banks. Since a large part of the foreign debt was contracted with floating interest rates, Brazil became increasingly dependent on international decisions that escaped the immediate control of the government.

One of the reasons for the continued growth of the foreign debt proved to be the tendency of the government to guarantee short-term loans to be used almost exclusively to pay past debt installments and interest rates. Increasingly, the government encouraged state corporations to borrow in the international market, not to cover trade transactions and oil purchases, as happened in the past, but rather to cover the government's balance-of-payment deficits. By the end of 1981, the government had contracted a further US\$ 11.8 billion. By October 1982 the net total of the short-term loans had reached US\$ 16 billion.[88] These new loans were contracted to cover the cost of interest payments and diminish the overall outstanding deficit of US\$ 3 billion to 4 billion in the balance of payments.

The overall profile of the debt would place Brazil in increasingly difficult circumstances. One of the most crucial aspects of the growth of the short-term debt after 1979 is the country's dependency on constant renegotiation of rescheduling terms. The short-term debt contracted for normal trade reasons accounts for less than a third of the total debt. Most of the rest of the debt has been cash loans, with repayment periods of 180 days or less, hence, the constant liquidity crisis of the country that was characteristic of 1982 and 1983.

Hardly had the votes of the 1982 elections been counted, when the government began official negotiations with the International Monetary Fund (IMF). The same week in which President Reagan visited Brazil, the minister of finance, Ernane Galvêas, announced that the government was forced to appeal to the standby mechanisms of the IMF. According to Galvêas, this was necessary to obtain US$ 6 billion in parceled loans through 1983. The new loans would be used to lessen the extreme liquidity crisis of the country and to pay off outstanding debt servicing.[89]

It became a matter of wide press attention that Reagan's visit, while releasing a further loan to Brazil from the government of the United States, was meant to pressure the country into negotiations with the IMF and the international bankers worried about the extent of Brazil's debt. The seriousness of the involvement of the ten largest banks in the United States in Brazil's liquidity crisis pressured the Reagan government to act. As may be seen in table 32, Brazil represents the largest part of the total loans extended by American banks to countries in Latin America.

In November 1982 Brazil began a series of negotiations with representatives of the IMF. A "letter of intentions" (*carta de intenções*) was signed

Table 32
Loans Extended by Ten Largest U.S. Banks
(U.S. $Millions)

| Bank | Debtor Country | | | Total |
	Brazil	Mexico	Venezuela	
Citicorp	436	327	109	872
Bank of America	230	250	200	680
Chase Manhattan	236	168	101	505
Manhattan Hanover	201	173	110	484
Morgan Guaranty	168	108	54	330
Chemical	130	150		280
Bankers Trust	87	87	47	221
Continental Illinois	49	69	46	164
First Interstate	47	68		115
Security Pacific	49	52		101
Total	1,633	1,452	567	3,752

Source: *Veja* (6 April 1983), p. 106.

that programmed carefully the established economic goals to be reached during the next years. In fact, during 1983 there were three different agreements signed, each of which was made obsolete by the failure of the government to achieve the stated initial goals.

Although the IMF clearly resorts to orthodox monetarist policies and austerity measures that impose recession—curtailment of imports and severe control of government spending (with the argument that these measures are necessary to achieve an equilibrium in the balance of payments and reduce inflation)—it was not clear whether the IMF imposed specific policies on the Brazilian government. To a certain extent, the government used the excuse of resort to the IMF to reduce its own responsibility for the increasingly painful political and social costs of the policies implemented. It is relevant to cite from the testimony given by DIEESE to Congress in January 1983:

Much has been said with respect to the relation between Brazil's appeal to the IMF and the systematic readjustments of salaries. It is difficult to assert just what the relationship is.

Already in 1981, some segments of the national Brazilian business community were openly favorable to the alterations in the calculations of salary readjustments. The debate between the business community was intense through 1982. However, it is true that the discussion became more intense when Brazil went to the IMF in November, and ended up in Decree-Law 2012, of January 1983.

The IMF usually imposes austerity policies in the countries that resort to its financing so as to reduce the rate of inflation. According to the theoretical orientation of the IMF, one of the ways to achieve the lowering of the inflation rate is to adjust salaries at below-inflation rates.

Former Ministers Roberto Campos and Mário Henrique Simonsen, however, themselves claimed that the changes in the salary laws were only a suggestion of the IMF and not an imposition. It was up to the government authorities to take a position on the matter. It is interesting also to observe that, according to an article published in the newspaper *Folha de São Paulo* of 27 January 1983, when Argentina went to the IMF the "letter of intentions" that was signed included a real raise in salary of 5 percent. There exists also a report of the World Bank, which is a part of the international system of the IMF, drafted in 1982, that textually states that the salary policy that was developed in Brazil after 1979 was not a factor in the increase of inflation.[90]

To a certain extent the social and economic situation was a result of previous policies of the military governments since 1964. From the census of 1980 it was clear that the level of impoverishment of the population had already reached significant levels. Data made public by the IBGE, the official governmental statistical department, demonstrated clearly the impact of the pattern of distribution of income inherent in the economic model pursued by those in power. In 1980, 12.5 percent of the economically active population received a salary equivalent to one half or less the legal minimum wage. A further 20.8 percent of the economically active population received a salary between one half and one time the minimum wage. Of those employed, 31.1 received between one time the minimum wage and two times the legal amount established by law. The middle classes were composed of those salaried workers who earned between twice the minimum wage and five times (23.6 percent), between more than five times to ten times the minimum wage (7.2 percent), and more than ten times up to twenty times the minimum wage (3.2 percent). Only 1.6 percent of the salaried workers in Brazil earned more than the equivalent of twenty times the legal minimum wage of 1980.[91]

In addition, according to DIEESE's economist Walter Barelli, the plight of the unemployed aggravated the situation. The recessionist policy the military government imposed in 1980 resulted in growing unemployment, which, by 1981, amounted to 12.3 percent of the working-age population and a further 18 percent who were underemployed and lived from selling products in the streets, washing cars, or other means composing what has been called the "informal economy." Hence, in 1981, according to a study conducted by DIEESE, a total of 30.3 percent of working-age people were either unemployed or underemployed in Brazil and were not included in the official statistics of the IBGE.[92] In São Paulo itself, unemployment reached dangerous levels by 1983. State Secretary of Labor Almir Pazzianotto pointed out that in the Greater São Paulo area alone there were over 1 million persons unemployed. According to a DECAD study (Departamento de Estatística da Federação das Indústrias do Estado de São Paulo, the Statistical Department of the Federation of Industries of the State of São Paulo), the large industrial complex of São Paulo employed approximately 2 million persons in December 1980 but laid off 437,000 workers in the next two years. The service and commercial sectors were unable to absorb the industrial workers, and the reduced available income sharply cut sales, forcing further layoffs in these sectors, as well.[93] Because there is no program of unemployment compensation in Brazil, no government aid in the form of foodstamps, nor aid to dependent children or other welfare benefits that allow those who are unemployed to physically survive, the situation is exacerbated. Those who are out of work for more than a year also lose the right to become members of trade unions (and thus to apply for medical and dental care) or use state-run health system in the INPS (Instituto Nacional de Previdência Social, National Social Work Institute). They are left without any means of support, thus creating an explosive situation of social distress.

According to the government's own statistics, 70 percent of the population has a minimum daily calorie intake lower than necessary for human development. This amounts to approximately 71 million persons who are officially undernourished. Hunger and undernourishment, according to the IBGE, are responsible for 40 percent of the deaths of children in the country.[94] The infant mortality rate in the richer areas of Brazil in 1981 was 87.3 deaths for each 1,000 live births. In the Northeast this rate reached 130 per 1,000 live births. Among the higher-salaried population, life expectancy was sixty-two years, whereas among the poor it was only forty-nine years of age. The minister of health, Valdir Arcoverde, in an interview in the *Folha de São Paulo* (28 August 1983) recognized that the level of nutrition, housing, sanitation, and education in the country had immediate consequences for the health of the poorest:

One can state, then, that the risk of becoming sick and dying in Brazil is essentially determined by work relations and how the person is situated in the labor force, in the social class, and in consumption. Therefore, there are concrete possibilities, by aiding social development, of eliminating the diseases that are typical of poverty, such as malnutrition and most of the tropical contagious diseases.

Hunger, even in the developed regions, became a concern of the armed forces in 1983. Every year the armed forces must excuse from the service 45 percent of those registered because they do not have the minimum physical requirement, in weight and height.[95] The United Nations has established three thousand calories for a man and twenty-two hundred for a woman as the minimum caloric intake necessary for human development. A World Bank study, however, concluded that 79.5 percent of the population of the Brazilian Northeast received less than the minimum daily caloric intake. In the northern states this percentage was even higher, with 87.4 percent of the population undernourished. Even in the richest parts of the country, the South and the Southeast, the percentage of undernourishment among the population reached an alarming 57.9 percent.[96]

Because of the pressure to earn export dollars for the payment of debt servicing, the government increasingly emphasized fiscal incentives for agricultural crops for export. Although the production of soybeans between 1970 and 1979 increased at an average annual rate of 22.5 percent, sugarcane, 6.3 percent, cacao beans, 3.7 percent, and oranges for export, 12.6 percent, the production of basic staple foods for the internal market was abandoned for lack of government support and increased concentration of land used for the export crops. In spite of the growing internal demand for the basic foods, the production of black beans fell 17.32 percent, and wheat production fell 9.92 percent in the same period. Only the production of rice, which is also exported, increased, by 11.19 percent during these years.[97] The use of increasing millions of acres for the production of sugarcane in the alcohol program has further decreased the available space for cultivation of basic foods. Traditional staple foods such as rice, black beans, corn, manioc, and potatoes are no longer planted in the rich lands of the South.

Alcohol production for gasoline substitution has forced up the price of basic foodstuffs. The production of soybeans for export has been the second most important factor in the reduction of land area available for cultivation of basic foods. In the period between 1969 and 1979, for example, the total land area planted with soybeans increased from 906 to 8.3 million hectares (one hectare equals approximately 2.5 acres).[98]

The resulting inflationary pressures on food prices were severe. Between 1977 and 1980 the minimum salary was raised 203 percent but food prices increased by 428 percent.[99] Between September 1982 and September 1983, according to DIEESE, the prices of thirteen food products that are part of the minimum requirements for caloric intake increased by an average 28.5 percent, with an annual 246.4 percent increase. With the last price increases the minimum salary (Cr. 34,776, September 1983) became for the first time lower than the cost of the minimum food necessary for an adult man. Hence, in 1983 the minimum wage was not enough to buy food, not to mention housing, transport, and health expenses. Since the price of basic foodstuffs is higher than the minimum salary, a work load of 240 hours per month is no longer sufficient even to cover the cost of food, as can be seen in table 33. According to DIEESE, to afford the costs of food, housing, and transportation, a worker would have needed to earn Cr. 220,477.23 in September 1983, when the minimum wage was only Cr. 34,776. The cost of food alone for a man, his wife, and two children would have been Cr. 106,049.55, representing 48.1 percent of total domestic income.[100]

Although it is clear that the great majority of the population is not benefiting from the economic model and is suffering from the pressures of inflation and unemployment, there have been a series of controversial debates between business figures, bankers, and the government as to exactly who is responsible for the chaos of the Brazilian economy. The government has accused business owners of increasing the price of products above what is justifiable. Business leaders respond by counteraccusing the government of not carrying out a coherent economic policy, not resolving the problems of the balance of payments, not countering inflation, and provoking the highest unemployment rates in the history of Brazil. The bankers, for their part, accuse the government of doing nothing to prevent the high cost of money.

In fact, each has a portion of the responsibility. In the public services, which are controlled by the government, the price of electricity increased 108.1 percent between June 1982 and June 1983. Tariff rates for water and sewage were raised 132.3 percent in the same period. The price of bottled gas for industrial and consumer use was increased 103.5 percent during the year. On the other hand, products that are not controlled by the government also increased sharply: for example, medicine prices increased by 158.7 percent during the period and clothing by 104.9 percent.[101] Nonetheless, as the DIEESE study summarized in table 34 shows, the banking sector perhaps benefited most from the period of unbridled inflation, as the foreign bankers profited most.

One reason for the high profits of banks has been the extremely high interest rates charged. In Brazil banks charge between 250 and 400 percent per year, averaging 35 to 40 percent real interest (above the rate of inflation). This contributes to their high profit rate but has been constantly indicated by economists as the cause of bankruptcies, unemployment, and inflation. Foreign banks have profited from the floating interest rates, especially, which have been pegged to a large part of the Brazilian foreign debt. In the last thirteen years, Brazil has paid to developed nations' banks $50.7 billion in interest alone.[102] This is equivalent to approximately half the total amount of loans contracted by the country since 1964. Because of the pressures to maintain interest payments and debt servicing, Brazil has been forced to engage in increasingly recessionist policies, with tight wage controls, import limitations, and other measures to reduce internal consumption and turn most of production to exports and payment of the debt. When all fails, and a liquidity crisis threatens, the government has tended to take out short-term loans, which are used merely to pay outstanding bills. These add to the financial troubles by increasing the total debt as well as by forcing renegotiations every 180 days.

Even though there may have been some early lack of clarity as to whether the IMF imposed specific wage policies on the government, as 1983 developed, events showed that in fact the pressure of the IMF and international bankers became intense. The government of Brazil, however, could have utilized its influence to resist certain terms and impose conditions that were better for the country and would have required less sacrifice from its people. There was an apparent coincidence of interests, and the policy of recession and salary adjustment became the government's priority through 1983.

As we have seen, in November 1979 a new wage law was passed.[103] Salary readjustments were modified so that wages were raised every six months. In addition, there was a real gain of 10 percent for those workers who earned less than three times the minimum salary. Wage raises became pegged to different rates according to salary: those who earned up to three times the minimum salary received 110 percent of the Consumer Price Index (INPC, Indice Nacional de Preços ao Consumidor); workers with salaries of between three and ten times the minimum wage received 100 percent of the INPC; and those who earned more than ten times the minimum salary received 80 percent of the INPC. Percentage raises decreased in higher brackets, and those who earned more than twenty times the minimum salary were freed to negotiate directly with their

Table 33
Cost of Minimum Ration, São Paulo

Food	Quantity	Monthly Cost (Cr.)		% Variation	Work Time Necessary to Purchase	
		Sept. 1982	Sept. 1983		Sept. 1982	Sept. 1983
Meat	6.0 kg	3,733.44	13,733.82	267.9	53h57m	94h47m
Milk	7.5 l	472.50	1,237.50	161.9	6h50m	8h32m
Black beans	4.5 kg	634.73	4,566.42	619.4	9h10m	31h31m
Rice	3.0 kg	421.17	1,335.63	217.1	6h 5m	9h13m
Wheat flour	1.5 kg	117.21	423.83	261.6	1h42m	2h55m
Potatoes	6.0 kg	426.00	2,994.00	602.8	6h 9m	20h40m
Tomatoes	9.0 kg	1,097.46	2,331.99	112.5	15h52m	16h 6m
Bread	6.0 kg	979.38	2,885.22	194.6	14h 9m	19h55m
Coffee	600.0 g	468.71	1,012.50	116.0	6h46m	6h59m
Bananas	7.5 dz	572.48	1,995.23	248.5	8h16m	13h46m
Sugar	3.0 kg	285.00	591.00	107.4	4h 7m	4h 5m
Lard	750.0 g	248.81	862.90	246.8	3h36m	5h57m
Butter	750.0 g	749.07	1,379.81	84.2	10h49m	9h31m
Total		10,205.96	35,349.85	246.4	147h28m	243h57m

Source: DIEESE, "Salário mínimo não dá nem para comer," *Boletim do DIEESE* 2 (September 1983):4.
Note: Exchange rate in September 1983 was Cr. 780 per dollar.

Table 34
The Banking System, 1980 and 1981

Type of Bank	Profits (billions of Cr$)		Rise in Profit (%)		Rate of Profit (%)	
	1980	1981	Nominal	Real	1980	1981
Official state	182,672	464,401	154.2	21.1	77.8	94.6
Federal state	165,990	417,493	151.5	19.8	81.5	97.6
State	16,882	46,908	177.9	34.0	53.7	74.2
Private	68,588	270,901	295.0	88.2	47.8	80.6
National private	55,597	213,593	284.2	83.0	44.9	73.7
Foreign private	6,308	24,689	291.4	86.5	79.5	131.7
Associated	6,683	32,619	388.1	132.6	57.5	117.4
Total banking system	251,260	735,302	192.6	39.4	66.4	88.9

Source: DIEESE, "Banqueiros lucraram 917.5 bilhões em 1981," *Boletim do DIEESE* 1 (June 1982):5.

employers. The minimum salary was also readjusted every semester by 110 percent of the Consumer Price Index. Because all other salaries are based on the minimum salary of the period, it is evident that all wage brackets benefited from the 10 percent added to the base salary.

The 1979 wage legislation was a factor in the redistribution of income among the salaried population. Those workers who earned less than 11.5 times the minimum wage received real gains, and those with higher salaries lost real purchasing power. Nonetheless, the wage legislation was considered by most workers to be an advance, particularly because the biannual nature of raises allowed them to keep up with the cost of living.

In the last days of 1982 the dimensions of the economic crisis became public with the visit of President Reagan and the supplementary loan given by the U.S. government to allow Brazil to close accounts for the year. The salary policy then came under heavy attack by international bankers, by the officers of the Ministry of Planning, and by many Brazilian business leaders, who emphasized the need to control salaries. With this background, the government signed Decree-Law No. 2012, of 25 January 1983, modifying greatly the salary policy. First of all, the extra 10 percent raise above the Consumer Price Index was eliminated for workers earning up to three times the minimum wage. Other wage brackets were introduced with different percentage raises lower than the INPC. Therefore, only the lower-paid workers were to receive salaries equal to the cost of living. All other workers, especially the middle classes, suffered severe losses in terms of real salary and purchasing power.[104] The opposition parties protested strongly against this limitation on the wages of middle-class workers, pointing out its recessionist impact on the economy. The PTB, as the party that oscillates between the opposition and the government, reached an agreement with the government's PDS to change slightly the severity of the losses for middle classes. Decree-Law No. 2024, of 25 May 1983, was introduced in Congress and became effective in June. It specified that workers earning up to seven times the minimum salary would receive the full raise according to the cost of living (100 percent of INPC).[105]

This new modification, of benefit to workers, was of only passing importance. On 5 July 1983, the government signed the most controversial of its measures up to then. Without the approval or consideration of Congress, Decree-Law No. 8782 was signed, authorizing the IBGE to deduct from the calculations of the INPC increases in prices that were due to the measures just enacted by the government. This eliminated all subsidies for oil, wheat, sugar, petroleum and its by-products. It also directed the IBGE to not consider in its calculations the spectacular food price increases that resulted from the floods in the South and the drought in the Northeast.[106] The minister of planning justified this amazing measure, which publicly manipulated the official inflation statistics used to calculate salaries , by saying that the elimination of subsidies was an imposition of the IMF and that the government could not allow the resultant rise in prices to be reflected in salaries. The calculations of the INPC thereafter were "purged" from real increases in prices. Therefore, workers at all salary levels suffered severe losses in terms of real purchasing power because their salaries were corrected according to the new, "purged" (*expurgado*) INPC, and the reality of inflation rates was not affected.

In July 1983, the government introduced yet another decree-law in Congress under the *decurso de prazo* legislative mechanism. Decree-Law No. 2045 limited the percentage of raises for all workers—independent of their salary brackets—to 80 percent of the already-purged Consumer Price Index (INPC). All salaries, without exception, would be cut 20 percent immediately in relation to the monthly variation of the INPC after August 1983.[107] Those who earned salaries of up to seven times the minimum wage suffered the greatest losses.[108] Reduction in benefits of workers in state companies became part of another decree, No. 2036.

Increasing public outrage over the measures constantly being passed by the government exploded in major strikes during July 1983. On 6 July eleven hundred workers of the Paulínia state oil refinery, near Campinas in the state of São Paulo, went on strike to protest Decree-Law 2036. The refinery of Paulínia is the country's most important, concentrating one third of the country's oil-refining capacity. The Ministry of Labor took immediate action with the hope of avoiding the spread of the strike action. Using the strict labor legislation, which expressly forbids strikes in essential sectors, ministry officials intervened in the Oil Workers Union of Campinas and Paulínia, removed all officials from office—including the president, Jacó Bittar, who was also general secretary of the Partido dos Trabalhadores—and fired workers who remained on strike. In reality, the repressive measures served mostly to anger other workers. The next day, oil workers at the Mataripe refinery in Bahia, which supplies the whole of the Northeast, joined the strike in support of the Paulínia oil workers. The minister of labor immediately intervened in the union of Mataripe as well. On the morning of 7 July, however, seventy thousand metalworkers of São Bernardo do Campo and Diadema voted a "solidarity strike" and brought the automobile industry to a complete halt. The workers left the factories and marched down the major industrial streets of the area by the thousands, stopping at each factory gate to ask workers to join the strike. The metalworkers protested the doctoring of official statistics of the INPC and the changes in the wage law (decrees 2012, 2024, and 2045). They also indicated their willingness to strike in protest against the interference of the IMF in the economic policies of the country. The next day other laborers joined the strike in the ABCD region of São Paulo. Besides the metalworkers, bus drivers, chemical workers, leather goods and glass workers all stopped. The

Ministry of Labor reacted with another intervention—Jair Meneguelli and all other officials of the Metalworkers' Union of São Bernardo do Campo and Diadema were removed from office. This was the third intervention in the São Bernardo Metalworkers' Union in four years.[109] On Sunday, 9 July, the metalworkers assembled by the thousands in the Vila Euclides football stadium of São Bernardo do Campo and voted to go back to work temporarily and prepare for a general strike, which was set for 21 July.

The general strike against the economic policies of the government and the IMF would mark the first time that workers went out on strike for exclusively political reasons. The seriousness of the wage decreases spurred labor leaders to join efforts and temporarily stemmed the divisions in the labor movement that differing opinions as to union organization and strategy for fighting the economic policies of the government had sharpened. Jacó Bittar, *cassado* president of the Oil Workers' Union of Campinas and Paulínia, Jair Meneguelli and Luís Inácio Lula da Silva, both *cassado* leaders of the Metalworkers' Union of São Bernardo do Campo and Diadema, joined efforts with Joaquim dos Santos Andrade, president of the powerful Metalworkers' Union of São Paulo (representing 400,000 workers in the capital) and with Argeu Egydio dos Santos, of the São Paulo Metalworkers' Federation. The preparations for the general strike in São Paulo demonstrated that the government's actions to repress leadership by removing elected officials from union office were no longer effective. The *cassado* leaders, once removed from office, nonetheless continued to be the representatives whom the membership recognized. They remained the legitimate leaders and were active in the organization of the general protests of 21 July.

On the eve of the planned general protest, the government enacted an important new measure of political and social control: Decree No. 88540, signed by acting president Aureliano Chaves on 20 July 1983, extended the powers of the federal executive to convene military police forces in the states:[110]

The president of the republic, using the powers given to him in Article 81 of the Constitution, declares that:

Article 1: The convening of the military police, either totally or partially, in accordance with Article 3 of Decree-Law Number 667 of 2 July 1969 as altered by Decree-Law Number 2010, of 12 January 1983, will be considered effective:

   1. In case of external war.

   2. To prevent or repress a grave disturbance of the public order or the threat of its occurrence. . . .

Article 2: The convening or mobilization of the military police, in case of war, shall be according to specific legislation.

Article 3: The convening of the military police will be done by act of the president of the republic when:

a) There is urgent need to assume the proper training and arming of the military police to fulfill its role as an auxiliary force of the army. . . .

b) When the requirements of training, discipline, arming, competence, structure, organization, and number of conscripts in the military police of a state are not in conformance with the stipulations of Decree-Law No. 667, of 2 July 1969 as altered by Decree-Law No. 2010 of 12 January 1983. . . .

c) When the president of the republic deems necessary, in case of adoption of measures of emergency or state of siege, which are expressly allowed in Title II, Chapter V of the Constitution.

Article 4: When convened in the forms established in this decree, the command of the military police will be exercised by an active duty officer of the army, of the levels of brigadier general, colonel, or lieutenant colonel, or an active duty officer of the highest level of the corporation itself.

Article 5: The military police, when convened, will be placed under the direct supervision of the High Command of the Army [EME, Estado Maior do Exército] or placed under subordination of the army command or the military command of the area or state in which the convened military police is located.

Article 6: The convening of the military police, by stipulation of this decree, will be without impairment of:

1. The specific commitment of the military police, as a participant in the efforts of internal defense and territorial defense, in the cases which are predicted in Item 2 of Article 1 of this decree.

2. The normal competence of the military police as its duty in the maintenance of public order and in support of federal authorities for specific missions of internal defense. . . .

3. The convening of the military police, which is referred to in Item 2 of Article 1 of this decree, may also be undertaken whenever the state government does not take appropriate action to prevent or repress disturbances or the threat of occurrence of disturbances . . . for the planning and proper execution of the measures necessary, the military police should act with the state organization responsible for public security or its representatives.[111]

The decree stipulated a period of one year in cases where the military police of a state was placed under the control of the army for reasons of discipline, arming, or training. However, if the convening was for reasons of failure of the state governments to repress or prevent social disturbances, there was no prior established period, and the military police would remain under the direct control of the army until the president, by explicit action, declared otherwise.

This decree eliminated effective control of the state police forces while placing opposition governors in an extremely difficult position. In states governed by members of the opposition parties, the decree forced the governments to effectively repress any public disruption or be vulnerable to an immediate takeover of their state military police. On the other hand, the explicit regulations in Item 3 of Article 6, would make the state governments become directly involved in any repression because of the need to coordinate activities of the military police and the state security officials. This point would be a matter of controversy among members of the opposition and result in charges against the governors who had been elected by the PMDB and the PDT in 1982. The federal government in effect forced state governors, members of the opposition parties, to share the blame for any overt act of repression during strikes or other public protests.

The general strike was coordinated by the Pro-Central Union Organization (Pró-Central Unica dos Trabalhadores), federations, and trade unions in the country, mostly urban. Their main concerns were claimed as the following:

1. To protest the economic policies of the governments as responsible for unemployment, low salaries, and rising cost of living.

2. To protest the attempts to end other salary benefits, particularly of the retired.

3. To favor a moratorium on the question of the debt, with an immediate break with the IMF and the freezing of payments with renegotiation.

4. To seek job security and safety.

5. To seek controls of food prices, particularly staple foods.

6. To seek the end of government interventions in trade unions and the return of all unions to their democratically elected leaders.

Not all states, however, decided to strike as a means of demonstrating their protest. July 21 was thus organized as a "national day of protest" with different activities, depending on the locality.

In São Paulo, 21 July was like a holiday. The trade unions had distributed over 1 million pamphlets to the population, urging them to stay home. The streets were completely empty. In the downtown business district an estimated 70 percent of commercial establishments were closed for the day. Banks, hospitals, and all public departments worked at only 30 percent capacity. In the city of São Paulo 300,000 of the total 400,000 metalworkers joined the strike. In the ABCD industrial region the strike was almost total, with approximately 95 percent of workers stopping.[112] The most significant strikes occurred in the states of São Paulo, with an estimated 2 million workers joining the strike, and Rio Grande do Sul, where 1 million workers stopped.[113] In the state of Pernambuco only thirteen metalworker factories were stopped, one textile factory, and the garbage collectors. In Espírito Santo there were some strikes in the construction industry, among public-health workers, graphics workers, and journalists. In Rio de Janeiro the strike was concentrated in the large shipbuilding industry, Ishibrás, and in factories in Nova Iguaçú and Caxias. In Goiás construction workers and most state and federal employees stopped. In Paraná the strike was limited to construction workers.

In most other cities the national day of protest was marked more by rallies than by strikes. In most capitals schools were closed and public transportation was affected by the strikes, and there were public rallies and marches in almost all. The most important occurred in Rio de Janeiro, where an estimated fifty thousand persons marched down the main street, Avenida Rio Branco, and concentrated for a public protest in Cinelândia. This was the largest demonstration in the city of Rio de Janeiro since the 1968 "March of the 100,000." In Rio Grande do Sul thousands of workers marched in protest from Canoas to Porto Alegre, 20 kilometers. They were followed by military police but were not arrested.

However, many public rallies and strikes that had been planned did not occur because of the total mobilization of the military police in all states. Police violence, particularly in the industrialized ABCD region, marked the day of the general strike in São Paulo. Over eight hundred persons were arrested and many wounded by the indiscriminate beating. The repression was most severe in São Bernardo do Campo, known to be the most organized area of the state. Workers took refuge from the troops in the Cathedral of São Bernardo do Campo, but it was invaded and bombed in spite of the protests of the local bishop, Dom Cláudio Hummes. One of the severest problems of those who tried to protect workers during that day was to find out just who was in command of the troops. Because of the ambiguities of the decree-law passed the day before, it was not clear whether the state security department, the governor, or the army was in control of the military police. This was the element that most frustrated Dom Cláudio Hummes, who at one point commented that the repression that day was worse than he had witnessed during the metalworkers strikes in 1978, 1979, and 1980. The government also intervened in two other trade unions: the Bankworkers of São Paulo and the Subway Workers of São Paulo.[114]

The demands of the trade unions were not met nor were they expected to be met. But, although only partially successful, the national day of protest was an important step in the organization at all levels. Particularly in São Paulo, trade unionists, church members, neighborhood associations, and political parties came together in a vast joint action to organize the strike. However, the strikes also showed the weaknesses of the labor movement, which is clearly strongest in São Paulo and Rio Grande do Sul. The coordination mechanisms at the national and state levels, in spite of the many state congresses that were held during the year, proved ineffective. Clearly, the labor movement has a long way to go before a general strike is able to paralyze a country with over forty million workers.

The mobilization of the population to protest the wage decrees took on the form of direct lobbying in Congress. Trade unionists from all over the country assembled in the Congress to pressure members who were considering a positive vote. In particular those trade-union members connected to the PTB, as was for example the case of Joaquim dos Santos

Andrade of the Metalworkers' Union of São Paulo, used their influence to convince congressional representatives to vote against the two decrees that were simultaneously being considered. The first sign of a new resistance in Congress to impositions of the executive came with the defeat of Decree No. 2024. This decree-law resulted from a previous agreement between the PTB and the PDS. Although it is true that the government applied less pressure for the approval of this compromise decree, nonetheless, the defeat marked the first time that Congress had been able to summon sufficient opposition strength to stop an executive decree introduced under the *decurso de prazo* mechanism. The members of Congress were emboldened by their newfound independence and encouraged by the amount of popular support from the galleries and in daily visits to Congress. When Decree No. 2045, which kept all salaries at 80 percent of the INPC, came to the floor for a vote there were at least forty-five members of the PDS now willing to cross party lines and vote with the opposition. The pressure of organized labor on the representatives and senators was even more intense than had been the case with the milder salary-control version of the decree just defeated. In addition, the effect of the mass mobilizations, public rallies in the cities, strikes and protests against the economic policies of the government were not lost upon the members of Congress, who now worried about their own political futures. September and October were almost completely taken up by the legislative battle in Congress fueled by increasing public pressure to strike down Decree No. 2045.

On the eve of the vote in Congress, President João Figueiredo signed a declaration of "state of emergency" in accordance with the safeguard clause included in the Constitution in exchange for the revoking of Institutional Act No. 5 in 1979. This was the first time the emergency safeguards were invoked. The "emergency declaration" was limited to Brasília, with an explicit validity period of sixty days. However, the constitutional clause allows the executive almost unlimited powers through the temporary suspension of civil guarantees, prohibition of assemblies, public demonstrations and rallies, explicit authorization of press and mail censorship, unlimited entry and seizure powers, and the explicit allowance for the appointed executor of the decree to enforce whatever other measures are deemed necessary. General Newton Cruz, who had been head of the SNI agency in Brasília, was appointed by President Figueiredo as the commander of the operations permitted by the extraordinary powers of the emergency declaration. He proceeded, during the first two days, to carry out the duties with enthusiasm. A complete blockade of the roads leading to Brasília was set up to prevent the members of trade unions from coming into the city and lobbying in Congress. Document searches were carried out. An assembly of lawyers in the local headquarters of the OAB was broken up by troops under the command of General Cruz. The outcry against the emergency was so widespread, however, that the government backed down, and the commanding general was told to not enforce the emergency decree to its fullest potential. Even in this climate of tension, Congress voted to defeat Decree No. 2045.

Two significant political interpretations should be pointed out here. First, Congress found new strength in enforcing an independent position vis à vis the executive, in spite of the overt coercive measures passed in the declaration of a state of emergency in Brasília. The members of Congress were not intimidated. On the contrary, the outrage over the exceptional coercive measures perhaps further emboldened a rebellious Congress. Second, the executive was unable to exercise fully all of the potential coercive powers available to it under the decree of emergency. The national security state was sufficiently weakened by internal contradictions and external opposition so that it contradicted itself within a few days. First a declaration of emergency was signed, troops were placed in the streets, and a hard-line general was given complete flexibility in enforcing the measures. Shortly thereafter, when General Newton Cruz began to apply his powers fully, the government backed down and retreated to a less coercive position. The government's lack of legitimacy made it difficult for the repressive apparatus to be utilized fully. The contradictory nature of the impasse between the force of the opposition and the institutionalized coercive powers of the state became evident in the events surrounding the defeat of Decree No. 2045.

The immediate introduction of two other decree-laws in Congress deepened the confused and contradictory political scenario. First the government introduced Decree-Law No. 2064, which was almost immediately replaced by Decree-Law No. 2065. Only in 1983, therefore, there were a total of five modifications introduced in the calculation of salaries. The confusion of the wage policy, with all the different decrees being enforced, at times concomitantly, became a source of irritation to workers as well as to corporations, which had trouble keeping up with all the differing requirements. The profusion of different and contradictory measures introduced in Congress, and then immediately replaced, also made evident the disorientation and weakness of the government. However, the government was able to negotiate an agreement with the PTB by which, in exchange for top posts in government administration and at least one ministerial position, that party would support Decree-Law No. 2065. With the votes of the PDS, quieted by the milder version of the decree, added to the votes of the PTB the government was finally able to assure passage of a wage-limitation bill.

Decree-Law No. 2065, approved in Congress, established in reality three different salary policies. The first, valid until 31 July 1985, establishes a salary readjustment according to four different salary brackets. Salary readjustments are still to be made every six months, using as a base the Consumer Price Index, and any real raise, for productivity, is to be limited to the growth of the national product. Workers earning up to three times the minimum salary are to get 100 percent of the INPC; from three to seven times the minimum salary, 80 percent of the INPC; from seven to fifteen times the minimum salary, 60 percent of the INPC, and for salaries over fifteen times the minimum salary only 50 percent of the INPC. The second part of the salary policy included in the decree is to last from 1 August 1985 until 31 July 1988. According to this part, from 1 August 1985 until 31 July 1986 all salaries will be readjusted at only 70 percent of the INPC, every six months. From 1 August 1986 to 31 July 1987, the percentage of readjustment falls to 60 percent of the INPC. From 1 August 1987 to 31 July 1988, the percentage readjustment of salaries falls even more, to 50 percent of the INPC.[115] Trade unions and employers may negotiate the difference between the percentages of automatic readjustment and the INPC, for those workers with higher salaries.

The difficulty in measuring the impact of this new decree, now in effect, lies in the uncertainty of the political scenario in Brazil. Although the decree predicts a continuing wage policy up to 1988, it is impossible to know whether in reality the decree will remain in effect, be modified, or even revoked altogether in response to the differing degrees of opposition that will develop. A coherent economic policy, with a government that lacks legitimacy and even the ability to enforce its own legislation, is impossible to maintain. In the immediate future it is likely that the force of Decree-Law 2065 will greatly affect salary levels. This, as DIEESE points out, is particularly true because it utilizes as a base for the calculations of salary readjustments the "purged" Consumer Price Index (INPC). In no way does the purged version of the cost of living calculations reflect real rates of inflation, and thus the loss in terms of real purchasing power for all salaried workers will be severe (see table 35).

The reaction to the measures was almost immediate. In the ABCD region, 53,000 workers went on strike. The confusion of the wage policy was demonstrated by the statement of the National Association of Vehicle Production (ANFAVEA, Associação Nacional dos Fabricantes de Veículos Automotores): "All the industries," according to the official note, "rigorously applied the law. The majority readjusted salaries by 49.9 percent—or 80 percent of the INPC, in accordance to Decree-Law No. 2045." In fact, workers were now demanding that the decree just approved (No. 2065) be enacted in spite of their general opposition to its terms. This decree guaranteed them at least 100 percent of the INPC, which they wished to have applied to all salary brackets. Ford and Volkswagen readjusted their employees' salaries by utilizing a mixture of Decree-Law No. 2065, for those who earned up to three times the minimum salary, and Decree-Law No. 2045 for those who earned more than that.[116]

Table 35
Purged INPC Effect on Wage Readjustments
April–September 1983

Adjustment Allowed by D-L 2065 (% of INPC)	% of INPC Represented by Purged INPC	% of Cost of Living as Calculated by DIEESE Represented by Purged INPC
100	93	88
80	74	70
60	56	53
50	47	44

Source: DIEESE, *Divulgação*, 07/83, p. 8.
Note: During the period the purged INPC was 64.2 percent; the INPC without the deductions was 69 percent; DIEESE's calculation of the cost of living was 72.9 percent.

The strike succeeded almost immediately. São Bernardo metalworkers utilized their temporary advantage to press corporations into negotiations. First they realized that companies such as Ford, for example, were dependent on uninterrupted production to meet their schedules of car exports to the European markets. Ford was pressing for time to manufacture thirteen hundred Escort cars scheduled for delivery to Finland, Norway, and Sweden. This program alone was expected to raise over $5 million in profits. Through 1983 Ford had to deliver two thousand new Escorts and could not afford to stop the production process. For 1984 Ford plans to export ten thousand Escorts, already sold to the European markets, at an estimated value of $40 million.[117] Therefore, the metalworkers' threat to completely, and indefinitely, paralyze production was taken seriously by all the large automobile corporations, which, as was the case with Ford, are dependent on exports for profits. Negotiations were also eased by the confusion of the different wage decrees, confusion that did not allow the government to declare the strike illegal. Finally, in spite of the fact that the union was intervened, the metalworkers maintained a unity and a degree of organization, led by Jair Meneguelli and Lula, that allowed them to be completely successful. As to the government, the contradictions and weaknesses of the economic program and the political coercion powers became evident:

It [the government] has its hands and feet tied. It fought for the laws, managed to approve them, ran the risk of becoming even more unpopular, and now it watches these same laws, which were approved against the expressed will of the workers, be used by the leaders themselves against the economic policy of Minister Delfim Neto, a policy that was elaborated with the idea that it would be valid to plan the long-term development of the industrial sector. He was clearly wrong, however, at least insofar as the automobile production sector is concerned. And that sector, for the most part, regulates all other activities in the economy.[118]

Conclusion

Although the government, by the end of 1983, was in a situation of disarray and confusion—both politically and in terms of economic policies—it nonetheless still maintained a considerable amount of power within the complex institutional framework that was built after 1964. The military was divided as to specific policies to be followed, some even beginning to question the Doctrine of National Security and Development.[119] On the other hand, the basic structures of political power remained intact. Congress had regained some of its influence, but it remains to be seen whether the opposition can muster a sufficient majority to make institutional changes in the Constitution so as to return to the Congress its full power. The National Security Law was modified but not revoked or profoundly affected in its basic elements.[120] Negotiations with key elite groups, with more flexible mechanisms of power characteristic of the policy of *abertura*, were the major element that would allow continuity through stronger alliance with sectors of the opposition.

As the year developed, the contradictions within the opposition parties became more sharply defined. Within the PMDB, some argued for immediate negotiation with the military, which would allow a consensus candidate to be elected through the indirect Electoral College (under the present legislation, it is to elect the president in 1985). Others agreed with the need to negotiate, but not to capitulate (the strategy became popularized as "*conciliação*"). This, in essence, meant that there should be extensive negotiations for further liberalizing measures, which would include—as the primordial goal—direct elections for president and the calling of a Constituent Assembly. Governor Leonel Brizola, of the PDT of Rio de Janeiro, proposed still a third alternative: that President Figueiredo remain for another two years with the expressed purpose of organizing direct elections for president. The PTB, no longer to be considered an opposition party, had sealed a direct alliance with the government's PDS in exchange for promised top positions in the administration. The PT maintained a united program calling for the revoking of the National Security Law (as opposed to its reform), for direct and immediate elections for president, and for the end of all the institutional legality of the military governments.

In addition to all the different proposed reforms and negotiations with the military, the contradictions within the opposition governments added to the general confusion of the political scenario. Governors of the opposition were caught in the web of having to exercise political and administrative power within an authoritarian system, with centralized federal tax controls, limited access to resources, and little possibility of changing the major precepts of the economic policies that were federally elaborated but that affected the states and municipalities in a most direct manner. That so many members of the opposition parties now shared local political power, at the state and the municipal levels, in practice meant that they shared with the central government the responsibility for the economic and social situation. It is indicative of the population's interpretation of the situation that, only a few weeks after taking office, Governor Franco Montoro of São Paulo (PMDB) already faced the most serious riot in the history of the state. The angered population stormed the governor's palace to demand implementation of policies that would relieve unemployment and increase salaries. Montoro, unable to change the recessive policies that caused unemployment and financially limited by the state of bankruptcy of the government's finances, reacted with fear and repressed the population.[121]

In fact, a coherent police policy has been consistently the most difficult area of administration for the opposition governments. The resistance of the local police and the only partial influence that the state governments have on the military police increase the difficulty of handling a situation of increasing violence. However, the fact that, even under democratically elected governments, unemployed and strikers are still arrested and beaten in the streets has caused sharp criticism of the opposition governments. The governors of the opposition, and their parties, as a consequence, suffered significant loss of prestige in 1983. Unable to control their police forces and to plan their finances and economic programs, the opposition governors became managers of a growing political, economic, and social crisis. The population tended to see them as partially responsible for the general paralysis at all levels of government. Because they now shared so much municipal and state power also forced them to share in the blame. In the process of attempting to govern within the strict parameters imposed by the authoritarian system, the opposition governments became more conservative in bent and paralyzed in concrete political, social, and economic alternatives. The proposition of participation in matters of government was abandoned in most municipal and state governments. The population, however, recalled the hopeful campaign slogans and pressured the state governments into more direct overt actions. What was then seen, in 1983, was an adaptation to the general authoritarian structure, so that the governments of the opposition became almost indistinguishable from the state governments of the PDS. The elite sectors, which now shared local power, adapted to the previous administrative and power structures rather than attempting to modify them profoundly in the general context of social crisis.

The opposition parties, affected by the performance of their members in power, suffered a loss of prestige. Divided in terms of strategy, as well, they were still unable to develop a consistent alternative plan, common to all parties, that would be forceful enough to unite all the different sectors in opposition to the central government. The dialectical relation between the state and the opposition, in 1983, developed into a frantic pace, keeping both sides suspended in indecision and contradictory positions. In essence, the dialectical relation between the state and the opposition transformed both totalities. The government began slowly to unravel further mechanisms of negotiation, which would allow the basic system to continue while making greater concessions toward incorporating key elite opposition groups. On the other hand, the elite members of the opposition, now holding considerable power themselves, retreated in their demands and began also to search for a consensual position that would allow them to have greater flexibility in local government. It has become clear, however, that, with a consensus and a deeper negotiation, the government's lack of legitimacy could also affect the legitimacy of the opposition parties.

Conclusion: The Opposition and the State in Perspective

The Dialectic of State and Opposition

With the crisis of formal democracy in 1964, the clientele classes in Brazil—associated with international capital—moved decisively to transform the structures of the state so as to continue an exploitative-dependent model of capitalist development. When the civil-military coalition took power in 1964, there was a general blueprint for the institutionalization of the state. The ideology of national security provided an important organizational framework and served, at the same time, as a justification for the need to build repressive mechanisms to control civil society. Having carefully developed a basic program to control civil society in order to curb the danger of the "enemy within," state planners began the work of institution building.

The attempt to organize the totality of Brazilian society within the framework of the Doctrine of National Security and Development was, however, blocked by a constant resurgence of opposition. The national security state, therefore, was not constructed according to blueprint but rather emerged from a dialectical relationship between the forces in power and the organized opposition. Specific controls had to be created in response to challenges from civil society, for opposition developed in social groups, in the judiciary, in the legislature, and even within the "internal public" of the military itself. These challenges became particularly pressing during those periodic upsurges of dissent in which the various opposition sectors united to form a vast social protest movement. These periods forced a reorganization of state structures to develop new mechanisms of control sufficient to bring about a new conformity.

The national security state has never succeeded in eliminating opposition and resistance to its policies and to its very existence. The application of coercion to a particular target has tended to generate support from previously inactive groups and thereby actually to increase the overall strength of the opposition. Furthermore, targeted opposition groups have not been eliminated but only temporarily disbanded, to surface again as part of a more coherently organized and experienced totality. And, the main structural contradictions implicit in the attempt to institutionalize the national security state on a stable and permanent basis have defied resolution; they have instead been continually displaced from one locus of opposition to another: labor against capital (both private and publicly organized); formal politics of elite parties against the government; popular-based social movements against the state; national capital against international capital; moral protest against the repressive apparatus. The fundamental tension between the state's need for legitimation and the repressive organization of production required by its economic model has meant that neutralization of one form of opposition has entailed the activation of another.[1]

The displacement that occurred as a result of the state's attempt to crush all resistance can be seen throughout the different development phases of the opposition. In the first period, the opposition took a largely defensive stance against the excesses of the 1964 purges and denounced maltreatment and torture of political prisoners. The national security state's attempt to install a parallel legal system alienated the judiciary, which resisted encroachment by exerting its independence in judgments of those indicted by the IPMs. After the 1965 elections and the passage of Institutional Act No. 2, the opposition was reinforced by new groups offended by the abolition of the political parties and encroachment on legislative and judicial prerogatives. The beginning of dissent among elite sectors can be traced to that period.

In 1966 the national security state went on the offensive, laying the foundation of the economic model with a series of laws for wage control and incentives to multinational investment. Attacks on the autonomy of the universities and against student organizations fueled resistance in that sector. Although its original effect was to dismantle workers' organizations, a policy of continuing intervention in the trade unions spurred an increase in efforts to organize and win back control of the unions. One union official I interviewed remarked that the period of state intervention was the one in which workers participated most actively in union affairs, stimulated by the desire to regain control.[2] During 1967 and 1968 opposition spread from one sector to another, until accumulated dissatisfaction with state policy erupted in a social movement, catalyzed by the death of Edson Luís and the violence of state repression of students and workers. To those groups already involved in opposition activities was added the support of members of the middle class and the Catholic church. Church participation, at this point, was limited to defending the right to protest rather than organizing opposition directly.

The period of armed struggle was dominated by the symbiotic violence of armed opposition groups and the security forces of the national security state. Although the state did succeed in eliminating the challenge of the armed revolutionaries, it increasingly displaced opposition to middle sectors, to the church, and to elite groups concerned with torture, violence, disappearances, and severe violations of human rights, which now directly touched their own members. The extreme physical violence with which the state crushed the armed challenge laid the foundations for the period of "formal" politics after 1974. This period saw the political remobilization and increasingly vigorous opposition activity of elite sectors, acting though traditional civil organizations such as the OAB, the ABI, and the CNBB and united around the issues of freedom of expression, freedom of the press, freedom of association, and the protection of civil, political, and human rights. The political space created by such activity in turn made possible a resurgence of the student movement (in the reorganized UNE) and of the popular sector (both industrial workers and peasants). The opposition at this point became a multiclass movement of resistance to the overall framework of the national security state, its parallel legal system, its restrictions on civil society, and the limits of its economic model.

During the liberalization periods, the opposition was able, in many (often ingenious) ways, to participate at the level of formal politics, using existing institutions, including even some that the military itself had established. The military was thus continually forced to change the rules of the game, with the result that its credibility, legitimacy, and popular support were further weakened. Thus while the April Package in 1977 may have succeeded in its objective of maintaining control over Congress, it accomplished this goal by means so obviously manipulative as to negate the legitimacy of the result; the creation of "bionic" senators earned the government widespread, loudly voiced, and persisting ridicule. Similarly, the Lei Falcão had the unexpected and contradictory consequence of forcing the MDB to develop its organization at the base. From that point on, the Catholic church, the OAB, the ABI, and the MDB worked in earnest to establish connections with the base and among the different opposition groups. Two of these institutions, the church and the Bar Association, traditionally had been prominent in the legitimation of the state. The church came to deny support to the state largely because of human rights questions, the lawyers because of a commitment to traditional legality, opposition to the dual legal system, and an inability to function professionally as a result of that system.

By the end of the Geisel period, then, the state had suffered a sharp decline in political, moral, and legal legitimacy, as evidenced in the open and increasingly vigorous opposition of Congress, the church, the press, and the legal profession. In addition, growing difficulties in implementing the economic model, rising inflation, and skyrocketing foreign debt brought substantial sections of the national bourgeoisie into the fray, demanding greater participation in economic decision-making. The *abertura* policy, according to Golbery, was necessary to avoid the "black hole" of overcentralized power. The state was isolated; it was in trouble economically; it was concerned about the parallel power of the security forces and the inefficiency of the overcentralized bureaucratic apparatus. For its own survival, it needed to decentralize and become more flexible. For its own legitimacy, it had to liberalize enough to recover some base of support. However, by this time the grass-roots movement had raised a further challenge by making demands that required the transformation of the economic model itself.

Unlike their counterparts in Chile, Uruguay, or Argentina,[3] Brazilian generals used the language of democracy to implant a dictatorial system. The disparity between the language and the practical need for repression has had two important consequences. First, it has forced the military government to seek legitimacy based on consensus established in formal institutions of political representation. The government has thus not been able to abolish such bodies as Congress, state and municipal assemblies, and political parties. Although elections have been manipulated, they have nonetheless been held regularly, for they have continued to be necessary to maintain a minimum of legitimation. Similarly, although the judiciary was brought under control, it managed to retain a degree of autonomy, which it exercised to varying degrees in different periods. Second, the gap between the language and the institutional reality has opened space for the opposition to maneuver, organize, and even negotiate within the system. It has been able to use this space to force further liberalization and to organize a vast social movement at the grass-roots level.

In the dialectical relationship with an opposition movement that it could not destroy and whose relationship with the state was continually changing, the national security state was constantly forced to incorporate some of the demands of opposition sectors. Hence, after each period of repression (which reflected the view of the "internal security" sector within the military) the state would implement a policy of gradual liberalization in order to lower the level of tension created by the violence of the repressive apparatus. An analysis of the formative years of the national security state discloses various characteristics (see fig. 9). First, every president since 1964, with the exception of General Médici, has initiated a policy of liberalization intended to ease or repair the previous policy of violent repression or legislative controls. All presidents, including General Médici, began their terms with a promise to restore democratic forms of government before leaving office. All were at some point forced to apply the full force of the repressive apparatus, and none, in fact, restored democracy.

Second, the strategy of the repressive apparatus changed over the different periods. The first wave of repression in 1964 was intended to destroy all political connections to the former government and to social

Fig. 9. Repression and Liberalization Cycles

REPRESSION CYCLES	LIBERALIZATION CYCLES
1964: First wave of repression, to eliminate those connected to past political and social movements.	*1965*: Castello Branco's policy of "return to normalcy" after, Institutional Act No. 1.
1966-1967: Completion of political purges after Institutional Act No. 2.	*1967-1968*: Costa e Silva's "policy of relief," including negotiations with opposition sectors.
1969-1973: Comprehensive and most severe cycle of repression, to deal with armed rebellion and to implant the repressive apparatus.	*1974-1976*: Geisel's "decompression" policy, which ended with the April Package of 1977.
1975-1976: Repression most localized in state of São Paulo, to deal with an emerging broad national front of opposition.	*1977-1979*: Geisel's "distension" policy resumed and negotiations with opposition for reforms and for end to Institutional Act No. 5.
1979-1982: Class-based repression, targeted to destroy social movements of workers and peasants.	*1979-1982*: Figueiredo's policy of *abertura*, or political opening. Includes broader negotiations with elite opposition sectors and church.

movements. Repression was nationwide and cut across class lines. Only those with ties to past governments or to populist social movements were defined as "internal enemies." Politicians with links to former governments—the primary targets of the repression—were generally from the middle or upper classes, but repression was also aimed at working class and peasant leaders and militants, and at members of Catholic social movements that had supported the organization of the poor in the pre-1964 period. In the 1966-1967 period, repression was applied to complete the purges that had not been carried out to the satisfaction of the guardians of internal security. Fewer arrests were made, but the purges were extended to include some of those who had been saved from conviction by the independent stance of the judiciary. After Institutional Act No. 5, during the 1969 to 1973 period, the situation changed. The state was confronted with armed opposition, and it fully implanted the repressive apparatus on this excuse. All citizens were considered suspect until they could prove otherwise, and repression reached all groups, with little distinction between classes or political affiliation.

During the early phase of General Geisel's "decompression" policy, there were two important aspects to the strategy of repression. First, a massive nationwide campaign by the armed forces was specifically aimed at the destruction of the organizational framework of two surviving underground parties: the Brazilian Communist party (PCB) and the Maoist Communist Party of Brazil (PC do B). Second, repression in 1975-1976 became particularly concentrated in São Paulo, where human rights and other broad-based grass-roots movements were rapidly organizing to challenge the national security state in its economic heart.[4] During the *abertura* years, the repression strategy became increasingly class-selective. The *abertura* policy did not prepare for the growth of the grass-roots and labor movements, both developing increasingly close ties to the church. The intent of the policy had been to build an institutional framework flexible enough to provide the state with a "new social pact," with an enlarged base of support in upper- and middle-class sectors, but not so flexible as to admit the possibility of alternative social, economic, or political policies. The Figueiredo government was thus most concerned with setting the bounds of acceptable and of intolerable opposition. Working class and peasant social movements, and those who supported them, were clearly not tolerable in that they constituted a challenge to the economic model.

A third point of interest in examining the sequence of repression and liberalization cycles is their placement in time. Until the beginning of the decompression policy in 1974, liberalization cycles chronologically followed repression cycles. With the beginning of the third stage of institutionalization, during the Geisel government, this no longer held true. Because of its more selective character, repression could exist simultaneously with a period of liberalization. Thus the sharp distinction between repression and liberalization was blurred, and selective acts of coercion could be carried out at the same time as increased political liberalization and negotiations with key sectors of the elite opposition. This has been one of the most important elements of a policy designed to eliminate pressure from elites and to attain long-term stability without losing political and economic control.

Finally and perhaps most important, the *abertura* period has been characterized by increased use of paramilitary and clandestine forms of repression. Undercover terrorist actions have been carried out against important opposition groups: bombs have been placed in the headquarters of the OAB, the ABI, in the municipal chamber of Rio de Janeiro, in the Cathedral of Nova Iguaçú, in dozens of newspaper stands selling opposition publications, and (in what was probably the most significant incident) an attempt was made to place a bomb at an opposition benefit concert where twenty thousand young people were gathered.[5] Furthermore, an increase in the activities of the underground death squadrons and the Mão Branca (White Hand) organization suggest a decentralization of repression and a new reliance on covert operations that are not formally recognized by authorities of the state but that maintain the climate of terror necessary for effective political control over marginalized populations.

Thus the dismantling of centralized or official repressive organizations such as the CODI-DOI and the SNI would not necessarily signify an improvement in the human rights situation (a similar move was made in Chile with the dismantling of the Chilean secret police, the DINA, and its replacement by more decentralized and hidden kinds of physical repression). There are even indications that Brazil's repression strategy may move closer to the decentralized structure of the repressive apparatus in Argentina, which was both more effective in dealing with widespread and diffuse social protest movements and less visible as a target for internal and international public opinion. The Argentine "doctrine of war" is a possible model for repressive action, a prospect with clearly ominous implications for the future of the Brazilian state.[6]

Dismantling the machinery of the repressive apparatus in Brazil will be a definite step toward democracy only when it is conducted within the context of shared political, economic, and social power in a transition period that decisively breaks with the Doctrine of National Security and Development. Indeed, the dismantling of the repressive apparatus must be accomplished simultaneously with the end of the national security state itself. Structures of decentralized repression could lead Brazil into a violent skirmish, which could well escalate into an undeclared state of social and political civil war.

The Search for Stability

The national security state in Brazil has been engaged in a constant search for institutional stability. The development of its institutional framework followed three distinct stages of institutionalization. In the first stage, an attempt was made to apply the formal blueprint and lay the foundation for a lasting state structure. President Castello Branco put in place the first elements of the economic development model and attempted to institutionalize its political and social priorities in a new constitution. But developing contradictions in the relations between the state and the opposition, as well as within the state itself, made it impossible to follow the original plans. The guardians of internal security and the repressive apparatus temporarily resolved the institutional crisis of 1968 by assuming control. The combination of contradictions within the economic model, contradictions within the state, and the confrontation with both armed and nonviolent opposition, forced the state to seek new forms of stability. Abandoning the effort to institutionalize the national security state through achieving a broader base of support, the coalition in power sought stability by means of extensive and explicit use of coercive force.

The second stage of institutionalization, which began with the passage of Institutional Act No. 5 in 1969, was centered around the development of the security apparatus. Stability was sought by means of terror and the suppression of dissent on the one hand, by the implementation of a capitalistic economic development model on the other. This meant that the achievement of long-term stability was linked to continued high rates of economic growth (to demonstrate the success of the model), and, consequently, the state was confronted with a deep crisis when the first signs of economic trouble appeared.

The third stage of institutionalization of the national security state began in 1974 with the government of General Ernesto Geisel and the policy of decompression. At this point, the state resumed its previous effort to find a balance between selective repression and more flexibile mechanisms of representation that would allow it to extend its base of support among middle- and upper-class groups, now disaffected because of the violence of the repression and the end of the economic miracle. The search for legitimacy was the major characteristic of the Geisel period, and the post-1979 *abertura* period, during the Figueiredo presidency, must be understood not as a stage of transition to democracy but rather as a continuation of the policy of controlled decompression of society in the interests of long-term institutionalization of the national security state. The *abertura* policy has been bounded by the Doctrine of National Security and Development, and thus has not been open to participation of marginalized sectors of the population, which have demanded substantial modification of the economic development model.

The constant search for stability and long-term institutionalization reveals the inherent fragility of the national security state. This fragility is caused by a combination of three main elements: the state's inability to achieve legitimacy and its increasing isolation from civil society; its inability to develop stable and effective mechanisms for the transfer of power; and its inability to overcome dissent and contradiction within its own main base of support, the military. The continuing legitimacy crisis has reflected the state's inability to disguise the disparity between the language of democracy and the practice of repression. Even during periods of relative relaxation of physical repression, the need to employ rather obvious means of electoral manipulation continually has undermined the state's legitimacy claims. The persistence of extreme and very visible social inequality and the continued severe—if selective—application of violence have undermined efforts to secure stability by means of the more flexible mechanisms of representation developed in the third stage of institutionalization.

New Dilemmas and Challenges

The economic model has imposed extremely heavy burdens on the majority of the population; these burdens weigh increasingly on the middle class. The trend toward ever-greater concentration is most pronounced in rural areas, where the poorest 50 percent of the population has suffered a 33 percent reduction in its share of national income. On the other hand, the richest 1 percent has seen its share rise by 179 percent.[7] Whereas, during the time of the economic miracle, Minister Delfim Netto had dismissed the growing foreign debt as unimportant, it became, by the 1980s, a major bottleneck. In 1980 the debt service absorbed as much as 61 percent of total export earnings. In addition, two thirds of the debt was contracted with floating interest rates, meaning that rising interest rates in other countries seriously affect Brazil's debt position.[8] By December 1982 the Brazilian foreign debt had officially reached $91 billion.[9] Inflation also continued to plague the country, reaching 110.2 percent in 1980 and maintaining a rate of over 95 percent for the next two years. In 1983 it reached over 200 percent.[10] Economic troubles upset the balance of forces in a continuing institutional crisis of social unrest and instability.

Looking at the national security state's policies in perspective, to what extent have they succeeded in achieving the goals of institution building and long-term stability? What contradictions have developed between the state and the organized opposition and what do they suggest for the future? Although the state has been haunted by contradictions and is in many ways institutionally fragile, it has, nonetheless, achieved a remarkable degree of control over civil society. Two important facets need to be considered. The first is the penetration of national security ideology within the military itself. The three major components of the doctrine—the theory of internal security, the economic development model, and the orientation toward the permanent national objectives—structure military training in the ESG, the ECEME, and particularly in the Intelligence School. These three training centers form the system of the intelligence community. The second aspect to consider is the impact of the military on the state apparatus itself. Since 1964 the presidency has been occupied by five military men. In 1981 as many as one fifth of the top administrative posts in Brazil were held by members of the military and, among the top executive posts, thirteen of twenty-six ministers of state and top advisers came from the military.[11] The military has also taken control of the top state-owned corporations, mostly those corporations linked to the military-industrial complex or to the control of strategic minerals.

The military's influence in shaping politics has been demonstrated in the consistent ability of hard-line sectors to impose their points of view in moments of crisis. Legislation demanded by those sectors has shaped relations with civil society. The generals most closely involved in the actual running of the state are the authors of 76 percent of the legislation passed since 1964:

Between April 1964 and 11 December 1980, the president of the republic signed a total of 2,572 laws. Of these, a total of 1,956 were written by the executive power itself, and only 590 originated in the legislative branch, with a further 26 coming from the judiciary. In addition, a relevant aspect is the number of decree-laws issued by the executive without any input or power from the legislative branch: from 1964 to 9 March 1981, the executive issued 1,866 decree-laws, of which 186 were during the presidency of João Figueiredo. During the period of congressional recess between 6 December 1980 and 28 February 1981, Figueiredo issued exactly 50 decree-laws.[12]

The legislative influence and economic power of the military is a factor that must be considered in analyzing the national security state. It is within the military that the state finds its strongest base of support, a base powerful enough to determine the format of legality. Within its continuing dialectical relation to the opposition, the state has three potential alternatives: higher levels of physical repression and political coercion; a renewed attempt to broaden its base of support so that it does not rely so heavily on military power—something that might be accomplished by further development of clientelistic ties and state-influenced organization at the grass-roots level; and continued application of selective repression against intolerable opposition while engaging in negotiations with elite sectors of the opposition and co-opting support.

The potential consequences of the first alternative limit its long-term feasibility. A renewal of heavy political repression would entail high stakes. It would require nationwide military mobilization, which might elicit resistance from some groups of the military. The coercion would have to be extended to cover sectors of the elite opposition and members of the

Catholic hierarchy who have become strongly connected to opposition activities. The legitimation problems posed by recourse to such an act of internal war would be vast and the international repercussions enormous. In addition, although such a policy might appear attractive in the short run, it would be extremely difficult for the central government to keep the organisms of repression under control, and this, together with the adverse international implications, make it a difficult alternative for the state in the long run.

The second alternative amounts to, in a sense, "playing the game of the opposition" by becoming involved in grass-roots politics. Such a policy would involve use of the bureaucratic apparatus to foment and control neighborhood associations, clubs, collectives, cooperative organizations, peasant and urban labor unions. A corporative policy of social control, similar to Mexico's, might use clientelistic and patronage relations to promote greater support for state policies at the base level, but although such a policy is promising for the long-term institutionalization and legitimation needs of the state, it is limited by the real economic constraints posed by the crisis. An economy troubled by the weight of the foreign debt and high inflation does not allow policymakers to engage in sufficiently flexible clientele arrangements to co-opt significant numbers at the grass-roots level. There are, in reality, even indications that the economic concessions granted during the strike period of 1979 will have to be reversed to comply with the austerity program imposed by the International Monetary Fund. The salary policy, for example, has already been significantly modified, eliminating the incremental increases above inflation for those wage earners who earn up to three times the minimum monthly wage.[13]

The third option would be a combination of policies, in a continuation of the dialectical relation with the opposition. There would be a number of elements in this alternative: first, there would be a policy of selective or underground repression; second, the social base would at least be somewhat expanded by developing more flexible clientelistic and patronage patterns; third, there would have to be a sharing of power and negotiation with certain opposition groups, at least on municipal and state levels; fourth, control over the electoral process would be maintained with new manipulative mechanisms to guarantee continuing feasibility for the PDS; and finally, new measures would have to be enacted to keep the process of constitutional reform under the control of the state planners. These measures, taken together, would succeed in buying the state more time, in spite of its isolation and lack of legitimacy. A measure of stability could be obtained in a continuing dialectic with the opposition.

From the point of view of the opposition, the reality of continuing state power marks the boundaries of possible negotiation and modification of the political, social, and economic models. In spite of an inherent institutional instability, the state retains sufficient influence to pass significant measures to ensure its own continuation. The opposition, although with greater popular support and legitimacy, is still divided and lacks adequate forms for mediation. Political parties are in their infancy; they are fragile, and could be disbanded by the state at any moment because, ultimately, the initiative remains in the hands of the state. In addition, the opposition is locked into the framework of "strong democracy" and is in a defensive position, often reacting to the initiatives of the state. To continue to develop influence and organization, the opposition will have to find ways to escape the circle that surrounds it. Mechanisms must be developed to allow social and political participation in the decisions of state in order to transform, from the bottom, the structures of political and economic society in such a way that it becomes responsive to the needs of the population. The dialectic of state and opposition has become a prison to both.

Appendix

Table A-1
Rates of Inflation

Year	Rate of Inflation	Year	Rate of Inflation
1960	26.3	1972	17.4
1961	33.3	1973	20.5
1962	54.8	1974	31.5
1963	78.5	1975	32.7
1964	87.8	1976	41.9
1965	55.4	1977	44.1
1966	39.5	1978	40.8
1967	28.8	1979	77.2
1968	27.8	1980	110.2
1969	20.3	1981	97.0
1970	18.2	1982	99.7
1971	17.3	1983*	239.0

Sources: 1960–1977: World Bank Country Study, *Brazil: Human Resources Special Report* (October 1979)
1978: *O Estado de São Paulo* (3 January 1978), p. 23.
1979: *Latin America Regional Reports* (5 February 1982), p. 6.
1980: *Latin American Weekly Report* (6 February 1981), p. 8.
1981: *Latin American Regional Reports* (5 February 1982), p. 6.
1982: *Latin America Regional Reports* (11 February 1983), p. 6.
1983: Luiz Carlos Bresser Pereira, in "Os limites tecnoburocráticos-burgueses da abertura brasileira." Paper presented at the XI International Congress of the Latin American Studies Association (Mexico City, 29 September–1 October 1983), p. 32.
*There have been different estimates for the 1983 inflation rate partly because the official government statistics now do not include price rises in food due to the mid-year end of food-crop subsidies or to the consequences of weather conditions. Thus economists vary in their estimates. For example, Julian Chacel, economist of the Fundação Getúlio Vargas of Rio de Janeiro, which is responsible for the calculation of the INPC (Consumer Price Index), estimates 1983 inflation at 180 percent. *Isto E*, 10 August 1983, estimated inflation at 112.5 percent by taking into account price rises until August 1983. Marcelo Antinori, an economist of the Fundação Getúlio Vargas of São Paulo, estimates the 1983 inflation rate at 305 percent in an article in *Folha de São Paulo* (28 November 1983), p. 6.

Table A-2
Foreign Debt, Reserves, Export Earnings
(Billions of U.S. Dollars)

Year	Gross Foreign Debt	Reserves	Net Foreign Debt	Export Earnings	Net Foreign Debt ÷ Export Earnings
1960	3,071.0	345.0	2,726.0	1,270.0	2.15
1961	3,080.0	470.0	2,610.0	1,405.0	1.86
1962	3,183.1	285.0	2,898.1	1,215.0	2.39
1963	3,185.5	219.0	2,966.5	1,400.0	2.12
1964	3,101.1	245.0	2,856.1	1,430.0	2.00
1965	3,478.4	484.0	2,994.4	1,595.5	1.88
1966	3,702.4	425.0	3,277.4	1,741.4	1.88
1967	3,372.0	199.0	3,173.0	1,654.0	1.92
1968	3,917.0	257.0	3,660.0	1,881.3	1.95
1969	4,403.3	657.0	3,746.3	2,311.2	1.62
1970	5,295.2	1,187.0	4,108.2	2,738.9	1.50
1971	6,621.6	1,722.9	4,898.7	2,904.0	1.69
1972	9,521.0	4,183.2	5,337.8	3,991.0	1.34
1973	12,571.5	6,415.8	6,155.7	6,199.0	0.99
1974	17,165.7	5,269.1	11,896.6	7,951.0	1.50
1975	21,171.4	4,040.5	17,130.9	8,670.0	1.98
1976	27,600.0	6,400.0	21,200.0	10,100.0	2.10
1977	32,037.0	7,256.0	24,781.0	12,120.0	2.04

1978	43,511.0	11,895.0	31,616.0	12,659.0	2.50
1979	49,904.0	9,689.0	40,215.0	15,244.0	2.64
1980	53,847.0	6,913.0	46,934.0	20,132.0	2.33
1981	61,411.0	7,505.0	53,906.0	23,293.0	2.31

Sources: *Conjuntura Econômica* 26 (April 1976); *Boletim do Banco Central do Brasil.*
Note: The amount for foreign debt and reserves refers to the end of each year. On 8 December 1982 the Brazilian foreign debt had reached $91 billion (US). The New York branch of Banco do Brasil was short of funds to cover its operation. The shortfall was variously estimated at $50 million (US) by government officials and $350 million by U.S. bankers. An overnight rescue operation was organized by Bankers Trust, Citibank, and other banks. See the report in *Latin America Weekly Report* (15 December 1982), p. 1.

Table A-3
Growth Rates, by Sector

Year	Growth Rate Agriculture (%)	Industry (%)
1960	4.9	9.6
1961	7.6	10.6
1962	5.5	7.8
1963	1.0	0.2
1964	1.3	5.2
1965	13.8	− 4.7
1966	−15.0	9.8
1967	9.2	3.0
1968	4.5	13.3
1969	3.8	12.1
1970	1.0	10.4
1971	11.4	14.3
1972	4.1	13.4
1973	3.5	15.8
1974	8.5	9.9
1975	3.4	6.2
1976	4.2	10.8
1977	9.6	3.9
1978	− 0.9	5.9
1979	3.8	6.3
1980	6.5	8.0
1981	6.8	− 8.0
1982	3.5	1.0

Sources: For 1960–1977, World Bank, Country Study, *Brazil: Human Resources Special Report* (October 1979), p. 66, Annex II; for 1978–1979, *Latin America Regional Reports* (1 January 1982), p. 8; for 1980, ibid. (20 November 1981), p. 8; for 1981–1982, ibid. (7 January 1983), p. 8.

Table A-4
Private National, Multinational, and Public Sector Firms
in Economic Sectors, 1978
(%)

Sector	Type of Firm		
	Private National	Multinational	Public Sector
Predominantly national			
Civil construction	100.0	—	—
Communications	100.0	—	—
Supermarkets	98.3	1.7	—
Furniture	97.4	2.6	—
Clothing, shoes	96.9	3.1	—
Retail business	90.0	10.0	—
Heavy construction	88.7	8.5	2.8
Printing & publishing	73.8	26.2	—
Food	66.6	33.4	—
Pulp & paper	59.9	32.9	7.2
Nonmetallic minerals	58.0	42.0	—
Predominantly foreign			
Wholesale business	41.4	42.2	16.4
Machinery	41.5	48.8	9.7
Transportation equipment	37.7	53.6	8.7
Heavy vehicles	45.2	54.8	—
Petroleum distribution	11.0	60.8	28.2
Electronics	33.6	66.4	—
Textiles	31.8	68.2	—
Cleaning products	27.2	72.8	—
Plastics & rubber	21.5	76.1	2.4
Beverages & tobacco	23.6	76.4	—
Pharmaceuticals	15.6	84.4	—
Office equipment	13.8	86.2	—
Automobiles	0.6	99.4	—
Predominantly state			
Public service	—	—	100.0
Chemicals & petrochemicals	5.0	15.8	79.2
Steel	27.1	7.9	65.0
Minerals	29.5	12.0	58.5
Transportation	49.6	—	50.4

Sources: "Melhores e Maiores," *Exame* (Special edition, September 1979), p. 125 (these figures refer to the sales of the twenty largest firms in each sector); Sylvia Ann Hewlett, *The Cruel Dilemmas of Development: 20th Century Brazil* (New York: Basic Books, 1980).

Table A-5
Direct Private Investment

U.S. Direct Private Investment
(Millions of U.S. $)

| Year | Total | Book Value at Year End | |
		Manufacturing	Manufacturing as % of Total
1929	194	46	24
1940	240	70	29
1946	323	125	39
1950	644	285	44
1957	835	378	45
1961	1,000	543	54
1964	994	673	68
1967	1,326	891	67
1972	2,490	1,745	70
1974	3,760	2,578	69
1977	5,956	3,935	66
1978	7,170	4,684	65

Direct Foreign Investment by Country of Origin

| Year | % Distribution | | | | |
	United States	West Germany	France	United Kingdom	Japan
1961	43	9	4	4	4
1969	48	10	2	6	3
1975	33	12	4	6	12
1977	31	14	4	5	11
1978	29	15	4	5	10

Source: Sylvia Ann Hewlett, *The Cruel Dilemmas of Development: 20th Century Brazil* (New York: Basic Books, 1980).

Table A-6

Average Monthly Income, Persons 10 Years of Age or Older, 1980

Average Monthly Income (multiple of minimum wage)	Total No. of Persons	% of Total	White	% of Total White	Color Black	% of Total Black	Yellow	% of Total Yellow	Brown	% of Total Brown
Men	43,342,266	99.5	23,972,876	99.5	2,673,825	99.3	332,199	99.5	16,271,228	99.5
Up to 1	10,542,721	24.3	4,296,339	17.9	886,920	33.1	29,785	8.9	5,307,797	32.6
Between 1 and 2.9	13,790,604	32.5	7,809,270	32.5	962,290	35.9	49,714	14.9	4,946,104	30.3
Between 3 and 4.9	3,829,195	8.8	2,673,864	11.1	152,321	5.7	42,511	12.8	956,970	5.9
Between 5 and 10	2,616,443	6.0	2,026,380	8.4	61,102	2.3	56,704	17.0	469,242	2.9
More than 10	1,816,860	4.2	1,562,907	6.5	12,976	0.5	57,464	17.3	180,792	1.1
No income	10,746,443	24.7	5,604,116	23.3	598,216	22.3	96,021	28.9	4,410,323	27.0
Women	45,570,033	99.5	25,730,913	99.5	2,676,525	99.53	305,001	99.4	16,107,523	99.5
Up to 1	7,738,129	17.3	3,731,759	14.7	765,474	28.50	21,074	6.9	3,201,240	19.8
Between 3 and 4.9	1,022,934	2.3	828,884	3.3	22,106	0.80	14,712	4.8	155,223	1.0
Between 5 and 10	628,887	1.4	535,607	2.1	12,538	0.50	11,354	3.7	68,661	0.4
More than 10	227,280	0.5	207,049	0.8	907	0.03	3,121	1.0	15,798	0.1
No income	29,999,574	67.1	16,696,921	65.6	1,582,528	58.90	223,345	72.9	11,416,597	70.7

Source: IBGE, Census data for 1980. Published in Deputado Eduardo Matarazzo Suplicy, speech, 12 April 1982, "As Sequelas da Escravidão," Assembléia Legislativa de São Paulo.

Note: The census did not separate Japanese and Chinese; all are included in "yellow." Similarly, Indians are included in the color brown, together with lighter blacks. There have been criticisms as well of the separation of the classification "black" into "brown" and "black," hence diminishing the actual numbers of black people. I have maintained the classification as originally included in the census.

Table A-7

Income Distribution among Economically Active Population with Declared Income

Economic Sector	1960		1970			1972	1976			1980		
	% of Total Income	% of Urban Income	% of Total Income	% of Urban Income	% of Rural Income	% of Total Income	% of Total Income	% of Urban Income	% of Rural Income	% of Total Income	% of Urban Income	% of Rural Income
Poorest 20%	3.9	3.2	3.4		5.2	2.2	3.2			2.8	3.8	2.8
Poorest 50%	17.4	16.0	14.9		22.4	11.3	13.5			13.1	14.9	12.6
Richest 10%	39.6	43.7	46.7		33.8	52.6	50.4			48.1	53.4	50.9
Richest 5%	28.3	30.3	34.1		23.7	39.8	37.9			34.7	44.2	37.9
Richest 1%	11.9	13.0	14.7		10.5	19.1	17.4			14.0	29.3	16.9

Source: IBGE, Censuses for 1960, 1970, 1980; idem, *Pesquisa Nacional por Amostras de Domicílio* (PNAD), 1972, 1976. Published in Deputado Eduardo Matarazzo Suplicy, speech of 6 March 1982, Assembléia Legislativa de São Paulo.

Notes: The censuses refer to the entire Brazilian territory; the PNAD-1972 refers to the total economically active population in the states of Rio de Janeiro, São Paulo, Minas Gerais, Espírito Santo, regions of the South, the Northeast, and the Federal District. The PNAD-1976 refers to all of these plus the urban areas of the North region and the States of Mato Grosso and Goiás.

Table A-8
Education Data, Persons 5 Years of Age and Older, 1980

Years of Study	Total No. of Persons	% of Total	Color							
			White	% of Total White	Black	% of Total Black	Yellow	% of Total Yellow	Brown	% of Total Brown
Men	50,665,800	99.7	27,582,059	99.8	3,108,737	99.7	363,159	99.7	19,484,997	99.8
None to less than 1	17,669,832	34.9	6,711,556	24.3	1,454,913	46.8	49,951	13.8	9,399,277	48.2
1 to 4	21,007,162	41.4	12,287,282	44.5	1,263,079	40.6	104,761	28.8	7,303,545	37.5
5 to 8	6,964,431	13.7	4,637,251	16.8	298,398	9.6	82,195	22.6	1,932,503	9.9
9 to 11	3,215,395	6.3	2,389,975	8.7	76,607	2.5	72,937	20.1	669,608	3.4
12 or more	1,808,988	3.6	1,555,995	5.6	15,740	0.5	53,316	14.7	180,064	0.9
Women	51,712,225	99.7	28,972,794	99.7	3,075,301	99.7	335,377	99.0	19,195,601	99.7
None to less than 1	18,232,720	35.2	7,428,079	25.6	1,498,066	48.7	56,806	16.9	9,191,739	47.9
1 to 4	21,263,946	41.1	12,831,360	44.3	1,185,137	38.5	115,490	34.4	7,083,010	36.7
5 to 8	7,048,724	13.6	4,688,551	16.2	291,381	9.5	73,011	21.7	1,982,760	10.3
9 to 11	3,735,246	7.2	2,796,968	9.6	87,786	2.9	58,972	17.6	781,848	4.1
12 or more	1,431,589	2.8	1,227,836	4.2	12,931	0.4	31,098	9.3	156,244	0.8

Source: IBGE, Census data for 1980. Published in Deputado Eduardo Matarazzo Suplicy, speech of 12 April 1982, "As Sequelas da Escravidão," Assembléia Legislativa de São Paulo.

Note: See table A-6.

Table A-9
Strikes, Demands, Results, 1978

Sector/Locale (State)	No. of Workers on Strike	Primary Demands	Results	Government Reaction
Metallurgical/				
São Bernardo, Sto. André, São Caetano (São Paulo)	76,843	20% raise above official index	24.5% raise above official index	No interference
São Paulo, Osasco, Guarlhos (São Paulo)	250,000	70–74% raise above official index; recognition of factory committees	58% raise above official index	No interference in union, but police repression
João Monlevade (Minas Gerais)	4,200	20% raise above official index	10% raise above official index plus 5% early pay	No interference
Betim, Belo Horizonte (Minas Gerais)	15,000	20% raise above official index	12% raise above official index	No interference
Rio de Janeiro (Rio de Janeiro)	11,000	10% raise above official index	10% raise above official index	No interference
Port/				
Santos (São Paulo)	1,200	20% raise above official index	No raise	Strong police repression
Urban transport/				
São Paulo (São Paulo)	170	39% raise above official index	39% raise above official index	Police repression
Tobacco/				
São Paulo (São Paulo)	400	20% raise above official index	20% raise above official index	No interference

Sector / Location	Number	Demands	Outcome	Government response
Glass/ São Paulo (São Paulo)	400	20% raise above official index	20% raise above official index	No interference
Ceramics/ Itu, Cabreuva (São Paulo)	2,000	34% raise above official index Better working conditions	15% raise above official index Working contract	Police repression
Textiles/ Bras. Fábrica de Alpargatas (São Paulo)	5,390	25% raise above official index Better working conditions	20% raise above official index Partial improvements	No interference
Chemical/ Goyana, São Paulo (São Paulo)	2,750	25% raise above official index	20% raise above official index	No interference
Banks/ São Paulo	10,000	65% raise above official index	No raise	Threat of intervention in union; police repression
Health/ São Paulo (São Paulo)	7,500	100% raise above official index	Inconclusive	Threat of intervention; police repression
Primary & secondary teaching/ All municipalities of Bahia, São Paulo, Paraná	138,634	Statute of Teachers Raise 27–38% above official index	Inconclusive	Threat to management associations of teachers; severe police repression
University teaching/ São Paulo (São Paulo)	800	20% raise above official index	Inconclusive	No interference

Table A-9 (continued)

Sector/Locale (State)	No. of Workers on Strike	Primary Demands	Results	Government Reaction
Medicine (doctors & residents)/ São Paulo (São Paulo), Rio de Janeiro (Rio de Janeiro), Belo Horizonte (Minas Gerais), Porto Alegre (Rio Grande do Sul), Brasilia (Distrito Federal), (Paraná)	11,500	5 times minimum salary Work contract in accordance with Labor Code	Inconclusive	No interference
Rural/ Banaurea, Mambu São Pedro Bariqui farms (São Paulo)	1,200	60% raise above official index Work tools Food Work contract Accident insurance Back pay	All demands met	No interference

Source: *Jornal do Brasil; Folha de São Paulo; Isto E; Veja; Movimento; O Trabalho; O Globo;* union newspapers and documents issued by strikers during assemblies and meetings.

Notes: Total number of workers on strike was 539,037; total number of strikes was 24. In Brazil a union calls a general strike for its entire territory; thus the total number of strikes, per factory, is greater than demonstrated by this table.

Table A-10

Strikes, Demands, Results, 1979

Sector/Locale (State)	No. of Workers on Strike	Primary Demands	Results	Government Reaction
Metallurgical/				
São Bernardo, São Caetano, Sto. André, Diadema (São Paulo)	240,000	70% raise above 1978 salary levels Shop stewards Trimonthly adjustments Base salary 3 times minimum wage	63% raise for those who earn up to 10 times minimum wage; 44% raise for wages above 10 times minimum wage	Intervention in unions, police repression toward picket lines
São José dos Campos, Jacareí, Cacapava (São Paulo)	35,000	78% raise over previous salary	67% raise over previous salary, in installments	No interference
Campinas (São Paulo)	20,000	78% raise of 1978 salary levels	67% raise over previous, in installments	No interference
São Paulo (São Paulo) Indústria Siam-Util	300	Back pay for 3 mos.	Back pay for 3 mos.	No interference (legal strike)
São Paulo, Osasco, Guarulhos (São Paulo)	280,000	83% raise Base salary of Cr. 7,200	67% raise in 3 installments	Strong police repression toward picket lines (1 death, Santo Dias da Silva)
São Bernardo, São Caetano, Sto. André, Diadema (São Paulo) Bordado	1,465	Back pay	Back pay	No interference

Table A-10 (continued)

Sector/Locale (State)	No. of Workers on Strike	Primary Demands	Results	Government Reaction
Metallurgical/(continued) Campo, Esmaltec, Elevadores Otis, Vaporint factories				
Niterói (Rio de Janeiro)	14,000	35% bonus for dangerous work Salaries from Cr. 4,680 to 13,000 40-hour week	69% raise for those earning less than 3 times minimum wage; 50% for others 30% bonus for dangerous work	No interference
(Rio de Janeiro) general strike	200,000	83% raise Salary base Cr. 6,114 1-year job security Right to union delegates in factories	75% raise 30% anticipated deduction from next raise	Threat of union intervention; military occupation of grounds around union headquarters; repression of picket lines
Rio de Janeiro (Rio de Janeiro) Fiat	3,900	1st strike: end to layoffs 2d strike: rehire union leader Giannini; 90% raise; job security for shop representatives	Rehired Giannini Job security for union representatives; 53% raise for those earning between 1 and 3 times minimum wage	No interference
Contagem (Minas Gerais) Toshiba	610	50% raise Free uniforms	Fixed raise of Cr. 7,000 Free uniforms	No interference

				Repression of picket lines
Contagem (Minas Gerais) Mannesmann	10,000	20% raise; End of system of work by turns; extra hourly pay; job security for Salary Committee	40% raise for those earning less than 3 times minimum wage; 20% for others; change in system of work by turns	
Belo Horizonte (Minas Gerais) Macife	300	35% raise for dangerous work 1 month extra pay	15% raise; 5% anticipated Bonus for dangerous work	No interference
Belo Horizonte (Minas Gerais) Nansem	600	30% raise 2-year job security for Salary Committee	20% raise 6-months job security	No interference
Ouro Branco (Minas Gerais) AcoMinas	21,000	Base salary of Cr. 4,000 for nonskilled, Cr. 9,000 for skilled, Cr. 18,000 for work chiefs	Base salaries of Cr. 3,600, 6,500, 12,000	No interference
Itaúna (Minas Gerais) Cimetal	600	80% raise Base salary of Cr. 3,600	30% raise Base salary of Cr. 3,300 Pay for strike days	No interference
Belo Horizonte (Minas Gerais) Brafer	160	80% raise	For 2 months, raises between 10 and 35%; followed by raises of 53%	No interference
Caetés (Minas Gerais) Cia. Ferro Brasileiro	2,500	50-80% raises	44-60% raises; after 8 months, raises of 80% Base salary of Cr. 5,150	No interference
Divinópolis (Minas Gerais)	7,500	80% raise	Anticipated salary of Cr. 1,000	Blocked union bank account
Nova Lima (Minas	4,200	Base salary for nonskilled of	No base salary	Police repression of strikers

Table A-10 (continued)

Sector/Locale (State)	No. of Workers on Strike	Primary Demands	Results	Government Reaction
Metallurgical/(continued) Gerais) Mineração Morro Velho		Cr. 8,000, for skilled between Cr. 9,000 and 12,000		and picket lines
Pacos (Minas Gerais) AcoMinas	1,500	80% raise	63% raise for those earning up to 3 times minimum wage	No interference
Belo Horizonte, Contagem (Minas Gerais)	35,000	80% raise Base salary of Cr. 8,000	65% raise	No interference
Pains, Belo Horizonte (Minas Gerais) Cia. Siderúrgica Pain	300	40% raise	30% raise	No interference
Contagem, Betim (Minas Gerais)	50,000	80% raise Base salary of Cr. 8,000	64% raise Cr. 4,000 base salary	No interference
João Monlevade (Minas Gerais)	10,000	Cr. 4,000 raise Base salary of Cr. 8,144	Cr. 2,700 raise Base salary of Cr. 5,200	No interference
Fortaleza (Ceará)	18,000	75% raise	70% raise	No interference
Cruciuma (Santa Catarina)	1,500	30% raise Base salary of Cr. 2,339	16% raise	No interference

Urban transport/

Location	Number	Demands	Outcome	Government action
Rio de Janeiro (Rio de Janeiro)	45,000	80% raise, to level of interstate drivers	41% raise (except ticket collectors, who got Cr. 4,000 bonus)	No interference
Rio de Janeiro, Niterói, Duque de Caxias, Nova Iguaçú (Rio de Janeiro) General strike	222,000	Raise to equal pay of interstate drivers	Raise from 5,350 to 7,200 for drivers; 2,204 to 4,110 for ticket collectors	Threat of union intervention; police repression of strikers
São Paulo (São Paulo)	60,000	80% raise	60% raise	Repression of strikers
Jundiaí (São Paulo)	1,400	20% anticipated	20% anticipated	No interference
Campinas (São Paulo)	1,800	20% raise	10% raise, 10% anticipated	No interference
São José dos Campos (São Paulo)	300	30% raise	20% anticipated	No interference
Belo Horizonte (Minas Gerais)	10,000	Cr. 7,500 salary for drivers, 3,700 for ticket collectors	Cr.7,000 and Cr. 2,600	Strong police repression of pickets and strikers
Vitória (Espírito Santo)	2,000	100% raise Overtime pay 1 hour for meals Free uniforms	60% raise 8-hour work day (from 13) Rehiring of 13 fired workers	No interference
Recife (Pernambuco)	8,000	80% raise Overtime pay Extra pay for nights	75% raise for drivers; 50% for ticket collectors	No interference

Table A-10 (continued)

Sector/Locale (State)	No. of Workers on Strike	Primary Demands	Results	Government Reaction
Urban Transport/(continued)				
Fortaleza (Ceará)	3,000	Base salary 4 times minimum wage 4 free days/month	All agreed to, but not being carried out	No interference
João Pessoa (Paraíba)	360	40% raise	25% raise	No interference
Salvador (Bahia)	3,000	Salaries of Cr. 7,000 for drivers; 4,000 for collectors; 8-hour day	Cr. 6,000 for drivers; 3,000 for collectors	Police repression, injuries, 1 death
Porto Alegre (Rio Grande do Sul)	8,500	Salaries of Cr. 8,400 for drivers; 6,350 for collectors; shop stewards	7,200 for drivers; 6,000 for collectors; recognition of union delegates	Police repression of picket lines
Major capitals (18 cities) Taxi drivers	40,000	No 40% rise in gasoline price	No rise	No interference
Pelotas (Rio Grande do Sul)	1,500	30% raise	20% raise	Police repression
Belo Horizonte (Minas Gerais) Coal truck drivers	3,000	Raise in truck rental price of 71%	71% raise	No interference
Minas Gerais, Paraná, São Paulo Rio Grande do Sul Truck drivers	30,000	Raise in truck rental price from 25-50%	Raise of 25-50%	No interference

Location	Number	Demand	Raise	Response
São Bernardo, São Caetano, Sto. André, Diadema (São Paulo) Auto transport drivers	2,300	70% rise in price paid by corporations	70% rise	No interference
Paraná (Paraná) Wheat truck drivers	1,000	50% rise in price	50% rise	No interference

Construction/

Location	Number	Demand	Raise	Response
Belo Horizonte (Minas Gerais)	80,000	Salaries between Cr. 5,000 and 8,000	Cr. 3,600 to 6,500	Police repression, 1 death Da Silva intervened and government agreed to cease repression and distribute food
Goiânia, Anápolis (Goiás)	40,000	100% raise Base salary of Cr. 6,000 to 20,000	30% raise for those earning less	Police repression
Brasília (Distrito Federal)	30,000	Base salaries of Cr. 5,000 to 20,000	2,600 to 3,900 base; 25% raise for those earning up to 5 times minimum wage	No interference
Porto Alegre (Rio Grande do Sul)	80,000	Raises between 25% and 80%	Anticipated 22.5% to 70% No punishment for strike leaders Job security for strike leaders	Police repression on approximately 70 sites
Vitória (Espírito Santo)	20,000	Base salary from Cr. 3,600 to 8,400	6% raise/month for 4 months; 50-70% raise for carpenters & masters	No interference
Volta Redonda (Rio de Janeiro)	12,000	70% raise	Raise from Cr. 16.20 to 17.80 per month	Police repression of street riots

Table A-10 (continued)

Sector/Locale (State)	No. of Workers on Strike	Primary Demands	Results	Government Reaction
Construction/(continued)				
Curitiba (Santa Catarina)	20,000	80% raise and base salary of Cr. 4,016	50% raise	Police repression
Minas Gerais AcoMinas	21,000	60% raise	30% raise	No interference
Wheat mills/				
Santos (São Paulo)	1,500	70% raise	66.23% raise	No interference
Textiles/				
Belo Horizonte (Minas Gerais)	350	Base salary of Cr. 5,000	Base salary of Cr. 5,000	No interference
Rio de Janeiro (Rio de Janeiro) De Millus	3,000	50% raise and end of frisking system of theft control	25% anticipated End of frisking	Police repression
Baking/				
São Paulo (São Paulo) Pullman	500	63% raise Base salary of Cr. 5,000	63% raise Base salary of Cr. 5,000	No interference
Food industry/				
(São Paulo) Swift Armour Foods	1,500	10% raise 15% anticipated	10% raise	No interference
Clubs/				
São Paulo (São Paulo) Jockey Club	3,000	54% raise	54% raise	No interference

		Demands	Results	
Ceramics/ Belo Horizonte (Minas Gerais) Klabin	1,050	80% raise / Better working conditions	70% raise / Partial improvement in conditions	No interference
Gravedigging/ Rio de Janeiro (Rio de Janeiro)	1,000	58% raise	43% raise	No interference
Gasoline/ Rio de Janeiro (Rio de Janeiro) Distribution	3,000	Salary base of Cr. 4,000	Salary base of Cr. 4,000	No interference
Gas/ São Paulo (São Paulo)	8,000	Minimum wage of Cr. 8,000 to 9,000	Minimum wage of Cr. 8,000 to 9,000	No interference
Paper & cardboard/ (Rio Grande do Sul)	2,000	62% raise	57% raise	No interference
Garbage collection/ Rio de Janeiro (Rio de Janeiro)	4,300	Base salary of Cr. 4,680 Cr. 1,577 raise 8-hour day	165% raise	No interference
Brasilia (Distrito Federal)	2,200	Salaries between Cr. 4,300 and 7,200	Salaries of Cr. 4,300-7,200	No interference
São Paulo (São Paulo)	3,000	70% raise	40% raise	Police repression
Belo Horizonte (Minas Gerais)	1,200	Salary of Cr. 6,000	Salary of Cr. 4,500	Police repression

Table A-10 (continued)

Sector/Locale (State)	No. of Workers on Strike	Primary Demands	Results	Government Reaction
Mining/(continued)				
Ouro de Morro Velho (Minas Gerais) Gold	3,800	Salary between Cr. 8,000 and 12,000	25% anticipated	No interference
Lauro Muller, Urussanga, Siderópolis, Rio Marina, Criciuma (Santa Catarina) Coal	12,000	100% raise Base salary of Cr. 4,014	17% raise 15% anticipated	Police repression of pickets
Ouro Velho (Minas Gerais)	3,800	Salary between Cr. 8,000 and 12,000	25% anticipated	No interference
Ouro Branco (Minas Gerais) AcoMinas	15,000	Salary between Cr. 8,000 and 12,000	20% raise	No interference
Electric/				
Recife, São Francisco (Pernambuco) Celpe, Cia. Hidroelétrica de Pernambuco	10,000	Rehiring of 5 strike leaders; raises between 53% and 81% Job security for labor leaders	All demands met	No interference
Commercial establishments/				
Belo Horizonte	40,000	100% raise	100% raise	No interference

(Minas Gerais)

Health/

São Paulo (São Paulo) 204 centers	10,000	1st demand: 70% raise, 2,000 fixed bonus; Lowered to 43% and 2,000	30% raise	No interference

Banks/

Belo Horizonte (Minas Gerais) general strike of all banks	16,000	70% raise and added Cr. 3,000	5% raise above official index	Intervention in union and removal of President Arlindo Ramos; police repression
Porto Alegre (Rio Grande do Sul) General strike involving 11 other municipalities, 22 other local unions	28,000	75% raise and union delegate in shop	15% raise; 5% above official index after 2 months	Intervention in union and removal of board of directors and arrest of President Olivio Dutra; strong police repression
São Paulo (São Paulo)	5,000	50% raise plus Cr. 3,000 fixed bonus	Raises between 8% and 18% above official index	Union intervention and removal of 3 directors; police repression, 300 arrests
Rio de Janeiro (Rio de Janeiro)	56,000	50% raise, Cr. 3,000 fixed bonus	Raise between 5% and 15% above official index	Union intervention and removal of board of directors

Security/

Belo Horizonte (Minas Gerais)	3,000	Minimum wage of Cr. 6,000 Cr. 4,000 insurance 5-day work week	Minimum wage of Cr. 5,000 250,000 insurance Rehiring of fired	No interference

Table A-10 (continued)

Sector/Locale (State)	No. of Workers on Strike	Primary Demands	Results	Government Reaction
Security/(continued)				
		Free uniforms	workers; payment for strike days	
São Paulo	9,000	100% raise; overtime pay Minimum salary of Cr. 7,000	10-44% raise; base salary Cr. 4,000; job security for labor leaders	No interference
Porto Alegre (Rio Grande do Sul)	8,000	8-hour day; base salary of Cr. 5,000	Base salary of Cr. 4,413; Cr. 200,000 insurance Free uniforms	No interference
Primary & secondary teaching/				
(Rio Grande do Norte) Public schools	4,000	200% raise	10% raise above raise of public employees	Police repression
(Goiás) Public schools	26,000	Raises between 202% and 313%; minimum wage between Cr. 5,000 and 19,000	65% raise after May 1979; 50% after February 1980	Police repression
(Rio Grande do Sul) Public schools	86,000	Base salary of 3 times minimum wage and 70% raise	Base salary of Cr. 4,000; 70% raise	Police repression
Brasília (Distrito Federal)	11,000	Base salary of 4 times minimum wage and 65% raise	No demands met	Intervention in union and removal of directors; police repression

Rio de Janeiro (Rio de Janeiro) SENAI professors	400	40% anticipated	43% raise after December 1979	No interference
Rio de Janeiro (Rio de Janeiro) Private schools	20,000	60% raise; 5-week month 100% raise in base salary	Raise according to official index; month of 4.5 weeks; base salary of 75%	No interference
Rio de Janeiro (Rio de Janeiro) Public schools, 1st strike	110,000	Base salary 4 to 6 times minimum wage; 30% raise Extra 10% for difficult-access areas	Promise to resolve difficulties in 1980; Niterói teachers received 97% to 137% raise	Police repression
Rio de Janeiro (Rio de Janeiro) Public schools, 2d strike	110,000	Same as 1st strike (agreements not fulfilled)	30% raise; reconsideration of cases of fired strikers	Intervention in and dissolution of Teachers' Association (Centro Estadual de Profesores); arrest of leaders; police repression
(Minas Gerais) Public schools	100,000	Base salary of Cr. 8,000	Base salary of Cr. 6,000	Police repression
(Mato Grosso) Public schools	20,000	100% raise	60% raise after July 1979 40% after January 1980	No interference
(Paraiba) Public schools	10,800	100% raise	No raise	Public repression
University teaching/ São Paulo (São Paulo) USP, UNICAMP, UNESP	6,200	70% raise plus Cr. 2,000	Cr. 2,000 paid irregularly	No interference
São Paulo (São Paulo) PUC	1,100	Raises of 12% and 20% over March's official index	Inconclusive	No interference
Salvador (Bahia)	539	Payment of agreed-upon	Payment in 2 installments	No interference

Table A-10 (continued)

Sector/Locale (State)	No. of Workers on Strike	Primary Demands	Results	Government Reaction
University teaching/(continued) PUC		wages of March 1978		
Rio de Janeiro (Rio de Janeiro) UERJ	6,300	60% raise; 100% raise in base salary	50% raise	Tribunal Regional do Trabalho judged strike legal
Public employees/ São Paulo (São Paulo) General strike	280,000	70% raise plus Cr. 2,000	See results by sector	Police repression
São Paulo (São Paulo) Municipal employees	30,000	70% raise plus Cr. 2,000	17% raise, which, added to 20% in 1978, gave 37%	Police repression
São Paulo (São Paulo) Education & health depts.	63,800	70% raise plus Cr. 2,000	Cr. 2,000 paid irregularly	Police repression
Belo Horizonte (Minas Gerais)	13,000	Base salary of Cr. 7,031	Base salary of Cr. 7,031	No interference
Belo Horizonte (Minas Gerais) Junta Comercial & City Hall	1,198	Base salary of Cr. 7,031	Base salary of Cr. 7,031	No interference
Medicine (doctors)/ São Paulo (São Paulo) Hospital das Clínicas	2,400	Base salary to equal work contract in negotiation	Inconclusive	No interference

Journalism/				
São Paulo (São Paulo)	1,500	25% raise	16% anticipated	No interference
Rural/				
Recife (Pernambuco) Sugarcane workers	20,000	100% raise	52% raise	No interference
São Paulo (São Paulo) Fazenda Barigui, Fazenda Banaurea in Itanhaem	162	Enforcement of contract	Court-enforced contract	Strike (2d in 8 months) declared legal
(Pernambuco) General strike of 24 unions	70,000	100% raise	100% raise	No interference (legal strike)

Sources: *O Globo; Jornal do Brasil; Folha de São Paulo; O Estado de São Paulo; Ultima Hora; Movimento; Veja; Isto E; Em Tempo; ABCD Jornal;* union newspapers and bulletins.

Notes: Total number of workers on strike was 3,207,994; total number of strikes was 113. In Brazil a union calls a general strike for its entire territory; thus the total number of strikes, per factory, is greater than demonstrated by this table.

Table A-11
Strikes, Demands, Results, 1980

Sector/Locale (State)	No. of Workers on Strike	Primary Demands	Results	Government Reaction
Metallurgical/				
São Bernardo, São Caetano, Sto. André, Diadema (São Paulo)	240,000	Base salary of Cr. 12,000 15% raise Same raise for those hired after November Readjustments every 3 months 100% pay for overtime 40-hour work week Job security and firing criteria Access to factory for union leaders Recognition of union delegates and job security for them	Base salary of Cr. 5,904 7% raise Same raise for those hired after November No readjustments 5% pay for overtime No 40-hour week No job security, but some negotiated firing criteria No access to factory for union leaders No recognition of union delegates or job security	Intervention in union of São Bernardo and appointment of government representative to run it; 64 leaders arrested; arrest of church lawyers of São Paulo Justice and Peace Committee; indictment of 13 strike leaders; sentencing of 11 to prison for 2 to 3.5 years (overturned by SMT); strong police repression; invasion of church where strikers met
Belo Horizonte (Minas Gerais) Belgo Mineira	4,500	Cr. 5,700 raise for productivity 40-hour work week	Cr. 5,700 raise No 40-hour week	No interference

Sector / Location	Number	Demands	Result	Government Response
Port/ Santos (São Paulo) Cia. Docas de Santos	12,500	Cr. 3,300 raise for productivity 15% raise over official index	10% raise over index	Government took conciliatory stance and negotiated
Oil & refinery/ Cubatao (São Paulo) Refinaria Presidente Bernardes	2,000	20% raise over official index	Inconclusive	No interference because only a slowdown operation
Construction/ Vitória (Espírito Santo)	10,000	Enforcement of 1979 agreement End of substitution of minors without contracts for workers	Inconclusive	Violent repression by military police; annulment of union elections of 1979
Primary & secondary teaching/ (Minas Gerais) General strike	60,000	104.1% raise Work contracts for 73,000 substitute teachers Base salary of Cr. 12,217	No concessions	Arrest of 7 strike leaders; indictment of 1 strike leader; severe and violent repression; refusal to negotiate
(Acre) General Strike	20,000	Enforcement of 1979 contract	Inconclusive	Military police repression
(Goiás) General Strike	30,000	Enforcement of 1979 contract	Demands not met	Enforcement of law prohibiting strikes in "essential" activities Military police repression

Table A-11 (continued)

Sector/Locale (State)	No. of Workers on Strike	Primary Demands	Results	Government Reaction
University teaching/				
Salvador (Bahia) PUC	1,000	Higher salary Consideration of study made by PUC professors on crisis in university	Demands met	No interference
Rio de Janeiro (Rio de Janeiro) Universidade Santa Ursula, PUC-Rio, Universidade Cándido Mendes, Universidade Hélio Alonso, Centro Unificado Profissional	2,000	Base salary of Cr. 18,000 20-hour week	Demands partially met	No interference
Campinas (São Paulo) UNICAMP	1,200	Rehiring of 8 union leaders fired	Inconclusive	No interference
Universities of Goiás, Minas Gerais, Juiz de Fora, Pará, Alagoas, Rio Grande do Norte Ceará, Paraíba, Bahia, Rural do Rio do Janeiro, Pernambuco, do Rio de Janeiro Fluminense, Espírito Santo, Santa Catarina Paraná, Santa Maria, Rio Grande do Sul, 8 other	35,000	Enforcement of 1979 contract; 48% raise above official index after March; Increase in federal union's % allocation from 4% of total budget to 12% Repeal of Law No. 6,733; Approval of	Raises averaging 117% Regularization project not totally approved and included clause leaving all hiring and promotion to joint committee of MEC-DASP-SEPLAN	Minister of Education Eduardo Portella began negotiations, but was fired as result of resistance from other government sectors; Colonel Ludwig appointed minister of education

Ministry of Education learning establishments	Ministry of Education's draft project for regularization of profession		Negotiations
Medicine (residents)/ 15 states General strike in state hospitals	6,500	Regularization of profession Inclusion of residents in Labor Law, i.e., subject to work contracts and salary regulations	Inconclusive	
Rural/ São Lourenço, Pandalho (Pernambuco) Strike of 42 rural unions	240,000	Right to 2 acres near home for planting 4% raise over official index for productivity Same pay rate for workers paid by hour or month Raise from 3,599 to 6,899 Right to union representation	Demands met, but enforcement only partial	Civil and military police repression

Sources: *Jornal do Brasil*; *Folha de São Paulo*; *Isto E*; *Veja*; *Movimento*; *O Trabalho*; *O Globo*; *ABCD Jornal*; union newspapers and documents issued by strikers.

Notes: Total number of workers on strike was 664,700; total number of strikes was 50. In Brazil a union calls a general strike for its entire territory; thus the total number of strikes, per factory, is greater than demonstrated by this table.

Abbreviations

AAB	Aliança Anti-Comunista do Brasil; Brazilian Anti-Communist Alliance
ABI	Associação Brasileira de Imprensa; Brazilian Press Association
ADESG	Associação dos Diplomados da Escola Superior de Guerra; Association of Graduates of the Superior War College
AI-5	Ato Institucional No. 5; Institutional Act No. 5
ALN	Aliança de Libertação Nacional; National Liberation Alliance
AP	Ação Popular; Popular Action
ARENA	Aliança de Renovação Nacional; Alliance for National Renovation
ASI	Assesoria de Segurança e Informação; Security and Intelligence Assistance Department
BNH	Banco Nacional de Habitação; National Housing Bank
CEB	Comunidade Eclesial de Base; Basic Christian Community
CEIS	Comissão Especial de Investigação Sumária; Special Investigation Committee
CENIMAR	Centro de Informações da Marinha; Navy Information Center
CGT	Comando Geral dos Trabalhadores; General Workers' Command
CIEX	Centro de Informações do Exército; Army Intelligence Center
CISA	Centro de Informações Secretas da Aeronáutica; Air Force Information Center
CMN	Conselho Monetário Nacional; National Monetary Council
CNBB	Conferência Nacional dos Bispos do Brasil; National Conference of Brazilian Bishops
CNTI	Confederação Nacional dos Trabalhadores na Indústria; National Confederation of Workers in Industry
CODI-DOI	Centro de Defesa Interna-Departamento de Ordem Interna; Center of Internal Defense-Department of Internal Order
CONCLAT	Confêrencia das Classes Trabalhadoras; Conference of the Working Class
CONTAG	Confederação Nacional dos Trabalhadores na Agricultura; National Confederation of Workers in Agriculture
CONTEC	Confederação de Trabalhadores na Educação e na Cultura; Confederation of Workers in Education and Culture

DECAD	Departamento de Estatística da Federação das Indústrias do Estado de São Paulo; Statistical Department of the Federation of Industries of the State of São Paulo
DIEESE	Departamento Intersindical de Estatística e Estudos Sócio-Econômicos; Interunion Department of Statistical Studies
DM	Departamento Municipal de Polícia; Municipal Police Department
DOPS	Departamento Estadual de Ordem Pública e Social; State Department of Social and Public Order
DPF	Departamento de Polícia Federal; Federal Police Department
DSI	Divisão de Segurança e Informação; Divisions of Security and Information
ECEME	Escola de Comando do Estado Maior do Exército; Army General Staff and Command School
EMFA	Estado Maior das Forças Armadas; High Command of the Armed Forces
ESG	Escola Superior de Guerra; Superior War College
FAFERJ	Federação das Associações das Favelas do Rio de Janeiro; Federation of *Favela* Associations of Rio de Janeiro
FAMERJ	Federação das Associações de Moradores do Estado do Rio de Janeiro; Federation of Associations of Residents of the State of Rio de Janeiro
FGTS	Fundo de Garantia por Tempo de Serviço; Time-in-Service Guarantee Fund
IBAD	Instituto Brasileiro de Ação Democrática; Brazilian Institute for Democratic Action
INPS	Instituto Nacional de Previdência Social; National Social Work Institute
IPES	Instituto de Pesquisas e Estudos Sociais; Institute for Research and Social Studies
IPM	Inquérito Policial Militar; Military Police Inquiry
MAB	Movimento de Amigos do Bairro de Nova Iguaçú; Movement of Friends of the District of Nova Iguaçú
MDB	Movimento Democrático Brasileiro; Brazilian Democratic Movement
MR-8	Movimento Revolucionário 8 de outubro; October 8 Revolutionary Movement
OAB	Ordem dos Advogados do Brasil; Brazilian Bar Association
OBAN	Operação Bandeirantes; Operation Bandeirantes
PC do B	Partido Comunista do Brasil; Communist Party of Brazil (Maoist)
PCB	Partido Comunista Brasileiro; Brazilian Communist party
PDP	Partido Democrático Paulista; Democratic Party of São Paulo
PDS	Partido Democrático Social; Social Democratic party

PDT	Partido Democrático Trabalhista; Democratic Labor party
PMDB	Partido do Movimento Democrático Brasileiro; Party of the Brazilian Democratic Movement
PNAD	Pesquisa Nacional por Amostragem Domiciliar; National Household Survey
PP	Partido Popular; Popular party
PRP	Partido Republicano Paulista; Republican Party of São Paulo
PRP	Partido de Representação Popular; Popular Representation party
PSD	Partido Social Democrático; Social Democratic party
PT	Partido dos Trabalhadores; Workers' party
PTB	Partido Trabalhista Brasileiro; Brazilian Labor party
SAB	Sociedade Amigos do Bairro; Friends of the Neighborhood Society
SEPLAN	Secretaria do Planejamento; Ministry of Planning
SNI	Serviço Nacional de Informações; National Intelligence Service
SUDAM	Superintendência do Desenvolvimento de Amazônia; Superintendency for the Development of Amazônia
SUDEPE	Superintendência de Desenvolvimento de Pernambuco; Superintendency for the Development of Pernambuco
UDN	União Democrática Nacional; National Democratic Union
UEE	União Estadual de Estudantes; State Student Union
UNE	União Nacional dos Estudantes; National Union of Students
VPR	Vanguarda Popular Revolucionária; Popular Revolutionary Vanguard

Notes

Introduction: Dependency and the National Security State

1. The economic tripod is an alliance of private national capital, international capital, and state capital. See the analysis of the structures of dependent capitalist development in Peter Evans, *Dependent Development: The Alliance of Multinational, State and Local Capital in Brazil* (Princeton, N.J.: Princeton University Press, 1979). For information on the predominance of American capital in Brazil, see, for example, the study conducted for the Report to the Sub-Committee on Foreign Relations of the United States Senate, Samuel Newfarmer and Willard F. Mueeler, *Multinational Corporations in Brazil and Mexico: Structural Sources of Economic and non-Economic Power* (Washington: United States Government Printing Office, August 1975). See also the study by Moniz Bandeira, *Presença dos Estados Unidos no Brasil: Dois séculos de história* (Rio de Janeiro: Civilização Brasileira, 1973); Jan Knippers Black, *United States Penetration of Brazil* (Philadelphia: University of Pennsylvania Press, 1977); Osny Duarte Pereira, *Um desafio à dignidade nacional* (Rio de Janeiro: Civilização Brasileira, 1967).

2. Fernando Henrique Cardoso and Enzo Falleto, *Dependency and Development in Latin America* (Berkeley & Los Angeles: University of California Press, 1979), p. xxii. For further analysis of the dependent model of capitalist development, see Susanne Bodenheimer, "Dependency and Imperialism: The Roots of Latin American Underdevelopment," in *Readings in U.S. Imperialism*, ed. K. T. Fann and Donald Hodges, pp. 155-182 (Boston: Porter Sargent, 1971); idem, "The Ideology of Developmentalism: The American Paradigm-Surrogate for Latin American Studies," Sage Professional Papers in Comparative Politics 2, 01-015 (Beverly Hills, Cal.: Sage, 1971); Cardoso, "Teoría de dependencia o análisis concreto de situaciones de dependencia?" (Mexico City: Asociación de Becarios del Instituto de Investigaciones Sociales de la UNAM, DT-1); Theotônio dos Santos, "The Structure of Dependence," in *Readings in U.S. Imperialism*, ed. Fann and Hodges, pp. 225-236. A useful reader in English on dependency is Ronald H. Chilcote and Joel C. Edelstein, eds., *Latin America: The Struggle with Dependency and Beyond* (New York: John Wiley & Sons, 1974).

3. Cardoso and Falleto, *Dependency and Development*, p. xvi.

4. The civilian-military coup began on 31 March but was not victorious until 1 April 1964, when President João Goulart left the country and a military junta took power. The opposition immediately labeled the coup "the worst April Fool's joke";

military governments have since tried to establish 31 March as the beginning date of their regime. For details on the military operations that led to the overthrow of President Goulart, see the report in General Olympio Mourão Filho's memoirs, *Memórias: A verdade de um revolucionário* (Rio de Janeiro: L&PM Editores, 1978).

5. For analyses of the organization in the countryside, see, for example, Joseph A. Page, *The Revolution That Never Was: Northeast Brazil 1955-1964* (New York: Grossman, 1972); Francisco Julião, *The Yoke: The Hidden Face of Brazil* (Middlesex, England: Penguin, 1972).

6. During the government of Miguel Arraes in Pernambuco, innovative health, education, and development programs were put into effect with the participation of the local population. One of the best-known efforts in increasing the literacy rate of the state was organized by Paulo Freire. The government of Arraes is well described by Page in *The Revolution That Never Was*. See also Miguel Arraes, *Brazil: The People and the Power* (Middlesex, England: Penguin, 1969); Antônio Callado, *Tempo de Arraes: Padres e comunistas na revolução sem violência* (Rio de Janeiro: Civilização Brasileira, 1963); Josué de Castro, *Documentário do Nordeste* (São Paulo: Brasiliense, 1959). The administration of Leonel Brizola has not been so widely covered. The importance of the role he played during this period lies in his confrontation with American capital in the episode of the nationalization of the electrical plants of the American Foreign Power Corporation in his state. For more information, see Thomas E. Skidmore, *Politics in Brazil, 1930-1964, An Experiment in Democracy* (New York: Oxford University Press, 1967), pp. 210-215, 228, 233, 244, 247, 25, 266-277.

7. Skidmore, *Politics in Brazil*. The penetration of international capital, with the increasing hegemony of American capital added to the growing organization of workers in industry and of the peasants in the countryside, brought to the surface a crisis of "populism," in the formal democratic state of the period. For extended information on this period, see, for example, Maria Victória de Mesquita Benevides, *O governo Kubitschek: Desenvolvimento econômico e estabilidade política, 1956-1961* (Rio de Janeiro: Paz e Terra, 1976); Francisco Weffort, "Populismo en la política brasileña," in *Brasil hoy*, ed. Jean Claude Bernadet et al., pp. 64-71 (Mexico City: Siglo XXI, 1968); John J. Johnson, *Political Change in Latin America: The Emergence of the Middle Sectors* (Stanford: Stanford University Press, 1965); Weffort, *O populismo na política brasileira* (Rio de Janeiro: Paz e Terra, 1978); E. Bradford Burns, *A History of Brazil* (New York: Columbia University Press, 1980); Octávio Iannni, *O colapso do populismo no Brasil* (Rio de Janeiro: Civilização Brasileira, 1971); and idem, *A formação do estado populista na América Latina* (Rio de Janeiro: Civilização Brasileira, 1975).

8. Jürgen Habermas, *Legitimation Crisis* (Boston: Beacon Press, 1973), pp. 27-28.

9. Ibid., p. 74.

10. See Alfred Stepan, *The Military in Politics* (Princeton, N.J.: Princeton University Press, 1971). See also Alexandre de Barros, "The Brazilian Military: Professional Socialization, Political Performance and State Building" (Ph.D. diss. University of Chicago, 1978); Edmundo Campos Coelho, *Em busca de Identidade: O exército e a política na sociedade brasileira* (Rio de Janeiro: Forense

Universitária, 1976); and Peter Flynn, *Brazil: A Political Analysis* (Boulder, Colo.: Westview Press, 1979).

11. For an analysis of the destabilization policy and the coordination of civilians and military officers in the planning of the coup, see, in particular, René Armand Dreifuss, *1964: A conquista do estado, ação política, poder e golpe de classe* (Rio de Janeiro: Vozes, 1981). Dreifuss's work is based on hitherto unpublished and unavailable documents from the archives of the IPES, ESG, and IBAD. See also Phyllis R. Parker, *Brazil and the Quiet Intervention, 1964* (Austin: University of Texas Press, 1979), for an analysis based on documents from the Lyndon B. Johnson and the Kennedy presidential libraries; A. J. Langguth, *Hidden Terrors* (New York: Pantheon Books, 1978); Moniz Bandeira, *O governo João Goulart: Lutas sociais no Brasil* (Rio de Janeiro: Civilização Brasileira, 1977); and Carl Oglesby and Richard Shaull, *Containment and Change* (New York: Macmillan, 1967).

12. See particularly the account of the activities of the IBAD and the IPES in Dreifuss, *1964: A conquista do estado*.

13. Article 1 of Law No. 785 of 20 August 1949, founding the Superior War College. See the account in Alfred Stepan, *The Military in Politics*, chap. 8.

14. *Manual básico da Escola Superior de Guerra* (hereafter *Manual básico da ESG*), published by the Estado Maior das Forças Armadas, Escola Superior de Guerra, Departamento de Estudos, 1976, p. 19.

15. Ibid.

16. Stepan, *Os militares na política* (Rio de Janeiro: Artenova, 1975), p. 129.

17. Ibid., p. 130. See also Dreifuss, *1964: A conquista do estado*, pp. 417-455.

18. Dreifuss, *1964: A conquista do estado*, p. 76.

19. Ibid., p. 74.

20. Ibid., pp. 362-372.

21. Stepan, *Os militares na política*, pp. 133-134. In footnote 27, Stepan refers to this conference prior to the 1964 coup d'état. He also relates his interview with General Golbery do Couto e Silva, who stated that "the ESG believed that the political parties had no authority and wished to reduce their numbers."

22. Dreifuss, *1964: A conquista do estado*, pp. 361-370. A complete list of the officers who were on the staff working with General Golbery in designing the security network can be found on pp. 365-368.

23. Ibid., pp. 281-337, and chap. 7.

24. Ibid.; see the account on pp. 417-455.

25. Ibid., pp. 199-204, on the funding of the ESG/IPES complex, and pp. 244-252 on the misinformation campaign in the mass media.

26. Ibid., pp. 417-455.

27. General Golbery do Couto e Silva, *Conjuntura política nacional, o poder do executivo e geopolítica do Brasil* (Rio de Janeiro: José Olympio, 1981), p. 106 of the section "Geopolítica do Brasil."

28. Ibid., p. 9. The entire quotation is as follows:

Leviathan awakens after having been asleep for many centuries. Awakened to the sounds of the new totalitarian mythologies, from the Right and from the Left, which incite and seduce humanity lost in an ominous fear. Within the framework of a world that no longer knows any frontiers that can separate the nations, we see the rise of a Universal State, as the solution that is cried for and proclaimed as the only possible solution to the insecurity. This state shall be the supreme *Leviathan*, the super-Leviathan, the uncontested owner of the planet Earth and of the human spirit.

(All translations, unless otherwise noted, are mine.)

Chapter 1. The Doctrine of National Security and Development

1. See Margaret E. Crahan,"National Security Ideology and Human Rights," paper presented at the Tenth Interamerican Congress of Philosophy of the Interamerican Society of Philosophy and the American Philosophical Association, Florida State University, Tallahassee, 18-23 October 1981, pp. 7-13.

2. Ibid., pp. 12-22.

3. Some of the books that deal specifically with the Doctrine of National Security and Development and ideology as it has been developed in Brazil include Eliezer Rizzo de Oliveira, *As forças armadas: Política e ideologia no Brasil, 1964-1969* (Rio de Janeiro: Vozes, 1976); Joseph Comblin, "The National Security Doctrine," in *The Repressive State: The Brazilian National Security Doctrine in Latin America* (Toronto: Latin America Research Unit, 1976); idem, *A ideologia da Segurança Nacional: O poder militar na América Latina* (Rio de Janeiro: Civilização Brasileira, 1977); José Alfredo Amaral Gurgel, *Segurança e democracia* (Rio de Janeiro: José Olympio, 1975); and the important research and analysis organized by Dom Cândido Padim, bishop of Bauru in the state of São Paulo, the smaller version of which was published in *SEDOC* (*Serviço de Documentação*), vol. 1 (Rio de Janeiro: Vozes, 1969), under the title "A doutrina de segurança nacional à luz da doutrina da igreja."

4. On the influence of the ADESG and its extensive role in the dissemination of the ideology of national security and the conspiracy to overthrow the government of João Goulart, see René Armand Dreifuss, *1964: A Conquista do Estado, Ação política, poder e golpe de classe* (Rio de Janeiro: Vozes, 1981), p. 456n.8, pp. 73-82, 417-455.

5. See Alfred Stepan, *Os militares na política* (Rio de Janeiro: Artenova, 1975), p. 133. See also Alexandre de Barros, "The Brazilian Military: Professional Socialization, Political Peformance and State Building" (Ph.D. diss., University of Chicago, 1978).

6. *Manual básico da ESG* (Estado Maior das Forças Armadas, Escola Superior de Guerra, Departamento de Estudos, 1976), pp. 20-21.

7. Ibid.

8. General Golbery do Couto e Silva, *Conjuntura política nacional, o poder do executivo e geopolítica do Brasil* (Rio de Janeiro: José Olympio, 1981). p. 24.

9. Ibid.

10. These definitions are taken from the basic training manual of the Superior War College. See *Manual básico da ESG*, particularly section 1, dealing with contemporary warfare: "Guerra contemporânea," pp. 65-82. All of the definitions of warfare, unless otherwise explicitly stated, come from this section of the basic training text.

11. Ibid., pp. 78-79.

12. Ibid., p. 79.

13. Ibid., p. 430. It should be added that the theory establishes that

insurrectionary war, also nondeclared and nonconventional, is closer to the traditional concept of civil war: "It is a type of war where part of the population—whether or not it is aided or reinforced from the exterior of the nation—opposes the government in power and rebels with the aim of deposing the government or of imposing upon it certain conditions" (p. 79). Because of the inescapable conditions of today's confrontation between the United States and the Soviet Union, most wars of independence or insurrectionary wars will not remain neutral and will be contaminated by the "Communist revolutionary war" (p. 79). Thus it believes that wars of independence, rebellions against unjust and oppressive dictatorships, or any other civil resistance to state power eventually become tainted by the cold-war struggle and by the all-encompassing fight to the death between the two superpowers.

14. Ibid., p. 431.

15. Ibid.

16. Ibid.

17. See General Golbery do Couto e Silva, *Conjuntura política nacional*, p. 25 of the section, "Geopolítica do Brasil."

18. Ibid.

19. See *Manual básico da ESG*, pp. 273-275. The emphasis is in the original.

20. Ibid., p. 288.

21. Ibid. See the discussion of the obstacles also included on pp. 288-289. For an analysis of these obstacles and their relationship to antagonisms, adverse factors, and pressures, see pp. 278-280.

22. A full discussion of the war maneuvers to be conducted to counteract each of the different levels of disturbances that may result from situations tied to adverse factors, obstacles, antagonisms, or pressures is found in the *Manual básico da ESG*, pp. 291-296. This particular citation is on p. 293. In the rest of this work I shall follow the actual application of the counteroffensive strategy against the opposition in various periods since 1964.

23. A full discussion of the term "political strategy" (*expressão política*) is contained in the *Manual básico da ESG*, Section 1, "Expressão política do poder nacional: O poder político," pp. 303-325. Mention of the four principal components of political expression is on p. 310.

24. The economic area, or the economic model, is carefully studied in Section 2 of the manual, "Expressão econômica do poder nacional: Poder econômico," pp. 329-351. The concepts included in this section have not changed very much from the early writings of ESG authors, prior to the takeover.

25. The psychosocial area is discussed in Section 3, "Expressão psicosocial do poder nacional: Poder psicosocial," pp. 355-371.

26. The military area is handled in Section 4, "Expressão militar do poder nacional: Poder militar," pp. 375-410. I shall discuss the military area more thoroughly in the analysis of the repressive apparatus of the national security state.

27. *Manual básico da ESG*, p. 319, "Inconformismo (Oposição e contestação)."

28. Ibid.

29. This is a brief summary of an involved and complicated argument. For details, including maps, graphs and military strategy, problems and planning, see Golbery do Couto e Silva, *Conjuntura política nacional*, section "*Geopolítica do Brasil*," pp. 95-138, in particular.

30. Ibid., p. 246.

31. Ibid., p. 52.

32. *Manual básico da ESG*, p. 338.

33. Golbery do Couto e Silva, *Conjuntura política nacional*, section "Geopolítica do Brasil," pp. 131-132.

34. Ibid., pp. 132-133.

35. *Manual básico da ESG*, p. 343.

36. Ibid., chap. 4, pp. 147-167.

37. This point will be examined in more detail in later chapters. It is interesting to point out that such an economic interpretation has resulted in what has been called the Brazilian "economic tripod" (see note 1, Introduction).

38. See, for example, the analysis in the *Manual básico da ESG*, p. 338:

One should make a special mention of the multinational corporations, which are unequaled examples of efficacy and economic efficiency. These corporations have great organizational flexibility and constitute powerful complexes that are capable of exerting large amounts of influence on the economy.

Although the present expansion of the multinationals has been the object of a growing preoccupation—even in the more developed nations—because of their potential to elicit protest, there is a consensus of opinion that ultimately the contribution of multinational corporations is positive.

39. Ibid., p. 339:

Nations that have achieved a rapid rate of development accumulated in the whole of their history considerable savings and an immense general effort. This effort may imply different degrees of sacrifice for *successive generations*, for it is clear that all enforced savings must correspond to an enforced reduction in consumption [my emphasis].

When an economic-financial policy—compatible with the permanent national objectives—brings about a sacrifice of the population in the way just mentioned, there is a certain degree of general consensus, if not ostensive then at least admitted, although there is always the potential for disequilibrium in the actual distribution of this sacrifice among the population.

Chapter 2. The Foundations of the National Security State

1. See John W. F. Dulles, *Castello Branco, the Making of a Brazilian President* (College Station: Texas A&M University Press, 1978); Hélio Silva, *1964: Golpe ou contragolpe?* (Rio de Janeiro: Civilização Brasileira, 1975); Luís Viana Filho, *O governo Castelo Branco* (Rio de Janeiro: José Olympio, 1976).

2. For a detailed account of these plans and statements, see Viana Filho, *O governo Castelo Branco*, pp. 3-45.

3. Ibid., p. 56.

4. *Diário Oficial da União* (9 April and 11 April 1964). Institutional Act No. 1 was signed on 9 April 1964 by General Arthur da Costa e Silva, Brigadier (Tenente-Brigadeiro) Francisco de Assis Correa de Mello, and Vice-Admiral Augusto Hamnn Rademaker Grunewald.

5. For an overview of press reaction, particularly after the passage of Institutional Act No. 1, see Thereza Cesário Alvim, *O golpe de 1964: A imprensa disse não* (Rio de Janeiro: Civilização Brasileira, 1979). See also Alceu de Amoroso Lima, *Revolução, reação ou reforma* (Rio de Janeiro: Tempo Brasileiro,

1964); and idem [Tristão de Athayde], *Pelo humanismo ameaçado* (Rio de Janeiro: Tempo Brasileiro, 1965). Lima is one of Brazil's most prominent Catholic philosophers and writes a column under the pseudonym "Tristão de Athayde."

6. *Diário Oficial da União* (9 April and 11 April 1964).

7. Ibid., article 7.

8. Ibid., article 8.

9. Ibid., article 10.

10. Viana Filho, *O governo Castelo Branco*, p. 59.

11. Decree-Law 53897of 27 April 1964. Passed by President Castello Branco, this law regulated and established the IPMs and stipulated the levels of organization and responsibility of the investigating committees.

12. Note the preoccupation with legality and the establishment of a legalist system capable of forming the basis for organization and coordination of a repressive strategy of control and purges.

13. See the extensive article on the IPM of Goiás, headed by Colonel Danilo Darcy de Sá Cunha Melo, who investigated the public employees of the state of Goiás and ended up by filing for the removal of the governor of the state. According to Colonel Cunha Melo, Governor Mauro Borges was conspiring to install in the state a "Communist paradise" and had surrounded himself and his administration with notorious Communists. The IPM's proofs had remained a secret until recently. See "Goiás: A incrível história do espurgo de 1964: Os relatórios do Coronel Danilo, uma aula de arbítrio," *Isto É* (4 April 1979), p. 30.

14. Ibid., pp. 30-31.

15. Viana Filho, *O governo Castelo Branco*, p. 55.

16. René Armand Dreifuss calls the different sectors the right-wing extremists, the traditionalists, and the ESG/IPES sector. Alfred Stepan prefers to call the hardliners "authoritarian nationalists." In reality, the nationalist ideology of the ESG and the hard-line sector did not differ to a significant degree, for both favored multinational investment and supported basically the same economic model. The nationalist sector of officers, those who supported an economic policy geared toward local capital and with strict control of multinational activities, was eliminated and kept from achieving positions of power through successive purges. See Dreifuss's definitions in *1964: A conquista do estado, ação política, poder e golpe de classe* (Rio de Janeiro: Vozes, 1981), pp. 339-373; and Alfred Stepan, *The Military in Politics* (Princeton, N.J.: Princeton University Press, 1971), pp. 159-183.

17. This estimate was reached after compiling data from interviews with different political actors who dealt closely either with lists of political prisoners that were reported to the press or with their defense. Of most particular value to me were interviews with journalist Antônio Callado, who was editor of *Correio da Manhã* at that time; Márcio Moreira Alves, a political journalist at that time on the same newspaper; former congressman Modesto da Silveira, then a lawyer who defended political prisoners; historian Hélio Silva; General Pery Bevilacqua; General Euclides Zerbini; and Catholic philosopher and journalist Alceu de Amoroso Lima. A search through the archives of the Brazilian Bar Association decisively indicated that repression was most concentrated in the states of Rio de Janeiro, Minas Gerais, São Paulo, Rio Grande do Sul, and Pernambuco. The largest number of denunciations of arbitrary arrests came from Pernambuco.

18. "Fine-tooth comb" (*pente-fino*) and "fishnet" (*arrastão*) operations are military-police maneuvers for widespread search-and-arrest campaigns with roadblocks, house-to-house search, and frisking of all individuals.

19. *Time* (17 April 1964), p. 21. A sample of the press reports may be found in *Correio da Manhã*, issues from May to November 1964.

20. See report of the International Committee of Jurists, reproduced in *Correio da Manhã* (8 September 1964), p. 1.

21. *Correio da Manhã* (14 July-9 October 1964).

22. For complete details on the different articles reporting the repression, see Maria Helena Moreira Alves, "The Formation of the National Security State: The State and the Opposition in Military Brazil" (Ph.D. diss., Massachusetts Institute of Technology, 1982).

23. Márcio Moreira Alves, *Torturas e torturados* (Rio de Janeiro: Idade Nova, 1966).

24. Data collected from the dossier of the Ministério da Aeronáutica, 1964-1967. I have counted only those names published under Institutional Act No. 1 for 1964. The dossier does not provide the party affiliations of all those who lost their political mandate. The sample provided is, however, sufficient for an adequate analysis of the effect of the purges on the political composition of Congress.

25. The sailors' revolt occasioned a deep crisis between the military and President Goulart, after the president granted amnesty to the mutinous sailors. The military charged him with interfering in the armed forces and of fomenting indiscipline and breaks in the hierarchy. It is now known that the leader of those revolts, "cabo Anselmo," was a covert *agent provocateur* who was explicitly ordered to incite the revolt that would deepen the crisis and thus facilitate the military coup d'état.

26. Dulles, *Castello Branco*, p. 297.

27. See *O livro negro da USP: O controle ideológico da universidade* (São Paulo: Brasiliense, 1979); *UFMG: Resistênca e protesto* (Belo Horizonte: Vega, 1979); and *Universidade e repressão: Os expurgos na UFRGS* (Porto Alegre: L&PM, 1979).

28. *O livro negro da USP*, p. 23.

29. The minister of justice at that time was Milton Campos, a liberal and respected jurist. He resigned from his post shortly after, to protest the *cassação* of the electoral mandates of state assemblymen in Rio Grande do Sul in order to maintain the government party's majority in the local legislature.

30. See *UFMG: Resistência e protesto*.

31. *Jornal do Brasil* (5 July 1964).

32. *Brazil: 1964 to the Present: A Political Analysis* (Québec: Editions Latin America, 1972), p. 17. Jean Marc von der Weid was elected UNE president in a clandestine congress held in Ibiúna, São Paulo, in 1968. His book analyzes the student movement in the early years of the national security state.

33. Francisco Juliaõ, *Cambaõ: As ligas camponesas* (Coimbra, Portugal: Centelha, 1975), published in English as *The Yoke: The Hidden Face of Brazil* (Middlesex, England: Penguin, 1972). See also, idem, *Brasil: Antes y después* (Mexico City: Nuestro Tiempo, 1968); Joseph A. Page, *The Revolution That Never Was: Northeast Brazil 1955-1964* (New York: Grossman, 1972); and Miguel Arraes, *Brazil: The People and the Power* (Middlesex, England: Penguin, 1969).

34. *Anuário Estatístico do Brasil* (Rio de Janeiro: Fundação IBGE, 1965). See also the tables in chap. 8 and the Appendix of this book on the total number of trade unions in Brazil and the total number of direct government interventions in trade unions.

35. See Kenneth Erickson, *The Brazilian Corporative State and Working Class Politics* (Berkeley & Los Angeles: University of California Press, 1977); and Argelina Maria Cheibub Figueiredo, "Política governamental e funções sindicais" (M.A. thesis, University of São Paulo, 1975).

36. See table 20.

37. Modesto da Silveira, a prominent lawyer who defended political prisoners from the first days after the coup d'état, told me that at least 80 percent of his clients in the first year were workers, peasants, and trade union leaders.

One of the most dramatic invasions of a union hall was that of the Rio de Janeiro Metalworkers' Union. The leadership and a great many union members inside the building were arrested. Union members still refer to that night as the "night of the boots."

38. See Figueiredo, *Política governmental,* pp. 40-98. Her study was based on data from 2,049 unions, federations, and confederations.

39. See *Correio da Manhã* (13 May 1964), p. 9. In Minas Gerais between 1 April and 5 May 1964 there were further interventions and arrests reported in *Correio da Manhã* (5 May 1964), p. 1.

40. Ibid. (5 May 1964), p. 1.

41. Ibid. (3 May 1964, p. 2; 6 May 1964, p. 2; and 27 June 1964, p. 51).

42. See Erickson, "Brazil: Corporatism in Theory and Practice," in *Latin American Politics and Development,* ed. Howard J. Wiarda and Harvey F. Kline, p. 144 (Boston: Houghton Mifflin, 1979).

43. *Informações* may be translated as "intelligence" or "information." This entails some confusion, even for Portuguese speakers. Brazilian newspapers commented, a few years ago, on the fact that the SNI often received phone calls from citizens inquiring (for example) whether the airport was open.

44. See *Manual básico da ESG,* p. 438.

45. Ibid., p. 439.

46. Viana Filho, *O governo Castelo Branco,* p. 72.

47. *Diário Oficial da União,* year 102, no. 113 (15 June 1964).

48. I shall discuss more thoroughly the connections between the SNI and the various organs of the repressive apparatus in chap. 8.

49. *Diário Oficial da União,* year 101, Sect. 1 (11 December 1964), p. 11336.

50. Ibid.

51. Ibid. See also *Correio da Manhã* (10 May 1964), p. 1.

52. Decree-Law No. 4341. Article 9 establishes the budget of the SNI. The exchange rate in 1964 was 2.20 cruzeiros per US dollar.

53. Dreifuss, *1964: A conquista do estado,* chap. 9 and note 20 on p. 492, where he states that "it was under the orientation of the Ministry of Planning that the reformulation of the productive and administrative structure of the state was conducted. . . . The Ministry of Planning transformed the state into a giant factor for the accumulation of capital, which benefited the multinational and associated block."

54. See *Programa de ação econômica do governo (1964-1966),* published by the Ministério de Planejamento e Coordenação Econômica, Brasília.

55. See Robert R. Kaufman, "Industrial Change and Authoritarian Rule in Latin

America: A Concrete Review of the Bureaucratic-Authoritarian Model," in *The New Authoritarianism in Latin America,* ed. David Collier, pp. 165-253 (Princeton, N.J.: Princeton University Press, 1979); Paul Singer, "Evolução da economia brasileira: 1955-1975," *Estudos CEBRAP,* no. 17 (July-September 1976), pp. 61-83; Werner Baer, "O crescimento brasileiro e a experiência desenvolvimentista: 1964-1974," *Estudos CEBRAP,* no. 20 (April-June 1977); Celso Furtado, *Diagnosis of the Brazilian Crisis* (Berkeley & Los Angeles: University of California Press, 1965); and Thomas E. Skidmore, "Politics and Economic Policy Making in Authoritarian Brazil, 1937-1971," in *Authoritarian Brazil: Origins, Policies and Future,* ed. Alfred Stepan, pp. 3-47 (New Haven, Conn.: Yale University Press, 1973).

56. Viana Filho, *O governo Castelo Branco,* p. 89.

57. Ibid.

58. Skidmore, "Politics and Economic Policy Making," p. 22.

59. Viana Filho, *O governo Castelo Branco,* p. 89.

60. Marcos Arruda, Herbet de Souza, and Carlos Afonso, *Multinationals and Brazil: The Impact of Multinational Corporations in Contemporary Brazil* (Toronto: Brazilian Studies, 1975), pp. 62-64. For a more comprehensive analysis of the system of fiscal incentives, see Alvaro Melo Filho, *Teoria e prática dos incentivos fiscais, introdução ao direito premial* (Rio de Janeiro: Eldorado Tijuca, 1976).

61. *Diário Oficial da União,* year 102, no. 104 (3 June 1964).

62. Kenneth S. Mericle, "Conflict Regulation in the Brazilian Industrial Relations System" (Ph.D. diss., University of Wisconsin, 1974), pp. 130-131.

63. Erickson, *The Brazilian Corporative State,* p. 159.

64. See *Cadernos do CEAS* (1977), pp. 34-36. The detailed compilation of strike actions for the 1973-1977 period included wildcat strikes and slowdowns.

65. Circular Número 10, Ministério da Fazenda, 19 June 1964. This was the first of a number of regulations establishing the formula for calculating wage adjustments, each of which was designed to fit the economic and political needs of the time. A chronology of the national security state's wage policy goes as follows: (1) 19 June 1964, Resolution No. 10 of the Ministry of Finance; (2) July 1964, Decree-Law No. 54018; (3) September 1964, Decree-Law No. 54228; (4) July 1965, Law No. 4725; (5) January 1966, Decree-Law No. 57627; (6) July 1966, Decree-Law No. 15; (7) August 1966, Decree No. 17; (8) July 1968, Law No. 5451; (9) November 1974, Law No. 6147; (10) October 1979, Six-Month Readjustment Law. See "Dez Años de política salarial," *Departamento Intersindical de Estatística e Estudos Sócio-Econômicos* (DIEESE), no. 3, (August 1975).

66. Ibid., p. 10.

Chapter 3. Building New Control Mechanisms: Institutional Act No. 2

1. According to the electoral legislation of the time, there were to be gubernatorial elections in the eleven states that had a five-year term for the office of governor, matching the presidential elections. The other eleven states in Brazil had four-year terms. Elections for the governors of the latter were held at the same time as congressional elections.

2. Decree-Law 55762, which regulates the Foreign Investment Law, passed on

17 February 1965. See Marcos Arruda, Herbet de Souza, and Carlos Afonso, *Multinationals and Brazil: The Impact of Multinational Corporations in Contemporary Brazil* (Toronto: Brazilian Studies, 1975), p. 59.

3. See Appendix, table A-1, for inflation rates in Brazil, 1960-1983.

4. World Bank, Country Study, *Brazil: Human Resources Special Report* (October 1979), p. 66. See also table A-3, Appendix, for growth rates by sector, 1960-1982.

5. *Correio da Manhã* (10 May 1964), p. 6.

6. The plebiscitary nature of elections has become one of the main characteristics of the national security state in Brazil. Forced to hold periodic elections because of its need for legitimacy, nonetheless it is torn by pressure from hard-liners to not allow the opposition to acquire any real measure of political power. Elections are therefore times of crisis, of inner conflict within the state, as well as times in which opposition groups can coalesce and express political dissent by voting against the government.

7. See "Dez años de política salarial," *Departamento Intersindical de Estatística e Estudos Sócio-Econômicos* (DIEESE), no. 3 (August 1975), pp. 12-13.

8. Decree-Law Number 57627 was regulated on the anticipated inflation rate as an element for the calculation of percentage raises in wages and established that, if for any reason an increase was granted over the official rate, half of the anticipated inflation had to be deduced from the increase. See ibid., p. 14.

9. Decree-Laws Nos. 15 and 17, July and August 1966. See ibid., p. 16.

10. Ibid., pp. 16-19.

11. Ibid., p. 15.

12. Data compiled from *Diário Oficial da União*, daily for 1965.

13. Interview with the leader of the group of IPM colonels, Colonel Martinelli. See *Correio da Manhã* (13 May 1965), p. 6. For other accounts of the hard-line IPM colonels' movement, see Luís Viana Filho, *O governo Castelo Branco* (Rio de Janeiro: José Olympio, 1976), pp. 315-338; Carlos Castello Branco, *Jornal do Brasil* (13 May 1965), p. 2; Marcus Figueiredo, *Legitimidade e coação no Brasil pós-1964* (Rio de Janeiro: Forense-Universitária, 1978), p. 130.

14. *Correio da Manhã* (6 February 1965), p. 2.

15. Ibid. Also discussed by Figueiredo, *Legitimidade e coação*, p. 130.

16. For the text of the Electoral Reform and Party Statute, see *Brazil: Election Factbook Number 2, November 1966* (Washington, D.C.: Comparative Study of Political Systems, Division of Operations and Policy Research, 1966), pp. 72-73.

17. The poll was published by Carlos Castello Branco in the *Jornal do Brasil* (20 June 1965), p. 2. Reprinted in his *Os militares no poder*, vol. 1, p. 266 (Rio de Janeiro: Nova Fronteira, 1976).

18. Viana Filho, *O governo Castelo Branco*, p. 313. The last point included in the law was intended to eliminate the secretaries of state of the governments of Miguel Arraes of Pernambuco and Mauro Borges of Goiás, as well as any member of the state government of Rio Grande do Sul under Leonel Brizola.

19. Ibid., pp. 304-340.

20. Reported to me by my brother, Márcio Moreira Alves, who was then a political journalist at *Correio da Manhã* and who followed the events closely. He commented that Hélio de Almeida was in fact the only person affected by that law.

21. Luis Viana Filho, *O governo Castelo Branco*, p. 315.

22. Carlos Castello Branco, *Jornal do Brasil* (14 May 1965), in the political column. Nelson Carneiro is now a senator from Rio de Janeiro.

23. See Carlos Castello Branco, *Os militares no poder*, vol. 1, p. 245, reprinted from his 14 May 1956 column in *Jornal do Brasil*.

24. The IPM colonels tried to include Negrão de Lima in the IPM investigation of the Communist party by claiming that he had been elected mayor of the city of Rio de Janeiro with the support of the Communist party. He was harassed and repeatedly arraigned for questioning, but the attempt nonetheless failed. Negrão de Lima was a close friend of President Castello Branco and as such had the president's discreet support, which strengthened his position.

25. There were 8,591,064 registered voters in 1965, but the actual number of voters in the 1965 elections was 6,574,226. In Brazil voting is required by law. However, because of migration and other factors, there is always a certain percentage of voters who request exemptions. The results of this election were reported in *Brazil: Election Factbook Number 2*, p. 90.

26. Ibid.

27. Ibid.

28. It is relevant to note that this pattern may be changing as a result of the rapid rural union organization and the social movements in the countryside organized by the Catholic church. See chaps. 7 and 8.

29. My information on the negotiations of this period comes from public documents, press articles, and in particular a series of conversations with my father, Márcio de Mello Franco Alves, who was a central participant in the events and was appointed finance secretary in the government of Negrão de Lima. He resigned his post during the cabinet crisis that followed the shooting of students in the streets of Rio de Janeiro in 1968.

30. Viana Filho, *O governo Castelo Branco*, p. 350.

31. *Diário Oficial da União*, year 103, no. 206 (26 October 1965).

32. Ibid. Article 16 was later made more repressive with the issuing of Complementary Acts Nos. 1 and 3. Complementary Act No. 1 made it a crime to disobey the provisions of the Statute of the *Cassados*, punishable with prison terms ranging from three months to one year. See Complementary Act No. 1, in ibid. Complementary Act No. 3 established a formal system of public denunciation that provided that all infractions of the Statute of the *Cassados* to be reported by the minister of justice or "any person of the population . . . by written denunciation of the infraction." See Complementary Act No. 3 in ibid. (4 November 1965).

33. Ibid. (26 October 1965).

34. See ibid., no. 208 (24 November 1965), for the text of Complementary Act. No. 4.

Chapter 4. Constitutional Reform and the Institutionalization of the New State

1. This description of the job stability program is largely based on Kenneth S. Mericle, "Conflict Regulation in the Brazilian Industrial Relations system" (Ph.D. diss., University of Wisconsin, 1974).

2. The FGTS has been analyzed by Vera Lúcia B. Ferrante, *FGTS: ideologia e repressão* (São Paulo: Atica, 1978). Much of the disscussion that follows is based on

this account of the origins and effect of the forced-savings fund system.

3. DIEESE has documented this policy in sectoral studies measuring the layoffs that occur in particular industries in periods immediately preceding and immediately following wage-salary deadlines. See the report in *Isto E* (30 April 1980), p. 91; and *Veja* (25 July 1979), pp. 100-101.

4. Brazilian lawyer, specialist in labor law, and University of Bahia professor José Martins Catharino emphasizes that the FGTS system was "not a choice but rather an act of coercion." In his experience there are only rare companies that will hire workers who have not opted for the system. See the account in *Veja* (7 April 1976), p. 71.

5. *Diário Oficial da União*, year 104, no. 36 (7 February 1966).

6. Ibid.

7. See Complementary Act No. 10, 4 June 1966, in *Diário Oficial da União* (7 June 1966), which provided for the cancellation of the electoral mandates of members of state, federal, or municipal governments who had their political rights cancelled; Complementary Act No. 11, 28 June 1966, in ibid. (30 June 1966), which provided for federal intervention in municipalities; Complementary Act No. 12, 30 June 1966, in ibid., which declared intervention in the state of Alagoas; Complementary Act No. 13, 28 June 1966, in ibid., which changed an article in Complementary Act No. 9; Complementary Act No. 14, 30 June 1966, in ibid., which stipulated that there would be no substitution for members of state, municipal, and federal legislatures who resigned their mandate; Complementary Act. No. 15, 15 July 1966, in ibid. (18 July 1966), which regulated municipalities; Complementary Act No. 16, 18 July 1966, in ibid. (20 July 1966), which established a party discipline rule whereby if a legislator voted for the candidate of the opposing party, that vote would be considered void; Complementary Act No. 17, 29 July 1966, in ibid. (1 August 1966), which contained new party registration rules; and Complementary Act No. 18, in ibid., which limited further the legislative power of Congress on matters of budget.

8. See Complementary Act No. 19, of 9 August 1966, in ibid. (9 August 1966). This act was meant to prevent ARENA dissent voting.

9. This was a part of the conclusion of the military-police inquiry (IPM) into the activities of the Communist party. The inquiry consisted of 157 volumes and annexed documents, with an extensive list of almost one thousand persons indicted. The records of the IPM of the Communist party were published by the Biblioteca do Exército Editora, in four large volumes entitled *O inquérito policial militar número 709*. For the names of those who were prevented from running for office, see *Ultima Hora* (14 October 1966).

10. See Osny Duarte Pereira, *A constituição do Brasil de 1967* (Rio de Janeiro: Civilização Brasileira, 1967), p. 330. The term "gorilla" was used to describe a member of the military in power.

11. The six federal congressmen who lost their mandates were opposition MDB politicians: Doutel de Andrade, Sebastião Paes de Almeida, César Prieto, Abraão Moura, Humberto El Jaick, and Adib Chamas. For an account of this crisis, see Carlos Castello Branco, *Os militares no poder*, vol. 1, pp. 579-582 (Rio de Janeiro: Nova Fronteira, 1976).

12. Castello Branco, *Jornal do Brasil* (16 October 1966), p. 2; reprinted in *Os*

militares no poder, vol. 1, pp. 581-582.

13. Ibid.

14. *Diário Oficial da União* (20 October 1966). For an account of the military troop operation used to close down Congress, see Carlos Castello Branco's columns, *Jornal do Brasil*, reprinted in *Os militares no poder*, vol. 1, pp. 586-587.

15. *Diário Oficial da União* (20 October 1966).

16. Pereira, *A constituição do Brasil de 1967*, p. 331.

17. For complete information on elections from 1966 to 1978, see table 19.

18. Cited in the *Correio da Manhã* (25 November 1966).

19. *Diário Oficial da União* (7 December 1966), p. 14187. Under the terms of the act, the committee would have seventy-two hours in which to discuss and vote on the constitution project, *in toto*. Then Congress, in a joint session, would have four days to discuss the project. After this period it would return to the committee for consideration of amendments for another twelve days. Finally, a joint session of Congress would have to discuss all of the amendments proposed and vote as a block within twelve days.

20. For an account of the voting process and events that preceded the passing of the 1967 Constitution, see Pereira, *A constituição do Brasil de 1967*, pp. 274-355.

21. Ibid., p. 336.

22. Ibid., p. 364, Article 6.

23. Ibid. See particularly Article 34, p. 419, Article 36, p. 422, Article 64, p. 459, Article 81, p. 475, and Article 56, p. 445.

24. Ibid., Article 57, p. 445, and Article 58, p. 446.

25. Ibid. See Article 106, p. 492; Articles 111, 112, 113, and 114, pp. 493-499; Article 116 regulating the Tribunais Federais de Recursos, on p. 499; and Articles 120, 121, and 122 regulating the Military Supreme Court, pp. 505-506. These articles deal with the controls of the judiciary and include many of the provisions of the extraordinary institutional acts.

26. Ibid., Article 83, p. 477.

27. The Constitution of 1967 included a section entitled "Tax System" ("Sistema Tributário"), from Articles 18 to 28. These established the precise tax rights of the states and the exclusive rights of the federal government in the centralization of tax collection and distribution. This was a way of weakening the federative system by giving the central government the exclusive right of charging and collecting tax tributes and of deciding on the redistribution of taxes among the states and the municipalities. This subordinated the states to the central federal government, thereby increasing its political control. See ibid., Articles 18 to 28, pp. 393-416.

28. Ibid., Article 157, p. 550, Item 8.

29. Ibid., Article 163, Items 1, 2, and 3, p. 553.

30. Ibid., Article 161, pp. 552-553, and Article 162, p. 553.

31. Ibid., Article 162, p. 553.

32. Ibid.

33. Ibid., Article 157, Item 7, p. 550.

34. Ibid., Article 158, Item 13, p. 551.

35. Ibid., Article 158, Item 10, p. 551. There has been an increasing tendency in corporations to replace adult labor with child labor, for, legally, a minor receives a smaller minimum wage than an adult.

36. Ibid., Section 5, pp. 180-184. This section is entirely devoted to the concept of national security and its effective structural implementation. In previous conceptions, national security was defined as the defense of the territory of the nation against the aggression of other nations. This was reinterpreted.

37. Ibid., Article 89, p. 480.

38. Ibid., Article 91, p. 481. The description of the measures, powers, and members of the National Security Council that follows is in this article of the Constitution of 1967.

39. Ibid., Article 148, p. 527. These may also be found in Article 143, p. 523, and Article 144, p. 524.

40. Ibid., chap.4, "On the Rights and Individual Guarantees." See, particularly, Article 150, Items 1 to 35, for the Bill of Rights, pp. 532-536.

41. Ibid. Pereira provides an interesting comparison of the Constitution's text as it was originally drafted by the executive with the amended text eventually passed by Congress. The account of the congressional debate on the question of individual rights may be found on pp. 536-542.

Chapter 5. Liberalization, Opposition, and State Crisis: Institutional Act No. 5

1. Costa e Silva was elected by Congress, in accordance with Article 9 of Institutional Act No. 2 and Article 5 of Institutional Act No. 3. His vice-president was Pedro Aleixo. The president was elected with 295 votes, divided in the Electoral College as follows: 252 votes from ARENA federal deputies, 3 votes from MDB deputies, and 40 votes from ARENA senators.

2. Carlos Castello Branco, *Jornal do Brasil* (16 March 1967); reprinted in his *Os militares no poder*, vol. 2, p. 13 (Rio de Janeiro: Nova Fronteira, 1976).

3. See Thomas E. Skidmore, "Politics and Economic Policy Making in Authoritarian Brazil, 1937-1971," in *Authoritarian Brazil*, ed. Alfred Stepan, pp. 20-22 (New Haven, Conn.: Yale University Press, 1971); Albert Fishlow, "Some Reflections on Post-1964 Brazilian Economic Policy," in ibid., pp. 70-77; Robert R. Kaufman, "Industrial Change and Authoritarian Rule in Latin America: A Concrete Review of the Bureaucratic-Authoritarian Model," in *The New Authoritarianism in Latin America*, ed. David Collier, pp. 171-173 (Princeton, N.J.: Princeton University Press, 1979).

4. "Dez años de política salarial," *Departamento Intersindical de Estatística e Estudos Sócio-Econômicos* (DIEESE), no. 3 (August 1975), p. 64.

5. Alceu de Amoroso Lima, in an interview with me on 20 May 1978, was responding to my question as to whether one could consider the opposition to be a united and well-orchestrated social movement, or whether it was composed of fragmented and isolated groups.

6. These agreements, which became known as the MEC-USAID agreements, were signed in 1966. They aimed at a complete reform of the university system in Brazil to privatize educational institutions. The university reform was to be carried out under the direction and coordination of planning committees set up in the terms of the agreement. These were mostly composed of North American technicians and were to establish guidelines for all education policy, for agricultural education, and for textbook publication. The reforms would completely transform the Brazilian university system, bringing it closer to the model followed in American universities. The agreements were a source of protest because they were considered a threat to

university autonomy. See Márcio Moreira Alves, *Beabá dos MEC-USAID* (Rio de Janeiro: Gernasa, 1968); Betty Antunes de Oliveira, *O estado autoritário brasileiro e o ensino superior* (São Paulo: Cortez, 1980); Florestan Fernandes, *Universidade brasileira: Reforma ou revolução?* (São Paulo: Alfa-Omega, 1979); and Irene de Arruda Ribeiro Cardoso, "A reforma universitária e a Universidade de São Paulo," *Educação e Sociedade*, no. 3 (May 1979).

7. The national organization is the Board of Directors and the Political Council. State organizations are the state student unions (União Estadual de Estudantes, UEE). Local university organizations are the central directorates (Diretório Central dos Estudantes, DCE) and the academic centers (Centro Acadêmico, CA). These organizational networks persisted as parallel underground organizations. At the same time, students increasingly organized to take control of the official structures of representation set up by the Lei Suplicy. Thus there was a dual system of organization, one legal and one illegal.

8. For an account of the secret 1967 National Congress of Students, see *Folha de São Paulo* (11 August 1967).

9. See Jean Marc von der Weid, *Brazil: 1964 to the Present: A Political Analysis* (Québec: Editions Latin America, 1972); Luiz Henrique Romagnoli and Tânia Gonçalves, *A volta da UNE*, Historia Imediata Series (São Paulo: Alfa Omega, 1979); and Alfredo Syrkis, *Os carbonários: Memórias da guerrilha perdida* (São Paulo: Global, 1980).

10. A description of the events surrounding the student demonstrations of this period can be found in the press of the time. See especially *Jornal do Brasil* (5 April 1968), on the mass at the Candelária. For the riot and street battle referred to as "Bloody Friday," see extensive coverage in *Correio da Manhã* (22 June 1968), and *Jornal do Brasil* (22 June 1968). The demonstration in Rio de Janeiro known as the "March of the 100,000" was reported in *Jornal do Brasil, Correio da Manhã,* and *Ultima Hora* (25 and 26 June 1968).

11. *Jornal do Brasil* (5 April 1968), p. 1.

12. *Correio da Manhã* (7 April 1968), p. 1.

13. The "March of the 100,000" was preceded by violent street battles in downtown Rio de Janeiro, which involved thousands of people in direct confrontations with the military. As the students demonstrated peacefully, the military police attacked them. Office workers and construction workers who witnessed the attack came down to help the students. This developed into an all-out street battle, including the setting up of barricades, which lasted for over six hours. The damage done and the number of wounded in this street battle earned it the name "Bloody Friday." The American Consulate was damaged in the fighting (see *Correio da Manhã* [22 June 1968]).

As a result of popular protest against the violence of the police attack on unarmed demonstrators, however, the government finally removed the military from the streets, and the "March of the 100,000" took place peacefully. See *Jornal do Brasil* (26 June 1968), and *Correio da Manhã* (25 June 1968). See also the personal testimony of the members of the Committee of the 100,000 published in *Flagrante* (March-April 1978). The negotiations with the government quickly reached a stalemate.

14. For more information, see chap. 8.

15. Information on the Cobrasma Factory Committee is based on interviews with

Roque Aparecido da Silva (interview with the author, 5 August 1979) and José Ibrahim (interview with the author, 3 November 1979). See also interview with José Ibrahim in *Veja* (12 April 1978).

Both José Ibrahim and Roque Aparecido da Silva were leaders of the Cobrasma Factory Committee. Both were forced to spend many years in exile. José Ibrahim, in addition, was in prison for a period and was finally banished from Brazil in 1969 as one of the prisoners exchanged for American Ambassador Charles Burke Elbrick, who was kidnapped by participants in the armed opposition.

The Cobrasma Factory Committee began with the organization of "Groups of 10" in each sector of the factory. Workers would set up groups in their own sections to discuss plant problems. Then they would elect their own sector leaders. These in turn coordinated and elected representatives to a larger group, for coordinating the work of all sections of the factory.

In 1965 the management of Cobrasma accepted the legality of the committee, which up to then had existed semiofficially. It was established that the committee would be composed of one effective representative and one alternate for each section of the factory. These would be elected by their fellow workers in each section. The Cobrasma Factory Committee was constituted of thirty persons from the nineteen different sections of the factory.

16. Ibid.

17. For information on the MIA, see "Dez anos de política salarial," p. 17; see also Francisco Weffort, "Participação e conflito industrial: Contagem e Osasco, 1969," *Cadernos do CEBRAP*, no. 5 (1972), pp. 26, 34-35. For information on the parallel structures, see idem, "Partidos, sindicatos, e democracia: Algumas questões para a história do período 1945-1964" (M.A. thesis, Universidade de São Paulo).

18. See Weffort, "Participação e conflito industrial." See also articles in *Flagrante* (March-April 1978), p. 14, and *Reporter*, no. 4 (March 1978), pp. 22-23.

19. *Diário Oficial da União* (14 June 1968).

20. "Dez anos de política salarial," pp. 17-19.

21. Information on the Osasco strike comes from interviews with leaders and participants in the strike, as well as from Weffort, "Participação e conflito industrial."

22. Roque Aparecido da Silva, interview with the author, 5 August 1979.

23. The first real indication of the government's worry about the activities of the Frente Ampla came with an order that prohibted mention of the front's activities in the mass media. For more information on this movement, see Marcus Figueiredo, *Legitimidade e coação no Brasil pós-1964* (Rio de Janeiro: Forense-Universitária, 1978), vol. 2, particularly pp. 15-16. For a reprint of the program of the Frente Ampla and articles from September 1967 to April 1968, see Carlos Lacerda, *Depoimento* (Rio de Janeiro: Nova Fronteira, 1978).

24. Castello Branco, *Os militares no poder*, vol. 2, p. 183. See also his political analysis column in *Jornal do Brasil* (12 October 1967).

25. Cited by Carlos Castello Branco, *Jornal do Brasil* (12 October 1967).

26. Castello Branco, *Os militares no poder*, vol. 2, p. 189, and his column in *Jornal do Brasil* (22 October 1967).

27. Figueiredo, *Legitimidade e coação no Brasil pós-1964*, pp. 137-138.

28. For an insider's account of this period and the efforts of Pedro Aleixo and other more liberal members of the Costa e Silva government to continue the liberalization process and draft a new constitution, see Carlos Chagas, *113 dias de angústia: Impedimento e morte de um presidente* (Rio Grande do Sul: L&PM Editores, 1979).

29. See Márcio Moreira Alves, *A Grain of Mustard Seed: The Awakening of the Brazilian Revolution* (New York: Doubleday Anchor Press, 1973), pp. 14-25. This gives an account of the tactics and analysis made at the time of the political conjuncture and correlation of forces by a group of opposition members of Congress.

30. Ibid., and accounts in the press of the time. My own information also comes from long conversations and analyses of the event with Márcio. The provocative attitude that this small group of radical members of Congress adopted is placed in the context of the time, of the euphoric feeling of opposition offensive and the real belief that not only would armed struggle be the sole alternative, but that the population was ready to rise up against the national security state. It was even believed in many opposition circles at the time that the military would become divided, and dissidents would distribute arms to the people—as had just happened in the Dominican Republic. Márcio Moreira Alves paid for his speech with eleven years of exile. He was forced to leave the country to escape a major manhunt, and returned only after the partial political amnesty was won in August 1979.

31. See the report in *Isto E* (7 December 1977), p. 11; *Coojornal* (April 1978), p. 31; and *Veja* (21 December 1977).

32. Institutional Act No. 5 in *Atos institucionais, atos complementares e decretos lei*, vol. 4, Diretoria de Informação Legislativa, Senado Federal, Brasília. Also in *Diário Oficial da União*, year 106, no. 241 (13 December 1968).

33. Figueiredo, *Legitimidade e coação no Brasil pós-1964*.

34. See *Jornal do Brasil* (13 December 1977), p. 8, and *Isto E* (7 December 1977), pp. 9-10.

35. General Golbery do Couto e Silva, *Conjuntura política nacional, o poder do executivo e geopolítica do Brasil* (Rio de Janeiro: José Olympio, 1981), p. 9.

Chapter 6: Armed Struggle and the National Security State

1. Régis Debray, *Revolution in the Revolution? Armed Struggle and Political Struggle in Latin America* (New York: Grove Press, 1967). Debray's book assessed the situation in Latin America. He was highly critical of the political strategy of peaceful transition to socialism, which had been espoused by the Moscow-oriented Communist parties in Latin America. Debray fought with Che Guevara in Bolivia and was serving, at that time, a period in prison in Bolivia for his advocacy of guerrilla war. He is considered one of the main theoreticians of *foquismo*, which is explicitly described in his writing. Debray no longer supports his earlier theories of armed struggle as the only path to socialism.

2. Ibid. For more detailed discussions of *foquismo*, see also João Quartim, *Dictatorship and Armed Struggle in Brazil* (New York: Monthly Review Press, 1971), particularly chap. 3; Debray, "The Long March in Latin America," *New Left Review* (September/October 1965), pp. 45-60; idem, *Strategy for Revolution: Essays on Latin America* (New York: Monthly Review Press, 1970); Leo Huberman and Paul Sweezy, eds. *Régis Debray and the Latin American*

Revolution: A Collection of Essays (New York: Monthly Review Press, 1968); Michael Lowy, *The Marxism of Che Guevara: Philosophy, Economics, and Revolutionary Warfare* (New York: Monthly Review Press, 1973).

3. See Carlos Marighela, *For the Liberation of Brazil* (Middlesex, England: Pelican, 1971); Richard Gott, *Guerrilla Movements in Latin America* (New York: Doubleday Anchor, 1972); Antônio Caso, *A esquerda armada no Brasil (1967-1971)* (Lisbon: Moraes Editores, 1976); and Alfredo Syrikis, *Os carbonários: Memórias da guerrilha perdida* (São Paulo: Global, 1980).

4. Carlos Chagas, *113 dias de angústia: Impedimento e morte de um presidente* (Rio Grande do Sul: L&PM Editores, 1979); and Carlos Castello Branco, *Os militares no poder: O baile das solteironas*, vol.3 (Rio de Janeiro: Nova Fronteira, 1979).

5. Chagas, *113 dias de angústia,* pp. 65-67. The Brazilian military show an unending devotion to legal formalities. Thus, the succession problem was first resolved by the issuing of Institutional Act No. 12, which installed the military junta in power. Institutional Act No. 16 reopened Congress to ratify the choice of General Emílio Garrastazú Médici. The texts of both these institutional acts can be found in the appendix of Chagas's book.

6. Ibid., pp. 76-173. This electoral college was composed of sixteen generals from the First Army, eleven from the Second Army, twelve from the Third Army, seven from the Fourth Army, fourteen from the army's General Provisions Department of Construction, seven from the army High Command, ten from the ESG, four from the Armed Forces High Command, and eight from the staff of the minister of the army. The power structure was clearly slanted toward the army, eclipsing the influence of the other two branches of the armed forces. This would fuel internal dissent and rivalry.

7. For statistical information on Brazil's foreign debt and reserves, see Table A-2 in Appendix.

8. See Edmar Bacha, *Política e distribuição de renda* (Rio de Janeiro: Paz e Terra, 1978); Luiz C. Bresser Pereira, *Desenvolvimento e crise no Brasil* (São Paulo: Brasiliense, 1977); Shelton H. Davis, *Victims of the Miracle: Development and the Indians of Brazil* (New York: Cambridge University Press, 1977); Celso Furtado, *Obstacles to Development in Latin America* (New York: Anchor, 1970); idem, *Formação econômica do Brasil* (São Paulo: Companhia Editora Nacional, 1972); idem, *Diagnosis of the Brazilian Crisis* (Berkeley & Los Angeles: University of California Press, 1965); Albert Fishlow, "Some Reflections on post-1964 Economic Policy," in *Authoritarian Brazil: Origins, Policies, and Future*, ed. Alfred Stepan (New Haven: Yale University Press, 1973); Rodolfo Hoffman and João Carlos Duarte, "A distribuição de renda no Brasil," *Revista de Administração de Empresas* 12, no. 2 (June 1972); Maria de Lurdes Scarfon, *Crescimento e miséria* (São Paulo: Símbolo, 1979); Mário Henrique Simonsen, *A nova economia brasileira* (Rio de Janeiro: José Olympio, 1974); and Delfim Netto, *Agricultura e desenvolvimento no Brasil*, Estudos AMPES, no. 5 (São Paulo, 1966).

Of particular relevance to the debate between the "productivists" and the "distributivists" and the critique of the economic miracle model of development is the collection of articles included in *A controvérsia sobre a distribuição de renda e desenvolvimento* (Rio de Janeiro: Zahar, 1975). See also Paulo Singer, "O milagre brasileiro: Causas e conseqüências," *Cadernos CEBRAP*, no. 6 (1972); idem, *A crise do milagre: Interpretação crítica da economia brasileira* (Rio de Janeiro: Paz e Terra, 1977); José Carlos Duarte, "Aspectos da distribuição de renda no Brasil em 1970" (M.A. thesis, Universidade de São Paulo, 1971).

9. See *Manual básico da EG*, p. 339: "Nations that have achieved a rapid rate of development accumulated in the whole of their history considerable savings and an immense general effort. This effort may imply different degrees of sacrifice of successive generations, for it is clear that all enforced savings must correspond to an enforced reduction in consumption."

10. See Mário Henrique Simonsen, *A nova economia brasileira*, pp. 39-41.

11. *Anuário Estatístico do Brasil*, 1969 and 1974.

12. The controversy over the denationalization of the Brazilian economy has produced abundant literature. See, for example, Marcos Arruda, Herbet de Souza, and Carlos Afonso, *Multinationals and Brazil: The Impact of Multinational Corporations in Contemporary Brazil* (Toronto: Brazilian Studies, 1975); Moniz Bandeira, *Cartéis e desnacionalização: A experiência brasileira: 1964-1975* (Rio de Janeiro: Civilização Brasileira, 1975); Jan Knippers Black, *United States Penetration of Brazil* (Philadelphia: University of Pennsylvania Press, 1977); Luciano Martins, *A nação e a corporação multinacional: A política das empresas no Brasil e na América Latina* (Rio de Janeiro: Paz e Terra, 1975); Kurt Mirow, *A ditadura dos cartéis: Anatomia de um subdesenvolvimento* (Rio de Janeiro: Civilização Brasileira, 1978); Sylvia Ann Hewlett, *The Cruel Dilemmas of Development: Twentieth Century Brazil* (New York: Basic Books, 1980). See also the Report to the Subcommittee on Multinational Corporations of the Committee on Foreign Relations of the United States Senate, August 1975, *Multinational Corporations in Brazil and Mexico: Structural Sources of Economic and non-Economic Power* (Washington: Superintendent of Documents, United States Printing Office, 1975).

13. See Delfim Netto, *Agricultura e desenvolvimento no Brasil*, and Langoni, *A distribuição de renda*.

14. See *A situação da criança no Brasil* (Rio de Janeiro: Muro, 1979).

15. Carlos Marighela, *For the Liberation of Brazil*, p. 21.

16. See Institutional Act No. 13. *Diário Oficial da União*, year 107, no. 172 (9 September 1969). The text of this institutional act may also be found in the appendix of Carlos Chagas, *113 dias de angústia*, p. 233.

17. Institutional Act No. 14, in *Diário Oficial da União*, year 107, no. 173 (10 September 1969). The text is included in Carlos Chagas, *113 dias de angústia*, pp. 233-234.

18. Decree-Law No. 898, entitled Segurança Nacional: Decreto Lei Número 898 of 29 September 1969, in *Diário Oficial da União*, year 107, no. 174 (29 September 1969). It became known as the National Security Law of 1969, for it defines the crimes against national security and the public and social order as well as the legal process of trial judgment and the penalties to be imposed for each crime. It is also found separately in a publication of the Departamento de Imprensa Nacional da República Federativa do Brasil of 1978, *Segurança nacional: Decreto lei número 898 de setembro de 1969 e decreto lei número 975 de outubro 1969 e decreto lei número 5,786 de 27 de junho de 1972.*

The first national security law was passed as Decree-Law No. 314 on 13 March 1967, and was regulated by Decree-Law 510 of 20 March 1969. These were specifically revoked by the 1969 National Security Law known as Decree-Law 898. The latter piece of legislation greatly extended the repressive force of the previous, more timid efforts to set up controls.

On 17 December 1978, President Ernesto Geisel modified the National Security Law. As we shall see later, however, the text remained the same as that of the National Security Law of 1969. The main modifications concerned shorter prison terms, for it was felt that the law as it stood was too stringent to be effectively applied as a mechanism of control.

19. See *Diário Oficial da União* (20 October 1969), republished on 30 October.

20. Articles 8-16.

21. Articles 22-28, 39, 31-33, 35, 37, 42, and 46.

22. Articles 24-25.

23. I refer here to the Press Law (Lei de Imprensa) and to direct prior censorship. The National Security Law also contains specific articles for the punishment of press infractions, in Articles 16, 34, 36, 39, 47, 53, and 54.

24. The Secret Decree-Law, as it is popularly called, is Decree-Law No. 69534. See *Diário Oficial da União* (11 November 1971). This decree-law is still in effect. I have counted ten secret decrees that have been published only by their numbers since 1971. The greatest number—seven—were passed in the government of General Figueiredo, and three under Médici. See *Movimento* (6-12 April 1981), p. 9.

Veja (24 November 1971), cites reactions to the law: "Finding himself surrounded by other congressmen who were anxious for explanations, the leader of the MDB, Oscar Pedroso Horta, had only this to say: 'In my opinion, Decree-Law No. 69534 is a unique piece of legislation in Brazilian juridical tradition. I cannot understand how one can possibly obey a law, a decree, or even a regulation, of which one is totally ignorant.' "

25. See accounts in *Jornal do Brasil* (22 October and 17 September 1971).

26. See *A Report to Senator John Tunney* (Democrat-California), for information on this occurrence and mass arrests in Rio de Janeiro prior to Rockefeller's visit (U.S. Senate, January 1972, p. 5).

27. Ibid. Also reported in Carlos Castello Branco, *Os militares no poder,* vol. 3, pp. 709-718 (Rio de Janeiro: Nova Fronteira, 1976).

28. The military operation was intended to surround and capture a group of nine men led by Captain Carlos Lamarca; the group was forming a *foco* in the area. Lamarca and seven of his men managed to break out of the encirclement and flee, using military uniforms and an army truck that they captured in an ambush. Lamarca was later killed after a long and large-scale military pacification campaign in the interior of the state of Bahia in 1971. The Vale da Ribeira operation is described in detail in a well-documented article based on reports from the army. This article was written by Osmar Trindade and Elmar Bones and published in *Coojornal* (February 1980), pp. 15-24 (*Coojornal* is a publication of the Cooperative of Journalists of Porto Alegre, Rio Grande do Sul). A detailed, book-length account of the campaigns in Vale da Ribeira and the later pacification program in Bahia to capture and kill Carlos Lamarca in 1971 is described in Emiliano José and Oldack Miranda, *Lamarca, O Capitão da Guerrilha* (São Paulo: Global, 1980).

29. See Marcos Arruda, Herbet de Souza, and Carlos Afonso, *Multinationals and Brazil: The Impact of Multinational Corporations in Contemporary Brazil* (Toronto: Brazilian Studies, 1975), pp. 79-88.

30. Ibid., pp. 85-86. See also the full report of the congressional committee investigating land purchase (*CPI da Terra, 1968*), which can be obtained from the Press and Documentation Department of the House of Representatives in Brasilia. Also published in *Jornal do Brasil* (5 July 1970).

31. Arruda, de Souza, and Afonso, *Multinationals in Brazil*. One of the largest landowners was D. K. Ludwig Corporation, in the Jari Project in the Amazon region. For a report on this project, see the well-documented account written by Congressman Modesto da Silveira, a member of the congressional committee investigating the Jari Project, *Ludwig: O imperador do Jari* (Rio de Janeiro: Civilização Brasileira, 1980).

32. The Amazon area contains, among other things, zinc, nickel, chromite, bauxite, manganese, aluminum, iron, tin, copper, uranium, precious stones, diamonds, and gold. The mountains of Carajás contain one of Brazil's richest mineral deposits. The Carajás Project, developed by the Figueiredo government, involves the towns of Marabá, Barsarena, Paragominas (Pará), and São Luís do Maranhão. The corporations that are currently exploiting the minerals in the region are Brazil's state-owned Vale do Rio Doce mining company, in association with the U.S. Steel Corporation, Alcoa, Kennecott Corporation, Kaiser and Reynolds corporations, and more recently, the Utah Corporation, which has bought the manganese mining rights from U.S. Steel Corporation. In 1981 the Brazilian government signed a contract with a consortium of thirty-two Japanese companies, which are to come into the area to produce aluminum. The new corporation has been named Albrás/Alunorte. The Carajás Project will also include specific grants for multinational corporations to mine the vast gold deposits. For full details on the Carajás Project and the corporations involved, see *Bulletin Number 6* (10 May 1981), of the Anthropology Resource Center, Boston, Massachusetts.

33. Arruda, de Souza, and Afonso, *Multinationals in Brazil*, p. 173.

34. The problem of Indian land, speculation, and conflict in the area is well handled in Davis, *Victims of the Miracle*. Extensive documentation on land conflicts that have resulted from the land speculation and corporation takeovers of Indian land can be found in publications of the National Conference of Brazilian Bishops (CNBB). The data have been carefully gathered through the years by the Conselho Indigenista Missionário (CIMI), an organization tied to the CNBB and responsible for work with the Indians.

The method of illicit influence-peddling and land purchase from squatters who have a traditional right to the land is known in Brazil as *grilagem*. A corporation, or rich individual, many purchase large amounts of land by agreement with the National Security Council. Sometimes this may involve as much as one million acres, as in the case of the Jari Project and the Volkswagen projects in the Amazon region. Peasants who have lived in the area over ten years have legal squatter's rights, but most of the time do not possess a deed to the land. The forced eviction of peasant families has been the cause of the conflicts in the region. Conflicts have become so violent that they have involved priests, lay pastoral agents, and the hierarchy of the Catholic church in an attempt to defend the peasants from armed eviction.

Bulletin Number 6 (10 May 1981), of the Anthropology Resource Center, Boston, provides a detailed account of the Figueiredo government's new forest and agricultural projects, which will increase speculation and violence in the region. The forest project, which covers approximately 2.4 million hectares of land, will involve coal and lumber exploitation. The agricultural project will cover another 7 million hectares, and involves the planting of soybeans, sugarcane, and manioc. The agricultural project is to be developed by 10,000 Japanese immigrant families, who are being brought to Brazil especially for that purpose.

There are currently an estimated 100,000 Indian and peasant families living on this land. They are to be dispossessed and removed from the area. In fact, the government is applying in full the methodology of the American military in Vietnam: to entirely replace the population of an area in order to bring that area under complete control.

35. For information on the guerrillas of the Araguaia as well as on the three different military campaigns conducted in the area, see Fernando Portela, *Guerra de guerrilhas no Brasil* (São Paulo: Global, 1979); Palmério Dória, Sérgio Buarque, Vincente Carelli, and Jaime Sautchuk, *A guerrilha do Araguaia, História Imediata*, No. 1 (São Paulo: Alfa-Omega, 1979); Clóvis Moura, *Diário da guerrilha do Araguaia* (São Paulo: Alfa-Omega, 1979); and the articles in *Movimento* (17 July 1978), p. 5, "Guerrilha do Araguaia, and "Uma história secreta que começa a ser revelada."

36. Interviews conducted with people in the region showed that the Paulistas were well liked because they provided technical assistance and medical care. It was also clear that the residents became aware of the underground activities of the Paulistas only when the army moved in and occupied the area in a search for the guerrillas.

37. Cited in Dória et al., *A guerrilha do Araguaia*, p. 5. A colonel who was interviewed stated that the war carried out in the region was a "dirty, secret, disgusting, and undeclared war where the rules of the Geneva Convention were never obeyed." These and other interviews with military commanders and participants in the struggle are also found in Portela, *Guerra de guerrilhas no Brasil*, esp. pp. 27-29.

38. See in particular Portela's extensive account of the situation in the region as late as 1982 in his *Guerra de guerrilhas no Brasil*, part 2.

39. Personal accounts of residents in the area, of pastoral agents of the Catholic church, of priests and bishops, as well as documents of the period may be found in the archives of the CNBB. In ibid., Portela provides evidence and interviews of torture victims in the area.

40. *O Estado de São Paulo* (24 September 1972).

41. Ibid.

42. Officially, the military justified the maneuvers by claiming to be fighting a large-scale civil war in the area. The need to maintain complete censorship of the press about the events in Araguaia was justified by Colonel Jarbas Passarinho as necessary to avoid the "multiplying effect" and provide an example of a rural guerrilla *foco*. See the interview with Passarinho in Dória et al., *A guerrilha do Araguaia*, pp. 21-27. See also Portela, *Guerra de guerrilhas no Brasil*, particularly chap. 15, "O governo em silêncio," pp. 89-95.

43. Portela, *Guerra de guerrilhas no Brasil*, part 2.

44. "A igreja e os problemas da terra," resolution of the National Conference of Brazilian Bishops, 1980, in the archives of the CNBB. See the report of the studies

of the Pastoral da Terra in *Isto E* (30 September 1981), p. 26.

45. Reported in the study of the Comissão Pastoral da Terra, published in *Isto E* (30 September 1981), p. 26.

46. Amnesty International, *A Report on Allegations of Torture in Brazil* (London: T. B. Russell, 1972).

47. Documentation on the use of torture and the disappearance of prisoners during this period may be found in the reports of international organizations. See, for example, International Association of Democratic Jurists, *Dossier Brésil* (April 1971); Amnesty International, *Torture of Political Prisoners in Brazil*, Report no. 5 (13 March 1970); idem, *A Report on Allegations of Torture in Brazil*; and periodic Amnesty updates; International Commission of Jurists, *Report on Police Repression and Tortures Inflicted upon Political Opponents and Prisoners in Brazil* (22 July 1970); Amnesty International, *Document and Prisoners in the Presídio da Justiça Militar Federal* (28 October 1975); World Federation of Trade Unions, Commission of Churches on International Affairs of the World Council of Churches, and International Commission of Jurists, *A Study of the Situation in Brazil which Reveals a Consistent Pattern of Violations of Human Rights: Official Version* (19 March 1971); Bertrand Russell Tribunal Session, Brussels, Belgium, *On Repression in Brazil, Chile and Latin America* (Nottingham, England: Bertrand Russell Peace Foundation, 1975).

48. International Commission of Jurists, Geneva, *Report on Police Repression and Tortures*.

49. For the complete text of Frei Tito's letter, see the appendix of Pedro Celso Uchoa Cavalcânti and Jovelino Ramos, eds., *Memórias do exílio: Brasil 1964- 19??* (Lisbon: Arcádia, 1976).

50. Amnesty International, various documents.

51. The legislation allows for detention of up to ten days, which may be extended for another ten.

52. The meeting took place in São Paulo and was filmed and taped by Joan Baez during her trip to Brazil in May 1981.

53. This interview was conducted in April 1979, during a major metalworkers' strike in São Bernardo do Campo and Diadema.

54. Not all the military are involved in torture or directly active in the repressive apparatus. In fact, many have opposed such deeds and have been a part of the various opposition movements within the military.

55. Further detailed information on the agencies and the machinery of the repressive apparatus may be found in, for example, Ettore Biocca, *Estratégia do terror: A face oculta e repressiva do Brasil* (Lisbon: Iniciativas Editoriais, 1974); Antônio Carlos Fon, *Tortura: A história da repressão política no Brasil* (São Paulo: Global, 1979); Reinaldo Cabral and Ronaldo Lapa, eds., *Os desaparecidos políticos: Prisões, sequestros, assassinatos* (Rio de Janeiro: Opção, 1979). Two collective works of political prisoners also contain detailed information on the workings of the various agencies and organizations of the repressive apparatus: *A esquerda armada: A luta continua (Testemunho dos presos políticos do presídio Milton Dias Moreira, no Rio de Janeiro)* (Vitória, Espírito Santo: Edições do Leitor, 1979); and *Dos presos políticos brasileiros: Acerca da repressão fascista no Brasil* (Lisbon: Edições Maria da Fonte, 1976).

See also the important articles in *Isto E* (3 March 1978), pp. 9-15; *Veja* (15 May 1978), pp. 45-55; *Veja* (13 September 1978), pp. 20-26; and *Isto E* (14 February 1979), pp. 26-34.

56. See Cabral and Lapa, eds., *Os desaparecidos políticos*, pp. 43-45.

57. Prior to 1969 the military police of the various states were not directly engaged in the repression of popular dissent. In 1969 the military junta signed a decree that reorganized all of the military police in the country. Decree no. 667, of 2 July 1969, centralized the operational control of the military police of all states in the army as well as changed its objective to that of keeping "internal security" rather than being engaged in preventive policing. The military police were henceforth connected to the army and put under the command of an army general.

58. According to the World Bank Country Study, *Brazil: Human Resources Special Report* (October 1979), the official inflation rates during this period were

1968	27.8 percent	1971	17.3 percent
1969	20.3 percent	1972	17.4 percent
1970	18.2 percent	1973	20.5 percent

However, the rates have been a matter of intense debate among economists in Brazil, and one is apt to find a variety of different indices, in particular during the period of the economic miracle. In 1977 the Metalworkers' Union of São Bernardo do Campo and Diadema filed a successful suit against the federal government claiming that the inflation rates of the period of the economic miracle had ben purposely distorted and that the statistics were doctored to decrease the salaries of workers further. It will be recalled that the inflationary residue is part of the formula that is used by the government to calculate the official salary index of raises for each year.

59. Instituto Brasileiro de Geografia e Estatística (IBGE), *Pesquisa nacional por amostra de domicílio (PNAD),* 1973.

60. For a complete account of the succession of General Médici and the expressed commitment of General Ernesto Geisel to a policy of "decompression," see the excellent documentary work of André Gustavo Stumpf and Merval Pereira Filho in *A segunda guerra: A sucessão de Geisel* (São Paulo: Brasiliense, 1979), pp. 18-27.

61. The new regulations for the election of a president and the formation of the Electoral College were established in accordance with paragraphs 1 and 2 of Article 74 of the Constitution of 1969, as regulated by Complementary Law No. 15, of 13 October 1973. President Geisel was the first president to be chosen by the institutionalized framework set up for dealing with the succession problem. The Electoral College was composed of 3 delegates from each state assembly and one more delegate per 500,000 voters registered in the state. The voting process was not secret and the session was public. In 1973 the presidential Electoral College was composed of a total of 503 members, of which 127 were delegates from the state assemblies, 66 were senators, and 310 were members of the House of Representatives.

62. Ulysses Guimarães, speech at the Sixth National Convention of the MDB, in Brasília, 23 September 1973. Published in the MDB's official report of the presidential and vice-presidential campaigns of 1973 and collected in a book of speeches of Ulysses Guimarães and Barbosa Lima Sobrinho, *Navegar é preciso: Viver não é preciso* (Brasília: MDB, 1973).

63. Barbosa Lima Sobrinho, interview with the author (16 March 1978), in Rio de Janeiro.

64. Thales Ramalho (secretary-general of the MDB), "Enquanto restar um homem há esperança de liberdade," in *Relatório de Deputado Thales Ramalho, secretário geral do MDB: Campanha 21 de septembro de 1973 a 15 de janeiro de 1974-do Deputado Ulysses Guimarães e do Professor Barbosa Lima Sobrinho, candidatos pelo MDB a presidente e vice-presidente da república* (Brasília, 1974).

Chapter 7: The Geisel Government: Decompression

1. For information on the "policy of decompression," see General Geisel's speech at the ARENA convention on 15 September 1973, published in *Opinião* (2 September 1974), p. 3. See also his speech during the first meeting of his cabinet, 19 March 1974, published in ibid., and his speech during a meeting of ARENA on 30 August 1974, in ibid. A complete account of Geisel's government and the policy of decompression, from an insider's viewpoint, is contained in General Hugo Abreu, *O outro lado do poder* (Rio de Janeiro: Nova Fronteira, 1979), and idem, *Tempo de crise* (Rio de Janeiro: Nova Fronteira, 1980). A history of the period is in Walder de Góes, *O Brasil do General Geisel* (Rio de Janeiro: Nova Fronteira, 1978).

2. Most articles prior to the 1974 elections expected an ARENA victory. Politicians of both parties said they expected the MDB to win the Senate seats in only three states: Guanabara, Rio Grande do Sul, and São Paulo.

3. Senator Marcos Freire of Pernambuco; cited in *Opinião* (3 January 1975), p. 12.

4. See *Visão* (18 November 1974), pp. 20-27, and *Veja* (27 November 1974), for the complete breakdown of electoral results by state.

5. *Opinião* (3 January 1975), p. 12.

6. *Veja* (10 November 1976) reports on this study.

7. For the text of the law and an analysis of its effect on the electorate, see *Veja* (17 November 1976), p. 24; and *Veja* (10 November 1976), p. 23.

8. "O relatório sobre a censura no rádio e na televisão," paper presented at the National Congress of Journalists in Curitiba, Santa Catarina, 1976.

9. Detailed information on the 1976 campaign may be found in the press of the period. See, for example, *Veja* (26 May 1976), p. 21; *Veja* (28 July 1976), p. 22; *Veja* (20 October 1976), pp. 20-26; *Veja* (17 November 1976), pp. 20-58; *Opinião* (16 August 1975), p. 3; *Opinião* (26 March 1976), p. 3; *Opinião* (2 July 1976), pp. 3-4; *Opinião* (12 November 1976), p. 8.

10. *Veja* (24 November 1976), p. 22.

11. *Latin America Political Report* 10, no. 41 (3 December 1976):371. See also *Veja* (7 January 1976), pp. 19-28, with a detailed map of the cities that were electoral strongholds of ARENA and the MDB.

12. Amendment No. 7, later passed by decree, has resulted in a situation of almost complete impunity for members of the military police. Military police who are indicted for crimes, including homicide, are tried in special courts composed of officers of the military police itself. Cases are handled in the State Military Tribunal, not the civil courts. Results of trials, furthermore, are considered classified material, not available to the public. Although in 1980 and 1981 there were 2,533 indictments in the military tribunal of São Paulo, for example, and a total of 300 persons killed by

the military police in the city of São Paulo, not a single conviction was publicly acknowledged. According to State Congressman Eduardo Matarazzo Suplicy, this is a situation that may be directly linked to the impunity of the police who commit crimes while on duty. For a full report on the military police of São Paulo, see Congressman Suplicy's speech in the State Assembly of São Paulo, 29 April 1982 (published in *Diário Oficial do Estado de São Paulo* [2 May 1982]).

13. For more information on this aspect and the OAB's position on the matter of the proposal, see *Veja* (6 April 1977), pp. 28-30, and (20 April 1977), pp. 19-25.

14. On judicial reform, see B. Calheiros Bomfim, *A reforma do judiciário, projeto do executivo—exposição de motivos, substitutivo Accioly Filho—emenda constitucional número 7—comentários* (Rio de Janeiro: Edições Trabalhistas, 1977). For a description of the voting, see *Veja* (6 April 1977), pp. 26-27.

15. There is evidence that Geisel's government fabricated the entire judicial reform crisis to force the MDB to reject the project *in toto* and to give the government a pretext to close down Congress and enact a series of new electoral reforms that would guarantee ARENA's continuing political control. For information on this point, see, in particular, the account of the then-chief of military staff, General Hugo Abreu, in *O outro lado do poder*, pp. 68-73; and André Gustavo Stumpf and Merval Pereira Filho, *A segunda guerra: A sucessão de Geisel* (São Paulo: Brasiliense, 1979), pp. 105-122.

16. For an account of the twelve days and the drafting of the final version of Constitutional Amendments Nos. 7 and 8, see Abreu, *O outro lado do poder*, pp. 68-71 and Stumpf and Pereira Filho, *A segunda guerra*, p. 117.

17. The text of both amendments to the Constitution of 1969 may be found in *A Constituição da República Federativa do Brasil, promulgada em 17 de outubro de 1969, contendo emendas de números 1 a 12* (Rio de Janeiro: Kennedy Editora e Distribuidora, 1980), pp. 99 (for Amendment No. 7), and 107 (for Amendment No. 8).

18. For the complete text and an analysis of Amendment No. 8 to the Constitution of 1969, see Paulino Jacques, *As emendas constitucionais números 7, 8 e 9: Explicadas* (Rio de Janeiro: Editora Forense, 1977).

19. The Constitutions of 1967 and 1969 had maintained the principle of direct popular elections for the governors of the states. In 1972, however, General Médici's government became worried about the elections for governor due in 1974 and enacted a specific constitutional amendment that would extend the indirect electoral process to governors of states for that election only: Constitutional Amendment No. 2, of the Constitution of 1969, published in the *Diário Oficial da União* (11 May 1972). Article 13 extended this measure and made it a permanent aspect of the Constitution.

20. The system of indirect elections of state governors was first introduced in Brazil after the victory of the opposition in Minas Gerais and Guanabara in the 1965 elections. The reforms of the April Package were meant to strengthen the government's control over the process of choosing governors by limiting the choice to a more easily controlled electoral college.

21. For an analysis of this point, see *Veja* (6 April 1977), p. 29.

22. Jacques, *As emendas constitucionais números 7, 8 & 9*, pp. 65-66.

23. Ibid., p. 68.

24. This measure was introduced as a modification of Article 48 of the

Constitution of 1969, dealing with the voting process required for constitutional amendments to pass. See ibid., pp. 69-70.

25. See Alencar Furtado, then-leader of the MDB in the House of Representatives, speech delivered on 16 April 1977 and published in the *Anais do Congresso Nacional* of 16 April 1977, pp. 1771-1774.

26. The speakers on the program were Franco Montoro of São Paulo, Alceu Collares of Rio Grande do Sul, Alencar Furtado, leader in the House of Representatives and the president of the party, Ulysses Guimarães. The program reached an estimated 21 million persons. See the report in *Veja* (6 July 1977), pp. 25-28.

27. See *Jornal do Brasil* (28 June 1977), p. 10. See also *Veja* (6 July 1977), pp. 25-28.

28. See the account in *Jornal do Brasil* (1 July 1977), p. 14, and the report on Guimarães's indictment in *Veja* (2 November 1977), p. 24.

29. *Jornal do Brasil* (1 July 1977), p. 14; *Veja* (2 November 1977), p. 24. The state congressmen indicted were Dalton Canabrava and Aroldo Lopes da Costa, both of Minas Gerais. President Geisel would use Institutional Act No. 5 to cancel the political rights and the mandates of representatives twelve times during his term in office. In only two cases were the mandates canceled for reasons of corruption— and both involved members of ARENA. In addition, President Geisel used AI-5 to close down the State Assembly of Acre in 1975 and to close Congress in 1977 to pass the April Package.

30. Complementary Act No. 104. An account may be found in *Veja* (2 November 1977), p. 24.

31. The emphasis of the MDB on the plebiscitary nature of the vote could be seen in the slogans used by opposition candidates in 1978: "The vote is your only weapon, put the vote in your own hands"; "Vote against the government, vote MDB"; "Vote against the wage squeeze"; "Vote against repression and torture."

32. Data from Márcio Moreira Alves, "As eleições no Brasil 1978," *Revista Crítica de Ciências Sociais*, no. 3 (December 1979), pp. 42-61.

33. Election results and analysis may be found in *Veja* (27 December 1978), p. 16; *Veja* (22 November 1978), pp. 19-35; *Isto E* (22 November 1978), pp. 3-21; *Movimento* (20-26 November 1978), pp. 3-11; Luiz Navarro de Britto, *As eleições nacionais de 1978*, vol. 2 (Brasília: Fundação Milton Campos, 1979).

34. *Jornal do Brasil* (1 September 1978), p. 4.

35. For electoral data for each state, see Britto, *As eleições nacionais de 1978*, vols. 1 and 2.

36. Originally, only a small group of bishops worked to gather evidence of the repression and convince others that the occurrence of torture was not isolated, but rather a systematic mechanism of control. Slowly, others joined the original group. The collection of documents from the CNBB shows the process of gradual change. See the account and the documents in *A realidade brasileira, Extra* 1, no. 3 (February 1977) (São Paulo: Símbolo, 1977).

37. See *Arquidiocese de São Paulo: Segundo plano de pastoral, 1978-1980*. The plan (published in 1978) established five programs of activities for the church in São Paulo for those years.

38. Interview with Dom Paulo Evaristo Arns, 3 September 1979. This interview

focused particularly on how the archdiocese is organized and the different levels of coordination.

39. The cost of living movement began in 1973 but reached its full organizational strength in 1978 with the cost of living petition. See the accounts in *Em Tempo* (6-12 November 1978); *Isto E* (22 March 1978), pp. 3-12; and *Caderno do CEAS*, no. 57 (September/October 1978), pp. 20-33.

40. Interview with Cardinal Arns, 3 September 1979.

41. Dom Paulo Evaristo Arns, interview with Getúlio Bittencourt and Paulo Sérgio Markum, published in *História imediata*, no. 4, *Dom Paulo Evaristo Arns: O cardeal do povo*, esp. p. 29.

42. See *The Amnesty International Report 1975-1976*, "Brazil," pp. 90-92.

43. Ibid., pp. 90-91.

44. Cited in the interview with Cardinal Arns by Bittencourt and Markum, *Dom Paulo Evaristo Arns*, p. 34.

45. See *O manifesto dos jornalistas, em nome da verdade* (January 1976) in the archives of the Brazilian Press Association, Rio de Janeiro. Also published in Bittencourt and Markum, *Dom Paulo Evaristo Arns*, pp. 24-28.

46. Excerpts from the document approved in the regional assembly of the Bishops of the São Paulo area, 26-30 October 1975, *Não oprimas teu irmão*, in *Secretariado da Comissão Episcopal Regional Sul-1, Conferência Nacional dos Bispos do Brasil-CNBB* (Brasília, 1975).

47. Quoted in Fernando Jordão, *Dossiê Herzog—Prisão, tortura e morte no Brasil* (São Paulo: Global, 1979).

48. The case of Manoel Fiel Filho is described in detail in a special Amnesty International report, *Amnesty International Newsletter* (February 1976).

49. The swift measures taken by President Geisel to offset a possible conspiracy are described in Abreu, *O outro lado do poder*. See also the article in *Opinião* (23 January 1976), p. 3.

50. See the report of Luiz Henrique Romagnoli and Tânia Gonçalves, *A volta da UNE*, in *História Imediata*, no. 5 (1979).

51. On the military police's invasion of São Paulo's Catholic University and the burning of the students, see *Em Tempo* (3-9 July 1978), pp. 3-5; *Veja* (28 September 1977), pp. 31-35; *Isto E* (28 September 1977), pp. 6-14; *Isto E* (1 October 1980), p. 18; *Reporter*, no. 7 (June 1978), p. 24.

52. See the report on this unit in *Em Tempo* (3-9 July 1978), pp. 3-5, and in *Isto E* (1 October 1980), with the report of the decision of payment of damages and medical care.

53. The case and the sentence are described in the study of the suit, "Clarice, Ivo e André Herzog, contra a união," in *Caso Herzog: Sentença: A integra do processo movido por Clarice, Ivo e André Herzog contra a união* (Rio de Janeiro: Salamandra, 1978).

54. See Jordão, *Dossiê Herzog* and *Amnesty International Newsletter* report (February 1976).

55. Interview with Antônio Modesto da Silveira, 10 March 1978. Modesto da Silveira is one of the main lawyers to defend political prisoners since 1964.

56. Interview with Dr. Eduardo Seabra Fagundes, at the time president of the Brazilian Bar Association, 8 February 1980. See also the article in the *Jornal do*

Brasil (2 February 1979), "Novo presidente da OAB diz que classe cansou dos muitos e confusos decretos."

57. Interview with Dr. Eduardo Seabra Fagundes, 8 February 1980.

58. President Ernesto Geisel signed two decree-laws that brought the OAB under the administrative control of the Ministry of Labor. See Decree-Law 7400 of 1 May 1974 and Decree-Law 74296 of 16 July 1974. The suit and justification for the autonomy of the OAB and its struggle to remain independent of governmental control are described in a book published by the OAB in 1975: *As razões da autonomia da Ordem dos Advogados do Brasil: Seu enquadramento na estrutura do estado de direito, a missão constitucional e outras atribuições—Os direitos do homem e seu defensor: A tradição* (Rio de Janeiro: Conselho Federal da OAB, 1975).

59. All works and resolutions of the Seventh National Conference of the OAB may be found in *Anais da VII Conferência Nacional da OAB, Curitiba, Paraná, 7 a 12 de maio de 1978* (Rio de Janeiro: Conselho Federal da OAB, 1978). Most of the works dealt with the question of human rights, the right to habeas corpus, the constitutional guarantees, and the "state of law" (*estado de direito*).

60. See, for example, the articles in *Folha de São Paulo* (2 February 1979); *Jornal do Brasil* (2 April 1979); *Isto E* (17 August 1977), p. 4; *Veja* (17 August 1977, p. 16. The explanation of what constitutes a "legitimate legal framework of a state of law" and an "illegitimate legal framework of a state of exception" was delivered in an open address to lawyers at the time of the celebration of sixty years of legal studies in Brazil. See Goffredo Carlos da Silva Telles Júnior, "Carta aos brasileiros: Em homenagem ao sesquicentenário dos cursos jurídicos no Brasil," São Paulo, 11 August 1977.

61. The analysis of a priori and a posteriori forms of censorship is based on the study by journalist Perseu Abramo prepared for the Committee for the Defense of Freedom of the Press and presented at the National Congress of Brazilian Journalists in 1976. See the records on censorship in the Congressional Investigation Committee on Censorship, House of Representatives, 1978-1979. The material was made available to me by Congressman Modesto da Silveira, for whose help I am grateful.

62. Orders are transmitted directly by the Federal Police Department (DPF) and, if not obeyed, other punishments may be imposed, such as prohibition of sale or even cancellation of the program. An account of censorship may be found in Senator Freitas Nobre, *Constituinte* (Rio de Janeiro: Paz e Terra, 1977), pp. 55-78; "A história da censura prévia em Movimento," *Movimento, Especial* (12 June 1978, 19 June 1978, 26 June 1978); *Folha da São Paulo* (5 March 1978), with special documentation of all the orders it received in 1972, 1973, and 1974; *Jornal do Brasil* (26 June 1978), with the list of its own censorship orders from 1972 to 1975.

The death of the newspaper *Opinião* is described in J. A. Pinheiro Machado, *Opinião versus censura: Momentos da luta de um jornal pela liberdade* (Porto Alegre: L&PM Editores, 1978). The *Correio da Manhã* was economically strangled. Other newspapers suffered severe economic losses: *Movimento* reported a total loss of 18 million cruzeiros (1978) and the *Tribuna da Imprensa* estimated its losses due to censorship at between 300 million and 400 million cruzeiros (1978). See the report on economic losses in *Visão* (26 June 1978), pp. 23-24.

63. For further analysis of the relationship between the National Security Law

and censorship, see Guido Fidelis, *Lei de Segurança Nacional e censura: Comentários* (São Paulo: Sugestões Literárias, 1979); and Heleno Claudio Fragoso, *Lei de Segurança Nacional: Uma experiência antidemocrática* (Porto Alegre: Sérgio Antônio Fabris Editor, 1980).

64. Two important pieces of legislation controlled the activities of the press: first, Law no. 5250 of 9 February 1967, passed by General Castello Branco to "regulate freedom of thought and of information" (in *Diário Oficial da União* [10 February 1964]); the second, enacted as Decree-Law No. 972, of 17 October 1969, "regulates the profession of journalism" (in ibid. [21 October 1969]) and is regulated by Decree No. 65912 of 19 December 1969 (in ibid. [22 December 1969]).

65. See the report on censorship in radio and television presented at the National Congress of Brazilian Journalists (Curitiba, Santa Catarina, 1976), and written by Décio Nitrini, Eurenides Pereira, Gabriel Romeiro, Márcio Guedes, Mônica Teixeira, Odair Redondo, Sérgio Leal Maia, and Vera Ataxo. It may be obtained from the Union of Professional Journalists of São Paulo or in the archives of the Brazilian Press Association. Other information may be found in *Index on Censorship: Brazil* 8, no. 4 (July-August 1979).

66. In 1979, while helping to organize a benefit concert for the strike fund of the metalworkers of São Bernardo do Campo, I had firsthand experience of the mechanisms of censorship. To have the show "cleared" by the federal police I had to obtain a package of forms. Each song had to be individually cleared with the federal police. I discovered that even though some of the songs had been generally cleared in other states they still could not be sung in Rio de Janeiro, for the requirement insisted that they needed to have the clearance of the local police department as well. In that case, the words could not be sung, but the music was played.

67. See the report on this specific legislation, the Lei Falcão, including its text, in *Jornal do Brasil* (30 July 1977), p. 13.

68. Barbosa Lima Sobrinho, then-president of the ABI, interview with the author, 16 March 1978.

69. For information on the "Portella Mission" and the reforms that resulted, see General Hugo Abreu's inside account in *Tempo de Crise*, pp. 115-143. See also *Latin America Political Report* 11, no. 13 (1 April 1977), 12, no. 25 (30 June 1978), 12, no. 37 (22 September 1978), 12, no. 48 (9 December 1977); *Veja* (19 May 1976; 9 March 1977); *Isto E* (7 December 1977), p. 7; *Folha de São Paulo* (27 June 1978).

70. For details on the measures included in Amendment No. 11, also known as the "Reform Package," see *Jornal do Brasil* (12 September 1978), p. 3; *Veja* (21 June 1978), pp. 20-24; *Jornal do Brasil* (24 June 1978), p. 1; and *O Estado de São Paulo* (21 June 1978), p. 6.

71. *O Estado de São Paulo* (21 June 1978), p. 6, "O que muda na constituição com as reformas."

72. See the analysis in *O Estado de São Paulo* (26 February 1978), p. 5, "Segurança nacional: O limite da reforma." See also *Jornal do Brasil* (17 May 1978), p. 3, "O projeto para a emergência."

73. The question of the state of emergency and the measures that were allowed the executive during its effective period is analyzed by jurist Goffredo da Silva Telles Júnior in a paper presented at the Seventh National Conference of the Ordem dos Advogados do Brasil, Curitiba, 7-12 May 1978. See *Anais da VII Conferência*

Nacional da OAB. See also Oscar Dias Correa, *A defesa do estado de direito e a emergência constitucional* (Rio de Janeiro: Presença Edições, 1980).

74. The OAB's criticisms were published in *Ultima Hora* (28 June 1978), p. 2; *Jornal do Brasil* (28 June 1978), p. 4; *O Estado de São Paulo* (6 June 1978), p. 2.

75. For an account of the power struggles as early as 1974, related to the succession of President Geisel, see Stumpf and Pereira Filho, *A segunda guerra.*

76. See *Latin America Political Report* 11, no. 45 (18 November 1977): 357, and the account in de Góes, *O Brasil do General Geisel,* particularly pp. 75-101.

77. The conflict between the SNI and the CIEX is described in Abreu, *O outro lado do poder* and *Tempo de crise,* and in Stumpf and Pereira Filho, *A segunda guerra,* pp. 126-133.

78. The dismissal of Frota was the most serious crisis of the Geisel government. Accounts of the episode are found in Abreu, *O outro lado do poder,* chap. 5, pp. 125-151; and de Góes, *O Brasil do General Geisel,* pp. 73-101.

79. For more information on the opposition candidacy of Bentes Monteiro for president under the auspices of the MDB, see Abreu, *Tempo de crise,* which deals specifically with the military coordination of an alternative candidacy for the succession.

Chapter 8. The *Abertura* Period

1. An excellent summary of the variety of grass-roots movements that exist in Brazil is provided by Paulo Singer and Vinícius Caldeira Brant, eds., *São Paulo: O povo em movimento* (Rio de Janeiro: Editora Vozes and CEBRAP, 1981).

2. This number is only approximate. It was given to me by the coordinator of the Movement of Friends of the District of Nova Iguaçú.

3. The information on the Federation of Associations of Residents of the State of Rio de Janeiro (FAMERJ) was provided me by César Campos, at the time president of the FAMERJ.

4. See José Alvaro Moisés, "Experiência de mobilização popular em São Paulo," *Contraponto* 3, no. 3 (September 1978):84.

5. See *O Globo* (6 April 1980), p. 12, "Associações de bairro estão voltando: A cada semana surge uma."

6. Moisés "Experiência de mobilização popular," p. 71.

7. For an account of the events connected to the attempt of then-mayor of São Paulo, Olavo Setúbal, to apply clientelistic pressures on the associations of the district and their refusal to become connected in any manner to the administration, see José Alvaro Moisés, "SABs, uma nova força," *Opinião* (25 July 1975), p. 5.

8. César Campos, president of the FAMERJ in 1980. Cited in *O Globo* (6 April 1980), p. 12.

9. For a detailed analysis of participation and the strategies for activation of the associations, see the articles in Singer and Brant, *São Paulo.*

10. A study was conducted by the São Paulo mayor's office in 1970. This research found that 61.8 percent of the SABs in existence in the state of São Paulo in 1970 concentrated their work exclusively on the mobilization of pressure groups for improvements in social equipment, i.e., schools, day care centers, health clinics, playgrounds; urban equipment, i.e., light, water, paving, public transportation; public services, i.e., security, police, fire, and garbage removal. See the account in

Moisés, "Experiência de mobilização popular." See also the documents of the meetings of the SABs in São Paulo in the archives of Unidade de Ação Comunitária e Pesquisa Social, Empresa Metropolitana de Planejamento da Grande São Paulo, S.A. [EMPLASA]).: "A carta de São Paulo," document of the first Encontro da Comunidade, 1975, and the three different meetings, Seminários de Assuntos, Metropolitanos, "A Comunidade Pergunta," in 1975, 1979, and 1980. These contain the basic demands of the São Paulo organizations to collectively influence the decisions of state government. According to the official records of the government of São Paulo, there were, by December of 1980, 1,115 SABs legally registered with the city of São Paulo. See Governo do Estado de São Paulo, Secretaria dos Negócios Metropolitanos: Cadastro das Sociedades Amigos de Bairros da Grande São Paulo, December 1980 (EMPLASA).

11. A serious conflict developed in Belém, Pará, in November 1977 between the local authorities and the neighborhood organizations, which had been asking for streets to be paved. The residents set up barricades in all the unpaved streets. See the accounts of the conflict in *O Liberal* (1 November 1977; 2 November 1977; and 30 November 1977).

12. See *O São Paulo*, the newspaper of the Archdiocese of São Paulo (30 May-5 June 1980). For other accounts of collective work, see, for example, *Veja* (9 August 1978), on the work of the 145,000 dwellers of the Rocinha slum in Rio de Janeiro. See also Alejandro Portes, "Housing Policy, Urban Poverty and the State: The Favelas of Rio de Janeiro, 1972-1976," *Latin American Research Review* 14, no. 2:3-24; and the account of Pedro Porfírio in *O poder da rua* (Rio de Janeiro: Editora Vozes, 1981).

13. For an account of the history of the cost of living movement, see *Isto E* (22 March 1978). See also *Cadernos do CEAS*, no. 56 (July/August,1978). *Jornal do Brasil* of 28 August 1978, p. 3, describes the rally organized in the square of the Catedral da Sé to present the petition formally.

14. The Movimento de Amigos de Bairro de Nova Iguaçú coordinates the work of the different associations of neighborhoods in the area. The MAB began in the late sixties with discussion groups for problems of health and developed in coordination with the work of the Pastoral da Terra, the Justice and Peace Committee of the Diocese of Nova Iguaçú, and the local secular organizations of the area.

15. The problem of clandestine sales and paper buying in the BNH system is described in Lícia do Prado Valadares, *Passa-se uma casa: Análise do programa de Remoção das favelas do Rio de Janeiro* (Rio de Janeiro: Zahar, 1978).

16. I observed this episode and the work of the associations, the MAB, the diocesan Justice and Peace Committee and Bishop Dom Adriano Hypólito of Nova Iguaçú. Their example of organization and effective action has inspired other area neighborhood associations to learn from that particular experience. For more information on Rio de Janeiro's problems, see the research organized by the Archdiocese of Rio de Janeiro in 1978, "O problema habitacional do Rio de Janeiro" (unpublished, but available from archdiocese).

17. Almir Ribeiro Guimarães, O.F.M. *Comunidades de base no Brasil* (Rio de Janeiro: Editora Vozes, 1980), p. 92.

18. For more information on the history and transformation of the Catholic church in Brazil, see, for example, *A igreja na atual transformação da América*

Latina à luz do concílio: Conclusões de Medellín (Petrópolis: Vozes, 1979); Luiz Gonzaga de Souza Lima, *Evolução política dos católicos e da igreja no Brasil: Hipóteses para uma interpretação* (Rio de Janeiro: Vozes, 1979); Paulo José Krischke, *A igreja e as crises políticas no Brasil* (Rio de Janeiro: Vozes, 1979); Márcio Moreira Alves, *A igreja e a política no Brasil* (São Paulo: Brasiliense, 1979); Thomas Bruneau, *The Political Transformation of the Brazilian Catholic Church* (Cambridge: At the University Press, 1974), and idem, *The Church in Brazil,* Latin American Monographs, no. 56 (Austin: University of Texas Press, 1982).

19. Padre Affonso Gregory and Maria A. Ghisleni, "Chances e desafios das comunidades eclesiais de base," *Cadernos de Teologia e Pastoral,* no. 13 (1979), pp. 28-29.

20. Further information on the origin and history of the CEBs may be found in Alvaro Barreiro,*Comunidades eclesiais de base e evangelização dos pobres* (São Paulo: Edições Loyola, 1977); Clodovis Boff, *Comunidade eclesial, comunidade política: Ensaios de eclesiologia política* (Rio de Janeiro: Vozes, 1978); *Uma igreja que nasce do povo: Comunidades eclesiais de base: O encontro de Vitória, Espírito Santo* (Rio de Janeiro: Vozes, 1975); Mariano Baraglia, *Evolução das comunidades eclesiais de base* (Rio de Janeiro: Vozes, 1974); Cândido Procópio Ferreira de Camargo, Beatriz Muniz de Souza, and Antônio Flávio de Oliveira Pierucci, "Comunidades eclesiais de base," in *São Paulo, O povo em movimento,* ed. Singer and Brant, pp. 59-81; Frei Betto, *O que é comunidade de base?* (São Paulo: Brasiliense, 1981); and the extensive study of Almir Ribeiro Guimarães, *Comunidades de base no Brasil: Uma nova maneira de ser da igreja* (Rio de Janeiro, Vozes, 1978).

21. *Uma igreja que nasce do povo,* and Frei Betto, *O que é comunidade de base?* p. 17.

22. "Comunidades eclesiais de base no Brasil," *Estudos da CNBB,* no. 23 (1978), pp. 22-23.

23. Ibid.

24. This questionnaire was published in the newspaper of the Archdiocese of São Paulo, *O São Paulo* (5-10 July 1980), p. 6.

25. See the description in Frei Betto, *O que é comunidade de base?* pp. 24-25.

26. For information on the legislation and the labor laws, see *Consolidação das leis do trabalho: Atualizada para 1978* (Rio de Janeiro: Gráfica Auriverde, 1978); Santos Campanhole, *Entidades sindicais: Legislação, jurisprudência, prática* (São Paulo: Atlas, 1978).

27. For more information on the trade union structure and the history of the trade union movement in Brazil, see, for example, Kenneth Paul Erickson, *The Brazilian Corporative State and Working Class Politics* (Berkeley & Los Angeles: University of California Press, 1977); Otávio Ianni, *A classe operária vai ao campo* (São Paulo: Caderno CEBRAP, Brasiliense, 1976); Leôncio Martins Rodrigues, *Trabalhadores, sindicatos e industrialização* (São Paulo: Brasiliense, 1974); José Albertino Rodrigues, *Sindicato e desenvolvimento no Brasil* (São Paulo: Símbolo S.A. Indústrias Gráficas, 1979); John Humphrey, "Auto Workers and the Working Class in Brazil," *Latin American Perspectives* 6, no. 4 (Fall 1979):71-90; idem, "The Development of Industry and the Bases for Trade Unionism: A Case Study of

Workers in the Car Industry in São Paulo, Brazil" (Ph.D. diss., Sussex University, 1977); and Luiz Werneck Vianna, *Liberalismo e sindicato no Brasil* (Rio de Janeiro: Paz e Terra, 1975).

28. Interview with the author, São Paulo, 6 September 1978.

29. These regulations are established in Articles 548 to 557 of the Labor Code. See *Consolidação das leis do trabalho*, pp. 114-118.

30. The data on the rural unions come from a study conducted by the Juridical Department of CONTAG for the years up to 1980.

31. Ibid. See also the introduction to José Francisco da Silva, ed., *As lutas camponesas no Brasil: 1980* (Rio de Janeiro: Editora Marco Zero, 1981).

32. *Movimento* (30 August-9 September 1981), p. 11.

33. José Alvaro Moisés, "Current Issues in the Labor Movement in Brazil," *Latin American Perspectives* 6, no. 4 (Fall 1979):51-70; see also the interview with Luís Inácio Lula da Silva, same issue.

34. Interview with Luís Inácio Lula da Silva, president of the Metalworkers' Union of São Bernardo do Campo and Diadema until 1980, ibid., pp. 90-100.

35. For an account of the congress in Rio de Janeiro, see Abdias José dos Santos and Ercy Rocha Chaves, *Consciência operária e luta sindical: Metalúrgicos de Niterói no movimento sindical brasileiro* (Rio de Janeiro: Vozes, 1980). The authors are leaders of the metalworkers in Rio de Janeiro and were officers of the union at the time.

36. Literally, "pelego" refers to an expression used by the *gaúchos* of Rio Grande do Sul to refer to the lambskin placed on the saddle to cushion the impact of the horse's trot. In union language, the term is used to refer to those union officials who serve to soften the conflict between workers and management.

37. See the "Carta de princípios," published at the Fifth National Congress of Workers in Industry in Rio de Janeiro on 29 June 1978. This document also called for increased emphasis on public education, housing, public health, and legal services. The points were refined in subsequent congresses and conferences organized to bring about a consensus to reflect the union movement's basic concerns.

38. "Carta de princípios" may be obtained from the archives of the Metalworkers' Union of São Bernardo do Campo and Diadema.

39. This point was emphasized by John Humphrey in "Auto Workers and the Working Class in Brazil."

40. See the text of the agreement in the *Tribuna Metalúrgica*, official newspaper of the Metalworkers' Union of São Bernardo do Campo and Diadema, and reproduced in *Isto E* (7 June 1978).

41. See the analysis of the strike in *Tribuna Metalúrigca* 8, no. 46 (June 1978), "Greve, o primeiro teste foi positivo."

42. Interview with Luís Inácio Lula da Silva, then president of the Metalworkers' Union of São Bernardo do Campo and Diadema, in *Jornal dos Metalúrgicos*, official paper of the Metalworkers' Union of Rio de Janeiro (July/August 1978), p. 4.

43. *Latin America Economic Report* 6, no. 36 (22 September 1978):296.

44. In *Movimento* (11 September 1978), p. 14. The data are from DIEESE.

45. *Diário Oficial da União*, 5 August 1978. For an analysis of the double

penalty, in this decree and in the National Security Law, see *Latin America Economic Report* 6, no. 32 (18 August 1978):256.

46. Interview with Luís Inácio Lula da Silva, 8 September 1979.

47. For details of the 1979 wage legislation, see *Latin America Economic Report* 7, no. 35 (7 September and 28 September 1979). See also DIEESE, *Divulgação*, no. 1 (1979), "Reajustes e aumentos salariais: Análise da proposta governmental."

48. See DIEESE's analysis of the effect of the 1979 wage legislation on the wages of middle-class professional job categories in *Divulgação*, no. 1 (1979).

49. My analysis is based on conversations with rank-and-file and leadership and on observation of assemblies, debates, meetings, and discussions of the strike of 1979.

50. Information from Lula's comments in a speech during an assembly in the Vila Euclides stadium in 1979, and my field notes. The strikers' intention was to avoid picket lines so as to remove the justification for direct military and police repression.

51. The figure for the total amount of food distributed per week is an estimate made by the archdiocese and based on purchasing and distribution figures.

52. For an account of this strike, see da Silva, *As lutas camponesas no Brasil: 1980*.

53. Interview, 5 October 1980.

54. This speech of General Golbery do Couto e Silva at the Superior War College was at first secret but was leaked to the press. The conference, entitled "A conjuntura nacional e o poder executivo," was published in part by *Veja* (10 September 1980) and then included complete in the compendium of Golbery's writings, *Conjuntura política nacional, o poder executivo e geopolítica do Brasil* (Rio de Janeiro: José Olympio, 1981).

55. *Veja* (10 September 1980), p. 4.

56. Ibid.

57. Ibid., p. 5.

58. Ibid.

59. Ibid., p. 6. See also the article on Golbery's master plan in *Isto E* (16 January 1980), pp. 3-11.

60. For more information on the movement for political amnesty, see *Anistia: A história das nossas anistias, os exemplos internacionais e a campanha de hoje: A quem vai beneficiar* (São Paulo: Edição, 1978). See also the account by the president of the movimento feminino pela anistia, Thereza Godoy Zerbine, *Anistia: Semente da liberdade* (São Paulo: Movimento Feminino pela Anistia, 1979).

61. *Anistia*, Law No. 6683, 28 August 1979 (Brasília: Departamento de Imprensa Nacional, República Federativa do Brasil, 1979). Also Decree-Law No. 84143, 31 October 1979, *Regulamentação da Lei da Anistia* (Brasília: Departamento de Imprensa Nacional, República Federativa do Brasil, 1979).

62. *Nova Lei Orgânica dos Partidos Políticos*, Law No. 6767, of 20 December 1979 (Brasília: Departamento de Imprenta Nacional, 1979), Divulgação no. 1,327. Published in the *Diário Oficial da União* (20 December 1979). This law was regulated by the Superior Electoral Tribunal. See *Organização dos Partidos Políticos, Tribunal Superior Eleitoral* (Brasília: Departamento de Imprensa Nacional, 1980), Divulgação no. 1,328. Part of the text of the Party Reform Bill was published in the *Jornal do Brasil* of 19 October 1979, p. 4.

63. Articles 2 and 3 were added by the president after he had vetoed the version that had been approved. Article 2 abolished the MDB and ARENA. Article 3 provided that

the legislature at that time should organize itself in parliamentary blocks until the parties had a chance to receive final registration from the Superior Electoral Tribunal.

64. Article 5, Item 2, paragraph 1: "The name of the party must, by obligation, include the word party."

65. Article 5, Item 3, paragraph 3: "The party's name must not use the term and/or elicit the affiliation based on an appeal to religious beliefs or feelings of class or race."

66. Article 12: "The party that, in the period of 12 months from the decision of the Superior Electoral Tribunal has not conducted conventions in at least 9 states and in one fifth of the respective municipalities of each state shall have its preliminary registration automatically cancelled."

67. Article 35, Article 58, Items 1, 2, 3, 4, and 5, reading as follows:

Item 1: Two percent of the electorate in municipalities of up to 1,000 voters.
Item 2: The 20 mentioned in Item 1, plus 5 for each 1,000 voters in municipalities up to 50,000 voters.
Item 3: The 270 of the previous Item plus 2 for each 1,000 voters in municipalities of up to 200,000 voters.
Item 4: The 670 of the previous Item plus one for each 1,000 voters in municipalities of up to 500,000 voters.
Item 5: The 1,170 of the previous Item plus 1 for each 2,000 voters in municipalities of more than 500,000 voters.

68. Article 16 of the Party Reform Bill of 1979, p. 6: "A party that does not gain at least 5 percent of the support of the electorate in a congressional election, distributed in at least 9 states with a minimum of 3 percent of the votes in each state, shall lose the right to representation in the federal Senate, in the House of Representatives, and in the state assemblies."

69. Article 19, Item 4 of the Party Reform Bill, p. 7: "It is prohibited to form coalitions with other parties for the elections for the House of Representatives, the State Assemblies and the Municipal Chambers." Subsequently, a further regulation also prohibited coalitions for the election of governor and senators.

70. By October of 1980 the PMDB had already organized the minimum of 20 percent of the municipalities of all states. The PP had the following states organized; Bahia, Ceará, Mato Grosso, Minas Gerais, Pará, Paraíba, Paraná, Piauí, Rio de Janeiro, Rio Grande do Norte, and Rio Grande do Sul. The PDT organized in Espírito Santo, Maranhão, Mato Grosso, Mato Grosso do Sul, Pará, Paraná, Pernambuco, Rio de Janeiro, Rio Grande do Sul, and Santa Catarina. The PTB also had ten states: Alagoas, Amazonas, Espírito Santo, Mato Grosso, Mato Grosso do Sul, Pará, Paraná, Pernambuco, Rio de Janeiro, and São Paulo. The PT had Acre, Ceará, Espírito Santo, Goiás, Maranhão, Mato Grosso do Sul, Minas Gerais, Piauí, Rio de Janeiro, Rio Grande do Sul, Santa Catarina, and São Paulo. Like the PMDB, the government's party, PDS, had organized in all states.

71. Interview with the author, February 1982.

72. See *Veja* (3 September 1980), pp. 16-24, for a detailed account of all terrorist bomb attacks and the evidence of connection to extreme right-wing groups. See, in particular, the per-year analysis on pp. 20 and 21, "A história dos atentados e da negligência policial: A polícia matou as pistas do terror."

73. Ibid., pp. 15-24, "As bombas na OAB."

74. *Veja* (8 April 1981), pp. 20-21, "As bombas de abril."

75. For an account of the bombing of the convention center and the investigations that followed, see, for example, *O Globo* (2 May 1981); *Veja* (6 May, 27 May, 3 June, 8 July 1981); *Isto E* (6 May, 13 May, 27 may, 8 July 1981); *Movimento* (20 May 1981); *O Estado de São Paulo* (31 May 1981); *Jornal do Brasil* (2 July, 3 July, 4 July, 9 July 1981).

76. "Close question" is a parliamentary legal recourse that forces all members of a party to vote the same way. The party leaders define the vote, and any member who votes differently by law loses his or her mandate.

77. A full account of the episode and the electoral reforms of November 1981 may be found in *Isto E* (2 December 1981), pp. 22-29, "Eleições: Pacote para o PDS. Com ele o partido poderá vencer em 1982 mas o preço será alto." See also *Infobrazil* 3, no. 2 (December 1981), Center of Brazilian Studies, the Johns Hopkins University School of Advanced International Studies.

78. See *Isto E* (30 June 1982), p. 21, "Governo marca o gol, constituição só muda com dois terços a favor"; and *Latin America Regional Reports* (2 July 1982), RB-82-06, "The Government Is Willing to Lose Elections but Not Power."

79. Interview with author, 5 February 1983. The local press carried regular articles throughout the campaign on the state personnel, administrative resources, and equipment that were being used by members of the PDS in the campaigns for public office. In addition, opposition candidates in São Paulo, Rio Grande do Sul, Paraná, Mato Grosso, and the states of the Northeast filed formal complaints with the Regional Electoral Tribunals of their states denouncing the administrative abuse of PDS candidates. Administrative abuse was particularly strong in São Paulo, where former governor Paulo Maluf did not attempt to hide the overt use of state offices in campaigns.

80. Reported to me in a conversation with PMDB candidate for governor of Pernambuco, Senator Marcos Freire, and in a discussion with the candidate for vice-governor, Cid Sampaio, who gave me the details of how *voto formiguinha* worked.

81. For detailed analysis, see chap. 7.

82. Interview with Tancredo Neves, elected governor of Minas Gerais (PMDB), *Veja* (1 December 1982), p. 28.

83. Helival Rios, "As oposições vão governar o país rico," *Folha de São Paulo* (13 March 1983), p. 6.

84. See the report in *Folha de São Paulo* (26 November 1982), p. 5, "Ulysses afirma que partido pode pedir recontagem em Mato Grosso e Pernambuco."

85. See the report in *Isto E* (1 December 1982), p. 18, "Sobressaltos no sul." See also *O Estado de São Paulo* (26 November 1982), p. 2, "Impugnações, o recurso dos peemedebistas no Rio Grande do Sul."

86. See *Latin America Weekly Report* (3 December 1982), WR-82-47, p. 2. The Brazilian press gave ample coverage to the investigations of election fraud in Rio de Janeiro. See, for example, *Jornal do Brasil* (26 November 1982), "TRE admite que errou boletins e vai reprogramar computador"; *Folha de São Paulo* (28 November 1982), p. 5, "Jornal do Brasil denuncia pressões no Rio," and "O novo Riocentro"; *Folha de São Paulo* (30 November 30, 1982), p. 8, "Suspensa computação dos votos da eleição do Rio"; *Isto E* (24 November 1982), p. 26,

"Contagem regressiva, confusão e apreensão na apuração dos votos"; and *Veja* (1 December 1982), pp. 38-40, "O computador inimigo: Como a programação feita pela Proconsult sumia só com os votos dados a Leonel Brizola."

87. See the account of the military conspiracy in *Latin America Weekly Report* (3 December 1982), WR-82-47, p. 2.

88. *Latin America Regional Reports*, Brazil, RB 82-10 (26 November 1982), p. 2.

89. See *Isto E* (1 December 1982), pp. 70-78, "Reagan no Brasil e o Brasil no FMI." See also the report in *Latin America Weekly Report*, WR-82-45, (19 November 1982), p. 1.

90. From a statement made by the technical director of DIEESE, Walter Barelli, in testimony before Congress: *Divulgação* 01/83, "Política salarial e Decreto-Lei 2,012, de 25/01/83—Depoimento do DIEESE à Comissão Mista do Congresso Nacional."

91. In *Boletim do DIEESE,* Edição Especial (April 1983), p. 2.

92. Walter Barelli, research report delivered during debate organized by TV Globo, in São Paulo, "São Paulo-2,000" (June 1983).

93. See *Folha de São Paulo* (27 November 1983), p. 35, "Desemprego se expande e pode levar ao caos, diz Pazzianotto: Desde o início do ano foram dispensadas 122,050 pessoas no estado."

94. Data from IBGE and the Instituto Nacional de Alimentação e Nutrição (INAN), in *Folha de São Paulo* (28 August 1983), p. 10, "A herança do 'milagre': A crise deixa o país pobre, doente e endividado."

95. General Danilo Venturini, secretary of the National Security Council, became sufficiently alarmed to ask for a special meeting to report on the effect of hunger on the armed forces. See the report in *Isto E* (14 August 1983), p. 38, "O Brasil descobre uma nova fome."

96. *Isto E* (14 August 1983). See table on p. 40, "Quem come de menos: Os brasileiros com deficiência de calorias; em porcentagem da população das regiões."

97. See report in *Folha de São Paulo* (28 August 1983), p. 10, "O abastecimento interno é abandonado: desde 1973 a política agrícola do governo está voltada à exportação." See also table in *Isto E* (14 August 1983), p. 40, "Tudo para exportar."

98. *Isto E* (14 August 1983), p. 42.

99. Ibid.

100. See DIEESE, "O salário mínimo não dá nem para comer," *Boletim do DIEESE* 2 (September 1983):6. On 1 November 1983, the minimum salary was raised to CR. 57,120; the November 1983 rate of exchange was Cr. 883 per U.S. dollar.

101. DIEESE, "Governo e empresários levam inflação a 97.7 percent," *Boletim do DIEESE* (June 1982):3-4.

102. See the account in *Folha de São Paulo* (28 August 1983), p. 10.

103. Law No. 6708, of November 1979, as altered by Law No. 6886 of December 1980.

104. See DIEESE, "Política salarial e Decreto-Lei 2,012, de 25/01/83—Depoimento do DIEESE à Comissão Mista do Congresso Nacional," *Divulgação* 01/83, p. 5.

105. See DIEESE, *Boletim do DIEESE* 2 (July 1983):9.

106. See *Latin America Weekly Report*, WR-83-21 (3 June 1983), p. 2. See also DIEESE, *Boletim do DIEESE* 2 (July 1983):10, and *Isto E* (27 April 1983), p. 73, "O INPC de cara nova."

107. Decree laws introduced in Congress by the executive take effect immediately from the date of their reading and publication until they are voted on or the sixty-day period of *decurso de prazo* runs its course. Hence, Decree-Law 2045 became effective on 1 August 1983 and remained in effect until it was defeated in Congress in October. See *Boletim do DIEESE* 2 (July 1983), p. 10, "Desindexação e expurgo: Novos nomes para velhas práticas."

108. For an excellent analysis of Decree-Law 2045 and its effect on wages, see DIEESE, *Divulgação 03/83*, "Política salarial—Decreto Lei 2,045," and ibid., 04/83 "Decreto-Lei 2,045: O mais violento arrocho salarial." See also *Folha de São Paulo* (14 July 1983), p. 16, "Todos os reajustes salariais serao de 80% do INPC." According to the National Security Council, the new wage decree-law was an explicit recommendation of the International Monetary Fund. See the account in ibid., "Medidas foram sugeridas pelo FMI."

109. The Metalworkers' Union of São Bernardo do Campo and Diadema was first taken by the Ministry of Labor in 1979, during the strike led by Lula. Later, under pressure, Lula was returned to the union until another strike, in 1980. The second intervention permanently removed Lula and his board of directors from office. After one year workers forced the government to hold an election, and Jair Meneguelli, a friend of Lula, was elected president with 92 percent of the vote.

110. Vice-President Aureliano Chaves was then acting as president because General João Figueiredo was in Cleveland, undergoing heart surgery.

111. For the complete text of the decree and an explanation of events connected to it, see *O Globo* (21 July 1983), p. 6, "Decreto amplia intervenção do exército nas PMs." See also *Folha de São Paulo* (21 July 1983), p. 11, "Governo decreta normas para o controle das PMs."

112. See *Veja* (27 July 1983), pp. 28-32, for a description of the protests, "Sindicatos: Uma vitória geral."

113. See DIEESE, "As greves de julho de 1983: A greve geral do dia 21," *Boletim do DIEESE* 2 (July 1983), pp. 17-24. In São Paulo the strike was strong in the capital and almost total in the ABCD region. In addition, other smaller industrial areas of the state were also paralyzed: Osasco, Guarulhos, Limeira, Mogi das Cruzes, Sorocaba, Campinas, Itú, São José dos Campos, Cruzeiro, Taubaté, Jaú, Lorena, Araraquara, Setãozinho, Bauru, Franca, Caçapava, and Matão. In Rio Grande do Sul, besides the almost complete stoppage in the capital, Porto Alegre, the following cities were affected: Canoas, Cachoeirinha, Viamão, Gravataí, Esteio, Sapucaia, São Leopoldo, Pelotas, Novo Hamburgo, and Ijuí.

114. The day of protest also indicated the limits of local power in Brazil. The governor of the State of São Paulo either had to utilize the military police for repression of strikers or see the army do it. The local mayors in São Bernardo (PMDB) and Diadema (PT) were totally helpless in the handling of the repression. I witnessed the local commander of the military police in Diadema tell the mayor, a member of the PT and a former codirector of the Metalworkers' Union of São Bernardo do Campo and Diadema (with Lula) that "today you have jurisdiction over City Hall and the parking lot around it." As a result of the repression, seventy-two

trade-union officials were removed from office. Virtually all the unions that were intervened were connected to the PT, thereby demonstrating the selective nature of the repression.

115. For a full explanation of all the measures of Decree-Law No. 2065, see the excellent analysis, complete with tables of potential salary readjustments, in DIEESE, *Divulgação 07/83*, "2,065: O arrocho continua."

116. See *Isto E* (16 November 1983), p. 77, "Salários: ABC testa decreto." For other information on this strike, see also *Veja* (16 November 1983), pp. 94-95; *Jornal do Brasil* (14 November 1983), p. 11; and *O Estado de São Paulo* (18 November 1983), p. 3.

117. *Isto E* (16 November 1983), p. 77.

118. *O Estado de São Paulo* (18 November 1983), p. 3, editorial.

119. See Alexandre de S. C. Barros and Paulo Roberto Kramer, "The Brazilian Military and "Abertura", paper presented at the 1983 LASA meeting, held in Mexico City, 29 September to 1 October 1983. The authors make a very interesting argument on the influence of the Falklands/Malvinas War on the ideology of the military in Brazil. Basically, the reality of external war has brought the military into direct confrontation with the precepts of the National Security Doctrine, with its emphasis on the internal enemy and the automatic alliance of countries in Latin America with the West. In addition, the authors point out that, besides beginning to question the basic precepts of the National Security Doctrine, the military is interested in finding an institutional framework within which to survive if and when it gets out of government. The problem, as the authors put it, is that the military is also employed in government and in the state corporations and hence, to advance the process of democratization, one needs to deal with the "structural unemployment" of the military.

120. The new National Security Law was voted on in Congress on Friday, 3 December 1983, in a vote that managed to garner the required two-thirds majority for a constitutional amendment. The opposition parties, except the PT, which argued for the simple revoking of the law and not its amendment, joined the members of the PDS in the vote. The new law was the result of lengthy negotiations, and its final draft had been previously approved by the government within the context of the continuity of the *abertura* policy. Immediately after the vote was taken, PMDB House leader, Freitas Nobre, said that his party was against the existence of a National Security Law, for it believed that crimes against the state should be defined either in the Military Penal code or in the Common Law Penal Code. However, the PMDB decided to vote in favor of the compromise bill because it represented a liberalization of the previous law and in fact would amount to a new amnesty with the immediate release of many prisoners who had been condemned under Law No. 6620 of 1978. Senator Fernando Henrique Cardoso, of the PMDB of São Paulo, also pointed out that the Brazilian Bar Association (OAB) had requested that this new National Security Law be approved. According to Congressman Dante de Oliveira (PMDB, Mato Grosso), after the Amnesty Bill of 1979 there were fifty-six new persons indicted under National Security Law No. 6620 of 1978. Of those, thirty-three (among whom are the French priests François Gouriou and Aristides Camio and thirteen squatters from the region of São Geraldo do Araguaia) have appeals to the Supreme Court pending. Another twenty-three (including the owner of *O Estado*

de São Paulo, journalist Júlio de Mesquita Neto, and the trade-union leaders Jacó Bittar, Jair Meneguelli, José Francisco da Silva of CONTAG, and Luís Inácio Lula da Silva) have suits under the National Security Law of 1978 about to be tried at the first-level court. In an interview with the lawyer of most of those who are currently being tried, Luís Eduardo Greenhalgh, I was told that the new legislation is a big improvement and that he expects most of his clients to either not be convicted or to be set free immediately. For more information on the new National Security Law, see *O Estado de São Paulo* (3 December 1983), p. 4, "O Congresso aprova LSN mais branda"; *Jornal da Trade* (3 December 1983), p. 7, "Nova LSN vai libertar 22 presos"; and *Folha de São Paulo* (3 December 1983), p. 6, "Aprovada a LSN, con 8 alterações."

The changes in National Security Law No. 6620 of 1978 include the following:

1. Article 4, Item 1: eliminated an aggravating circumstance (alínea A), which considered a heavier penalty if the person was "military or a public employee." Both situations are now considered to have sufficient penalty provided in special laws.

2. Article 7: an added paragraph established that youths less than eighteen years old cannot be charged under or tried by the National Security Law.

3. Article 13: added another type of crime, "industrial espionage." It is now a crime for those who "obtain or reveal, for espionage goals, drawings, projects, photographs, news or information in respect to techniques or technologies, of components, of equipment, of installations, or of processing systems that are in use or being developed in the country and that are considered essential for the defense, security, or economy, having for this reason to remain secret."

4. Article 22, Item 2: considered it a crime to propagate hatred of race, religion, or class. The new words are "of racial discrimination, fight for violence between the classes, and religious persecution."

5. Article 23: Item 4 excluded, which considered it a crime to "incite to hatred or to racial discrimination."

6. Article 30: different wording. Where it read that it is up to "the Military Court [Justiça Militar] to enter a suit and judge crimes against national security," it now reads "the crimes included in this law."

7. Article 33, paragraph 2: the maximum period in which a prisoner may be held incommunicado was reduced from eight to five days.

8. Article 33, paragraph 4: the government is held responsible for the "physical integrity of the prisoner," replaced by "for the physical and mental integrity of the prisoner."

(O Estado de São Paulo [3 December 1983], p. 4).

121. See *Isto E* (13 April 1983), pp. 21-27; *Veja* (13 April 1983), pp. 21-33; and *Manchete* 20, no. 1., "O Quebra-quebra que abalou o Brasil," pp. 4-11.

Conclusion: The Opposition and the State in Perspective

1. The Brazilian experience throws a revealing light on the general theoretical problem of the nature of crisis in state-regulated capitalism; see Jürgen Habermas's discussion of the relationship between economic, rationality, legitimation, and motivation crisis tendencies within mature (postliberal) capitalist systems in *Legitimation Crisis* (Boston: Beacon Press, 1974), part 2, a discussion that is in turn indebted to James O'Connor, *The Fiscal Crisis of the State* (New York: St. Martin's Press, 1973).

2. Maurício Ellena Rangel, then president of the Electrical Workers' Union of Rio de Janeiro, interview with author, 5 May 1980.

3. Comparative research on the particular mechanisms of repression and the machinery of the repressive apparatuses of Uruguay, Chile, Argentina, and Brazil is scant. There is a need for comparative research dealing specifically with the interconnections and learning processes between the different intelligence networks of the Southern Cone.

4. The specific targeting of São Paulo was not entirely planned, however. Contradictions within the national security state caused a growing competition for power between elements connected to the repressive apparatus and the government of General Ernesto Geisel. This power struggle played an important role in the events leading to the deaths of Herzog and of Manoel Fiel Filho.

5. I refer here to the terrorist activities that culminated in the bombing of Riocentro on the night of 30 April 1981.

6. For an excellent analysis of the Argentinian "doctrine of war" and the workings of the decentralized repressive apparatus in Argentina, see Emilio Mignone, "Desapariciones forzadas: Elemento básico de una política," *Punto Final, Suplemento de la Edición no. 174* (June 1981).

7. See *Latin America Regional Reports Brazil*, RB-81-09 (16 October 1981), p. 4. Data from IBGE 1970 and 1980 censuses. See also tables A-6 and A-7 in Appendix.

8. See Peter T. Knight, "Brazilian Socioeconomic Development: Issues for the Eighties," pp. 21-22 (prepared for Commission on U.S.-Brazilian Relations; in press, *World Development*).

9. See *Latin America Weekly Report* (15 December 1982). See also table A-2, Appendix.

10. See table A-1, Appendix.

11. See the special study conducted by *Movimento* on the militarization of the Brazilian state apparatus and of the state corporations, *Movimento* (6-12 April 1981), *Especial*, "O estado militar."

12. Ibid., p. 9.

13. See the report of the changes in the salary law in *Isto E* (26 January 1983), pp. 14-20, "A nova guerra dos salários: Decidido a impor um novo arrocho salarial o governo se apronta para a primeira grande luta política desde as eleições. A oposição e os sindicatos se organizam para resistir em todo o país."

Index